S0-CRS-052

Teacher's Handbook on Diagnosis and Remediation in Reading

SECOND EDITION

Eldon E. Ekwall

University of Texas at El Paso

Allyn and Bacon, Inc.

Boston · London · Sydney · Toronto

Library of Congress Cataloging in Publication Data

Ekwall, Eldon E.
Teacher's handbook on diagnosis and remediation in reading.

Bibliography: p.
Includes index.
1. Reading—Remedial teaching. 2. Reading—Ability testing. 3. Reading—Remedial teaching—Computer programs. 4. Reading—Remedial teaching—Computer programs—Directories. I. Title.
LB1050.5.E384 1986 428.4′2 85-28616
ISBN 0-205-08595-4

Printed in the United States of America

10 9 8 7 6 5 4 3 2 1 91 90 89 88 87 86

To:
Sylvia Arroyo Campa, Trini Mendoza,
and to
Sister Martha Torres

Contents

Preface ix

Using Appendices A through F and J to Make Your Own Diagnostic Kit xi

CHAPTER 1 SCOPE AND SEQUENCE OF THE READING SKILLS **1**

A Framework of the Reading Skills 2
The Subskills of Understanding Words and Ideas 3
The Skills Usually Taught in Remedial Reading 7
Competencies That Students Should Achieve in Their Progression Through the Grades 7

CHAPTER 2 PRINCIPLES OF DIAGNOSIS AND REMEDIATION **13**

Important Procedures in Diagnosis 14
Important Procedures in Remediation 16

CHAPTER 3 DIAGNOSIS AND REMEDIATION OF LETTER KNOWLEDGE AND SIGHT WORDS **23**

Diagnosing Students' Knowledge of the Alphabet 24
Diagnosing Students' Knowledge of Basic Sight Words 24
Diagnosing Students' Knowledge of Sight Words in General 25
Remediation Procedures for Letter Knowledge 26
Remediation Procedures for Sight Words and Basic Sight Words 27

CHAPTER 4 DIAGNOSIS AND REMEDIATION OF THE USE OF CONTEXT CLUES **39**

Diagnosis of Students' Knowledge of Context Clues 40
Remediation Procedures for Context Clues 41
The Progression of Difficulty in Using Context Clues 44
Other Types of Context Clues Exercises 45

CHAPTER 5 DIAGNOSIS AND REMEDIATION OF PHONICS AND STRUCTURAL ANALYSIS SKILLS 47

A Sequence for Testing Phonics and Structural Analysis Skills 48
Remediation Procedures for Sound-Symbol Correspondence 51
Remediation Procedures for Hard and Soft *C* and *G* Rules 54
Remediation Procedures for *R*-, *W*-, and *L*-Controlled Vowels 56
Remediation Procedures for Blending 56
Remediation Procedures for Vowel Rules 58
Remediation Procedures for Syllabication Principles 60
Remediation Procedures for Contractions 63
Remediation Procedures for Word Endings 64

CHAPTER 6 DIAGNOSIS AND REMEDIATION OF COMPREHENSION AND VOCABULARY SKILLS AND MATCHING STUDENTS WITH THE RIGHT LEVEL OF READING MATERIALS 67

Factors Affecting Comprehension 68
Methods of and Problems with Testing Comprehension 70
Some Recommended Procedures for Measuring Reading Comprehension Level and for Matching Students and Reading Materials 70
Remediation Procedures for Developing Comprehension 82
Commonly Used Procedures for Measuring Students' Vocabularies 100
Strategies for Increasing Students' Vocabularies 103

CHAPTER 7 SELECTION OF STUDENTS AND OPERATION OF THE REMEDIAL READING PROGRAM 109

Common Problems in the Selection Process 110

CHAPTER 8 FORMS FOR COMMUNICATION IN A REMEDIAL READING PROGRAM 121

Using Reports and Record Keeping 122

CHAPTER 9 EVALUATING AND PURCHASING MATERIALS FOR REMEDIAL READING 151

Important Questions in Evaluating Materials 152
Recommended Books for Remedial Reading 153

CHAPTER 10 USING MICROCOMPUTERS IN THE DIAGNOSIS AND REMEDIATION OF THE DISABLED READER **175**

Some Cautions to be Observed 176
Present Status of Microcomputers in the Diagnosis and Remediation of Disabled Readers 180
The Evaluation of Computer Software 184
The Evaluation of Computer Hardware 188
Guidelines of the International Reading Association 190
Summary 193
Software Directories 193
Magazines with Information about Computers and Computer Software 195
Computer Programs 196
Companies That Publish or Distribute Software Materials for Use in Reading Education 213
Computer Terminology 215

APPENDIX A Preparing and Using the Materials for Testing Letter Knowledge **223**

APPENDIX B Preparing and Using the Materials for Testing Basic Sight Words **229**

APPENDIX C Preparing and Using the Materials for Testing Context Clues **235**

APPENDIX D Preparing and Using the *Quick Survey Word List* and the *El Paso Phonics Survey* **245**

APPENDIX E Preparation and Use of Materials for Testing Knowledge of Vowel Rules and Syllable Principles **261**

APPENDIX F Preparation and Use of Materials for Testing Knowledge of Contractions **271**

APPENDIX G Tests Useful in Diagnosing and Remediation of Disabled Readers **275**

APPENDIX H Materials for Teaching Reading Skills in a Remedial Reading Center **297**

APPENDIX I Companies That Publish Materials in Reading **319**

APPENDIX J *Ekwall Reading Inventory* *ERI i*

Index *I-1*

Preface

This handbook was written to be a practical guide for teachers who are actively involved in the diagnosis and remediation of students with reading disabilities. Included might be remedial reading or learning disabilities teachers in the public schools or students in a practicum actively working with disabled readers. The book has been kept as brief as possible to emphasize the application of skills and knowledge of activities that a teacher will use on a daily basis. It includes very little quoted research and theory. Most practical knowledge comes from theory and research, however, and Dr. James L. Shanker and I have covered those aspects of diagnosis and remediation much more thoroughly in a book entitled *Diagnosis and Remediation of the Disabled Reader* (2nd ed.), published by Allyn and Bacon, 1983.

The second edition of this handbook contains the latest findings on methods of teaching comprehension, including such things as metacognition and the use of story frames. Also included in this edition is the *Ekwall Reading Inventory* (a commercial informal reading inventory designed for measuring students' oral and silent reading levels from grades one through nine). In the appendices are a number of other assessment devices devised by the author. These should be adequate to meet many diagnostic needs in a remedial reading classroom or in a learning disabilities classroom where the emphasis is on the teaching of reading. Included in these assessment devices are materials for measuring students' knowledge of the alphabet, basic sight words, context clues, and students' knowledge of phonics and structural analysis. Other appendices include a listing of many types of tests useful in remedial reading, a comprehensive listing of materials useful for remedial and developmental reading programs, and companies that publish materials for use in remedial and developmental reading.

Chapter 1 is on the scope and sequence of the reading skills. It presents a framework for understanding the most commonly recognized reading skills. The latter part of the chapter contains a comprehensive listing of the reading skills and the points where each should be mastered. This scope and sequence chart was developed on the basis of seven of the most commonly used basal reading programs currently marketed in the United States.

Chapter 2 presents some principles with which the diagnostician and remedial reading teacher should become familiar in order to avoid some of the pitfalls often encountered in the diagnostic-remedial process. Chapter 3 is on the diagnosis and remediation of students' problems with letter knowledge and sight words. Chapter 4 is on the diagnosis and remediation of students' problems with context clues. Chapter 5 discusses the diagnosis and remediation of various phonics and structural analysis skills. As with the other chapters on the teaching of skills, materials are contained in the appendices for assessing knowledge in this area. Chapter 6 pertains to the diagnosis and remediation of students with problems in comprehension and vocabulary and also includes material on how to properly match students with the right level of reading materials. Chapter 7 presents information on the selection criteria for students, as well as information for developing a caseload in a remedial reading program. Chapter 8 presents various forms that should prove helpful in record keeping and communicating information in a remedial reading program. Chapter 9 gives criteria for evaluating and purchasing materials to be used in a remedial reading program. It also includes a comprehensive listing of high-interest low-vocabulary books for a remedial reading program. Finally, Chapter 10 presents information on the use of the computer in the diagnosis and remediation of the disabled reader. It contains a listing of useful sources of information.

This handbook is designed to be used by teachers who are working with disabled readers at any grade level. As any experienced diagnostician knows, you are likely to find some students—even at the high school or adult level—who do not know the alphabet or certain basic sight words. Therefore, while the diagnostic procedures presented herein are applicable at any grade level, some older students will not want to do activities that they perceive as childish. Only experience and a knowledge of the personality of each student, along with a knowledge of his or her particular reading disability, will enable you to determine which of the remedial activities are appropriate for each student.

E. E. E.

Using Appendices A through F and J to Make Your Own Diagnostic Kit

As stated in the preface, this handbook is designed to provide the user with many of the assessment devices likely to be needed in a remedial reading program or in a learning disabilities classroom where remedial reading is a central focus of attention. Appendices A through F each contain three sections. The first explains how to prepare the materials in that section for use in testing; the second presents directions for use of that particular assessment device; and the third section provides additional information needed in using that assessment device. The *Ekwall Reading Inventory* comprises Appendix J. It is much more comprehensive than the other assessment devices, and its use will require more preparation.

This handbook has been punched, so that any of the materials can be taken from the book and placed in a three-ring notebook. This will enable the user to develop his or her own diagnostic kit. The pages are perforated as well, making them easy to remove for laminating and/or duplicating.

1

Scope and Sequence of the Reading Skills

In the first part of this chapter you will find various diagrams illustrating a framework of the reading skills along with a discussion of the way these component skills appear to fit together. In the latter part of the chapter you will find a scope and sequence chart of various reading skills. This chart shows the points at which various skills should be firmly established and the points where they would continue to be extended and refined. The scope and sequence chart is preceded by a discussion of its purpose and use.

A FRAMEWORK OF THE READING SKILLS

The Basic Skills

Reading might generally be considered to be composed of two main categories of skills: "Recognizing and Analyzing Words" and "Understanding Words and Ideas." Thus, the beginning of our framework would appear as in Figure 1–1.

Two Subskills of Recognizing Words

"Recognizing and Analyzing Words" is usually broken down into two subdivisions: *Sight Words* and *Word Attack Skills* (often called Word Analysis Skills). The framework now appears as shown in Figure 1–2.

If a reader has come in contact with a word enough times, it will have become a sight word, and he or she will know it instantly without applying word attack skills. On the other hand, if the student has not encountered the word enough times so that it is instantly known, he or she must apply one of the word attack skills. There are five commonly used word attack skills. They are *Configuration Clues, Context Clues, Phonetic Analysis, Structural Analysis* (now often called *Morphology*), and *Dictionary Skills.* The use of the encyclopedia is sometimes referred to as a *Study Skill.* Since students sometimes analyze the pronunciation of words by looking them up in an encyclopedia (a Study Skill), we might consider study skills as a sixth, but not so closely related, word attack skill. With these additions, our framework appears as shown in Figure 1–3.

Under the *Sight Word* category are two subcategories: *Basic Sight Words* and *Other Sight Words.* The term *Basic Sight Word* usually refers to a certain list of high utility words (words that appear most often in print) compiled by writers and researchers in the field of reading. Examples of some of these are the Dolch List (1942), the *Ekwall Basic Sight Word List* (1983), that appears on pp. 231 to 234 of this book, the Harris-Jacobson (1980), and the Fry List (1980). All of the words on the *Harris-Jacobson List* are designated as pre-primer, primer, or first reader. Fry's list contains three hundred words that Fry indicates would probably not be mastered by most readers until they had at least a third-grade reading

FIGURE 1–1 *Two basic categories of reading skills*

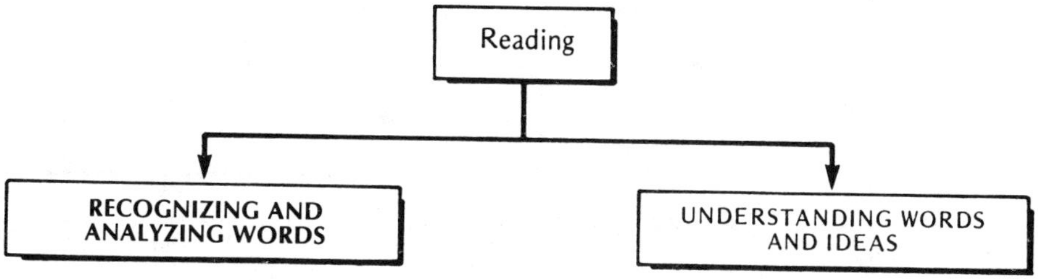

level. The author would recommend any of the four lists that have been mentioned as appropriate for the teaching of basic sight words.

Listed under *Sight Words* is another category called *Other Sight Words,* which includes all words known instantly or known without the use of word attack skills. The number of other sight words would, of course, vary from reader to reader and would vary within any one reader as he or she continues to come in contact with new words time after time. For example, a word such as *establish* might require the application of word attack skills for quite a number of times in which a student encounters it, but it would eventually become a sight word. It would then be classified here as one of the Other Sight Words—that is, it would be known instantly by the student, but it would not be of such high utility that it would appear on the list as a Basic Sight Word for that student.

The scope of the reading skills as explained thus far now appears as diagramed in Figure 1–4.

THE SUBSKILLS OF UNDERSTANDING WORDS AND IDEAS

The problem of deriving subcategories to illustrate the skills for "Understanding Words and Ideas," or what is usually referred to as comprehension, is much more complicated and less clear-cut than the area of word attack or word analysis skills. The technique that is usually used to attempt to identify the subskills of comprehension is one called *factor analysis.* Perhaps one of the best known of these studies was done by Frederick B. Davis (1944). About his own study Davis (1972) stated,

> Davis' study points to the general conclusion that comprehension among mature readers is not a unitary ability but that it is largely dependent on knowledge of word meanings and on ability to reason in verbal terms. Other more specific skills are involved but to a small extent.

In discussing the Davis and other studies Dale D. Johnson, Susan Toms-Bronowski, and Ray R. Buss (1983) stated,

> Further investigation of the critical skills of comprehension is sorely needed, especially at the elementary-school level. Nonetheless, the works

FIGURE 1–2 *Two basic categories of reading skills plus two subcategories of recognizing words*

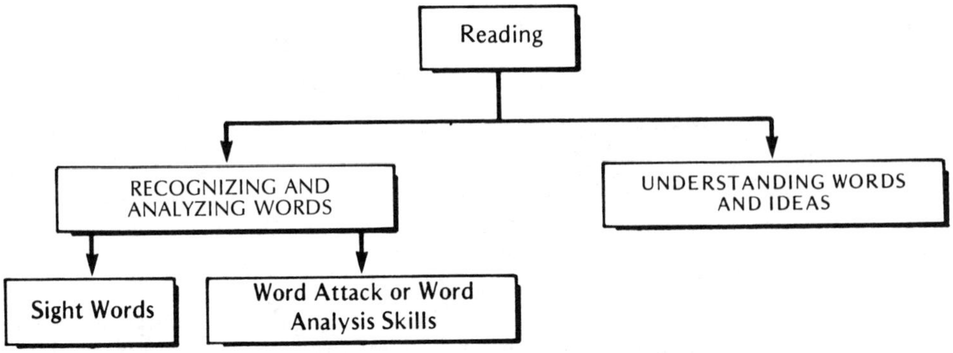

FIGURE 1–3 *A breakdown of the word attack skills*

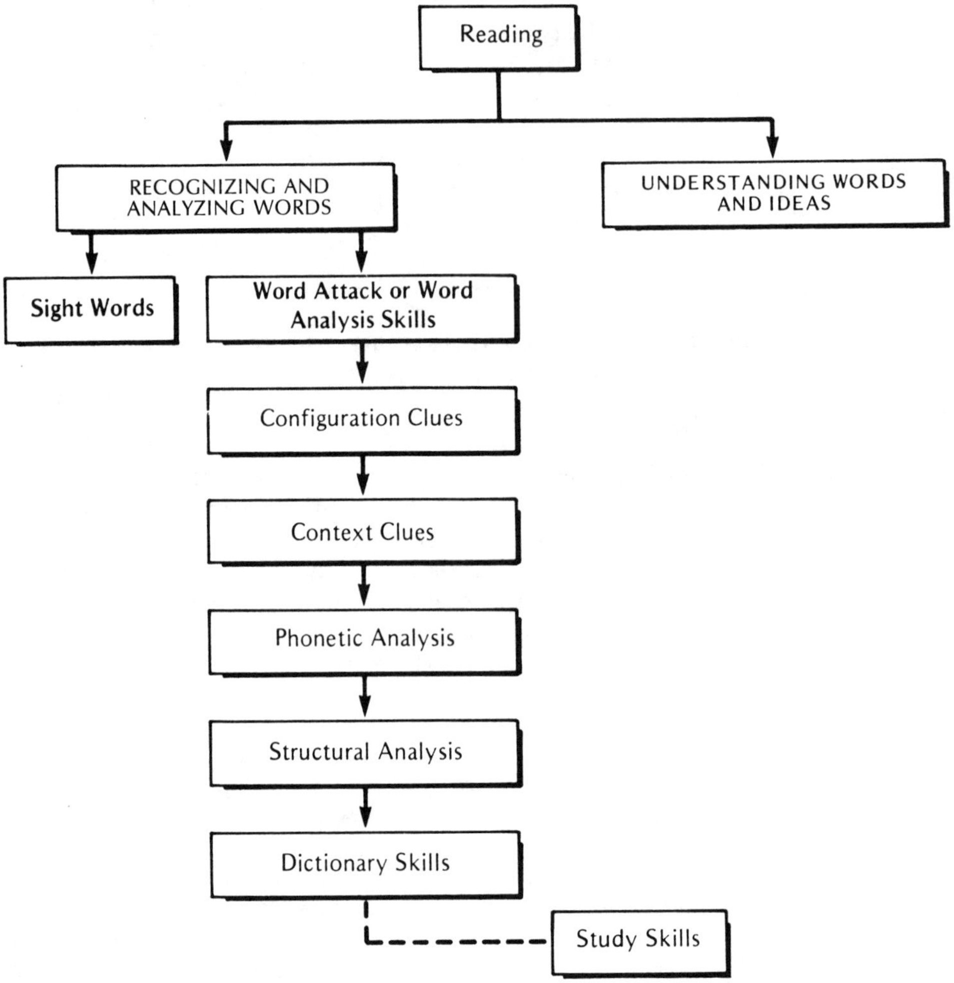

FIGURE 1–4 *A complete breakdown of the skill of recognizing words*

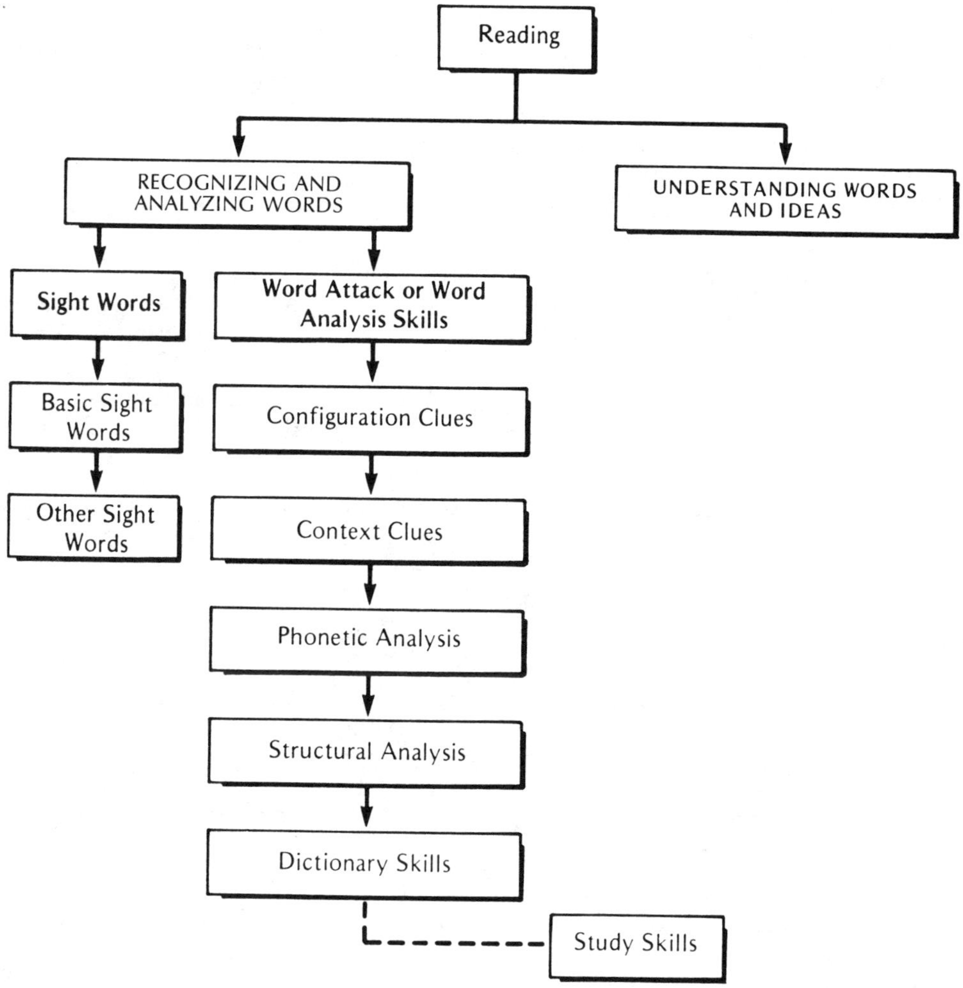

> reviewed here indicate that vocabulary knowledge *is* critical to comprehension. If you don't know the words, you're not going to understand the passage. (p. 254)

Because of the complexity of the skills of comprehension, many writers have simply lumped comprehension skills into two broad categories. They are *vocabulary* and *other comprehension skills.*

Thomas Barrett (1967) suggests that the cognitive dimension for comprehension categories might be classified as "(a) literal meaning, (b) inference, (c) evaluation, and (d) appreciation" (p. 21). *Literal meaning,* as defined by Barrett, would be concerned with ideas and information explicitly stated in a reading selection. The first of these, in terms of pupil behavior, would be "recognition," and the second would be "recall." *Inference,* as Barrett states, occurs when the student, ". . . uses the ideas and information explicitly stated in the selection, his intuition, and his personal experience as a basis for conjectures and hypotheses" (p. 22).

In explaining his concept of *Evaluation,* Barrett states: "Purposes for reading and teachers' questions, in this instance, require responses by the student which indicate that he has arrived at a judgment by comparing ideas presented in the selection with external criteria provided by the teacher, other authorities or written sources, or with internal criteria provided by the reader's experiences, knowledge, or values. In essence, evaluation deals with judgments and focuses on qualities or correctness, worthwhileness, or appropriateness, feasibility, and validity" (p. 22).

Barrett's last category, *Appreciation,* not only involves all of the other mentioned levels of thought, but goes beyond them. Barrett states, "Appreciation, as used here, calls for the student to be emotionally and aesthetically sensitive to the written work and to have a reaction to its psychological and artistic elements. For example, when a student verbalizes his feelings about part or all of a reading selection in terms of excitement, fear, dislike, or boredom, he is functioning at the appreciational level" (p. 23).

It should be noted here that other authors have added to these subskills of comprehension mentioned by Barrett by listing such other

FIGURE 1-5 *The framework of the reading skills*

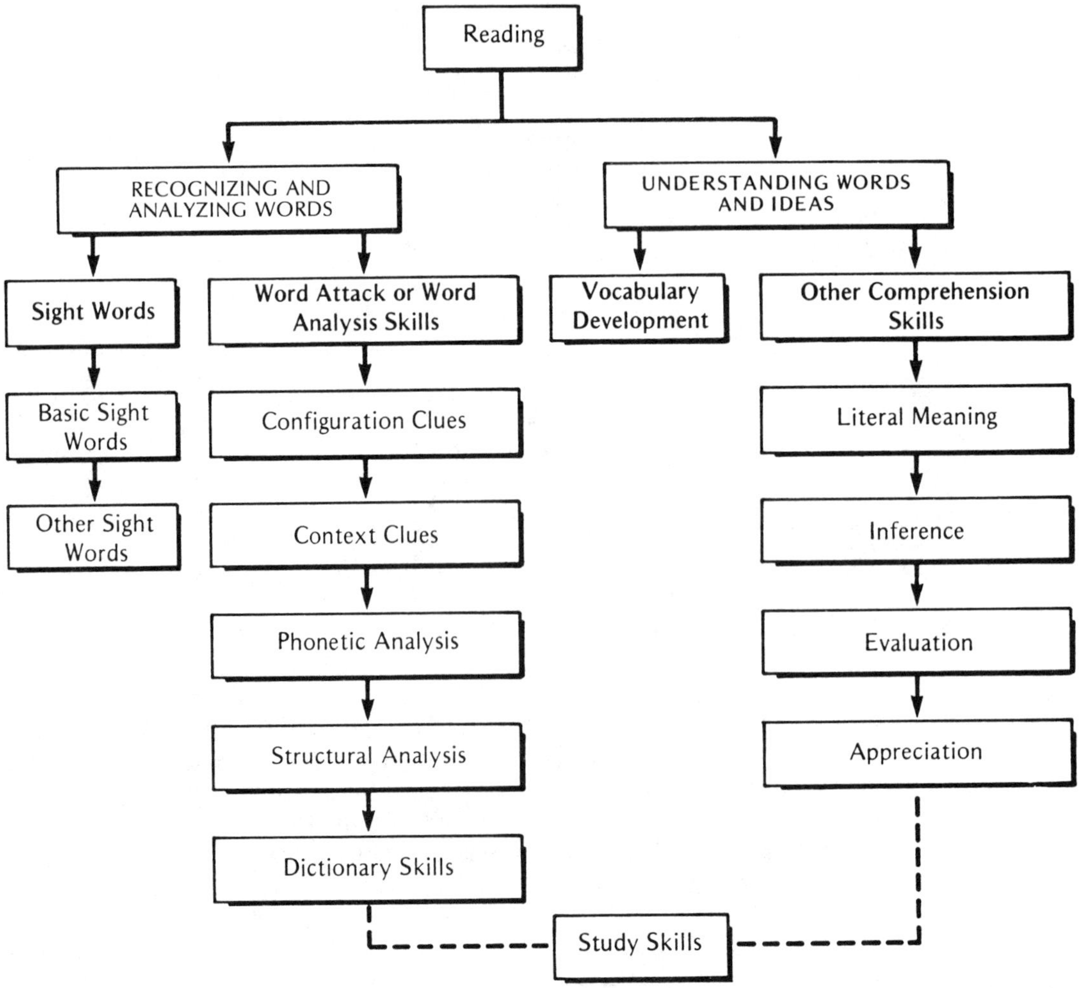

categories as the ability to see "Main Ideas," "Important Details," and "Author's Purpose," and the ability to "Develop Mental Images," "See a Sequence of Ideas," and "See the Author's Organization." It should also be kept in mind that while Barrett's taxonomy of skills for comprehension is emphasized here, it could not necessarily be defended in terms of factoral analysis studies dealing with concretely measured categories. His categories do, however, add meaning to our goals for viewing and teaching these skills.

The addition of Vocabulary Development as a main subskill of comprehension and the listing of Barrett's subcategories under a second main subdivision, Other Comprehension Skills, completes our framework of reading skills as shown in Figure 1–5. Note the broken line from Comprehension to Study Skills. This again indicates that the study skills have a relationship to, or contribute to, reading comprehension. This relationship is, however, less direct than the relationship between comprehension and the other subcategories previously mentioned.

THE SKILLS USUALLY TAUGHT IN REMEDIAL READING

Chapters 3 through 6 deal with the diagnosis and teaching of important reading skills as shown in Figure 1–5. These chapters deal with the teaching of sight words, context clues, phonics and structural analysis, and comprehension. There are no separate chapters on configuration clues, study skills, or dictionary skills.

Very little is known about "how" to teach configuration clues. We do know, however, that the top coastline, or top half of a word written in lower case letters, gives us more clues in identifying it than the bottom costline, or bottom half of the word. This can easily be illustrated by alternately covering the top and bottom of one or more words. Recent studies have also shown that children depend very heavily on the first one or two letters of a word when attempting to identify it. The implication from these studies would seem to be that we should urge students who miscall words with similar beginning letters to look carefully at the whole word before attempting to say it.

As stated earlier, there are no separate chapters on the diagnosis and remediation of either dictionary skills or study skills. Both dictionary and study skills are important and should be learned by a competent reader. However, in remedial reading we are usually more concerned with the basic skills that are absolutely necessary for students to begin to read. Neither the dictionary skills nor most study skills are considered as absolutely necessary in the beginning stages of reading.

COMPETENCIES THAT STUDENTS SHOULD ACHIEVE IN THEIR PROGRESSION THROUGH THE GRADES

Waiting until a secondary student is seriously retarded in reading will eliminate the need to be concerned about which of the various skills should be tested. That is to say, you could simply assume that at a given

FIGURE 1-6 *Competencies that students should achieve in their progression through the grades.*

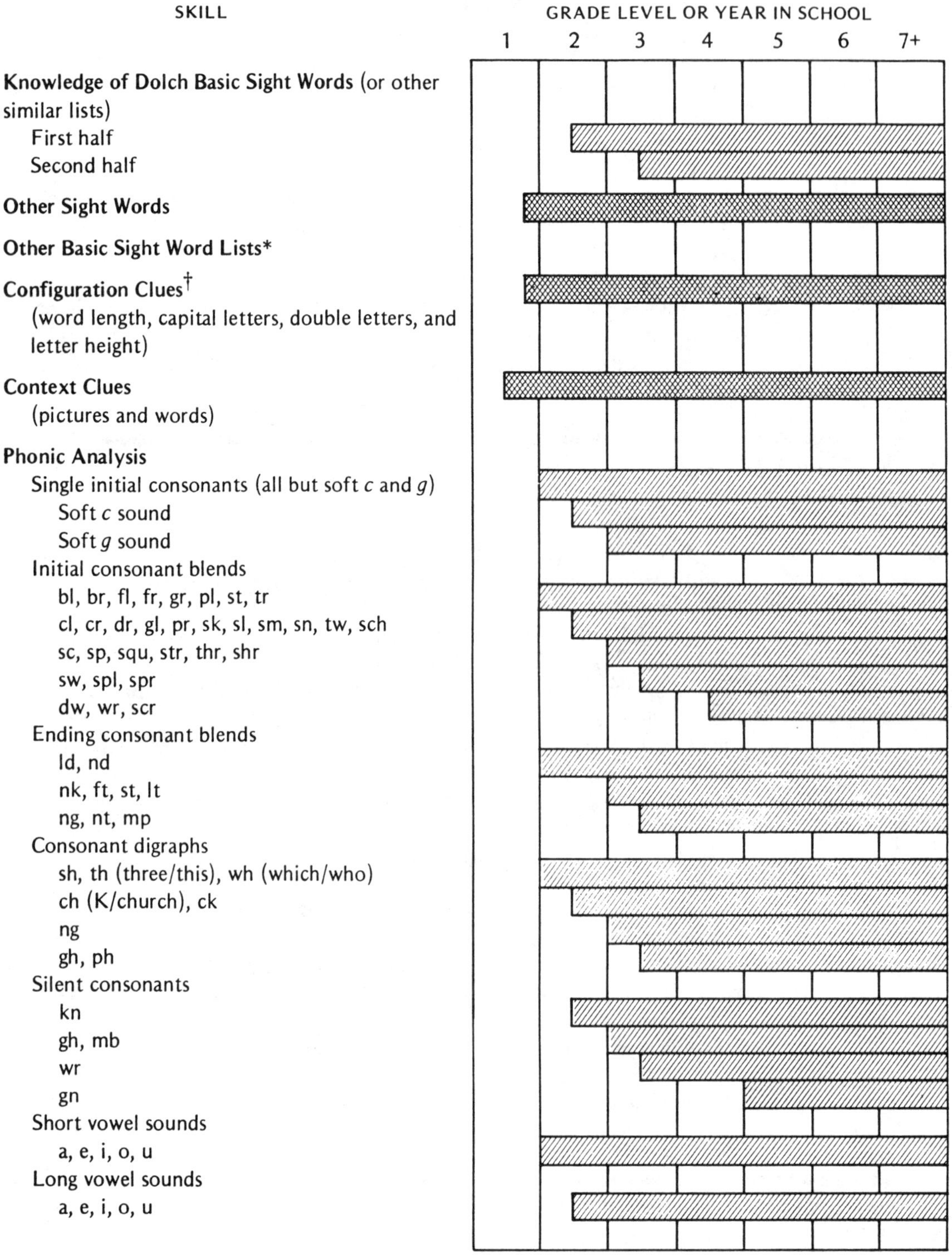

SKILL
GRADE LEVEL OR YEAR IN SCHOOL
1 2 3 4 5 6 7+
Knowledge of Dolch Basic Sight Words (or other similar lists)
First half
Second half
Other Sight Words
Other Basic Sight Word Lists*
Configuration Clues†
(word length, capital letters, double letters, and letter height)
Context Clues
(pictures and words)
Phonic Analysis
Single initial consonants (all but soft c and g)
Soft c sound
Soft g sound
Initial consonant blends
bl, br, fl, fr, gr, pl, st, tr
cl, cr, dr, gl, pr, sk, sl, sm, sn, tw, sch
sc, sp, squ, str, thr, shr
sw, spl, spr
dw, wr, scr
Ending consonant blends
ld, nd
nk, ft, st, lt
ng, nt, mp
Consonant digraphs
sh, th (three/this), wh (which/who)
ch (K/church), ck
ng
gh, ph
Silent consonants
kn
gh, mb
wr
gn
Short vowel sounds
a, e, i, o, u
Long vowel sounds
a, e, i, o, u

*See the list of basic sight words compiled by the author that appears in Chapter 3.

†The use of configuration clues is taught in grade one, but older students continue to use and improve in this skill as their knowledge of structural analysis increases.

Key:

Skill Firmly Established   Skill Extended and Refined (but has been introduced)

Competencies That Students Should Achieve in Their Progression Through the Grades

SKILL

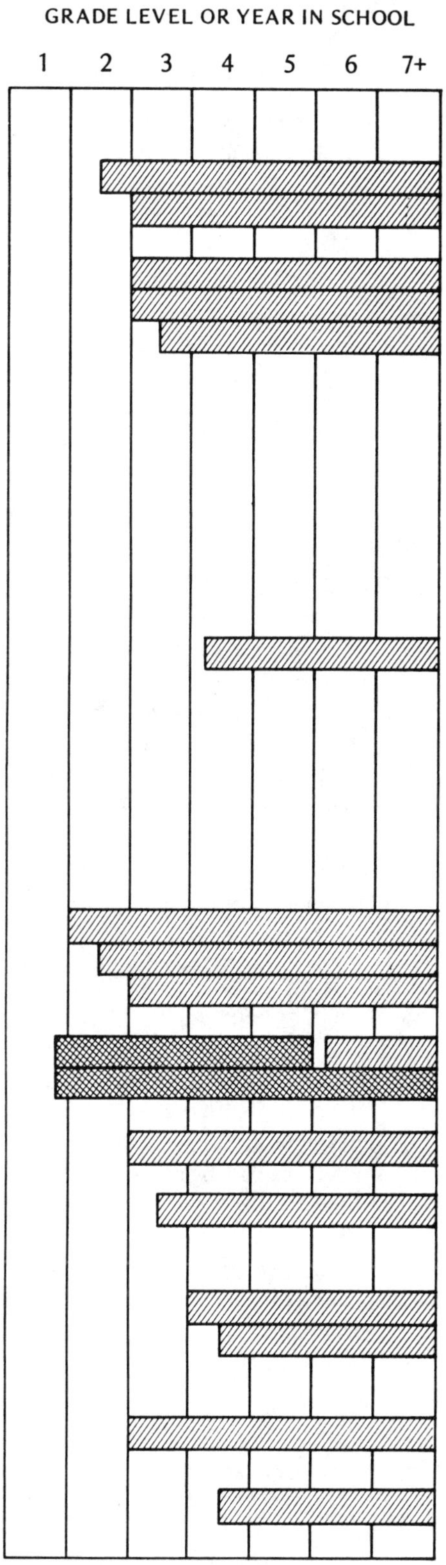

Phonic Analysis (continued)

Vowel teams and special letter combinations

oo (look/moon), ea (each/bread), ay, eo, ai, ee

oa (oats), ow (o/cow), ir, ur, or, ar, aw, ou (trout), oi, oy, al, er, au, ew

Rules for *y* sound

Vowel rules for open and closed syllables

Syllable principles (1, 2, & 3)

1. When two like consonants stand between two vowels the word is usually divided between the consonants.
2. When two unlike consonants stand between two vowels the word is usually divided between the consonants (unless the consonants are digraphs or blends).
3. When a word ends in a consonant and *le*, the consonant usually begins the last syllable.

Syllable principles (4, 5, & 6)

4. Compound words are usually divided between word parts and between syllables within these parts.
5. Prefixes and suffixes are usually separate syllables.
6. Do not divide between the letters in consonant digraphs and consonant blends.

Structural Analysis

Word endings

ed, ing, 's, d

er, es

est

Word families

all, at, et, em, etc.

Word roots

Contractions

let's, didn't, it's, won't, that's, can't, wasn't, isn't, hadn't

don't, I'll, we'll, I've, he'll, hasn't, haven't, aren't, I'm, he's, we're, you're, what's, there's, she's, wouldn't, she'll, here's

ain't, couldn't, they're, they'd

you'll, she'd, weren't, I'd, you've, you'd, we'd, anybody'd, there'll, we've, who'll, he'd, who'd, doesn't, where's, they've, they'll

Possessives

Accent Rules*

1. In two syllable words, the first syllable is usually accented.

*At present, no definitive research is available as to which accent generalizations are of high enough utility to make them worthwhile to teach. The four listed here are believed to be quite consistent and also of high utility.

Scope and Sequence of the Reading Skills

SKILL

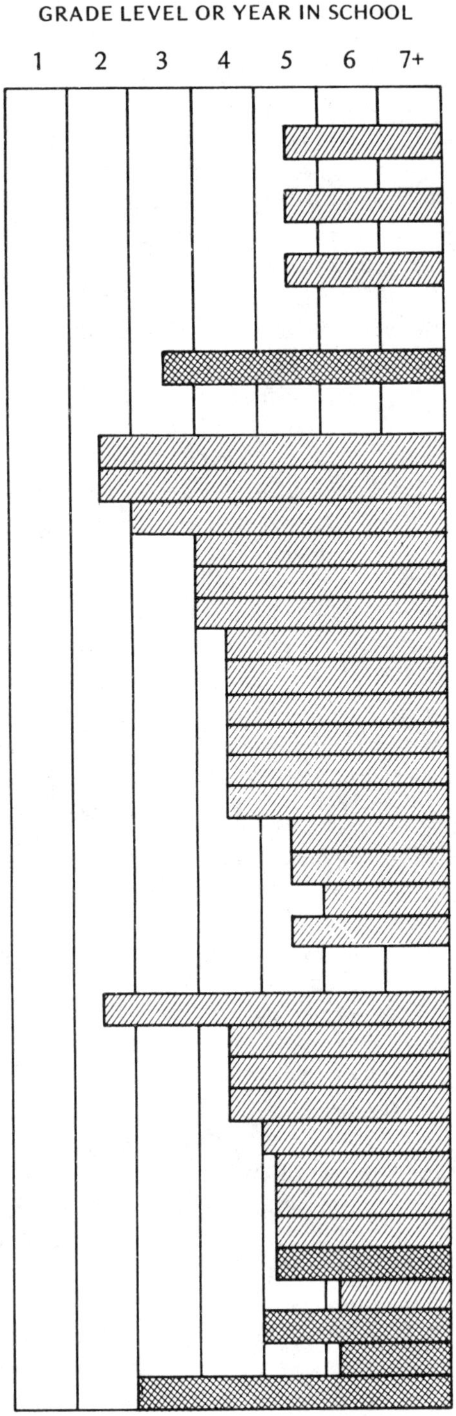

Accent Rules (continued)

2. In inflected or derived forms, the primary accent usually falls on or within the root word.
3. If two vowels are together in the last syllable of a word, it may be a clue to an accented final syllable.
4. If there are two like consonants within a word, the syllable before the double consonants is usually accented.

Suffixes and Prefixes

Dictionary Skills*

- Say alphabet in order
- Alphabetize letters
- Alphabetize words to first letter
- Alphabetize words to second letter
- Alphabetize words to third letter
- Estimate location of a word in the dictionary
- Derive word meaning
- Use guide words
- Interpret syllables
- Interpret accent or stress
- Select word meaning from context
- Interpret pronunciation key
- Use cross reference
- Preferred spellings
- Investigate word origin
- Parts of speech

Study Skills

- Table of Contents
- Index
- Glossary
- Encyclopedia (find topic)
- Encyclopedia (use index volume)
- Encyclopedia (use cross reference)
- Almanac
- Telephone Directory
- Interpret tables
- Library card index
- Read maps
- Read graphs, charts, and diagrams
- Skimming

*The prefixes *a* and *un* should be known by the middle of the third year in school. From that point on, the student should continue to extend and refine his knowledge of prefixes. This extension and refinement would continue throughout his elementary and high school years. The suffixes *er* and *ly* should be known by the middle of the second year of school. From that point on, the student should continue to extend and refine his knowledge of suffixes. This extension and refinement would continue throughout his elementary and high school years. (The author suggests that "known" in this case only means that the student recognizes the prefix and/or suffix, but that he not be required to know its meaning.)

age-grade level the student should have mastered all of the commonly tested reading skills and, therefore, it is appropriate to test any or all of the reading skills. On the other hand, with a younger and less disabled reader you must be more familiar with the scope and sequence of the reading skills in order to avoid testing beyond the point at which that student should have normally progressed. It is imperative, then, that the reading diagnostician be familiar with the scope and sequence of the reading skills. In this section, reference will again be made to the skills and subskills presented in Figure 1–5. This time, however, we will be more concerned with a further breakdown of these skills and the points at which each of the various skills should have been mastered by a student with normal achievement.

It is also imperative that classroom teachers become familiar with the scope and sequence of the reading skills in order to be able to identify students with incipient reading problems. For example, a teacher who does not know when his or her students should have mastered the basic sight words is not likely to notice a student with a mild disability in this area until somewhat later when the problem becomes obvious. At that time, the problem will, of course, be more difficult to correct, and the student will not only be more retarded in his or her reading ability, but may also have developed concurrent psychological problems resulting from his or her difficulty with reading.

In order to determine the point at which each of the reading skills should be mastered, seven sets of basal readers were analyzed. As one might expect, the points at which the authors of the various series of basal readers chose to introduce each of the skills varied to some extent. For the diagnostician, however, these minor disagreements as to time of introduction of the reading skills are not extremely important. What the diagnostician must be concerned with is the latest point at which all authors agree the skills should have been taught. This is the point at which the diagnostician can test for any particular skill and safely assume the student has been taught that skill.

An important point for the diagnostician to keep in mind is that some of the reading skills should definitely be mastered and others will be extended and refined ad infinitum. For example, the basic sight words (Dolch's list) should definitely be known by average students by the end of second grade or, at latest, middle of their third year of school. On the other hand, a student's knowledge of other sight words will continue to expand throughout his or her lifetime. Likewise, there is no point at which one can assume the comprehension skills are completely mastered. The ability to make inferences from a paragraph, for example, continues to improve as vocabulary and background of experiences continue to expand. Skills that are extended and refined rather than completely mastered should then be learned by the student and should also be tested; however, we should keep in mind that a student who continues to learn will also continue to improve in his or her ability to use these skills.

In the breakdown of reading skills in the scope and sequence chart (pp. 8–10), you will note the use of single and crosshatched lines that appear under various grade levels (see the chart's key). The level at which either of these appears is opposite the listing of a particular skill or subskill and indicates the general point at which you could assume that the skill had been taught and, likewise, the point at which you could logically assume the student should have mastered (in some cases) or should have a knowledge of the use of that skill.

In interpreting the chart, you should keep in mind that the designation of grade level serves only as a general guideline. Also, in using the scope and sequence chart several precautions need to be observed. First, you should not consider any one skill that appears on the chart to be necessarily a prerequisite to a child's learning to read. For example, knowledge of vowel rules is only necessary if a child cannot correctly pronounce various short and long vowel sounds. The learning of vowel rules is only a means to an end. If the child can pronounce various vowel sounds and combinations of vowels and vowel-controlling letters, then there is no need for the child to master that skill. Many very good adult readers can pronounce almost any word or syllable; however, it would be very difficult for many of these same adults to give the vowel sound in isolation. *It should again be emphasized that the following chart does not attempt to point to a specific time when a skill should be taught. The points of time illustrated represent the stage when nearly all of the basal reader programs examined agree that the skill should be known.*

A last, but very important, consideration is that there are often considerably different levels of development of a certain skill. For example, a child may be able to recognize and circle one of four phonemes that is the same as the initial sound heard in a word pronounced by a tester; however, he or she may not be able to pronounce the same phoneme in a strange word that is encountered in reading. This would, of course, be the level of competency that would be necessary in actual reading. This point will be emphasized again in later chapters as methods of testing for various competencies are discussed.

REFERENCES

Davis, Frederick B. Fundamental factors of comprehension in reading. *Psychometrika,* 1944, 9, 185–97.

Davis, Frederick B. Psychometric research on comprehension in reading. *Reading Research Quarterly,* Summer 1972, 7 (4), 628–78.

Dolch, Edward W. *Basic sight word test.* Champaign, Illinois: Garrard Press, 1942.

Fry, Edward. The new instant word list. *The Reading Teacher,* December 1980, 34, 284–89.

Harris, Albert J., and Sipay, Edward R. *How to increase reading ability.* New York: Longman, 1985, 376–78.

Johnson, Dale D.; Toms-Bronowski, Susan; Buss, Ray R. A critique of Frederick B. Davis' study: fundamental factors of comprehension in reading. In Lance M. Gentile; Michael L. Kamil; Jay S. Blanchard (Eds.), *Reading Research Revisited.* Columbus, Ohio: Charles E. Merrill, 1983, 247–55.

2

Principles of Diagnosis and Remediation

IMPORTANT PROCEDURES IN DIAGNOSIS

Gather Enough Initial Diagnostic Information to Begin a Program of Remediation, But Make Sure Program Remains Flexible

There is some danger in gathering too little diagnostic information before remediation is begun. In such a case, the student may be subjected to considerable repetition of material with which he or she is already familiar. Yet a very small amount of repetition in the beginning can be beneficial in bolstering the self-confidence of the student. It is important to remember that, in correcting a student's reading disabilities, the reading teacher will be filling in, or teaching, information that the student has forgotten or failed to learn. This differs from developmental reading where the teacher might expect to start from the beginning and cover all of the reading skills. For this reason, considerable diagnosis should be done before a remedial program is begun.

There is, however, an equal danger in gathering too much diagnostic information before beginning a program of remediation. Since the student will be learning and changing during the first few months of the remediation period, there is little value in subjecting a student to the testing of upper-level skills long before he or she is likely to be taught these skills. Furthermore, some of these skills may be learned while the initial remediation is in progress. When a great deal of diagnosis is done before any remediation is begun, there is also a danger that the program of remediation will become so inflexible that it will not meet the changing needs of the student.

Make the Diagnosis as Efficient as Possible

It is quite easy for a reading teacher or reading diagnostician to fall into the trap of administering the same battery of tests to every student regardless of his or her reading level or apparent reading problems. In order to make the diagnosis as efficient as possible, you should consider each individual student in terms of the type of problem he or she obviously exhibits. For example, if a student is doing quite well in mathematics or other subjects and is doing poorly in reading, very little is likely to be accomplished by giving the student an intelligence test. Or, a fifth- or sixth-grade student who has poor comprehension but can pronounce words up to and above grade level is not likely to need to be given a basic sight word test, nor is that student likely to need testing on a number of phonics skills. Therefore, before succumbing to the temptation to give every test in your kit, ask yourself whether giving any particular test is likely to change the course of the student's remediation. If the answer is no, then that test should be omitted from the diagnostic battery.

Test in a Situation That Is Similar to Actual Reading

A major problem with most group diagnostic tests and even with many individual diagnostic tests is that they do not really measure what they purport to measure. For example, the author's own research[1] has shown that students are quite likely to respond differently on tests for the same letter sound or basic sight word depending on how the stimulus is presented. Following are some examples:

A	B
The student is shown a word on a card and asked to pronounce it.	The student is given a choice of four words such as: dog like go be He or she is then asked to circle the word that is the same as the one called by the teacher.
The student is taught, or the teacher makes sure he or she knows, a word such as *at*. The student is then shown the following: g at gat The student is asked to say the name of the letter, then the middle word, and then the nonsense word.	The student is given a sheet of paper with numbers and blanks on it as follows: 1.______ 2.______ The teacher then says some words, and the student is to write the beginning sound he or she hears in each word, in each blank.

Obviously the type of test items shown under column B could be done in a group situation, but they do not test in a situation that is similar to what the student actually does when he or she reads. In the tests under column A the student is required to perform a task similar to what he or she would have to do when actually reading. Tests such as those shown under column B are often accurate enough to tell which students are generally poor or good in their knowledge of basic sight words or in their phonics knowledge. However, tests similar to those under column A are needed for more accurate prescriptive teaching.

The important question to keep in mind in examining any diagnostic test is: Does the student have to perform in a situation similar to what he or she would have to do when actually reading?

Removing a student from his or her classroom environment for any length of time is obviously a major change in the life of that student. Be-

1. Eldon E. Ekwall, "An Analysis of Children's Test Scores When Tested With Individually Administered Diagnostic Tests and When Tested With Group Administered Diagnostic Tests," *Final Research Report* (El Paso: University of Texas, University Research Institute, 1973).

fore a student is sent to a classroom for children with special learning problems, school personnel concerned with making such decisions should develop procedures for appropriate placement. A diagnostic-referral procedure such as the one outlined in Figure 2–1 will enable school personnel to place children according to the best information that can be derived from all sources.

IMPORTANT PROCEDURES IN REMEDIATION

Ensure That the Remedial Reading Program Is Highly Individualized

Terms such as a "well-balanced program" or "well-rounded program" sound good and are appropriate for a developmental reading program, but they do not describe the type of reading program that is desirable in remedial reading. In most cases, the remedial reading program must be highly individualized and directed toward correcting certain individual reading deficiencies rather than giving a child a well-rounded program.

Many children found in remedial reading classes are simply delayed a year or more in almost all of their reading skills; however, a large percentage of children are delayed a year or more only in certain areas of reading. For those students who are lacking only in certain reading skills, providing a remedial program that covered all reading skills would prove inefficient. These children can be brought up to reading grade level much more rapidly in an intensive instructional program that concentrates only on those skills in which they are deficient. One might think of a child's progression in developmental reading as the steps or rungs on a ladder, or as a continuum of skills, with each step representing the accomplishment of a certain skill such as learning the initial consonant sounds, the initial consonant blends, the short vowel sounds, and so forth. Whenever a child fails to learn one of these important skills, a step is omitted from the ladder or continuum of skills. The task of the corrective or remedial reading teacher is to fill in these omitted steps or rungs in the ladder or continuum of reading skills rather than to build a whole new ladder. For this reason, the reading teacher must be very specific in his or her diagnosis and equally specific in the remediation provided for noted weaknesses in order to provide for efficient use of both teacher and student time.

Start with the Student's Strongest Area

In order to establish rapport with a reader who has constantly failed, it is often desirable to begin instruction in an area in which he or she is already fairly strong. For example, if a student knows almost all of the initial consonant sounds, the teacher might begin by reviewing these and at the same time reinforce any that are not known as thoroughly as they should be.

FIGURE 2–1 *Student diagnostic-referral procedure*

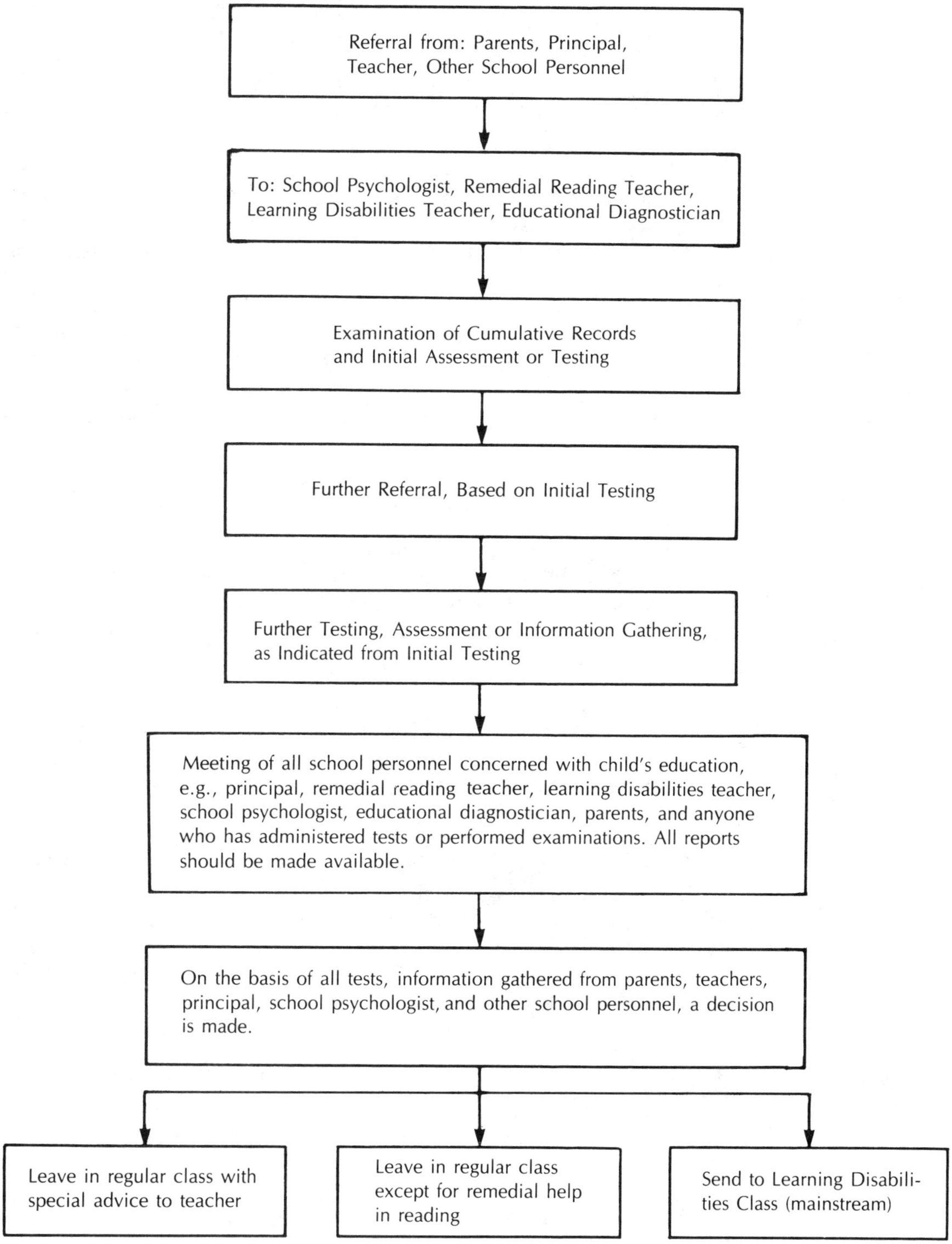

Referral from: Parents, Principal, Teacher, Other School Personnel
To: School Psychologist, Remedial Reading Teacher, Learning Disabilities Teacher, Educational Diagnostician
Examination of Cumulative Records and Initial Assessment or Testing
Further Referral, Based on Initial Testing
Further Testing, Assessment or Information Gathering, as Indicated from Initial Testing
Meeting of all school personnel concerned with child's education, e.g., principal, remedial reading teacher, learning disabilities teacher, school psychologist, educational diagnostician, parents, and anyone who has administered tests or performed examinations. All reports should be made available.
On the basis of all tests, information gathered from parents, teachers, principal, school psychologist, and other school personnel, a decision is made.
Leave in regular class with special advice to teacher
Leave in regular class except for remedial help in reading
Send to Learning Disabilities Class (mainstream)

Help the Disabled Reader to Recognize and Verbalize His or Her Problem

Some disabled readers may simply not realize that they have problems, while others may realize that they do not read as well as their peers and yet not know why. It is important for the disabled reader to be able to recognize his or her problem and to tell you what it is. Students can be helped to do this in a number of ways. For example, a student who reads word by word can listen to his or her reading via a tape recorder and then compare that reading with that of one of his or her better-reading peers whose reading was also recorded. A student who makes omissions can be given a copy of the material he or she has read incorrectly and told to circle all words that were omitted while listening to the tape-recorded passage.

Once the student is aware of a reading problem, you should then discuss it with him or her. During the discussion you should attempt to question the student closely enough to get him or her to tell you what seems to be wrong with his or her reading. This technique will not only make the student aware of the particular problem, but is also likely to provide an incentive for overcoming it.

Make the Disabled Reader Aware of His or Her Progress

It is often difficult for students to realize that they are actually improving in their reading ability. Since reading growth, like physical growth, often takes place rather slowly, a student may not really perceive any growth at all. The student can be made aware of his or her reading growth in a number of ways. Three of these techniques are discussed below.

1. After the student has improved in reading, he or she can read material that has been previously read and coded while the various types of errors are again coded by the teacher. The student can then be shown the reduction in each type of error from the first to the second readings. Tape recordings of the first and second readings also provide an excellent way of demonstrating improvement to a student. A tape recording in conjunction with a coded series of reading passages is still better.
2. Students who make a number of errors on the basic sight words can be given cards with known words on them. Each time a student learns a new word, he or she can be given a new card. In this way a student is easily able to watch his or her basic sight word vocabulary grow. Alternatively, the teacher can elect to take cards from the student when he or she has mastered troublesome words. In this way, the student sees the pile of cards gradually disappear until all basic sight word "troubles" are gone.
3. In phonics, the teacher can simply check or circle phonic elements not known. This checklist can then be shown to the student. As the various phonic elements are learned, the check marks or circles can be erased by the student.

By seeing active growth in his or her own reading skills, the student is much more likely to be motivated. And the student who is aware of progress is more likely to take an active interest in increasing his or her rate of progression.

Make the Learning Process Meaningful to the Child

Children, until they reach the junior high level or beyond, will seldom question why they are being taught various concepts and subject matter. However, the fact that they do not question why something is being taught does not mean that they believe in the necessity of learning it. In fact, the attitude that children often demonstrate confirms that they do not.

Most children, just as adults, when told that they must learn the basic sight words because they account for over half of the words that they will ever need to read, can understand the importance of thoroughly learning them. Children can also understand, if told, that they must do comprehension exercises to help them understand what they are reading so that they can get more out of their science and social studies books. Likewise, children need to be shown how learning the various word attack skills helps them unlock new words.

Use Materials Appropriate to the Needs of the Child

The reading program in many classrooms is dictated by the kinds of materials found within each classroom. This sort of situation is not desirable even in a developmental reading program, but it is completely intolerable in remedial reading. Excellent reading materials are no better than poor materials if they are not appropriate to the needs of the learner. Many reading programs have failed because an untrained teacher simply gave the disabled reader "more of the same."

The reading teacher must remember that students are, for the most part, delayed only in certain areas and that the weak areas must receive special attention. For example, a readily available book designed to improve a child's comprehension skills is of little value to a child who is experiencing problems with word attack skills.

Teachers and administrators should be extra cautious when buying materials to be used in remedial reading. Some materials attempt to do too many things to be really worthwhile in any one area of difficulty. For example, materials that attempt to enrich vocabulary, improve comprehension, and improve word attack skills in each lesson are likely to be of questionable value in remedial reading since a child is more likely to need an intensive saturation in one area rather than a well-rounded program of teaching each of these three skills. Educational research has also shown that many of the devices designed to speed up reading are of questionable value in developmental reading and may very well be detrimental to a disabled reader. In most cases, there is simply no valid reason for using them. Materials appropriate for the remedial reading classroom should contain lessons that are designed to remedy specific reading difficulties.

It is also important that the materials used be at the independent *or* instructional *reading level of the student and* not *at the student's* frustration *reading level.* (*For an explanation of these levels see pp. ERI 3 and 4.*)

Continue the Diagnosis While You Teach

A student who is being tested will often fail to perform as well as he or she does in the somewhat more relaxed day-to-day reading situation. If this happens, there is, of course, the danger that the student will fail certain items, while being tested, that he or she may know and thus will be channeled into unnecessary remedial work. For example, after testing a child, you may discover that a number of phonic elements and a number of basic sight words were missed and the student may also have missed a number of comprehension questions. You are quite likely to find that later in a normal classroom atmosphere the student will know some of the phonic elements and basic sight words and may improve a great deal in his or her comprehension. Such improvement in the area of phonics and basic sight words is often accounted for simply by the absence of stress that is present during the testing situation or by the difference in performance criteria between testing and actually reading. In the area of comprehension a child is likely to show improvement simply because he or she knows more about subject matter in general than was demonstrated on a particular passage or on a set of passages on a test. The prevalence of such cases emphasizes the need for continual diagnosis during the remediation period.

Maintain a Relaxed Attitude

Students who come to remedial reading have often experienced years of failure. When entering the remedial reading class, they are often greeted by a teacher who tests their reading ability as a beginning activity. Many of these students are likely to be highly defensive. During this time it is especially important that the teacher maintain a relaxed attitude that will, in turn, usually calm the tensions of students who are resentful or fearful.

Do Not Be Too Authoritative

Although the reading teacher may be firm in demanding certain standards, he or she should strive to create a climate in which students feel free to express themselves. This expression may take the form of discussing negative feelings about reading or any other tasks at which they feel unsuccessful. In discussing these negative feelings, a student should not be forced to hear a sermon on why he or she should like to read or why the student should like school. The importance of being able to read can be discussed at a later time when the student is not irritated.

Have Confidence in the Student's Ability to Learn

Not only must the reading teacher have confidence in the student's ability to learn, but he or she must also transfer this belief to the student so that the student will have confidence in his or her own learning ability. Several studies have shown that when teachers believe a student or even a group of students will be successful, they are more likely to be successful. Other studies have shown that teachers can be negatively influenced by seeing low IQ scores or achievement scores previously made by their students. However, still other studies have shown that teachers' positive thinking need not be changed even though they have been told a student or a group of students are not likely to achieve well. In summary then, the reading teacher must constantly search for the key that will unlock each student's learning potential.

Direct the Student toward Self-Instruction

Although the specific instruction that students may get in a reading classroom is almost always certain to be of considerable benefit to them, the amount that children learn on their own is often of equal or greater importance. This is, no doubt, true of almost any class that a student attends regardless of the subject matter. The learning that takes place within the classroom is, of course, of greater importance in the beginning, but it only serves as a stepping stone to the broadening of the student's knowledge. One might say that the classroom learning points the student in the right direction from which he or she then proceeds to expand and broaden that knowledge. Often the amount of time available for special tutoring sessions is severely limited due to the lack of an adequate teaching staff. In this situation the reading teacher must direct the child toward self-instruction.

Self-instruction may take many different forms depending on the age-grade level of the student, the nature of the reading disability, and a host of other factors. For example, a teacher may diagnose a child as having a very limited sight vocabulary and, as a result, spend many hours teaching words that the student should have learned during his or her progression through the grades. Such effort, however, can be quite futile if the child does not begin to read on his or her own, so that he or she is continually exposed to new words learned during the remedial sessions.

Begin Each Period with a Summary of What You Intend to Do; End Each Period with a Summary of What You Did and Why

As parents, most of us have at some time or another asked our children what they learned at school today. An all-too-common answer to this question is "Oh nothing." As teachers, most of us also realize the "Oh nothing" statement is probably incorrect. What we must remember, however, is that the "Oh nothing" represents the child's perception of what was learned. In order to stimulate or motivate a child to want to learn, the teacher must be cognizant of how *the child* feels about it. A child may, in reality, be learning a great deal, but if *he* or *she* does not really believe that learning is taking place, then chances are he or she will take little active interest in what is being taught.

In order to avoid the "Oh nothing" response, the child should be briefed on what is going to be taught and why the student needs to learn it, and then at the end of the tutoring session, the teacher should review what has been learned and why it was necessary to learn it. If you follow this procedure, you will find an overall improvement in students' attitudes toward learning, and, in addition, you are likely to improve your public relations program with the parents of the children you teach.

Provide for a Follow-Up Program

Remedial reading programs in which the disabled readers have been kept for a considerable length of time have tended to be more successful than those that have only brought children in for short periods of time. This is especially true where some sort of follow-up program was not instituted for children who were terminated from short-term remedial reading programs. The follow-up program may be one in which the student is brought back into the remedial reading classroom for only one-half or one-third of the amount of time he or she spent in it during the more intensive tutoring. However, research clearly illustrates that students who have been in intensive remedial reading programs are quite likely to regress if some sort of follow-up program is not instituted.

3

Diagnosis and Remediation of Letter Knowledge and Sight Words

In this chapter you will be introduced to methods of testing students' knowledge of the letters of the alphabet, their knowledge of basic sight words, and knowledge of sight words in general. Methods are then given for remediation of students who are lacking in their knowledge of these skills.

DIAGNOSING STUDENTS' KNOWLEDGE OF THE ALPHABET

In diagnosing students' knowledge of the alphabet, the reading teacher should remember that there are several competencies that students should possess. They should be able to match upper and lower case letters. They should be able to say and write the alphabet in order, and they should be able to identify letters as someone points to them. Students' ability to say the alphabet in order can, of course, be tested by simply asking them to recite the alphabet. They can be further tested by giving them a piece of paper and asking them to write the alphabet. In this case you may wish to specify whether you want them to write the alphabet in upper or lower case letters, or perhaps, both ways.

Students' ability to identify the letters, in both upper and lower case, can be tested using the stimulus sheet and answer sheets provided in Appendix A. You will note in using these materials that the letters are written in both upper and lower case. Another line is also provided for those students who are unable to identify letters to determine whether they have the ability to match like letters, which is the lowest level of the alphabet skills. Complete directions for the use of these materials is contained in Appendix A.

DIAGNOSING STUDENTS' KNOWLEDGE OF BASIC SIGHT WORDS

Basic sight words are those words of very high utility or that appear very often in written material. For example, one study showed that the words *a, and,* and *the* account for about 10 percent of the written words in most printed materials. Many studies have been done to determine just how many words might best be used to develop a core list for testing and teaching purposes. As a result of these studies, most of the better-known lists contain somewhere between 200–300 words. One of the earlier, and still widely used, is the Dolch list referred to in Chapter 1. It contains 220 words. One of the more recent lists is the Harris-Jacobson list also referred to in Chapter 1.

The Ekwall Basic Sight Word List, used in this handbook, contains 299 words. It contains words common to eight sets of widely used basal readers, all of the Dolch list, and all of the words found common to the eighty most frequently read children's books, as shown in a study by William Durr (1973).

All materials necessary for the testing of basic sight words will be found in Appendix B.

DIAGNOSING STUDENTS' KNOWLEDGE OF SIGHT WORDS IN GENERAL

Graded sight word lists are usually used to assess students' knowledge of sight words in general, or their reading level as it relates to word knowledge. The results of testing with a graded word list are, in many cases, a close estimation of a student's overall reading level. A number of graded sight word lists are available; however, one that the author has found to be useful is the San Diego Quick Assessment List (1969). It is found in the *Ekwall Reading Inventory* in Appendix J of this handbook. It is used in giving the *Ekwall Reading Inventory* to help in determining where students should begin reading in order to establish their independent reading level. If you wish to use it to determine a student's knowledge of sight words in general, you may wish to duplicate the stimulus sheet for these words from the *Ekwall Reading Inventory* found on pp. ERI 42 and 64. You may also wish to duplicate the answer sheet for the words. The answer sheet is found on pp. ERI 114 and 115.

If you are using this list to determine a student's knowledge of sight words in general, keep in mind that it is to be used differently than it is to be used in the *Ekwall Reading Inventory.* In using it in the *Ekwall Reading Inventory* any word that is pronounced correctly by the student is counted as being correct, regardless of the amount of time the student takes to pronounce the word. *On the other hand, if it is being used strictly to assess a student's knowledge of sight words in general, then words should be counted wrong that are not pronounced almost instantly.*

Other sources of sight word lists are as follows:

Bader, Lois A. *Bader reading and language inventory.* New York: Macmillan, 1983.

Burns, Paul C., and Roe, Betty D. *Informal reading assessment.* Chicago: Rand McNally, 1980.

Jacobs, Donald H., and Searfoss, Lyndon W. *Diagnostic reading inventory.* Dubuque, Iowa: Kendall/Hunt, 1979.

Johns, Jerry L. *Basic reading inventory.* Dubuque, Iowa: Kendall/Hunt, 1978.

Rinsky, Lee Ann, and de Fossard, Esta. *The contemporary classroom reading inventory.* Dubuque, Iowa: Gorsuch Scarisbrick, 1980.

Silvaroli, Nicholas J. *Classroom reading inventory.* 4th ed. Dubuque, Iowa: William C. Brown, 1982.

Woods, Mary Lynn, and Moe, Alden J. *Analytical reading inventory.* Columbus, Ohio: Charles E. Merrill, 1981.

In using graded sight word lists, you should keep their limitations in mind. For example, remember that you are only sampling a few words at each level as an overall estimate of a child's ability to pronounce words at that level. A child who is very good at word attack skills may tend to pronounce correctly quite a few words that are not in his or her sight vocabulary. You should, however, be able to determine whether this is happening, to some extent, based on the time and ease with which the child responds to each word. You should also remember that many children are disabled in reading because of their inability to comprehend what they read. For this type of child the graded word list is quite likely to be inaccurate in terms of placement level.

REMEDIATION PROCEDURES FOR LETTER KNOWLEDGE

If students are having difficulty with the alphabet, you should not attempt to teach more than one or two letters per day. Each time a new letter is introduced, be sure to review all of those already learned so as to provide many exposures to each letter.

A Basic Learning Technique

Give students prepared sheets of paper in which the lines appear as follows:

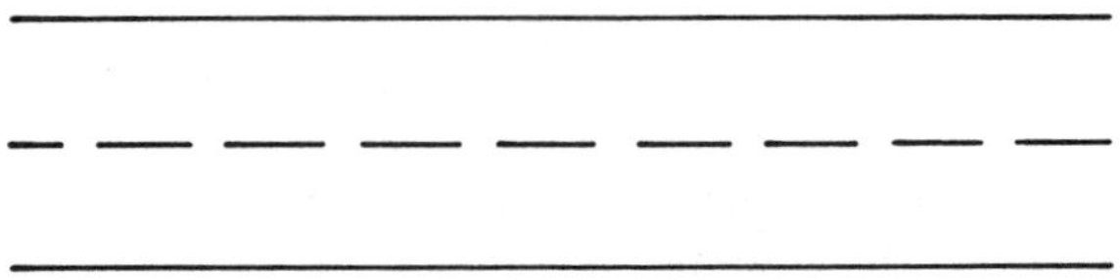

Write each new letter at the beginning of the line to illustrate its proper configuration as shown below:

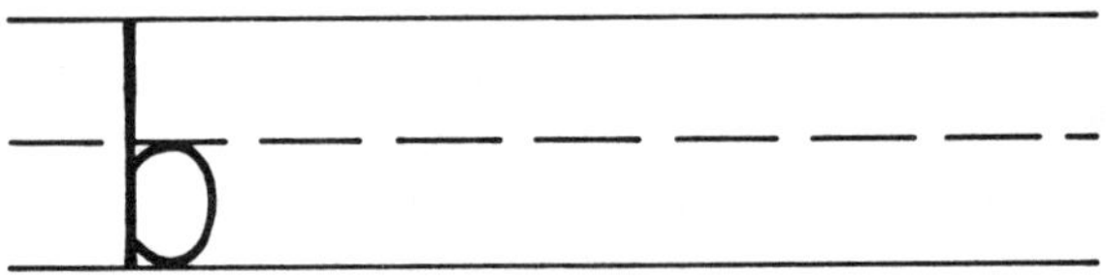

Tell the students the name of the letter and talk about its configuration. For older students above first grade, you may wish to discuss or have students name some words that start with the *b* sound. The teacher can then write these words on the chalkboard so that students get as many exposures to the letter as possible. After the letter appears on the sheet as shown previously, it might then appear several times using broken lines as shown below:

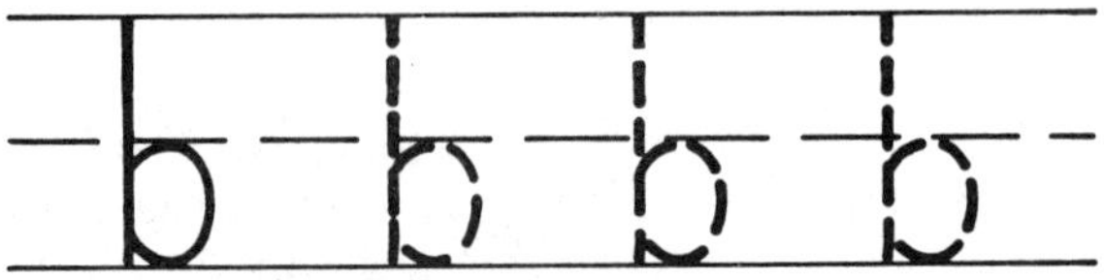

Have students trace over the broken lines to make the three letters with broken lines look like the first one that is solid. After they have done this, have them make a number of *b*'s on the same kind of lined paper. Ask them to say "b" as they trace or make the letter. Then have them practice making *b*'s on regular lined paper.

Other Teaching Techniques

1. Have students place a piece of paper over a piece of wire screen (the kind used on screen doors) and write the letter with a crayon. This will leave a series of raised or three-dimensional letters. Then have students trace over these raised letters with their fingers and say each letter as it is traced.
2. Give students three-dimensional letters such as those used on magnetic boards. Have them feel several letters that are being learned. Then blindfold them and have them identify the letters by feeling them. This can also be done with letters made with a baked mixture of salt, flour, and water.
3. Have students make letters of modeling clay.
4. Place cereals such as "Alpha-Bits" in individual bowls. Let students search for letters and eat each one they can name correctly.

For other ideas on teaching the letters of the alphabet, read the ideas for teaching sight words and ways of using the tape recorder to teach sight words. A number of these exercises can easily be adapted to teaching letter knowledge.

REMEDIATION PROCEDURES FOR SIGHT WORDS AND BASIC SIGHT WORDS

In the teaching of sight words there is little doubt that using any approach that focuses on one word at a time is bound to fail. It is recommended therefore that, in general, students who lack knowledge of a considerable number of basic sight words, as well as sight words in general, be exposed to two basic methods in the beginning stages of teaching. These two methods are the *language-experience approach* and the *neurological impress method.* Eldon E. Ekwall and James L. Shanker (1983) have described the use of the language-experience approach in a group situation as follows:*

1. Discuss some event of great interest. After discussing the event ask students if they would like to write a story about it.
2. As students dictate the story, write it on chart paper using the following methods:
   a. Use manuscript or cursive writing—whichever is common to the age-grade level of the group with whom you are working.
   b. Use a heavy writing instrument such as a felt-tip pen.
   c. Use the language of the students and do not attempt to alter it.

* From: Ekwall, Eldon E., and Shaker, James L. *Diagnosis and Remediation of the Disabled Reader* (2nd ed.). Newton, MA: Allyn and Bacon, Inc., 1983. (Reprinted by permission.)

d. Make sure students see the words as they are being written.
e. Try to adhere to the one important event and follow a sequence of events.
f. Use one-line sentences for severely disabled readers and gradually increase sentence length as improvement is noted.
g. In beginning each new sentence emphasize the fact that you start on the left and proceed to the right.
h. Emphasize the return sweep from the end of one sentence to the beginning of the next.

3. After the story has been completed, reread it as a choral exercise. Either you or a child may point to each word as it is read. It is important that the word being read is the same one being pointed to.
4. Have individual children take turns rereading the story sentence by sentence.
5. Duplicate the story on a large piece of tagboard and have students cut it into sentence strips. These can then be put in a pocket chart to form the original story. Go back to the original chart when necessary. Also let students rearrange the sentences to form a different order of events in the story.
6. After students have read the story over many times, you may wish to cut the tagboard sentences up into words and let students form the original sentences and new sentences.
7. As more stories are dictated and read and as students build a larger sight vocabulary, you may wish to duplicate stories on ditto paper and give each individual student a copy to be cut into sentences and/or words for building varying story order and new sentences.
8. As students' reading ability grows, you should begin to let each student write and illustrate his or her own stories. These can be bound into booklets with attractive covers indicating the "author" of each book. Students should then begin to read each other's books.
9. A great deal of emphasis should always be placed on rereading materials that were written earlier, as children require a great many exposures to each word before it becomes a sight word. After sight vocabularies begin to grow considerably, students can begin to read library or trade books.

When using the language-experience approach with an individual student you may wish to use a process somewhat similar to the following:

1. As with a group, find some event of interest to the student and ask the student to record the event on paper.
2. As the student dictates the events, you should write them on a piece of paper with the student seated so that the words can be observed as they are written. The same methods listed in steps 2 (a) through (h) above for a group should be observed, except the writing may be done on 8½″ x 11″ paper with a pencil or felt-tip pen.
3. After the story has been completed, you may wish to type it on a pica or primary-size typewriter as appropriate to the grade level of the student. (For third grade and above use regular pica type.)
4. Have the student reread the story, with either you or the student (if able to do it properly) pointing to each word as it is read. Depending on the ability of the student at this stage, the story may be reread sentence by sentence in varying order.
5. Let the student illustrate the story or apply stickers, pictures, or other decoration. Finally, the story should be placed in a booklet to be kept and reviewed each time you meet.
6. You may wish to duplicate the typewritten copies of these stories so that

students can cut them up and rearrange first the sentences and later the words within each sentence.

7. Bind groups of experience stories into booklets with illustrated covers and encourage all students to exchange and read each other's booklets.
8. Gradually encourage the student to branch out into the reading of trade books.

> The language-experience approach is especially appropriate for disabled readers because it is immediately meaningful to them—they are writing about events in their own lives and using their own speaking vocabularies. Another advantage is that it develops a feeling of security and success and keeps pace with their development. It also gives meaning to their reading because students learn to associate printed stories with their own experiences from having seen their own experiences transferred to print. (pp. 103–4)

The language-experience approach is also of great benefit to children with language difficulties. A deficit in language can cause children to experience little success in the comprehension of materials even if they do have the word attack skills to pronounce most words properly. When students with a language deficit read a story that they have dictated using their own vocabulary, they will immediately experience success in all phases of reading, including comprehension.

The *neurological impress method* was explained a number of years ago by R. G. Heckelman (1966). It has been extremely successful when used as described by him. In fact, it has been so successful and so easy to use that it is often overlooked as a method of teaching disabled readers because of its simplicity. It should be used as follows:

1. Sit the student with whom you will be working slightly in front of you so that you are in a position to be able to read directly into his or her ear and so that you can easily point to words as they are read by you and the student.
2. Begin by using materials that are rather easy for the student. Also in the beginning stages read at a slightly slower rate of speed than you would normally read when reading by yourself so that the student is able to keep up without a great deal of difficulty. After working with the student for a few sessions, the teacher may provide more difficult reading matter.
3. Explain to the student that you are going to read the material to be read and that the student is to read along with you, attempting to pronounce the word either at the same time as you pronounce it or slightly after you if the word is not known by the student. As you begin to read, be sure to point to each word as it is pronounced by you and by the student. *This is an extremely important part of the procedure. The student should be looking at the word as he or she is pronouncing it.* If the student tends to complain about the difficulty of the material, explain that you know the material being read is too difficult for the student to read by himself or herself but that soon he or she will be able to do much better.
4. In working with the student you are likely to begin to see a sharp increase in the student's ability to read. When this happens you may wish to increase your rate of speed slightly.

5. Heckelman suggests working with the student for periods ranging from five to fifteen minutes at a sitting. Keep a record of the total time spent in this activity. Heckelman suggests that it is not uncommon to cover from ten to twenty pages during one session.
6. Explain the procedure to a parent so that it may be continued at home in a similar situation. When explaining the procedure to parents make sure they understand that pointing to each word is necessary even if, for them, it seems awkward at first.

Heckelman cautions that teachers working with this method often make the mistake of moving into more difficult materials at too slow a pace and that it is not unusual to see growth rates of two years in an accumulated reading time of two or three hours. He suggests that after an accumulated time of six hours the student might be expected to have gained four to five levels in the ability to read.

Experiments have been done in which researchers have attempted to duplicate Heckelman's results using a tape recorder and having the student follow along with the reading as the words are pronounced on the recorder. However, most studies with which the author is familiar have failed. This, in the author's opinion, is because when students are reading in conjunction with a tape recorder, you have no way of ensuring that the student is actually looking at the word being read. The student's looking at the word as it is read seems to be the key to the success of this method.

Other Methods of Teaching Sight Vocabulary

No attempt will be made to differentiate between the teaching of sight words and basic sight words. In addition, in many of the games and exercises that follow, both sight words and basic sight words are simply referred to as sight words. However, since basic sight words are usually of higher utility than other sight words, primary emphasis should be placed on the learning of basic sight words before attempting to teach words of lower utility.

While the techniques for teaching sight words in a remedial reading program are essentially the same as those used in a developmental reading program, there are a few specialized techniques that may be used with students who have a great deal of difficulty in learning. One of the most important things to remember in teaching any sight word is that before a student is likely to learn and remember it, he must come into contact with it many times. Studies have shown that some words may be learned with only a few exposures. However, you should generally not expect a word to become a known sight word until a student has read it at least twenty times. Some students who have more difficulty in learning may need as many as 100–140 exposures to a word before it becomes a known sight word.

Another important thing to remember in teaching sight words is that once the student has the ability to begin to read, he or she will be able to analyze many new words through the use of word attack or word analysis skills. At this point, the student should simply be encouraged to read a great deal on his or her own. This reading will enable the student to encounter many new words many times, and they will thus become a part of his or her sight vocabulary.

A Basic Method of Teaching Words

There are many ways to teach a new word to a student or to a group of students; however, a method somewhat similar to the following will often prove successful:

1. Write a sentence on the chalkboard in which the new word to be introduced is used in a meaningful context. Underline the word.
2. Let students read the sentence and attempt to say the new word using context clues along with other word attack skills. If you are introducing a new story that students are to read, it is especially important that they are not told each new word in advance as this deprives them of the opportunity to apply word attack skills themselves.
3. Discuss the meaning of the word or how it is often used in talking and writing. Try to tie it to something in their background of experiences. If possible, attempt to illustrate the word with a picture or some concrete object.
4. Write the word as students watch. Ask them to look for certain configuration clues such as double letters, ascenders, descenders, and so forth. Also ask them to look for any well-known phonograms or word families (e.g., *ill, ant, ake,* and so on), but do not call attention to little words within big or longer words.
5. Ask students to write the word themselves and to be sure and *say* the word while they write it. Research done by the Socony–Vacuum Oil Company has shown that we tend to remember about 90 percent of what we say as we do a thing, 70 percent of what we say as we talk, 50 percent of what we see and hear, and only 10 to 20 percent of what we simply read or hear.
6. Have students make up and write sentences in which the word is used in context. Have them read these sentences to each other and discuss them as they are read.

Flash Presentation of Words

Put several students in a group. Include some who know the sight words to be learned and some who do not know them. Then give students a tachistoscopic, or flash presentation, of the words. Try to expose each word for about one-half second. Ask students to yell out each word as it is flashed. They enjoy this activity even though it is rather noisy. The same group of words should, of course, be gone over quite a few times so that those students who do not know the words can learn them from the ones who do.

Who Gets It First

Do this activity essentially the same as the one above but with only three students in the group. Use sight words that are known by some students but that are not known to others. As each card is flashed, each student should call out the word as soon as he or she can. The first student to call out the word gets to keep the card with the word written on it. The student who gets the most cards is the winner.

Look-Alike Words

Research has shown that words that students often confuse, such as *through* and *though* or *county* and *country,* can be learned more easily through the use of color cues. In this case one might use either white or colored chalk to write the words on the chalkboard; however, the *r* in *country* and *through,* for example, would be written in a contrasting color and then discussed. The words would then be rewritten all in one color and again presented to the same students.

Words with Similar Beginning Letters

Research has also shown that students get their strongest clues to words by looking at the first one or two letters and to some extent the last letters. However, this often causes students to miscall words, such as *what* for *when* and *then* for *than.* When this happens, you should put both words on the overhead projector or chalkboard and let students point out the differences between each word. Then let students write each word as they *say* it. It is important that they also say the word as it is written.

Look-Alike Words in Context

When students confuse words that look alike, it is often helpful to use the words in context and to provide a choice situation for using the correct word in the particular context. Note the examples that follow:

Directions: Write the correct word in each blank from the choices given below each blank

1. Steve went ______________________ the tunnel.
   (though—through—thought)

2. John is taller __________ Robert.
   (than—then)

Sight Word Bingo

Cut cards of tagboard into squares about 8″ x 8″. Then divide each card into sections as shown below:

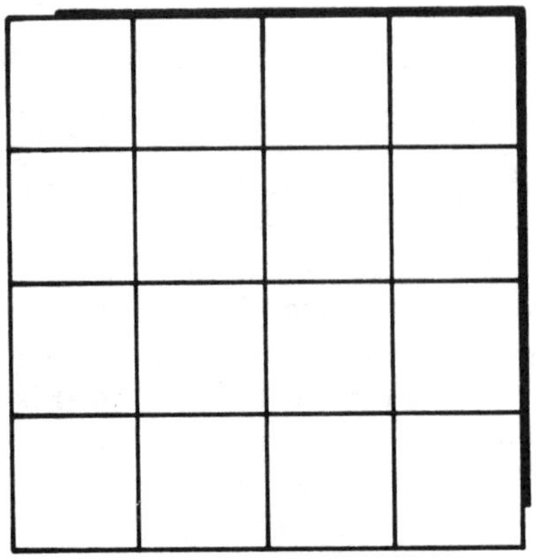

In each square, write a basic sight word. Make a number of cards, and include various basic sight words. Use the same words on several cards, but make sure they appear in different squares. Number each card. Then make a master list of all words used. Also make lists of words that can be called on certain cards so that you can ensure that certain students who need success will win.

To play the game, the teacher calls out words while students hunt those words on their cards. When a word is found, it is covered with a bean, button, or whatever. As in Bingo, the first student to cover four successive squares is the winner. Students should then be asked to read the words back to the teacher to make sure they can say the words when they see them as well as recognize them when they are called. If you have students playing who do not know all the words, you may wish to have a student who does know all the words help one who does not.

Pairs

Make about forty cards with a sight word on each card. Use only twenty words so that each word appears on two cards.

The game works well with two to six players. Each player is dealt six cards face down and then picks them up. The remaining cards are placed in a pile face down on the table. Players then look at their cards and attempt to find pairs of sight words. Each player in turn draws one card from the pile on the table, which he or she may either discard or keep and discard another from his or her hand. Discarded cards are placed face down on a pile. Players continue to draw and discard until one player gets three pairs. The student then says, "pairs," and must say each word. If the student can say each word, he or she wins the game.

Sight Word Donkey

Make about forty or fifty cards with a sight word on each card. On one card, draw a picture of a donkey. Place the word cards face down on the table and the donkey card beside it. Play then begins by having each player pick up one card from the word pile and try to say the word. If the student says it correctly, he or she keeps the card and the next player has a turn. If a player cannot say the word correctly, the student must take the donkey card and place it face up in front of him or her. The next player then continues. If the student cannot say the word on the card drawn, then he or she has to take the donkey card from the player who has it. Play continues in this manner until all cards have been picked up and the words pronounced correctly. The player with the donkey card in front of him or her when the last card is picked up is the "donkey."

Eraser Race

In this activity a number of sight words are written on the chalkboard and a vertical line is drawn on the board just above the chalk tray. Two students, each with an eraser, stand at opposite ends of the chalk tray facing the chalkboard. Each student places an eraser at the outside edge of the chalk tray. The teacher points to the sight words, one at a time, that are written on the chalkboard while the two students take turns trying to say the words. Each time a student says a word correctly, the student moves his or her eraser (the length of the eraser) toward the center of the chalk tray. The first student to get to the vertical line in the center wins. You will find it easier to gauge how far to move the eraser each time if short vertical lines are drawn at exact eraser lengths the entire length of the chalk tray. The game may also be played with several players on a team. This works well when students do not know the words too well and the rules allow any member of the team to call the word if he or she knows it. The students who do not know the words will, of course, learn them from the ones who do.

Move Up

Have students form two teams of equal numbers. The two teams line up and face the teacher who has a pack of sight words. The teacher then flashes a word and the two team members nearest the teacher each try to say the word first. The student who gets it first scores a point for his or her team. Both of these two students then move to the rear of the line and the next two students move up. If neither of the two students can say the word, it is inserted back in the pack and flashed again later. Play continues until all words have been pronounced correctly. The team with the most points at the time the teacher's word pack is gone is the winner. It is a good idea to have a scorekeeper and a judge who can decide who said a word first when the decision is difficult to make.

Using New Words in Context

Give students about five or six new sight words by listing them on the chalkboard or by using an overhead projector. Ask an equal number of students to go to the chalkboard and write a sentence in which each of the new words is used. Ask them to underline each new sight word. (More than one word may be used in each sentence.) Discuss each sentence with the group. Correct any that are wrong.

Making Three-Dimensional Words with Wire Screen

Give students a piece of wire screen (about 8″ x 12″) the same as that used on screen doors. Cover the sharp edges with a piece of bookbinding tape. Have students lay a piece of paper over the screen and write words on it with a crayon. This will leave a series of raised dots. Then have them remove the paper and trace over the raised dots, saying the word as they trace it.

Using a Kinesthetic Approach

For children who do not seem to learn through methods normally used, the kinesthetic approach is sometimes successful. Most teachers who use this approach usually follow the procedural steps discussed below.

Step 1. The child is shown a word, and the word is pronounced for him or her. The word may be written on the chalkboard, on a large sheet of paper, or on a flashcard approximately 3″ high by 9″ wide. Wherever it is written, the letters should usually be about two inches high. A very broad felt-tip marking pen works well for writing on tagboard flashcards. It may be written either in manuscript or cursive writing. The one chosen is usually that with which the child is most familiar or the one he or she is presently using in school.

Step 2. The child should be asked to trace the word while saying it. The student is to say each part of the word as he or she traces that part; however, the student is directed not to sound it out letter by letter. It is also important that the student's finger or fingers contact the surface of the paper or tagboard at all times while the word is being traced. Some teachers have children use only their index fingers. I would suggest, however, that you have the child use his or her middle and index fingers at the same time as though they, both together, were one large pencil or piece of chalk. The child should continue this tracing until both you and he or she are relatively sure the word is known.

Step 3. The child should then be asked to write the word while looking at the original copy. When the child writes the word, it should also be written in letters that are about two inches high. The student should also be directed to say each word part as it is written.

Step 4. In the final step of this procedure, the child should be told to write the word again, but this time from memory. The student should also be told to say the word again while writing it.

USING THE TAPE RECORDER TO TEACH SIGHT WORDS

Materials Envelopes, cards (approximately 3″ x 8″), cassette tape and player, and a numbered practice sheet.

Procedure 1 Write a sight word on each card, and on the other side of the card, put a number. Put eight cards in each envelope, and number the envelopes to correspond with the narrative on each tape. Program the tape recorder to say: "Now you will be given some words to be learned. Take the words from envelope number one. Place them in a pile on the table so that the numbers are showing. Number one should be on top, number two under number one, number three under number two [and so on]. Turn the tape recorder off until you have done this. [Pause four seconds] Now turn over card number one. This word is *was—was.* Now you say it. [Pause two seconds] Now listen to this sentence using *was.* 'I *was* going to go with Mary.' Now take your practice sheet and write the word *was* beside number one. You may look at the card if you need to. Turn the tape recorder off until you have done this. [Pause four seconds] Now look at the word you just wrote; it is spelled *w-a-s.* Say it again. [Pause two seconds]. Now turn over card number two. . . ," and so on for each additional word.

Materials Cards with sight words printed on the front and numbers on the back, cassette tape and player.

Procedure 2 Place the cards in a pile, numbered side up, so that number one is on the top, number two is next, and so forth. The tape recorder is programmed to say: "Number one is *dog,* [pause] number two is *then"* [and so on]. Each student takes a turn at drawing a card, turning it over, and trying to say the word. After saying it, the student turns on the tape recorder to check his or her answer. Students keep all the cards they get right and place missed cards on a pile in the middle of the table. Play should continue until all the words are mastered. (The number of word cards used will depend on the competence of the students.)

Materials Pocket chart, cassette tape and player, and a set of eight cards with sight words on one side and numbers on the other.

Procedure 3 Place the cards in the pocket chart so that the word side is showing. Program the tape recorder to say: "Now you will hear some words called. As you hear each word, try to find it in the pocket chart. When you find it, lay it face down on the table. When you find the next one, lay it face down on the first card. Do this until all the words have been called. Here is the first word: *was* [pause five seconds] *did* [pause five seconds] *go* [pause four seconds] *came* [pause four seconds] *from* [pause three seconds] *then* [pause three seconds] *but* [pause three seconds] *come.* Now look at the pile of cards. They should be numbered from number one on the top to number eight on the bottom. See whether they are in that order. If they are not, change them so that they are in that order. Turn the tape recorder off while you check carefully. [pause four seconds] If they were in the right order it means that you knew all of the words and you may rewind the tape and put the materials away. If they were not in the right order, turn them over and point to each word as you hear it. The first word is *was,* the next word is *did,* the next word is *go,* the next word is *came,* the next word is *from,* the next word is *then,* the next word is *but,* and the last word is *come.* Since you did not get them all right the first time, put the word cards back in the pocket chart and rewind the tape and begin again." (Note that the tape is programmed to give the students who need help continuous practice until all the words are mastered.)

The use of the computer for teaching basic sight words is becoming increasingly popular. In looking for programs that are appropriate for use with the computer keep in mind that if students are not able to recognize a number of *basic sight words,* then it is unlikely that they would be able to use the computer if the program requires that the student be able to read various directions for its use. It should also be remembered that a student is not likely to benefit from a program that uses various basic sight words in context since the words not known from the basic sight word list are likely to be at a lower level than the words that accompany them in context. Programs that would seem to be most effective for students with serious deficiencies in knowledge of basic sight words would be those that require a voice synthesizer to enable the student to hear each word as it appears on the screen.

REFERENCES

Bader, Lois A. *Bader reading and language inventory.* New York: Macmillan, 1983.

Burns, Paul C., and Roe, Betty D. *Informal reading assessment.* Chicago: Rand McNally, 1980.

Durr, William K. Computer study of high frequency words in popular trade juveniles. *The Reading Teacher,* October 1973, 27, 37–42.

References

Ekwall, Eldon E., and Shanker, James L. *Diagnosis and remediation of the disabled reader.* 2d ed. Newton, Massachusetts: Allyn and Bacon, 1983.

Heckelman, R. G. Using the neurological-impress remedial reading technique. *Academic Therapy Quarterly,* Summer 1966, I, 235–39.

Jacobs, Donald H., and Searfoss, Lyndon W. *Diagnostic reading inventory.* Dubuque, Iowa: Kendall/Hunt, 1979.

Johns, Jerry L. *Basic reading inventory.* Dubuque, Iowa: Kendall/Hunt, 1978.

Rinsky, Lee Ann, and de Fossard, Esta. *The contemporary classroom reading inventory.* Dubuque, Iowa: Gorsuch Scarisbrick, 1980.

Silvaroli, Nicholas J. *Classroom reading inventory.* 4th ed. Dubuque, Iowa: William C. Brown, 1982.

Woods, Mary Lynn, and Moe, Alden J. *Analytical reading inventory.* Columbus, Ohio: Charles E. Merrill, 1981.

4

Diagnosis and Remediation of the Use of Context Clues

DIAGNOSIS OF STUDENTS' KNOWLEDGE OF CONTEXT CLUES

As teachers, we have often used context clues so much in our reading that we take it for granted that students should be able to do the same. It is also true that many students become aware of, and use, context clues a great deal in their reading. This is evidenced by their frequent repetitions of words that precede a word they do not know. However, it is also important to remember that for some students the ability to use context clues does not come naturally. For these students, it is necessary to discuss how context clues can be used either to help them attack a strange word or to help them figure out the meaning of the word.

The first step in teaching students how to use context clues is to locate those students who do not possess this ability so that they can be given instruction in using this important skill. In Appendix C you will find passages written at each level from grades one through six. These passages can be used to give you a general idea of each student's ability to use context clues. Complete instructions for getting these materials ready for use are given on pp. 236–237 in Appendix C. Although the author knows of no "normed" test for students' ability to use context clues, some general guidelines in terms of whether the student's ability would be considered as *Excellent, Good, Fair,* or *Poor* are given in Appendix C. Some general guidelines for assessing students' ability to use context clues are as follows:

1. Do not expect students to be able to use context clues effectively in material that is written at one or more grade levels above their own reading level (not their grade level, but reading level).
2. With some students it may be necessary to give a little more explanation than is on the card. This is allowable, but do not give them the answers.
3. If a student can get only a few or no words at the grade level at which you think he or she is reading, then drop down to the next lower level. If the student is able to get most of the words at this level, it can usually be assumed that the surrounding words at the higher level were too difficult and thus kept the student from being able to use the context effectively. On the other hand, if the student cannot get most of the words, even on the easiest passage, providing that you know it is below that student's reading level, then you should assume that the student has difficulty with, and needs instruction in the use of, context clues.

REMEDIATION PROCEDURES FOR CONTEXT CLUES

In teaching students to use context clues you should remember that they may get clues from pictures and thus use *picture context clues,* or they may get the meaning of a word from the written context along with the initial sound of the word. It should be stressed that most students do not use context clues as a word attack skill in isolation; that is, they usually use context clues in conjunction with other word attack skills. Context clues that are derived from the written word are usually classified as either *semantic* or *syntactic* clues. Semantic clues are meaning clues that students get from the words, phrases, or sentences surrounding the word. Syntactic clues are those that the student gets from what would simply *sound right,* in terms of the way we speak. Thus it is conceivable that a student may use all of the above types of context clues, along with the first sound in a word to attack a new word.

Students in beginning reading often make extensive use of picture context clues. If you were to visit a first-grade classroom, near the beginning of the year before students had developed a sizable sight vocabulary and before they had learned much of other word attack skills, you would notice that as they read they would quite often look at the top of the page, if a picture appeared there, in order to attempt to derive a clue that would be helpful in pronouncing a new word. As students become more mature in their use of context clues, they tend to depend more on semantic and syntactic clues along with phonics and/or structural analysis.

One of the most important procedures that you can use in teaching students to use context clues, in the beginning stages, is to make them aware of the fact that they are able to figure out new or missing words from our language. For this reason the author recommends that with students in the beginning stages of learning context clues you make them aware of how the words are used in our oral language. This can be done by tape-recording passages with words that are rather obviously left out. The students can then listen to the passages and respond, in some way, to the words they believe were left out of the tape-recorded passages. An example of this type of exercise might be one in which the student is given a worksheet numbered from one to four as shown below. Each number is followed by a list of approximately three words from which the student is to choose as he or she listens to a tape.

1. of	to	be
2. to	of	in
3. of	an	him
4. the	get	do

A tape recording is played and each time a word is omitted it is replaced with a tone or beep sound. Each time the student hears the tone or beep he or she is to underline or circle the word that he or she believes would be most appropriate from the three choices. When doing this, be sure to wait a few seconds for the student to make his or her choice before reading the next sentence. The tape recording for the above list might appear as follows:

John and his father were going ___beep___ go camping.

John packed his sleeping bag ___beep___ a big box.

Father put a lot ___beep___ food in another box.

John could hardly wait to ___beep___ started.

If students are not at the point where they can read words such as those shown above, then the tape recorder can be stopped after each word and a discussion can be held to decide what word would properly fit the one omitted from each sentence.

Using Picture Context

Place several pictures at the top of a page. Then write sentences leaving out one word, except for the last letter, that stands for the meaning represented by the picture. Have students fill in the blanks. To make this exercise a little more difficult, you may wish to have several pictures that end in the same letter. An example might be as follows:

1. Frank s ____t ate some grass.
2. He gave the present to the ____y.
3. He put the ____t in a box.
4. Irma got a new ____y for her birthday.
5. The boy and ____l went to the store.

Stress the Importance of Context Clues While Children Read

Most adults, if asked whether they were ever given instruction in the use of context clues, will usually admit that this was never mentioned by their teachers. As mature readers, we are so used to getting both semantic and syntactic context clues that we take it for granted that students will be able to do the same with little or no help. One of the most important things the teacher can do is to constantly make students aware of the possibility of deriving clues from the context. As students read aloud you may wish to ask them, as they encounter strange words, to read up to the word and then read a line past the word in order to derive a clue. Whenever the opportunity arises, make it a point to discuss how clues may be derived about the pronunciation as well as about the meaning of words through the use of context.

Learning about Semantic and Syntactic Clues

A number of research studies have shown that students will learn very little about the use of context if their work in filling in blanks is not followed by a discussion by the teacher. An excellent way of providing for immediate feedback is to put sentences on the overhead projector with a word left out that is covered by a small piece of tagboard such as the material that manila file folders are made of. Put a piece of Magic tape across the top of the tagboard to fasten it to the overhead transparency so that it acts as a hinge. Then when you wish to disclose the word to the students, you simply lift the tagboard flap and the word that has been covered will be exposed. Show the sentence with the missing word to the students and ask that each of them write the word they think is covered by the tagboard. Asking each student to write what he or she thinks is the proper answer will also force all students to participate. See the example below:

Example 1

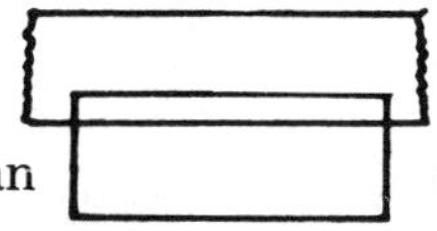

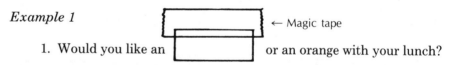

1. Would you like an ______ or an orange with your lunch?

Call on various students to discuss why various answers might or might not be feasible in terms of various semantic and syntactic clues. In the example shown above some logical answers would be as follows:

a. The missing word must be a noun since *a* and *an* are noun markers. (syntactic clue)
b. In this case the noun must start with *a, e, i, o,* or *u* since the word preceding the missing word is *an.* (syntactic clue)
c. The word must be something to eat since it is to go with lunch. (semantic clue)
d. It is quite likely that the missing word is a fruit since it is a choice of that or an orange. (semantic clue)
e. The missing word must be singular. (syntactic clue) (The missing word is *apple.*)

Example 2

2. Jim got in the ______ his father had bought and went for a ride.

In example 2 some logical answers might be as follows:

a. The missing word must be a noun since it follows a noun marker *the.* (syntactic clue)
b. The missing word is something rather large since Jim was able to get in it. (semantic clue)
c. It must be something that moves since Jim went for a ride. (semantic clue)
(The missing word is *car.*)

Example 3

3. Frank [ ] home from school as fast as he could. In example 3 some logical answers might be as follows:

a. The missing word is a verb since there is no other verb in the sentence. (syntactic clue)
b. Although we cannot be sure, the word might be *ran* since Frank did it as fast as he could. (semantic clue)

In the beginning stages of teaching about context clues you may wish to furnish one more clue by showing the first letter of the word on the front cover of the tagboard flap, as shown in the sentence below:

Would you like an [a] or an orange with your lunch?

There are a number of classifications that have been used for types of context clues. For example, there is the "experience" context clue that might be illustrated as follows:

I heard the siren on the firetruck as it passed me.

This, of course, allows the student to get the word based on his or her past experiences. Another type of context clue is the "definition" clue. This would be illustrated as follows:

An obese person is often so heavy that his or her weight becomes a strain on the heart.

While these types of classifications seem somewhat useful for using the context to derive *word meaning,* the author believes that learning the classifications as a means to improving *word attack skills* may simply add an extra burden to the disabled reader.

THE PROGRESSION OF DIFFICULTY IN USING CONTEXT CLUES

After teaching students to listen for context clues in oral language and discussing their use in terms of semantic and syntactic classifications and their ramifications, you may wish to use a progression such as the following:

Context clues in which a word is omitted and replaced with the first letter of the word omitted and a short line for each of the other letters of the word

Would you like an a _ _ _ _ or an orange with your lunch?

Context clues in which a word is omitted and replaced with a short line for each letter of the word that was omitted.

Would you like an _ _ _ _ _ or an orange with your lunch?

Context clues in which a word is omitted and replaced with only a line

Would you like an ________ or an orange with your lunch?

Another approach much the same as the one above is to use x's instead of short blank lines as in the progression that follows:

Context clues in which a word is omitted and replaced with the first letter of the word omitted and an x for each of the other letters of the word

Would you like an axxxx or an orange with your lunch?

Context clues in which a word is omitted and replaced with an x for each letter that was omitted

Would you like an xxxxx or an orange with your lunch?

Context clues in which a word is omitted and replaced with only a line

Would you like an ________ or an orange with your lunch.

OTHER TYPES OF CONTEXT CLUES EXERCISES

Using Picture Context

Materials Large flannel board, pictures from magazines or books, and tagboard strips (about 3″ x 12″)

Procedure On each tagboard strip, write a sentence that describes one of the pictures. Place the tagboard strips on the left-hand side of the flannel board and the pictures on the right-hand side of the flannel board. Put them in a mixed-up order. Ask students to place the strip that describes each picture on an even horizontal line with that picture. If the pictures and strips are numbered or color coded on the back, students can then turn them over to see whether the colors or numbers match. This allows each student to check his or her own work.

The same type of exercise can easily be done by using envelopes with smaller strips and pictures in them. They should also be color coded or numbered so that students can check their own work.

Using Multiple Choice in Context

In the beginning stages of using context clues, it is also a good idea to give students a list of words that belong in the blanks in a reading passage. They must select the correct word for each blank. See the example that follows:

said to was forgot store got

Sally ________ going with her mother ________ the grocery ________. They ________ in the car. Mother ________, "Oh Sally, I ________ the keys."

Matching Sentence Parts

On the left-hand side of a sheet of paper, write the first part of a number of sentences. Place a number before each sentence. On the right-hand side of the page, write the completion of each sentence; however, place them in mixed-up order. Place a blank before the last part of the sentences on the right-hand side of the paper. Some examples are as follows:

1. Sue went with Larry	________	ran after the ball.
2. Dan's dog	________	read books.
3. I like to	________	lots of milk.
4. Some cows give	________	to the movie.

Getting the Right Look-Alike Word from Context

Write sentences omitting words that are often confused. Give students a choice from words that look very much alike, such as the following:

1. He went ________________ the tunnel.
   (though—thought—through)

2. He moved from the city to the ________________.
   (country—county)

3. Tom is taller ________ Dave.
   (then—than)

5

Diagnosis and Remediation of Phonics and Structural Analysis Skills

In this section you will be introduced to a sequence of testing for the important skills in the areas of phonics and structural analysis (now often referred to as morphology). The tests appear in Appendices D, E, and F. Appendix D contains directions and materials for preparing and using the *El Paso Phonics Survey* and the *Quick Survey Word List.* The *Quick Survey Word List* is used with students whose phonics and structural analysis skills are thought to be equivalent to those of a student of approximately fourth-grade level or higher. Students who do well on this test will not need to be tested on the various subskills involved in phonics and structural analysis. Appendix E contains directions and materials for preparing a test for knowledge of vowel rules and syllable principles, and Appendix F contains directions and materials for testing knowledge of contractions. The suggested sequence of testing for knowledge of phonics and structural analysis is outlined in a flowchart that follows on pp. 49 and 50. In Appendix D you will find a discussion of the most common methods of testing for students' phonics knowledge and why the author suggests that you use the *El Paso Phonics Survey.*

A SEQUENCE FOR TESTING PHONICS AND STRUCTURAL ANALYSIS SKILLS

A logical place to begin in phonics testing is with the testing of sound–symbol or phoneme–grapheme correspondence such as a student's knowledge of initial consonant sounds, initial consonant clusters, and vowel sounds. Testing in this area is often done using a number of methods that the author's research has found to be invalid. For this reason I urge you to read the information included under the heading "Advantages of Using the El Paso Phonics Survey" very carefully so that sometime in the future you will not fall into the trap of using a phonics test that is not valid and/or reliable. Some students who learn sound–symbol correspondence then seem to do quite well in attacking new words. However, certain students who know the various sound–symbol relationships still do not have the ability to attack words. For this type of student it may be necessary to teach certain vowel rules and syllable principles. Appendix E contains directions and materials for preparing a test for knowledge of these structural analysis skills.

In noting the types of errors that students make in their oral reading it will be seen that a number of contractions are not known. Appendix F contains directions and materials for testing students' knowledge in this area.

A suggested sequence of testing for knowledge of phonics and structural analysis is as follows:

FIGURE 5-1 *Sequence for testing students whom you suspect have phonics skills equivalent to fourth-grade level or higher*

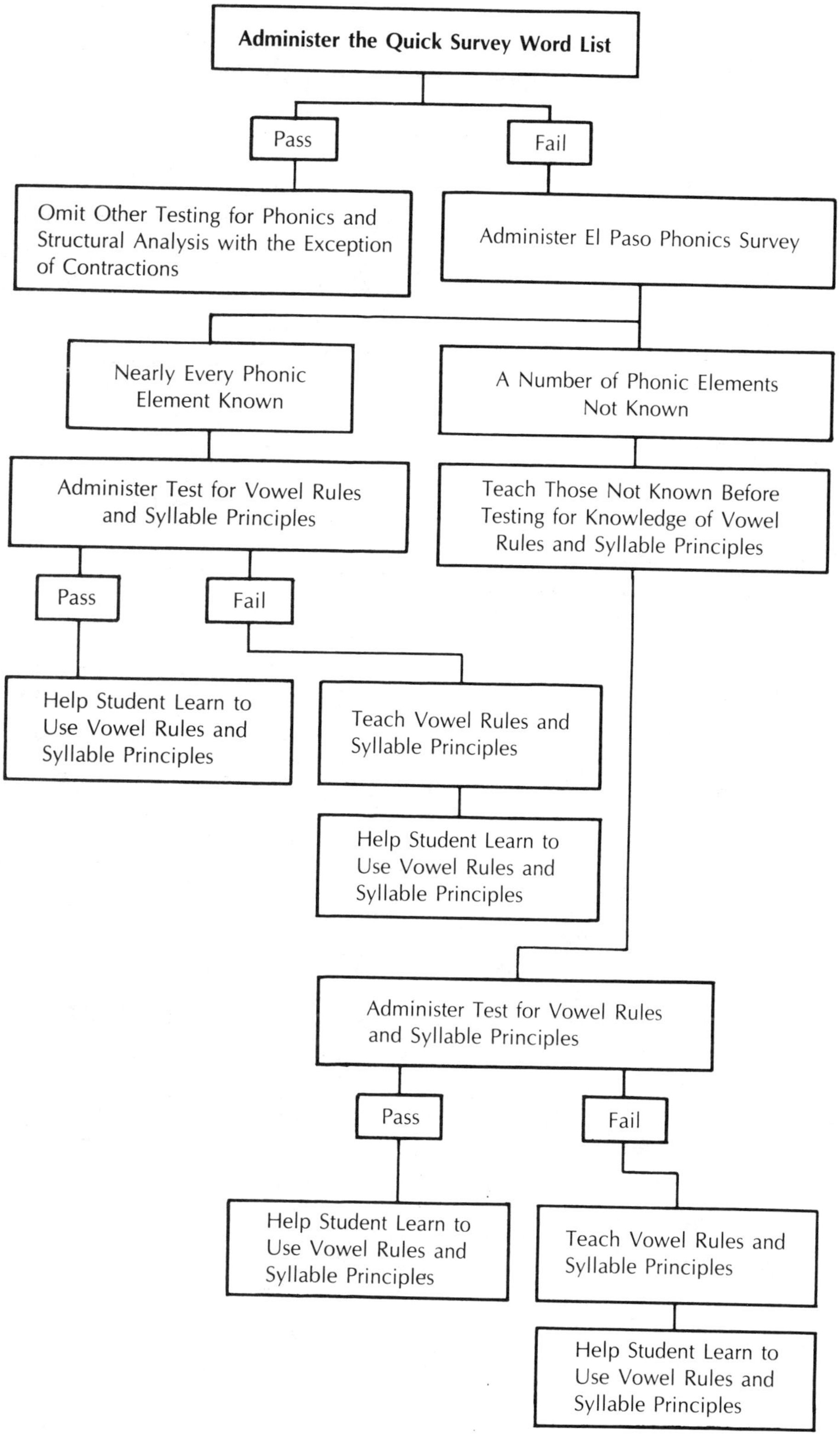

FIGURE 5-2 *Sequence for testing students whom you feel relatively sure have phonics skills below fourth grade level*

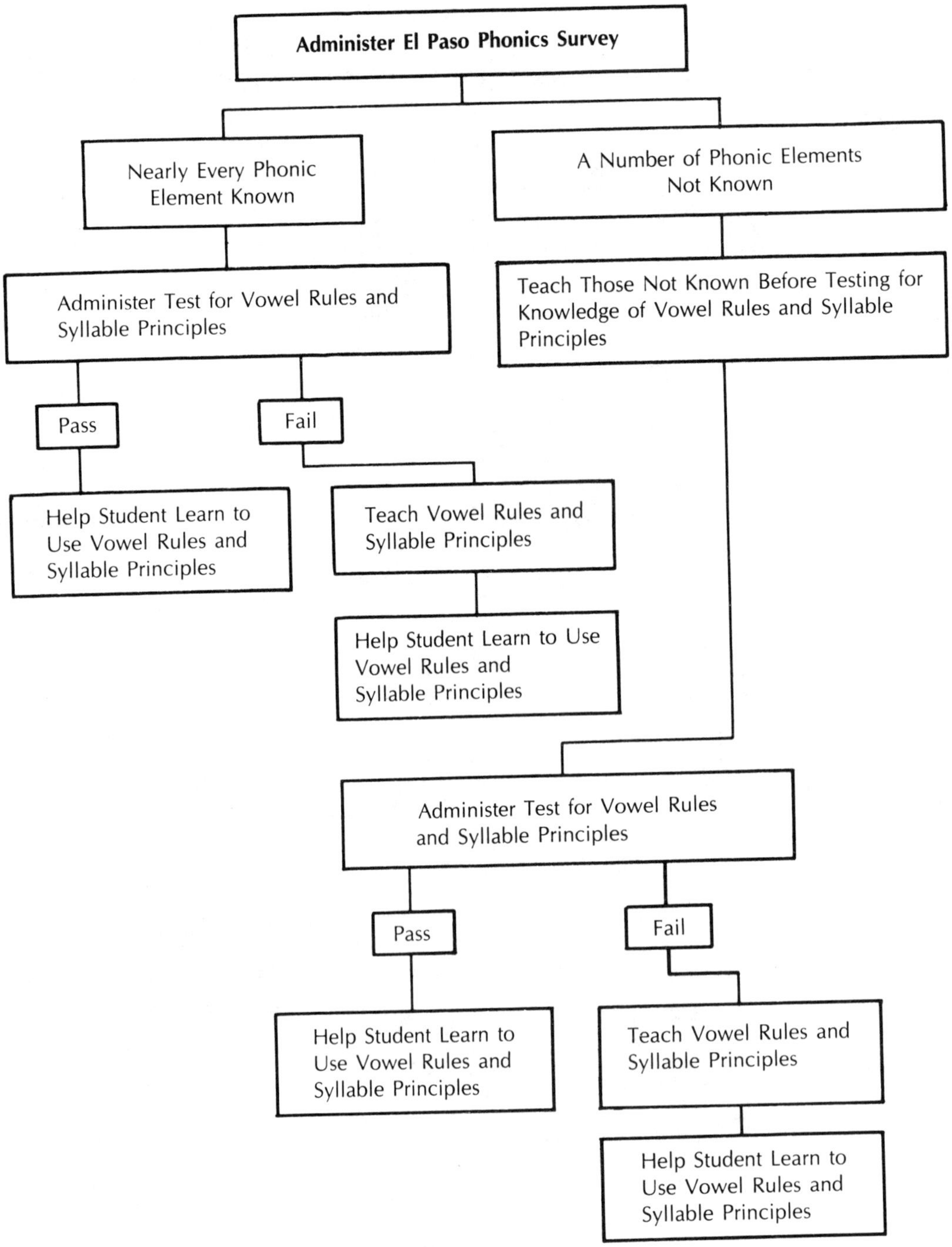

REMEDIATION PROCEDURES FOR SOUND-SYMBOL CORRESPONDENCE

Exercises for Sound-Symbol Hearing

One of the first procedures in teaching students sound-symbol or phoneme-grapheme correspondence is to develop an awareness of sounds. The two exercises below and the activities that follow are designed to do this.

Exercise 1. Show students a number of pictures of things that start with the same sound (for example, "man," "monkey," and "money"). Ask them to say the name of the picture and listen for the sound they hear at the beginning of the word.

Exercise 2. Do the same type of exercise as that described in Exercise 1, but use a list of *words* (rather than pictures of things) with the same beginning sound. You can also do the same exercise with words with the same ending sound and the same medial consonant or vowel sounds.

Picture Dictionaries

Have students construct picture dictionaries by searching through old books and magazines and finding pictures of objects that start with various consonant sounds, end in various consonant sounds, and have various vowel sounds in them. Let them cut out these pictures and paste them in a notebook to make their dictionaries.

A Tape-Recorded Exercise

Tape-record exercises in which students listen to words while looking at a stimulus sheet. The stimulus sheet can be constructed as follows:

A.	b	d	c	n
B.	f	g	b	p
C.	n	m	z	h

The tape script would say, "Look at the letters in row A. I am going to say a word, and you are to circle the letter that stands for the beginning sound that you hear on the word. Ready, row A, the word is *cat—cat.* [pause five seconds] Row B, the word is *goat—goat.* Row C, the word is *map—map* [and so on]." The tape can then give the answers as follows: "Now we will check our answers. The first word was *cat,* and you should have circled the c in row A. If you did not, circle it now. In row B, the word . . ." [and so forth].

Sorting by Sound

Collect a number of shoe boxes or boxes of similar sizes. On each box write an initial consonant sound, blend, or digraph. Then collect a number of small objects such as a spoon, a pencil, small plastic animals, and so forth.

Have students work together to sort the objects so that the spoon goes in the box marked "sp," the pencil goes in the box marked "p," and so forth.

Three Word Dash

Materials A game board with spaces showing a start and finish position (see example below); a movable object for each student to mark his or her position on the board; a pack of flash cards with various initial consonants, blends, and so forth on them.

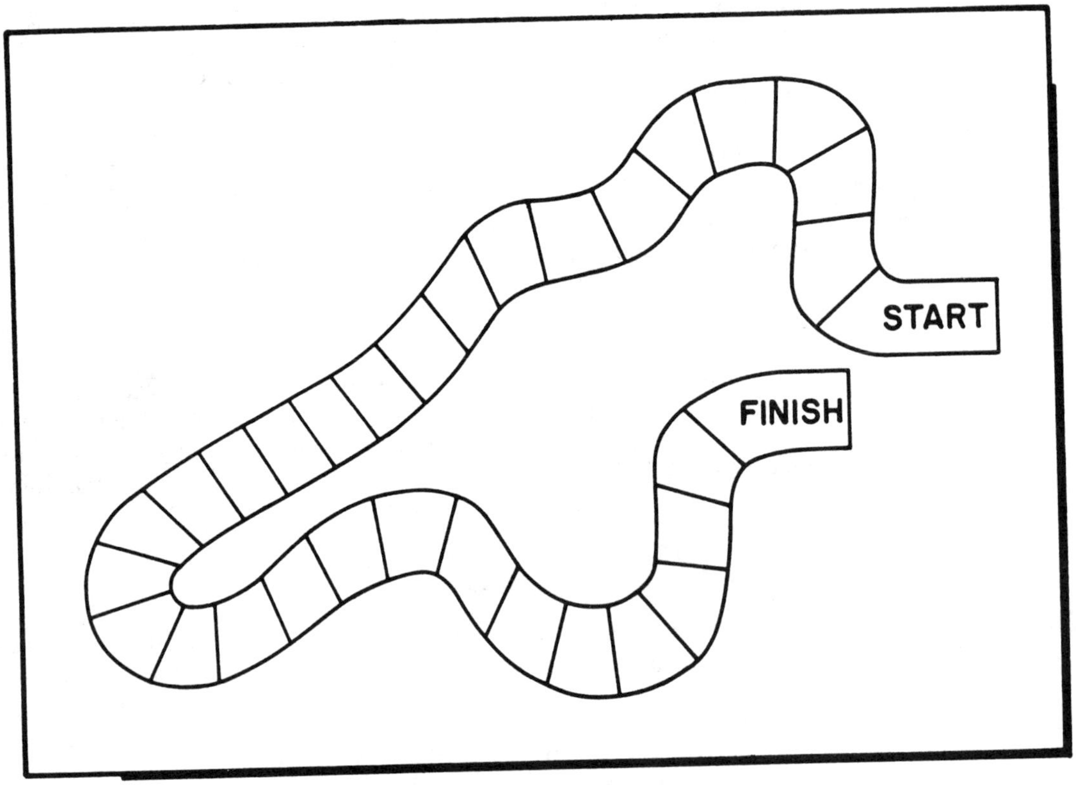

Procedure Show a flash card to students in turn. As each sees the letter(s) on the flash card, he or she must think of three words that begin with the same letter(s) in a period of ten seconds. If the student can, he or she gets to dash one space forward. If not, the student must stay in the same space. The first student to get to the finish line is the winner. The teacher acts as a timer and referee.

Matching Vowels or Consonants

Have students find a number of pictures with the same vowel sound such as a "bed" and a "head" or a "cake" and a "rake." Lay the pictures out on a table and have students match all pictures with the same vowel sound by placing them in the same row. The same exercise can also be done with initial consonants, blends, digraphs, and so forth. If you wish to make this a self-check type of activity, you can number the backs of the pictures so that the number 1 appears on all the long *a* sounds, 2 appears on the short *u* sounds, and so forth.

Diphthong Word Race

List some diphthongs on the chalkboard as follows: *au, ew, ey, oi, ou, ow, oy*. Have students see who can use these diphthongs in making words. The student with the most words wins the race, but must read his or her words when he or she has finished. Have the other students read their words also. Some examples are as follows: claw, new, boy, oil.

Changing Words

On the chalkboard place a list of words that can easily be changed to another word and then give oral instructions as in the example that follows.

Words:	Instruction:
cake	Change one letter to make something that you might use in your yard. (*rake*)
cool	Change one letter to make something to swim in. (*pool*)
an	Add one letter to make something that might help you keep cool. (*fan*)

Tape Recorder Exercise for Long and Short Vowel Sounds

Prepare a list of words containing either the short or long vowel sound. Number each word and place a short blank line after it as shown below:

1. fat ________
2. fun ________
3. top ________

Prepare a tape-recorded script as follows: "This is to help you hear long and short vowel sounds. I will read the words from the list you have been given, and you are to listen to the word and decide whether you hear a long or short vowel sound in it. If you hear a long vowel sound, then write *L* in the blank following the word. If you hear a short vowel sound, then write *S* in the blank. Here are the words. Number one is *fat.* [pause three seconds] Number two is *fun.* [pause three seconds] Number three is *top* [and so forth]. Now we will check your answers. If you did not get them right, circle the number beside each word that you got wrong. Number one was *fat.* You should have put an *S* in the blank. Number two is . . . [and so on]."

Bean Bag Sounds

Students and teacher sit in a circle. The teacher then says a word containing an initial consonant, consonant blend, vowel, digraph, diphthong, or whatever the students need to practice. As the teacher says the word, she tosses the bean bag to a student who catches it. When he catches it, he must say another word with the game's particular lesson objective in it within a period of ten seconds. If he can, he gets to say a new word and toss the bean bag to another student. If he cannot, he must give the bean bag back to the teacher who then begins the same procedure again.

Phonics Concentration

Make a concentration game board that has twenty squares out of tag-board. On an equal number of cards, write twenty words in which there are ten pairs having the same initial consonant sound, blend, vowel, and so forth. The cards are then placed face down on the game board, and the game proceeds like any concentration game.

REMEDIATION PROCEDURES FOR HARD AND SOFT *C* AND *G* RULES

Listening for the Soft and Hard *G* and/or *C*

Prepare worksheets with numbers in a vertical column. Beside each number write the words "hard" and "soft" as shown below.

1. hard soft
2. hard soft
3. hard soft

Prepare a tape recording with a script as follows: "I am going to say some words with the hard *g* sound as in the word 'game' and some words with the soft *g* sound as in the word 'gentleman.' I will say a number and then the word. If you hear the hard *g* sound in the word, circle the word 'hard' beside that number on your worksheet. If you hear the soft *g* sound in the word, circle the word 'soft' beside that number on your worksheet. Here are the words. Number one is *gate—gate.* [pause] Number two is *gem—gem.* [pause] Number three is *gone—gone* [and so forth]. Now we will check your answers. Number one was *gate.* You should have circled *hard.* Number two is . . . [and so forth]."

Inductive Learning of the Hard and Soft *C* and *G* Rules

This exercise should be done with either *c* or *g*, but do not do it with both letters at the same time. Let one or two students go to the chalkboard. Tell the rest of the students that you are going to try to develop a rule so that you know when to pronounce the letter *c* as a *k* sound or as an *s* sound. Have the students dictate as many words as they can think of that begin with *c*. They may look for words in a textbook if they cannot think of enough of them. As the students dictate words, the two students should write them on the chalkboard. Use about twenty or more words. When they finish, the words might appear as follows:

come	carpet	cut
cent	car	century
civet	cream	cyclone

civic	curve	cross
can	cymbal	crib
came	cylinder	circle

Then ask students to pronounce the words and see how many and what sounds they hear for *c* in all of the words. They will hear the *k* and *s* sounds. Then make two columns and label one with *"c=s"* and one with *"c=k."* Have the students at the chalkboard write all of the words with the *s* sound in a column under *"c=s"* and all of those with the *k* sound under *"c=k."* The list will then appear as follows:

"c=k"	"c=s"
come	cent
can	civet
came	civic
carpet	cymbal
car	cylinder
cream	century
curve	cyclone
cut	circle
cross	
crib	

Then have students look at the two lists and try to derive a rule for the *c* sound. They will usually come up with the correct answer—that is, *c* followed by *e, i,* or *y* usually has the soft *c* or *s* sound. If it is followed by any other letter, it usually has the hard *c* or *k* sound. Students are much more likely to remember the rule when they learn it this way. The same type of exercise can, of course, be done with the hard and soft *g* sounds.

Practice with the Hard and Soft *C* and *G* Rules

After students have been introduced to the hard and soft *c* and *g* rules, their knowledge of the rules can be reinforced by preparing a worksheet and giving them the following directions: "When *c* or *g* is followed by *e, i,* or *y,* they usually stand for their soft sounds. If they are followed by any other letter, then they usually stand for their hard sounds. Now look at the four words in capital letters at the top of the list of words. The words are *cent—came—goat—gentle.* Look at each word in the list and then write one of these four words that has the same beginning sound as that word in the blank by the word. The first one has been done for you."

CENT CAME GOAT GENTLE

1. cinder ____CENT____
2. cycle ____________
3. go ____________
4. gave ____________
5. come ____________
6. city ____________

7. gem ____________________
8. cat ____________________
9. gym ____________________

REMEDIATION PROCEDURES FOR *R*-, *W*-, AND *L*-CONTROLLED VOWELS

Discovering *R*-, *W*, and *L*-Controlled Vowels

Ask students to try to find as many words as they can in which the letter *r* follows a vowel. Then list these words on the chalkboard. The list might look somewhat as follows:

are	here	morning
corn	fire	never
fir	door	start
fur	far	warm
her	girl	car

From a list such as this, students will usually conclude that when the letter *r* follows a vowel it usually changes the vowel sound. (In this case, *here* and *fire* are exceptions.) They might also note that the sound heard in *fur* is the most common sound for the *er, ur,* and *ir* combinations; the sound heard in *corn* is the most common *or* combination; and the sound heard in *car* is the most common *ar* combination.

When doing this exercise it is important that you take plenty of time, if necessary, to develop the word list. And it is also important that students make these discoveries on their own. They are much more likely to remember them. This same exercise may also be done with vowels controlled by *w* (*a, o,* and *e*) and *l* (*a*).

REMEDIATION PROCEDURES FOR BLENDING

Instant Blending

First teach several initial consonant sounds, initial consonant blends, or digraphs, and several phonograms or word families. Then place them on the chalkboard as follows:

bl	and
m	end
s	at

First point to one of the initial consonants or blends and then quickly sweep across to the phonogram. As you do this, have students say the word that is formed. Let students yell these out as soon as they can. The ones who do not know how to do it will soon learn from the ones who do. It may become a noisy activity, but children enjoy it and quickly learn from it.

Double Consonant Substitution

Place lists of two words and then two blanks in a numbered row. Ask students to exchange the initial consonant sounds on each of the first two words and to say and write the two new words that are formed in the blanks. Some examples are as follows:

1.	sat	pick	____	____	(*pat—sick*)
2.	send	lake	____	____	(*lend—sake*)
3.	fell	call	____	____	(*cell—fall*)
4.	car	fat	____	____	(*far—cat*)

Apple Words

Draw a tree with apples on it. On each apple, write a beginning consonant blend or consonant digraph or an ending phonogram. Students are to gather the apples by finding any two that form a word. Let them write each word formed on their papers below the tree. After each pair is used, have them color the two apples red so they are not used again. See the example below.

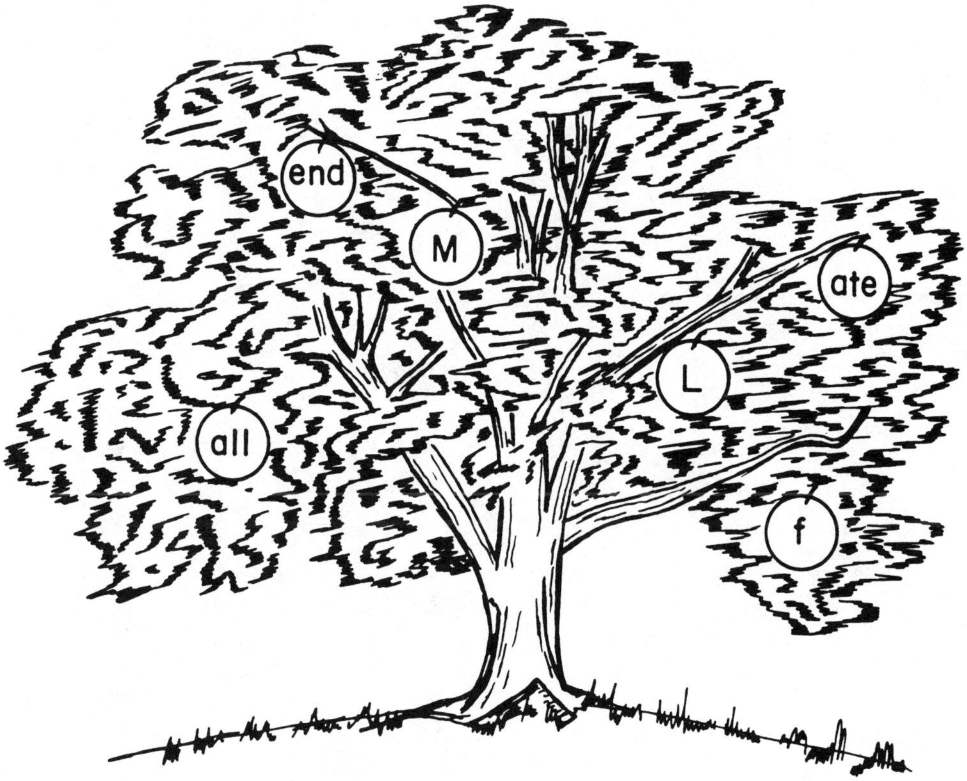

1. Late 2. fall

REMEDIATION PROCEDURES FOR VOWEL RULES

The Vowel-Consonant-Final *E* Rule

Exercise 1. Write a number of words as follows:

cak	long *a*	____
Pet	long *e*	____
rop	long *o*	____
rip	long *i*	____
mul	long *u*	____

Students are to write the word in the blank as it would appear using the vowel-consonant-final *e* rule.

cak	long a	cake
Pet	long e	Pete

Exercise 2. Write a number of words that conform to the vowel-consonant-final *e* rule, but leave a blank space for the vowel and the final *e*. Ask students to make words from each of these by filling in the blanks. See the examples that follow:

1. c __ k __
2. h __ p __
3. c __ m __
4. f __ d __
5. sn __ k __

Reinforcement for *EE, EA, OA, AY, AI* Rule

Exercise 1. Write a number of words containing the five vowel pairs listed above, but leave blanks in the spaces where these letters should go. Ask students to complete the words by filling in the blank spaces. See the examples that follow:

1. br __ __ k	6. m __ __ t
2. tr __ __	7. m __ __ n
3. h __ __	8. pl __ __
4. str __ __ ght	9. s __ __
5. c __ __ t	10. fl __ __ t

Exercise 2. Write a number of letters on the board including some consonants plus some of the combinations listed above. Students are to see

how many words they can form by using these combinations. An example of the jumbled letters and words students might make are as follows:

m i n e t q k y d o f

meat
mean
Fay
may

Exercise 3. Ask students to list as many words as they can that have these vowel combinations in them. Make sure that you give them plenty of time. The list may be somewhat as follows:

aid	tree	way	each	afraid
may	eat	please	float	near
hay	play	read	boat	appear
oats	green	head	coat	fear
each	see	clean	maid	tear

From this list they should conclude that when these combinations are found together, then the first vowel is usually long and the second one is silent. However, *ea* sometimes stands for the sound we hear in *head.* At this point, it would probably be a good idea to tell them that the older phonics materials used to quote this rule for all vowel combinations, but that recent phonics research has shown that the rule is really only good for these combinations.

The *OW* Sounds

Have students list a number of *ow* words on the chalkboard. Give them plenty of time. The list may look somewhat like the one that follows:

cow	mow
crow	plow
grow	low
blow	throw

Students will soon discover that *ow* usually stands for the sound heard in *cow* or the sound heard in *crow.* They should be encouraged to try one sound when they encounter a new word. And, if that doesn't sound right, they should then try the other sound.

Rules for *Y*

Do this exercise the same as the one for hard and soft *c* and *g* explained on pp. 54–55. In developing this rule inductively with students, make sure that they understand that *y* has the long *e* sound at the end of a multisyllable word *only when preceded by a consonant.* And *y* at the end of a single-syllable word has the long *i* sound *only when preceded by a consonant.*

Rules for *AU, AW, OU, OI,* and *OY*

Do this exercise the same as the *ow* exercise. In doing this, students will of course discover that these vowels blend to form a diphthong.

Rules for *OO*

Do this exercise the same as the one for *ow.* Students will discover two common sounds—that is, the short *oo* sound heard in *book* and the long *oo* sound heard in *moon.*

REMEDIATION PROCEDURES FOR SYLLABICATION PRINCIPLES

Develop a list of syllabication principles such as those shown on pp. 264–265. Then give students lists of two-syllable words that are not likely to be in their sight word vocabularies and ask them to draw vertical lines between the syllables. Give some students different words. Have one student who has done the exercise correctly go to the chalkboard, put his or her words on the board, and explain why he or she made each division. After this, have students, with words that should be divided in the same way as the first student's words, go to the chalkboard and list them under those put on the chalkboard by the first student. Then discuss the various principles in relation to the words.

Inductive Learning of Syllabication Principles

You may wish to start the learning of syllabication principles by having students make lists on the chalkboard of multisyllable words that are already in their sight word vocabularies. They can then say the words and listen for syllables. With guidance, they can then develop rules for the division of these words. It should be remembered, however, that the ultimate purpose of syllabication is to break words down into syllables so that students will then know the position of each vowel and thus know what the sound of each vowel letter should be. This, in turn, helps them pronounce new words.

Matching Syllables according to Rules

Place about two syllabication principles on a sheet of paper. Place one at the top and one in the middle. See the examples of these principles below.

1. When two consonants stand between two vowels, the word is usually divided between the consonants.
2. When a word ends in a consonant and *le,* the consonant usually begins the last syllable.

Cut a number of words printed on tagboard into syllables. Have students assemble the syllables into words and place them under the appropriate rule. Examples of words (to be cut where the dash appears) for this exercise follow:

tab-let	cab-in
ta-ble	ma-ple
ca-ble	map-ping

Practice with Vowel-Consonant Syllable Patterns for Students Who Encounter Difficulty with Polysyllabic Words

After teaching the various vowel rules and syllable principles, give students polysyllabic vowel-consonant patterns represented by nonsense words that may be divided according to various syllable principles. Ask them to draw a vertical line between syllables according to the rules. Also ask students to place a number over the vertical line that corresponds to the syllable principle so that they will become familiar with the rule and its application. After the words have been divided into syllables, ask students to mark the vowel sounds as short or *r, l,* and *w* controlled as shown in the list below. After marking each vowel sound, ask students also to place a number over each vowel mark that corresponds to the vowel rule applied in each case. As with the case of the syllable principles, this will make students more aware of the application of each rule. After students have mastered the application of the proper rule, then *do not* ask them to mark the number of each rule as this will become too burdensome. However, ask them to divide real and nonsense words into syllables and mark each vowel sound. The numbers placed above the division points and vowels correspond to the number assigned to each vowel rule and syllable principle following the list of nonsense words. After students have done the words as suggested above, discuss each point of division and then discuss the vowel sounds found in each syllable. In applying syllable principles, treat each consonant cluster (blend and digraph) as though it were a single consonant.

There is another vowel rule that is not covered in this list. That is that a single vowel in an unaccented syllable will tend to represent the schwa (a) sound. The problem in applying this rule is that accent generalizations are usually not taught until after the vowel rules and syllable principles. For older students you may wish to add this rule. However, for younger students the author would suggest that you tell students simply to mark a single vowel as "try the long sound first." Although this will not be the exact sound the word will probably have, it will be close enough for the student to derive the proper pronunciation of the word if it is used in context and is in the student's listening-speaking vocabulary.

Examples of marking system:
Long (–) Short (˘) Try the Long Sound First (⩱) R-Controlled (R) Schwa (a) L-Controlled (L) W-Controlled (W)

Nonsense words:

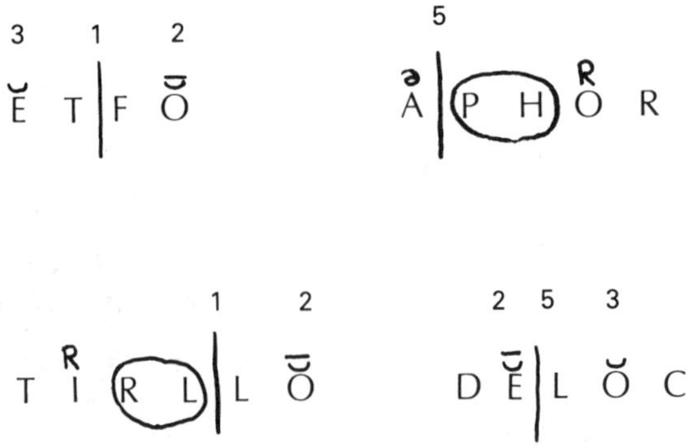

Note: In the words above, the "ph" and "rl" are circled to indicate that they are consonant clusters thus being treated as single consonants.

Syllable Principles*

1. Divide wherever there are two consonants surrounded by vowels, providing there are no consonant clusters between the vowels. (Examples: al/pil, opp/or, bot/nap, and cur/ro)
2. When a word ends in a consonant-*le,* the consonant preceding the *le* is included in the syllable with the *le.* (Examples: na/ple, fra/ble, da/ple, and sa/ple)
3. Divide between compound words and normal places in the words making up the compound words. (Examples: cow/per/son, dog/leg, cow/lick)
4. Do not divide between consonant digraphs or blends (consonant clusters). In this case treat the cluster as though it were a single consonant and divide the word so that the "cluster" goes with the second vowel as in #5 below, or as you would in #1 above. (Examples: ba/chop, ba/shil, and da/phod)
5. In vowel-consonant-vowel situations "VCV", first try dividing so that the consonant goes with the second vowel. (Examples: mo/nan, fa/dop, da/lop)

Vowel Rules

1. Single-syllable words with only one vowel at the end should usually be pronounced so that the vowel stands for its long sound. (Examples: me, he, she)
2. A single vowel at the end of a syllable in a multisyllable word should be given the long sound first. (Examples: *o* in *so* in con/so/nant, *o* in *pro* in pro/gram)
3. A single vowel in a closed syllable usually stands for the short sound of the vowel. (Examples: bad, hit, hot)
4. Wherever *r* follows a vowel, providing it is in the same syllable, it

* From: Ekwall, Eldon E. *Locating and correcting reading difficulties.* 4th ed. Columbus, Ohio: Charles E. Merrill, 1985. (Reprinted by permission)

usually changes the sound of the vowel. (They may be grouped as follows: *er, ur, ir* sound as *ur* in *fur; ar* sounds like the *ar* in *car;* and *or* sounds like *or* in *corn.*)

5. The letters *w* and *l* influence the vowel sound preceding them making the vowel neither long nor short. This is true more of the time when there is a double *l.* (Examples: owl, few, ball)
6. When a vowel-consonant-final *e* appears at the end of a word, the first vowel will usually stand for its long sound. Although this is not true a large percentage of the time, it is more true than not. (Examples: cake, made, code)
7. A *y* at the end of a single-syllable word, preceded by a consonant, usually stands for the long *i* sound. Be sure to note that the *y* must be preceded by a consonant and not a vowel. (Examples: fry, try, fly)
8. A *y* at the end of a multisyllable word preceded by a consonant usually stands for the long *e* sound. Be sure to note that the *y* must be preceded by a consonant and not by a vowel. (Examples: quickly, only)
9. A *y* at the beginning of a word usually has the *y* consonant sound as in the word *yard.* (Examples: yes, you, yield)

REMEDIATION PROCEDURES FOR CONTRACTIONS

Contracting Words

Give students a list of sentences and ask them to make contractions from any words that can be made into contractions. Leave a blank space behind each sentence for writing in the contraction and have students underline the two words from which they make the contraction. Some examples are as follows:

1. I can not go.
2. Henry said, "I have not been there."
3. Dennis said, "I do not think I can go."

Contraction Crossword Puzzles

Construct crossword puzzles using contractions in the puzzle and the two words standing for the contraction in the instructions across and down. See the example that follows:

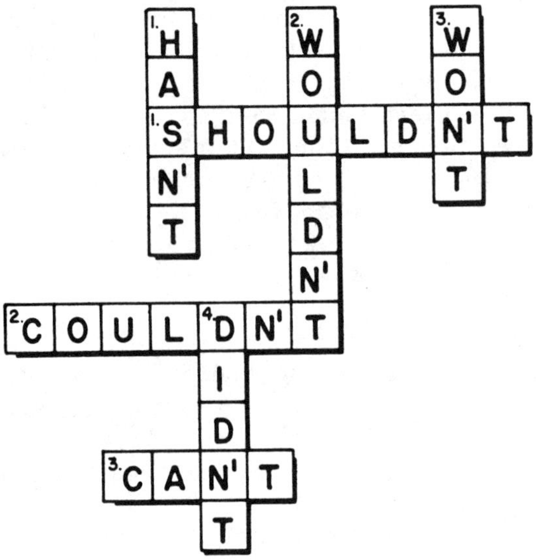

Across	Down
1. should not	1. has not
2. could not	2. would not
3. can not	3. will not
	4. did not

Furnish students with answer sheets when they have finished.

Changing Seats for Contractions

Give each student a card with a contraction on it, and then have each take a seat. Have one student stand up and remove his or her and all other empty seats. The teacher then says, "All students with contractions of words ending with *will,* change seats." Each time the standing student may take one of these seats, but one student will always be left standing. After doing this three or four times, have students exchange cards and then continue as before. Each time a student changes seats, he or she should be asked to read his or her contraction. (Other contractions might end in *not, are, is,* and *would.*)

REMEDIATION PROCEDURES FOR WORD ENDINGS

Picking the Correct Word Ending

Give students sentences with one word omitted and replaced with a blank. Let them fill in the word (from a choice of two or three words) with the correct ending according to the context of the sentence. See the examples that follow:

1. Dwight and Cindy were ______________ rope.
   (jumped—jumping—jumps)

2. Fred's father ______________________ at him yesterday.
(laughs—laughing—laughed)

Add the Correct Word Ending

Give students sentences with the word ending of some words omitted (as shown in the example below) and give the following directions: "In the sentences that follow there is one word from which the ending has been left off. Behind that word is a blank. Fill in the blank with the right ending. The right ending should be *s, ed,* or *ing.*"

1. Irma's horse run _____ very fast.
2. The girls were play _____ in the yard.
3. Dolly want _____ to go with John.

Word Ending Race

Print four or more root words on cards and place them in a pocket chart so that students cannot see them. Ask students to get a pencil and paper ready. Tell them that when you turn the cards over, they are to see how many words they can make from the root words by adding *s, ed,* or *ing* in a period of a few minutes. Then turn the words over, one at a time, and begin timing the exercise. After students have finished, have the winner(s) list their words on the chalkboard.

Detecting Wrong Endings

Write a paragraph or two using words with the wrong endings. Double-space the writing. Have students read the material and circle or draw a line through all wrong word endings and write the proper ending above each error. Discuss the changes with the class after you have finished.

Word Ending Bingo

Divide cards into squares with a free space in the center as in regular Bingo cards. Write various word endings in the squares as shown below.

ed	s	er
ing	free	est
s	er	es

Give each student a card with some markers such as buttons, corn, or whatever, and then call root words from a prepared list. If a student has an ending that will fit that word, he or she covers it with a marker. The first student to fill in three squares in any direction is the winner. When the teacher calls the root words, as a check the student must say each root word with the ending he or she has covered in order to win. Use words such as the following:

go	fast
throw	bus
duck	

6

Diagnosis and Remediation of Comprehension and Vocabulary Skills and Matching Students with the Right Level of Reading Materials

In this chapter you will first be introduced to the factors that tend to affect comprehension in terms of the reader and the materials being read. You will then be introduced to the most common ways of measuring students' comprehension and the strongpoints and weaknesses of each of these methods. Following this information, you will be given specific information on how to match students with reading materials using the criteria commonly applied to informal reading inventories. You will also find an explanation of the cloze procedure and how it can be used to match students with the right level of books or other instructional materials. In Appendix J you will find the *Ekwall Reading Inventory* which is a commercial informal reading inventory. It includes all materials necessary for testing students' oral and silent reading levels from low first-grade level (often referred to as pre-primer) through the ninth-grade level.

In the second part of this chapter you will find specific methods of improving students' ability to comprehend the materials they are required to read. Since the printing of the first edition of this text several rather promising methods of teaching comprehension have emerged that have been researched and proven very useful. These methods include the use of metacognitive approaches, including *story frames*. These are covered, in detail, as well as more traditional approaches that have proven beneficial.

In the last part of the chapter you will be introduced to the most commonly used procedures for measuring students' vocabularies and the strongpoints and weaknesses of each of these methods. You will then be introduced to various strategies that have proven beneficial in increasing students' vocabularies.

FACTORS AFFECTING COMPREHENSION

In reading the research on reading you may note the terms "bottom-up" and "top-down." There seems to be considerable controversy about whether comprehension is affected more by what is known as "top-down" or "bottom-up." The "top-down" model of reading sees the reader as bringing knowledge to the printed page and, therefore, being more important in the process. On the other hand, the "bottom-up" model sees the material being read as more important in the process of comprehension. It seems fruitless to argue whether one is more important than the other since both obviously contribute to the overall process of reading. On the other hand, it is useful to look at the factors that affect reading from both the "top-down" as well as the "bottom-up" so that the teacher can understand what he or she must do to improve the overall comprehension process.

The Reader

The factors that affect comprehension in terms of the reader could probably be classified into four main categories. The first of these would be the *knowledge that the reader brings to the material to be read.* A student with prior knowledge about a subject will, of course, be able to comprehend more of a passage than a student, with like abilities in reading, who has little or no knowledge of the material being read. Nearly everything that we are able to comprehend is the result of tying what is read, or learned in any way, to what has been learned in the past.

A second important factor, as it concerns the reader, is *the reader's interest in the subject.* If you stop to consider what you as an adult read, unless it is forced on you, you will find that it is material that is of interest to you. If the material is of interest to you, you are also, of course, likely to know more about the subject—which all goes hand in hand to improve your overall comprehension of the subject about which you are reading.

A third important factor is your *purpose for reading.* You will note that nearly all basal reader teacher's manuals recommend setting a purpose for reading before students are asked to read their assignments. If the reader has a purpose for reading, he or she is, of course, likely to comprehend more than if the material is being read for no particular purpose.

A fourth important factor affecting comprehension, especially at the beginning level, is *the ability of the reader to decode words rapidly.* A reader who has to spend time in thinking about how a particular syllable would sound, while holding other syllables in memory, will simply be bogged down in his or her thinking processes to the point that comprehension of the material being read will suffer. Therefore, a reader who has a large sight vocabulary as well as the ability to decode new words rapidly, will be likely to comprehend more than a reader with a smaller sight vocabulary and less facility in decoding skills.

The Material Being Read

The material being read is generally considered to be affected by three main factors. The first of these is the *number of hard words.* For our purposes here, the author will simply define number of hard words as the number of words with which the reader is not familiar. A number of readability formulae use the percent of "hard" or "unique" words as one of the factors in determining the reading level at which a passage is written. In this case the percent of "hard" or "unique" words is the percent of words that do not appear on a specified list of words from which the readability formula was originally derived.

A second factor that affects the difficulty of the material being read is the *length of the sentences.* We know that students, especially at the beginning reading levels, will have more difficulty with material that is written in longer sentences than the same material rewritten in shorter sentences.

A third factor that influences the difficulty of the material being read is *syntax.* This author would define syntax simply as the way we choose to string words together when we write. For example, we know that when adults write using nearly, if not exactly, the same words as first or second graders, the material written by adults would be likely to be more difficult for first- or second-grade students to read. An example of syntax affecting the difficulty level of material being read is the use of qualifying words such as *however* and *therefore;* adults would use such words more than a child.

METHODS OF AND PROBLEMS WITH TESTING COMPREHENSION

Some of the most commonly used methods of testing reading comprehension are the use of group standardized achievement tests, individual standardized tests, commercial informal reading inventories, teacher-made informal reading inventories, and the cloze procedure. All of the methods listed above present certain advantages and disadvantages; however, for the disabled reader the author would not recommend the use of group standardized achievement tests. Since some teachers will, no doubt, want to make use of certain group standardized achievement tests and individual standardized achievement tests, information on these instruments may be found in Appendix G. In Appendix G you will also find sources of a number of other types of tests such as commercial informal reading inventories, basic sight word inventories, etc.

The most commonly used method of measuring students' comprehension is through the use of group standardized reading achievement tests. This, however, offers some difficulties for disabled readers. One of the major problems is that group standardized achievement tests are designed to measure *group* achievement and not *individual* performance. In testing disabled readers we often find that group standardized achievement tests have a tendency to place these students considerably above their actual reading level. For example, it is possible for a student to score easily at or above the 3.5 grade level on the intermediate battery (grades 4–5, 6) of one of the most commonly used group standardized achievement tests without even being able to read—that is, by randomly marking the answer sheet. Where there are four choices for each answer, the student will usually get about 25 percent of the answers correct. And, by getting this many correct, he or she can score at, or near, the 3.5 grade level. For this reason you should generally use some other method of assessing a disabled reader's ability in terms of comprehension.

Another problem that teachers often face is in determining the level of various books or other materials in their classrooms. Some publishers of materials specifically designated for disabled readers include their own placement tests while others designate specific levels based on the use of one of the most commonly used and accepted readability formulas. However, all too many publishers simply state that their books are appropriate, for example, for students in grades three through six. Such a designation really has little meaningful value in attempting to match a student with material that he or she can actually read.

SOME RECOMMENDED PROCEDURES FOR MEASURING READING COMPREHENSION LEVEL AND FOR MATCHING STUDENTS AND READING MATERIALS

Individual Standardized Achievement Tests

The use of individual standardized achievement tests has the advantage of the test having gone through a period of writing and testing which, in most cases, is rather rigorous, thus ensuring the user that the levels are generally accurate. The author has found these, as well as other methods often used, to be rather time-consuming. However, it should be remembered that any accurate measure of a student's reading achievement level is likely to take a considerable amount of time. Since there are a number of individual standardized achievement tests, most of which have varying directions, their use will not be discussed here; you will find a list of these tests in Appendix G.

Commercial Informal Reading Inventories

One distinct advantage of a commercial or teacher-made informal reading inventory is that it will allow the teacher to listen to the student oral read (if the oral passages are administered). In listening to a student the teacher, trained to do so, will be able to diagnose strongpoints and weaknesses in the student's reading abilities, probably better than through the use of any other instrument, whether it be teacher-made or commercial.

Another advantage of commercial reading inventories is that the questions, in many cases, have been put through a much more rigorous testing than those of a teacher-made informal reading inventory. This may, at first, seem trivial; however, the author found in developing questions for his own commercial informal reading inventory, as well as in helping many teachers develop questions for teacher-made informal reading inventories, that developing valid questions is extremely difficult. We know very little about why some questions that appear to be valid are seldom ever answered correctly, while other questions that also appear valid are nearly always answered right by every student who reads the passage over which they were developed. The simple truth is that the development of valid questions for informal reading inventories is an extremely difficult task—so difficult, in fact, that many informal reading inventories are, in terms of the measurement of comprehension skills, probably meaningless.

A third advantage of commercial reading inventories is that the passages are usually written at the level for which they are designed. Even then there is often a discrepancy, in many cases, between the grade level at which a passage is written according to one readability formula and the grade level at which it is written according to another. On the other hand, passages taken from the materials from which a student will be working (which is supposed to be one of the major advantages of teacher-made informal inventories) may vary a great deal from page to page. For this reason if the materials are taken from a particularly easy page, then the teacher-made informal reading inventory will, of course, not be representative of that material at all. But it may work just the opposite, i.e., the readings may have been taken from a page that was much more difficult than the other materials in the book, or from whatever the material was taken. This would make the reading passage appear much more difficult than it actually is.

The *Ekwall Reading Inventory* appears in Appendix J. As stated before, it is a commercial informal reading inventory. It contains all of the materials necessary for its administration such as stimulus sheets, answer sheets, and complete directions for its administration. Other commercial reading inventories that you may wish to examine are listed in Appendix G.

Teacher-Made Informal Reading Inventories

One of the greatest advantages of teacher-made informal reading inventories is that they are constructed from the materials that the students will actually be using in the classroom. Although this is a distinct advantage, there are also some pitfalls to be avoided. One of the problems with teacher-made informal reading inventories, as pointed out in the section on commercial informal reading inventories, is that the material selected to use as reading passages is often not representative of the material as a whole. This problem can be avoided to some extent by the use of a readability formula. Since the use of the computer in the classroom has made complex computations and word searches much more simple, the teacher should be able to pick passages from which the teacher-made informal inventory will be constructed with more accuracy than in the past. For example, most of the more commonly used readability formulae are now available for use on the most commonly used computers in education. The teacher has only to type in a sample of the material (usually about 100 words) and the computer will automatically determine the readability level. This will enable the teacher to find five to ten passages from materials that he or she wishes to use to construct the informal reading inventory and determine the reading grade level of each passage. A passage that is representative of the average of all of the passages checked should then be used.

A second problem with the construction of teacher-made informal reading inventories is that it is difficult to write valid questions. As pointed out previously, the author found in constructing his commercial reading inventory that some questions that seemed perfectly logical were seldom answered correctly by students after reading the passages. On the other hand, some questions were consistently answered correctly even by students who could barely read the materials on which they were being tested. For this reason the author would caution the teacher who is developing his or her own informal reading inventory to be extremely careful to note whether certain questions are consistently missed or are nearly always answered correctly. It is also important to make sure that questions are passage-dependent, i.e., the questions should be such that they cannot be answered correctly by a student who has not read the material from which the questions were derived.

A Procedure for Using Teacher-Made Informal Reading Inventories to Match Students with Materials They Can Read

As noted in Chapter 1, reading is essentially a process of recognizing and analyzing words and understanding words and ideas. Or, said another way, in order to read efficiently we must reach a certain level of "word recognition" as well as a certain level of "comprehension." In reading, we normally designate the three levels described in the following section.

INFORMAL READING INVENTORY CRITERIA AND LEVELS

Probably the most commonly accepted set of criteria for administering and scoring informal reading inventories is that outlined by Marjorie Johnson and Roy Kress (1965). These criteria are as follows:

Free or Independent Level. Criteria (to be met without aid from examiner): Word Recognition—99 percent or better; Comprehension—90 percent or better.

This is the level at which children should be reading when they are reading a library book or the level at which they should read their textbooks *after* the teacher has introduced them to the new vocabulary and built up a proper background of experiences for comprehending the concepts in the material. In general, this is the level at which a student should be reading when there is no one around to help. Although placement is normally based on the criteria mentioned above, we normally associate certain behavioral characteristics with this level of reading. These characteristics are described by Johnson and Kress (1965, p. 6) as follows:

Rhythmical, expressive oral reading
Accurate observation of punctuation
Acceptable reading posture
Silent reading more rapid than oral
Response to questions in language equivalent to author's
No evidence of:

lip movement	vocalization
finger pointing	subvocalization
head movement	anxiety about performance

Instructional Level. Criteria (to be met without examiner aid): Word Recognition—95 percent; Comprehension—75 percent.

This is the level at which children would normally be reading in their textbooks (social studies, basal reading) before the teacher has introduced them to the vocabulary and built up a background of experiences for comprehending the concepts in the material. Again, placement is usually based on the criteria mentioned above, but the related behavioral characteristics while reading should be the same as for the Free or Independent Level of reading.

Frustration Level. Criteria: Word Recognition—90 percent or less; Comprehension—50 percent or less.

This is the level at which the material is too difficult for sustained reading and it is a level that we would hope to avoid. Placement is again normally based on the criteria mentioned above, but related behavioral characteristics, defined by Johnson and Kress (1965, p. 10), are as follows:

Abnormally loud or soft voice
Arhythmical or word-by-word oral reading
Lack of expression in oral reading
Inaccurate observation of punctuation
Finger pointing (at margin or every word)
Lip movement—head movement—subvocalization
Frequent requests for examiner help
Non-interest in the selection
Yawning or obvious fatigue
Refusal to continue

DETERMINING WHETHER READING MATERIALS ARE AT THE RIGHT LEVEL FOR THE STUDENT

In administering an informal reading inventory the examiner would usually sit to one side of a table while the student sits facing the examiner to the left or right side of him. The student would normally be given a set of graded passages, usually one oral and one silent, at each grade level. However, since we are only concerned here with placing a student in the right book or set of materials, the procedure would be as follows:

1. Make up questions (preferably at least eight) about the reading material. Try to sample vocabulary by asking questions such as, "What did the word ______ mean in this passage?" Also attempt to make up questions concerning main ideas, inference, and important details.
2. Give the student the material to be read and say: "Here is a passage [or story] I would like you to read. Please read it clearly and accurately and try to remember everything you read so you can answer some questions about it when you have finished. If you come across a hard word, read it as best you can and continue to read."
3. As the student reads, you should have a copy of what the student is reading to record any word recognition errors, hesitations, and so forth. Note that the examiner's copy is best when typed double- or triple-spaced so that ample room is available for recording the errors and that the prepared questions (step 1) should be typed below the passage on this copy.

A code for marking oral reading errors is shown below. While many people have learned another shorthand method of marking various kinds of word recognition errors, the author has found that students learn this code rather easily. In addition, by using this code, you can look at the recorded errors and accurately interpret them immediately following the reading or even six months or a year later. For this reason you should become thoroughly familiar with the code as shown below, or a modified version of it. Although you should mark oral reading errors as the student proceeds through the reading material, it is usually a good idea to tape-record the student's oral reading at the same time. The tape will then serve as a means for checking the accuracy of the coding. This is especially important when major decisions based on performance are to be made about the placement of a student.

Code for Marking Errors in Oral Reading Diagnosis

To be scored as errors in marking informal reading inventories:

1. Circle omissions. After the student has finished reading, it is suggested that you then determine whether the omission was deliberate or non-deliberate. If it is determined to be deliberate, then place a *d* over the circled word. If it is determined to be non-deliberate, then place the letter *n* over the circled word.

2. Show insertions with a caret (^).
3. Draw a line through words for which substitutions or mispronunciations were made and write the substitution or mispronunciation above the word. Determine later whether the word missed was a substitution or mispronunciation.
4. If the student reads too fast to write in all mispronunciation errors, draw a line through the words and write *P* for partial mispronunciation or *G* for gross mispronunciation above each.
5. Mark inversions the same as substitutions and determine later whether the mistake was really an inversion or a substitution. Examples of inversions are, *no* for *on, ont* for *not, saw* for *was,* and so forth.
6. Use parentheses ( ) to enclose words for which aid was given.
7. Underline repetitions with a wavy line.

Not to be scored as errors in marking informal reading inventories:

8. Make a check (√) over words that were self-corrected.
9. Use an arced line to connect words where there was disregard for punctuation.
10. Make two vertical lines (||) to indicate a pause before words.

An example of an oral reading passage with coded errors would appear as follows:

Cindy ~~wanted~~ to go visit ^ her friend Sally. She put on her coat and ~~overshoes~~ because it was snowing outside. She told her ~~mother~~ she ~~was~~ going and then || started (out) the door. Before she even started she (remembered) that Sally had told her that she ~~would~~ not be home all day.

After the student has finished reading the passage, the examiner should take the copy from him or her (as casually as possible) and then ask the comprehension questions that have been prepared ahead of time. These questions, which should be on the examiner's copy on which the student's word recognition errors were coded, can be marked with a plus (+) for correct answers or a minus (−) for wrong answers. If the student does not give a complete enough answer to score it accurately, you should then ask a neutral question to clarify the answer. Examples of neutral questions are "Can you tell me a little more about that?" or "Can you explain that a little more?" On the other hand, try to avoid questions that give the student a 50-50 chance of getting it right. For example, in a question calling for specific details such as "What color was the car?" you should not question further by asking 'Was it blue or green?" There are also times when you may wish to record verbatim what the student says in order to have more time to score his or her response later. On some answers, half credit is sometimes given where even after neutral questioning, the answer is still not clear-cut.

You are also likely to find some students who occasionally do not give an answer after they have had ample time to think about the question (usually 5–10 seconds at least). If after a period of time the student does not answer, you may wish to ask, "Do you think you know that?" If the student does not know the answer, he or she will usually say so, but if he or she thinks he or she may know it, he or she will often say, "Let me think about it a little longer." The point in doing this, of course, is to avoid wasting a great deal of time in waiting for answers from students who do not seem to take the initiative by simply saying, "I don't know."

After the student's Frustration Level in both oral and silent reading is reached, you may wish to begin reading to him or her in order to determine his or her listening comprehension level. In doing this, however, you may wish to use another set of graded reading passages so as not to spoil the original set for an administration at a later date.

Scoring and interpreting the student's reading performance

In coding oral reading errors, it often proves beneficial to code a passage exactly as a student reads it, although, as you will note, only the first seven types of errors listed in the code (pages ERI 10–11) are counted in computing the percentage of word recognition errors. The coding symbols shown in items eight through ten often provide information helpful to diagnosis of reading disability, but are not used in computing the percentage of word recognition errors. One of the main reasons that hesitations or lack of regard for punctuation are not counted as errors is that they simply cannot be objectively scored. For example, two scorers would seldom reach perfect agreement on the exact number of times a student disregarded punctuation or hesitated too long. Therefore, if these things were counted as errors, we would often have a low interscorer reliability (two or more people would not end up with the same number of errors). Items one through seven, however, are mistakes about which objective judgments can be made, and therefore, high interscorer reliability can be achieved, which can, in turn, make the informal reading inventory criteria valid.

After the student has read the material, you are then ready to determine whether it is at his or her Free or Independent, Instructional, or Frustration Level. To do this, follow the procedure outlined below.

1. Look in Table 1 where you will find numbers representing the total number of words in various passages in the left-hand column. Find the number or range that corresponds to the number of words in the passage just read. Place your left hand on this row. Look at the row of numbers across the top that represents the number of oral or word recognition errors. Find the number of errors made by the student and place your right hand on this number. Now find the point at which the row to which your left hand is pointing intersects with the column to which your right hand is pointing. This number represents the percentage of word recognition (percentage correct). Either remember or make note of this figure.

2. In Table 2 find the figure that corresponds to the number of questions asked and put your left hand on this figure. Then look across the top row of this table and find the figure that corresponds to the number of questions missed. Put your right hand on this figure. Find the point at which the row to which your left hand is pointing intersects with the col-

TABLE 6-1 *Guide for determining the correct percentage of word recognition*

Number of Words in Reading Passage	Number of Words Missed																			
	1	2	3	4	5	6	7	8	9	10	11	12	13	14	15	16	17	18	19	20
20–25	96	91	F	F	F	F	F	F	F	F	F	F	F	F	F	F	F	F	F	F
26–30	96	93	F	F	F	F	F	F	F	F	F	F	F	F	F	F	F	F	F	F
31–35	97	94	91	F	F	F	F	F	F	F	F	F	F	F	F	F	F	F	F	F
36–40	97	95	92	F	F	F	F	F	F	F	F	F	F	F	F	F	F	F	F	F
41–45	98	95	93	91	F	F	F	F	F	F	F	F	F	F	F	F	F	F	F	F
46–50	98	96	94	92	F	F	F	F	F	F	F	F	F	F	F	F	F	F	F	F
51–55	98	96	94	92	91	F	F	F	F	F	F	F	F	F	F	F	F	F	F	F
56–60	98	97	95	93	91	F	F	F	F	F	F	F	F	F	F	F	F	F	F	F
61–65	98	97	95	94	92	F	F	F	F	F	F	F	F	F	F	F	F	F	F	F
66–70	99	97	96	94	93	F	F	F	F	F	F	F	F	F	F	F	F	F	F	F
71–75	99	97	96	95	93	92	F	F	F	F	F	F	F	F	F	F	F	F	F	F
76–80	99	97	96	95	94	92	92	F	F	F	F	F	F	F	F	F	F	F	F	F
81–85	99	98	96	95	94	93	92	F	F	F	F	F	F	F	F	F	F	F	F	F
86–90	99	98	97	95	94	93	92	91	F	F	F	F	F	F	F	F	F	F	F	F
91–95	99	98	97	96	95	94	93	91	F	F	F	F	F	F	F	F	F	F	F	F
96–100	99	98	97	96	95	94	93	92	F	F	F	F	F	F	F	F	F	F	F	F
101–105	99	98	97	96	95	94	93	92	91	F	F	F	F	F	F	F	F	F	F	F
106–110	99	98	97	96	95	94	94	93	92	F	F	F	F	F	F	F	F	F	F	F
111–115	99	98	97	96	96	95	94	93	92	91	F	F	F	F	F	F	F	F	F	F
116–120	99	98	97	96	96	95	94	93	92	91	F	F	F	F	F	F	F	F	F	F
121–125	99	98	98	97	96	95	94	93	93	92	91	F	F	F	F	F	F	F	F	F
126–130	99	98	98	97	96	95	95	94	93	92	92	91	F	F	F	F	F	F	F	F
131–135	99	98	98	97	96	95	95	94	93	92	92	91	F	F	F	F	F	F	F	F
136–140	99	99	98	97	96	96	95	94	93	93	92	92	91	F	F	F	F	F	F	F
141–145	99	99	98	97	97	96	95	94	94	93	92	92	91	F	F	F	F	F	F	F
146–150	99	99	98	97	97	96	95	95	94	93	93	92	92	91	F	F	F	F	F	F
151–155	99	99	98	97	97	96	95	95	94	93	93	92	92	91	F	F	F	F	F	F
156–160	99	99	98	97	97	96	96	95	94	94	93	92	92	91	91	F	F	F	F	F
161–165	99	99	98	98	97	96	96	95	94	94	93	93	92	91	91	F	F	F	F	F
166–170	99	99	98	98	97	96	96	95	95	94	93	93	92	92	91	F	F	F	F	F
171–175	99	99	98	98	97	97	96	95	95	94	94	93	92	92	91	91	F	F	F	F
176–180	99	99	98	98	97	97	96	95	95	94	94	93	93	92	92	91	F	F	F	F
181–185	99	99	98	98	97	97	96	96	95	95	94	93	93	92	92	91	91	F	F	F
186–190	99	99	98	98	97	97	96	96	95	95	94	94	93	93	92	91	91	F	F	F
191–195	99	99	98	98	97	97	96	96	95	95	94	94	93	93	92	92	91	91	F	F
196–200	99	99	98	98	97	97	96	96	95	95	94	94	93	93	92	92	91	91	F	F

umn to which your right hand is pointing. This figure is the percent of comprehension questions that were correct.

3. Turn to the Reading Level Calculator and find the percentage of correct word recognition in one of the rows on the left-hand side and the percentage of correct comprehension in one of the columns on the top. Then find the point at which the row on the left intersects with the column on the top. If they intersect in one of the areas marked "F," the student is reading at his or her Frustration Level. If they intersect in the area marked "Inst," the student is reading at his or her Instructional Level. And, if they intersect in the area marked "Free," then the student is reading at his or her Free or Independent Level.

TABLE 6-2 *Guide for Determining the Correct Percentage of Comprehension Questions*

Number of Questions	Number of Questions Missed 0	1	2	3	4	5	6	7	8	9	10
10	100	90	80	70	60	F	F	F	F	F	F
9	100	90	80	65	55	F	F	F	F	F	F
8	100	90	75	65	F	F	F	F	F	F	F
7	100	85	70	60	F	F	F	F	F	F	F
6	100	85	65	F	F	F	F	F	F	F	F
5	100	80	60	F	F	F	F	F	F	F	F
4	100	75	F	F	F	F	F	F	F	F	F
3	100	65	F	F	F	F	F	F	F	F	F

Reading Level Calculator

Percent of Word Recognition	Percent of Comprehension 55*	60	65	70	75	80	85	90	95	100
100	Inst.	Inst.	Inst.	Inst.	Inst.	Inst.	Inst.	Free	Free	Free
99	F	Inst.	Inst.	Inst.	Inst.	Inst.	Inst.	Free	Free	Free
98	F	F	Inst.	Inst.	Inst.	Inst.	Inst.	Inst.	Inst.	Inst.
97	F	F	F	Inst.	Inst.	Inst.	Inst.	Inst.	Inst.	Inst.
96	F	F	F	F	Inst.	Inst.	Inst.	Inst.	Inst.	Inst.
95	F	F	F	F	F	Inst.	Inst.	Inst.	Inst.	Inst.
94	F	F	F	F	F	F	Inst.	Inst.	Inst.	Inst.
93	F	F	F	F	F	F	F	Inst.	Inst.	Inst.
92	F	F	F	F	F	F	F	F	Inst.	Inst.
91	F	F	F	F	F	F	F	F	F	Inst.

F = Frustration Reading Level   Inst. = Instructional Reading Level   Free = Free or Independent Level

* You will note in using this Reading Level Calculator that the student is not considered to be at his or her Frustration Level below 75 percent if his or her word recognition skills are still fairly high. The polygraph research referred to in this chapter indicated that if word recognition remains high, most students do not actually become frustrated until their comprehension level drops below the 50 percent level.

(Note: When using either Table 1 or Table 2, you will find that some rows and columns intersect in an area marked "F." Whenever this occurs, it means that the child is reading at his or her Frustration Level regardless of other scores. Therefore, there would be no need to use the Reading Level Calculator because his or her reading level would have already been determined.

In doing a quick check to determine whether certain materials are appropriate for a student you may often wish to omit the comprehension questions because of the time involved in both making up and asking these questions. Therefore, follow the same procedure previously described, but instead of asking questions, simply consider the student's comprehension to be at the 100 percent level when using the Reading Level Caculator as described in step 3.)

Briefly then, use the reading level guides as follows:

1. Determine the number of oral (word recognition) errors.
2. Convert this to a percentage by using Table 1.
3. Determine the number of comprehension errors.
4. Convert this to a percentage by using Table 2.
5. Find the corresponding percentages just derived on the Reading Level Calculator and determine the point at which these two percentages intersect. The coded intersection point represents the student's reading level.

If you are working with older students with whom you do not feel oral reading is necessary, or if they are hesitant to read orally, you may wish to modify the procedure just described. In this case simply hand them the material and tell them to read it silently, but remind them that you will ask them some questions about the material when they have finished. Then use Table 2 to calculate their percentage of comprehension. When this is found, go to the Reading Level Calculator and use it as described above; however, simply consider the student's word recognition as being 100 percent.

Using the Cloze Procedure to Match Students with Materials They Can Read

The cloze procedure is another technique that is useful for placing students in graded materials or for selecting materials to meet the needs of a particular group of students. In the following paragraphs some general information will be given that is necessary to understand in using the cloze procedure. Following this information, specific procedures are given for using the cloze procedure to match students with the materials they are to read.

The procedure consists of deleting every *n*th word and replacing it with a blank line. Students are then to read the material and attempt to fill in the blanks by using the correct word according to the proper context of the sentence. The percentage of correct answers is then calculated, and from these percentages Free or Independent, Instructional, and Frustration Levels of reading are derived. The Free or Independent reading level is the level considered appropriate for students who are expected to read material independently with no help from the teacher or other person. The Instructional level is that level that is considered appropriate for students who are reading in their textbooks such as a basal reader, a social studies, or a science book. It should, however, be stressed that this is a theoretical level that, in reality, should not be used when students actually read unless it is in a testing situation. That is, when tested, students may be reading at their instructional level when reading materials to which they have had no introduction on such things as new vocabulary and the building up of their background of experiences for reading the material. Therefore, if they place at their instructional level in testing, the material would be considered appropriate for them. However, it is only appropriate for them after the teacher has introduced the vocabulary to them and has laid a foundation for understanding the material in terms of building up their background of experience for the subject to be read. The point to be remembered is that students should not actually read, except in a testing situation, materials that are at their instructional level. What the teacher, of course, does in introducing the students to the vocabulary and concepts that they will encounter is to change the reading level of the material so that it becomes readable at the student's independent level. The frustration level is that level of difficulty where the student either encounters so many strange words and/or so many new concepts that he or she cannot adequately cope with reading the material.

DEVELOPING, ADMINISTERING, AND SCORING CLOZE PASSAGES

In constructing cloze passages, you could omit every third, fifth, or tenth word. However, most of the research that has been done is based on the deletion of every fifth word. As stated before, blank lines of equal length are then used to replace each of the words that have been deleted. It should also be stressed that the commonly used percentages for determining students' Free or Independent, Instructional, and Frustration Levels are based on the deletion of every fifth word. If every eighth or tenth word were to be deleted, these commonly used percentages would not apply.

Passages may vary in length depending on the grade level of the students; however, for students of ages equivalent to third- or fourth-grade level, or above, passages of about 250 words are often used. The entire first and last sentences are usually left intact. If passages of 250 words plus intact first and last sentences are used, and if every fifth word is omitted, then there will be fifty blanks, and every blank or answer will be worth two percentage points.

Cloze passages may be administered in a group situation much as one would do with standardized reading tests. However, in administering cloze passages there are usually no specific time limits for completion of the work.

For passages in which every fifth word has been deleted the percentages for the various reading levels are as follows:

Free or Independent Level	= 58 to 100 percent
Instructional Level	= 44 through 57 percent
Frustration Level	= 43 percent or below

In scoring the passages, only the exact word omitted is usually counted as correct—that is, correct synonyms are not counted as being correct. Research has shown that the overall percentages change very little regardless of whether synonyms are counted as correct or incorrect. Furthermore, if words other than the exact word omitted were counted, scoring would be much more difficult—that is, what one teacher might consider as an adequate answer another teacher may not and we would thus tend to lose interscorer reliability. In scoring cloze passages, however, students are not usually penalized for incorrect spelling as long as there is little or no doubt about which word was meant to be used.

A plastic overlay such as an overhead projector transparency can be made of each cloze passage with the correct answers appearing on the plastic overlay. When this is superimposed on the student's copy, you can readily check the number of right and wrong answers. These can, in turn, be converted to percentages. From these percentages you can then determine whether the material is at the student's Free or Independent, Instructional, or Frustration Level.

Using the Cloze Procedure to Place Students in Graded Materials

1. Select six to twelve passages from a book or material that students will tentatively be using. Pick them randomly but equally distributed from the front to the back of the book.
2. Give the tests to 25–30 students in a class in which the text is commonly used.
3. The mean score on each test is calculated and then the mean of the means is calculated.
4. Select the test that is closest to the mean of the means and throw the rest of the scores away.
5. When a test has been selected for each of the texts a teacher is likely to use, the tests can be duplicated and compiled into booklets that can be administered as group tests. When a student's score is 57 percent or higher, the student is reading at his or her Independent reading level. A score from 44 percent to 56 percent is equivalent to the student's Instructional reading level. A score of 43 percent or less is considered to be at the student's Frustration level. (In a textbook, of course, one is concerned with placing the student in the textbook that is represented by the passage in which the student scored at his or her Instructional reading level.)

Using the Cloze Procedure to Meet the Needs of the Students

1. Divide the book into sections and select two or more passages from each section. The same length passages as described earlier can be used.
2. Make a random selection of the students for whom the book will be used.
3. If you are using a great number of students, you may wish to put them into a number of groups and then let each group take some of the tests. (Make sure, however, that the selection of the subgroups is done randomly.)
4. If students are able to score at their Instructional level on the passages from the book, then it would be considered suitable for them. On the other hand, if most students scored at their Frustration level on the passages from the book, it would be considered too difficult for them.

The Reliability of the Cloze Procedure

The reliability of the cloze procedure will essentially depend upon the following four factors:

1. If longer tests are used, the students' scores will probably be more accurate, but it will take longer to correct them.
2. If a larger number of tests is used when selecting the one to represent the material, then the test selected will more accurately represent the difficulty of the material.
3. Some materials are uneven in difficulty. These materials should be avoided, if possible.
4. The procedure outlined herein must be followed exactly or the results will not be accurate.

REMEDIATION PROCEDURES FOR DEVELOPING COMPREHENSION

Unfortunately, most of the so-called teaching of the skills of comprehension has, if fact, not been teaching at all. If you were to remember what kind of instruction you as a teacher or parent had in improving your comprehension, you would probably recall that you were required to read a passage and then endless questions were asked over the content of the material. We do know that if teachers continually ask students questions over material they have read, the students ultimately improve in their comprehension skills. However, it should also be remembered that the students, in this case, were not taught how to comprehend. They were simply asked so many questions that they developed, in most cases, a comprehension strategy of their own. In recent years a few methods of actually helping or teaching students to comprehend better have been developed. Many of these strategies have been used by some teachers for years, but a much more systematic approach has now been developed. Many of these successful strategies fall into a category known as *metacognition.* Cognition is, of course, the process of thinking, and metacognition is the process of monitoring your thinking processes, or thinking about what you are thinking. Patricia Babbs and Alden Moe (1983) have defined metacognition in the following way:

> Metacognition refers to the ability to monitor one's own cognition; it is thinking about thinking. When applied to the act of reading, this definition suggests that the reader is able to select skills and strategies for the demands of the reading task. (p. 423)

Disabled readers appear to be unable to monitor their comprehension processes as well as more able readers. For example, Steve D. Rinehart and Jennifer M. Platt (1984) indicate that disabled or inefficient readers have difficulties with comprehension because they have deficits in metacognition. Rinehart and Platt also say that metacognitive deficits among young children, children with learning disabilities, and children who are generally poor readers have been evidenced in the following areas:

1. Understanding the purpose of reading;
2. Modifying reading strategies for different purposes;
3. Considering how new information relates to what is already known;
4. Evaluating text for clarity, completeness, and consistency;
5. Dealing with failure to understand;
6. Identifying the important information in a passage; and
7. Deciding how well the material has been understood. (p. 54)

Babbs and Moe, as well as other authors such as Oran Stewart and Ebo Tei (1983), have given some very practical suggestions for using metacognition for the improvement of students' comprehension skills. Some of these are as follows:

Changing Speeds in Relation to the Difficulty of the Material

The teacher should stress the need for students to change their reading speeds in relation to the nature of the material being read. Unfortunately, many adults, as well as students, have not learned to "shift gears" or change speeds in relation to the nature of the materials that they are required to read. This is often the kind of person one finds in so-called "speed reading" courses. That is, one might be likely to find new medical doctors or lawyers who have just graduated from law school. These people have been used to plodding through everything as though it were a law case book where every fact is extremely important, or medical doctors have been reading medical books where there are a great many facts to remember. After doing this type of reading, it is somewhat difficult to learn to read even the newspaper without feeling some sense of guilt for not reading every word. What most speed reading courses do, in reality, is to teach students of all ages to change their reading speeds, i.e., they learn to read a newspaper by skimming over the headlines to see if there is anything in various articles that interests them and, if there is not, then that section is skipped. Elementary and secondary school students, of course, need to be taught to read novels or the newspaper in a different manner than they would read their math book or the directions for a science experiment. Teachers should provide various kinds of materials and discuss which types should be read nearly word for word and which kinds can be skimmed simply to determine whether there is information of which the reader would want to take note.

Stressing the Importance of Obtaining Mental Images

The old adage that a picture can be worth a thousand words may be true in the monitoring of one's comprehension. Students should be provided with materials that depict a scene and then asked if they were able to get a mental image of what was being read, as the material was being read. If they report that they were not, then they should be given practice in the development of mental images while reading. It is often helpful, in the beginning stages, to ask students to close their eyes and attempt to get a mental image of something being read by the teacher. Students can be asked to draw a scene after being read a description of that scene. You may wish to have students do this on a transparency and then place it on an overhead projector. A discussion can then be held regarding certain details that were omitted by certain students in their pictures. Following this, have students read material of a very descriptive nature, about materials with which they are familiar, and discuss their ability to get a mental image of the material as it was being read. The author has taught college students to nearly double their ability to remember details of a story, in a very short period of time, simply by first asking them to close their eyes as something was read aloud. Following this, they were given descriptive material and asked to develop a mental image as they read.

Teach Students to Predict What May Lie Ahead

Asking students to get into the habit of predicting what may lie ahead in a passage or story will force students to monitor constantly what they are reading in order to make these predictions. This may be practiced by asking students to read up to a certain point in a story and then stopping to discuss what may be likely to happen based on what has been read up to that point. It is also important to read the material, following various predictions, to see which of the predictions were accurate. As a teacher, you are likely to find that with a certain amount of practice in this activity, students automatically begin to make predictions concerning the outcome. The whole process, of course, forces students to constantly monitor their reading comprehension.

Teach Students to Model the Questioning of the Teacher

Research has shown that one of the most effective strategies for teaching students to monitor their thinking or comprehension while reading is to model the questioning strategies of the teacher. In doing this activity, ask students to attempt to determine, while reading, what they think the teacher would ask them about the material after they have finished reading. You may wish to practice this by reading a paragraph at a time and then writing down what you would ask students about the material just read. Then ask students to ask you questions over the material just read. Following this activity, read the questions that you would have asked the students about the material. Discuss any difference in questions, and practice until students are able to emulate your questioning as closely as possible.

Make Students Aware of Difficult Words While Reading

Most of us, even as adults, have taught ourselves simply to omit or skip over words of which we do not know the meaning. For example, think about a time when you saw a strange word and looked up its meaning in the dictionary. Then did you not notice that word appearing several times during the next month or two? Chances are that the word did not suddenly begin to appear in the material that you were reading but that it had often been there before, but you simply had taught yourself to ignore it. There are several ways in which you may wish to make students aware of difficult words, or words for which they do not know the meaning. You may wish to read a story a paragraph at a time and ask students to write down any new word or word of which they do not know the meaning. After completing the paragraph, discuss these words and how lack of the knowledge of the meaning of these words may cause students to lack comprehension of the entire paragraph. You may also wish to have contests in which students attempt to find new words in daily activities that other students do not know.

Another activity mentioned by the authors above is the use of road signs such as YIELD before words with which you expect students may encounter difficulty. When students encounter these words, they will be reminded to pay careful attention to the meaning of that particular word.

Make Students Aware of the Importance of *Who, What, When, Where,* and *Why*

Many good teachers have been doing this for years; however, if you are not doing it, you will find that students tend to remember considerably more about material they have read if, while reading it, they are instructed to answer each of the questions posed by the words *who, what, when, where,* and *why.*

Make Students Aware of Having a Purpose for Reading

Although it may sound simplistic to an adult who is used to reading nearly everything for a purpose, it is extremely important to help students set a purpose for what they read. Since, in the process of schooling, many students are simply told to read a certain number of pages for "tomorrow's assignment" without being told why they are to read it, they quite naturally get into the habit of reading with no particular purpose in mind. Before students begin reading a passage or an assignment, discuss why it is important to know the material or what is expected of them when they complete the assignment. Attempt to get students in the habit of previewing material they will be reading to get an idea of what they will be learning from the reading material. Also attempt to get each student in the habit of asking questions such as, "Why am I reading this and what am I supposed to know when I finish?"

Help Students to Become Aware of Important Sentences

Although we have little or no positive research that would indicate that learning to locate the "main idea" of a paragraph is an important subskill of reading comprehension, you may find it helpful to instruct students to become more aware of sentences that are important and those that are of less importance. You may wish to do this by placing each of the sentences of a paragraph on the chalkboard or overhead projector and discussing, with the students, which sentences seem to be of greater and lesser importance.

Teach Students to Be Aware of Material That They Do Not Understand

You may wish to practice this skill with students by simply having them read a paragraph at a time from material that is somewhat new to them.

Ask them to stop and raise their hands each time they read a sentence or idea that does not make sense to them. Another way of providing practice in this skill is to rewrite certain sentences in a passage so that they do not make sense. These may then be duplicated and given to students to read. Ask them to underline any sentence that they feel is unclear to them while they are reading. In doing this activity you should also emphasize that any sentence that does not seem to make sense should be reread or, if necessary, perhaps reread the preceding two or three sentences to see if some important point was missed.

The Use of Story Frames

Gerald W. Fowler (1982) has illustrated how what he refers to as "story frames" can be used to help students monitor their comprehension processes as they read. Fowler suggests the use of five types of story frames that are illustrated in the material that follows. It is suggested that in the beginning stages only one frame be used. It may be displayed on an overhead projector following the reading of a story. Students may then be asked for their responses concerning the blanks in the story frames. Fowler stresses the point that there are often no exact responses for certain blanks in the story frames. As students learn how to use story frames, you may then wish to give them a story frame prior to reading a story and ask them to think about how they would complete the information called for as they read. As students progress in their ability to fill in the information in each story frame after completing a story, let them begin to work with more than one story frame, i.e., expose them to several frames before reading a story so they will monitor the information called for in each of the story frames as they read. In using story frames it should be kept in mind that not all frames are appropriate for certain stories. Following are five types of story frames as suggested by Fowler:*

FIGURE 6-1 *Story Summary with one character included*

____

Our story is about ____________________

____________________. ______________ is an

important character in our story. ______________

tried to ________________________________

The story ends when ______________________

___________________________________.

____

* Reprinted with permission of the author and the International Reading Association.

FIGURE 6–2 *Important Idea or Plot*

In this story the problem starts when ______ ______________________. After that, ______________________. Next, ______________________ ______. Then, ______________ ______________. The problem is finally solved when ______________ ______. The story ends ______________ ______________________. ______________________

FIGURE 6–4 *Character analysis*

______________ is an important character in our story. ________ is important because ______________________. Once, he/she ______________________. Another time, ______________________. I think that ______________ is ______________
(character's name) (character trait)
because ______________________. ______________________

FIGURE 6–3 *Setting*

This story takes place ______________ ______________. I know this because the author uses the words "______________ ______________." Other clues that show when the story takes place are ________ ______________________. ______________________

FIGURE 6–5 *Character comparison*

________ and ________ are two characters in our story. ______________
(character's name)
is ______________________ while
(trait)
______________ is ______________.
(other character) (trait)
For instance, ________ tries to ________ and ________ tries to ________. ________ learns a lesson when ________ ______________________. ______________________

* Reprinted with permission of the International Reading Association.

The Concept of Schemata Theory

Schema theory was explained by Michael Strange (1980). He stated,

> Schema theory seeks to explain how new information acquired while reading is meshed with old information already in our heads. It is helpful to think of schema (singular of *schemata*) as a concept, although a schema is meant to be more inclusive than a concept. (p. 393)

Margaret Stefferson, Chitra Joag-Dev, and Richard C. Anderson (1979) emphasized the importance of schemata. After doing research on the subject they stated,

> When a person reads a story, the *schemata* embodying his background knowledge provide the framework for understanding the setting, the mood, the characters, and the chain of events. It stands to reason that readers who bring to bear different schemata will give various interpretations to a story. (p. 11)

Stefferson, Joag-Dev, and Anderson had citizens from the United States and from India read about an Indian and an American wedding. They found that when subjects read material about their own culture they were able to read the material more rapidly, they were able to recall a greater amount of information, and they produced more culturally appropriate elaborations. This would indicate what many good teachers have known and been practicing for years, i.e., that in order to comprehend well the student must have a background of information on the subject about which he or she is reading. If students possess only a limited background of knowledge of the material being read, then the teacher can enhance their comprehension by building up their vocabulary and background of experience in order to help them comprehend information that is relatively new to them.

Chunking in Reading

Chunking in reading is the process of breaking sentences into what might be termed natural linguistic units or natural phrases. Chunking may be done by dividing natural phrases by the use of slash marks (/), by the use of dashes (–), or by simply leaving more space between natural phrases or linguistic units. William G. Brozo, Ronand V. Schmelzer, and Hillar A. Spires (1983) discussed the research on the use of chunking as a means of improving reading comprehension. They stated:

> Several studies have shown that poor readers' comprehension is improved when words are preorganized into meaningful groupings for them. . . . Few, however, have shown that grouping aids comprehension for competent readers. (p. 442)

An example of material that has been chunked by the use of slash marks appears below:

> Fred and his father/like to go fishing. One day/Fred said/to his father,/Father can we/go fishing/this Saturday?

There may be some debate as to where the exact phrases or natural linguistic units begin and end; however, the two sentences above indicate how the process is done.

Kathleen C. Stevens (1981) studied the use of the chunking procedure with eighty-five boys in the tenth grade. Stevens reported that students who read in the "chunked mode" read better than those who did not. In her conclusions Stevens stated,

> As a first step in teaching "chunking" teachers might present "chunked" reading material to students for discussion. Then, students might point out the phrase units in prose for themselves. The need to "chunk" for every reading task should make the discussion of phrasing and of thought units an ongoing activity. This can be emphasized to students by reading meaningfully and nonmeaningfully "chunked" materials. (pp. 128–29)

The Use of Questioning Strategies

As was pointed out earlier in this chapter, much of the so-called teaching of the comprehension skills is not actually teaching but questioning. Although it would, no doubt, be more productive if we knew more types of teaching exercises, in all fairness to the questioning process most research studies have shown that the constant use of questions over material that students have read does, in fact, increase their reading comprehension.

Perhaps one of the things that has made the questioning process even less meaningful is that most studies have also shown that an extremely large percentage of the questions that teachers ask their students are those calling for the simple recall of factual information. Gerard Giordano (1981) has suggested a taxonomy for questions consisting of four categories. These are as follows:

1. Recapitulative
2. Critical
3. Applied
4. Judgmental

Giordano illustrates this with the story of the three little pigs. For each of the categories he suggests asking the following questions:

Recapitulative: Who knocked on the doors of the pigs' house?
Critical: Why didn't all of the pigs build their houses out of bricks?
Applied: What would happen if your parents played instead of working?
Judgmental: How do you think the pig in the straw house felt when the wolf knocked at his door?

Ronald T. Hyman (1982) has suggested a number of techniques for improving your questioning strategies. Some of these are as follows:

1. Let all students know that they will be called on.

2. In addition to letting all students know that they will be called on, ask students not simply to call out the answers, but rather make sure that a specific student is called on to answer each question.

3. From time to time call on students to give their reactions to questions just answered by their classmates.

4. Do not call on volunteers more than 10 to 15 percent of the time. The author believes that this is an excellent suggestion, since in calling on only the answering or volunteering students, you do not get a true picture of the number of students who do not know the answers to various questions that are posed. The author has found that when he has persuaded his teachers to do this they have often been disappointed in the small percentage of students who knew the answers to various questions.

5. Call on volunteers mainly for those types of questions that ask a student to give his or her own opinion.

6. Make sure that questions are *passage-dependent,* i.e., that they can not be answered without the students having read the material. A question that is not *passage-dependent* can often be answered from the experiential background of the student.

7. Hyman suggests that the teacher use concise questions. For example, he states that one should not ask a question such as, "Why was Franklin Roosevelt elected president?" Hyman points out that the answer to this is simply that he got the most electoral votes. Hyman suggests that a much more meaningful question would be, "What did the article say were some of the reasons that people voted for Franklin Roosevelt?"

8. Hyman, as well as others, have also pointed out that teachers

often do not give students ample time to answer questions. Some studies have, in fact, found that many teachers give students less than five seconds to answer a question. It is suggested that you time the length of silence between your question and the time that you call on another student. Attempt to give at least five, if not ten seconds for students to gather their thoughts.

9. Hyman also suggests that all students be urged to answer at least some questions rather than letting them settle for "I don't know." He points out that if this is done, then the student will find it easy to avoid being asked questions by simple saying, "I don't know."

George and Evelyn Spache (1977) have made a number of suggestions concerning the use of questioning. Some of these are as follows:

1. They suggest that a session on building up student's background of experiences and vocabulary for a passage or story will probably be more effective in getting students to remember what they read than would questions posed prior to the students' reading of the material.
2. Ask questions, if you wish to use questions, after students have read material rather than before they read it. Spache and Spache point out that asking questions before students read a story tends to make them focus on those questions only, rather than on the overall information given in the story.
3. Have students set a purpose for reading that is not too narrow. As pointed out in number 2 above, if students are asked specific questions before reading a story, then they are likely to be able to answer those questions; however, their overall comprehension is likely to suffer. For this reason the purpose for reading the passage should not be too narrow.
4. Students should learn that not all questions actually have an answer. Some will be speculative and for other questions there may be no answer.
5. Teach students to learn to ask their own questions and to speculate on what the author is going to say.

Other Comprehension Strategies

STRUCTURED COMPREHENSION

Eldon E. Ekwall and James L. Shanker (1983) have described the structured comprehension strategy as follows:*

> For the student who has difficulty at the paragraph or sentence level a technique called "structured comprehension," described by Marvin Cohn (1969), works extremely well. For this technique Cohn suggests choosing factual-type material that is just difficult enough to be beyond the comprehension level of the students who will be reading it. Cohn suggests that students read the first sentence and then answer the question, "Do I know what this sentence means?" This forces each reader to be an active participant rather than a passive reader. If the reader does not understand all or part of the sentence, he or she is to ask the teacher or a peer as many ques-

* From: Ekwall, Eldon E., and Shanker, James L. *Diagnosis and Remediation of the Disabled Reader* (2nd ed.). Newton, MA: Allyn and Bacon, Inc., 1983. (Reprinted by permission.)

> tions as are necessary to fully comprehend the meaning. After all student questions have been answered, the teacher then asks one or more questions about the sentence. The students are to write the answers to each question asked by the teacher. This, of course, again forces all students to actively participate. After all answers are written, the question is then discussed and answers are checked. Cohn also points out that when answers are written the student cannot rationalize that a mental answer was right. He emphasizes the point that in the beginning you should stress literal meaning more than relationships. He suggests asking for the antecedent of every pronoun, the meaning of figurative expressions, and any new or uncommon vocabulary words. After the teacher has begun to set a pattern for questioning, the students should begin to use the same type of question in their search for meaning. Cohn stresses the fact that the book should remain open during the entire process. After ten questions have been answered, each student scores his or her own paper and compares it with those done previously. (p. 214)

REQUEST PROCEDURE

The *request procedure* was described by Eldon E. Ekwall and James L. Shanker (1983) and Anthony Manzo (1969).*

> In using the request procedure the teacher begins by telling the student to ask the kind of questions pertaining to each sentence that the student thinks the teacher might ask. The student is also told that each question is to be answered as fully and as honestly as possible and that it is considered unfair for the teacher to pretend not to know the answer to try to draw out the student and that it is also unfair for the student to say, "I don't know," since the student should at least explain why he or she cannot answer the question.
>
> The game begins by having the teacher and student both read the first sentences silently. The teacher then closes his or her book and the student asks questions concerning the content of the sentence. Then the student closes his or her book and the teacher asks questions about the material. The teacher should attempt to be a model for good questions, i.e., using thought-provoking questions that call for reasoning rather than strictly factual recall. After several sentences have been read, the teacher should ask questions that call for integration and evaluation of sentences read previously. Questioning is to continue until the teacher feels the student can answer the questions, "What do you think will happen in the rest of the selection?" "Why?" Manzo (1969) recommends specific types of questions as follows:
>
> 1. Questions for which there is an *immediate reference,* e.g., "What was the second word in the sentence?" or "What did John call his dog?"
> 2. Questions which relate to *common knowledge* and for which answers can be reasonably expected, e.g., "What kind of animal has been associated with the name Lassie?"
> 3. Questions for which the teacher does not expect a "correct" response, but for which he can provide *related information,* e.g., "Do you happen to know how many varieties of dogs there are? . . . well I just happen to . . ."
> 4. Questions for which neither the teacher nor the selection is likely to supply a "right" answer but which are nonetheless worth pondering or discussing; "I wonder why some animals make better pets than do others?"

* Reprinted by permission of the author and the International Reading Association.

5. Questions of a *personalized type* which only the student can answer, e.g., "Would you like to have a pet?", "Why?", "How did the different members of your family react to your first pet?"
6. Questions which are answerable, but are not answered by the selection being analyzed; *further reference* is needed, e.g., "I wonder what is the average height and weight of a collie?"
7. Questions requiring *translation.* Translation questions frequently call upon students to change words, ideas, and pictures into a different symbolic form, e.g., translation from one level of abstraction to another, from one symbolic form to another, from one verbal form to another. "In a few words, how would you summarize what happened to Lassie?" "What is happening in this picture?" "What do you suppose the ex-convict meant by 'up at the big house'?" (p. 126)

SQ3R

Ekwall and Shanker (1983) have also described the procedure known as SQ3R.*

> One of the most effective aids to comprehension that has ever been devised is the SQ3R technique. It was first described by Francis Robinson (1941), and since that time a number of variations have been devised. None of the variations, however, seems to have proven any more successful than Robinson's original technique. SQ3R stands for "survey, question, read, recite and review." This method is best adapted to material in which subject headings are used such as are commonly found in social studies and science books. In brief form the technique a student would use in reading a chapter or unit would be as follows:
>
> *Survey:* The student reads any introductory sentences that appear at the beginning of the chapter and then all boldface headings, captions under pictures, and questions at the end of the chapter. (Students who first use this technique should be timed to make sure they *only* survey. They have a tendency to simply read the material as they have been doing, if they are not put under some time pressure. A period of two to three minutes is usually sufficient; however, time will depend on the age and proficiency of the readers and the length of the chapter.)
>
> *Question:* Each heading is turned into a question. For example, the heading in a science book might read, "Iron is an important metal." This might then be changed to, "Why is iron an important metal?" (When students first begin to use this technique you should help them devise questions. One way to do this is to develop a list of common beginnings for questions such as, "When did," "Why are," "Why did," and "Why is.")
>
> *Read:* Students than read down to the next boldface heading to find the answer to the question.
>
> *Recite:* After reading down to the next boldface heading the student looks up from the book and attempts to answer the question. When students are first learning this technique, this can be done orally as a class procedure. After they have had a chance to practice, they should recite silently to themselves. If a student cannot answer a question, he or she should read the material under that boldface heading again.
>
> *Review:* After the entire chapter has been read, students go back and read only the questions derived from the boldface headings and see if they

* From: Ekwall, Eldon E., and Shanker, James L. *Diagnosis and Remediation of the Disabled Reader* (2nd ed.). Newton, MA: Allyn and Bacon, Inc., 1983. (Reprinted by permission.)

> can answer them. If any questions cannot be answered, they would read the material under that question again.
>
> Considerable thought about the nature of the material is required in order for the student to be able to change the boldface headings into questions. This technique also forces the student to actively seek answers to each question while reading. Some students find this method to be extremely rewarding, just as some find it to be rather burdensome. In teaching this method you should actually go through a number of chapters with students until they become adept at devising questions and following the other outlined procedures. You will find this technique to be generally suitable for students at the junior high school level and above. (pp. 216–17)

ILLUSTRATING PARAGRAPH STRUCTURE

Ekwall and Shanker have also described a method of helping students learn to differentiate sentences that tend to illustrate the main idea of a paragraph from those of less importance.*

> The drawing of various-sized rectangles to illustrate paragraphs showing the relationship between main ideas and important details is a technique that incorporates writing with reading. This is somewhat similar to having students underline key sentences and/or words but gives students a better overall understanding of the relationships that exist among sentences. In using this technique, main idea sentences are represented by rectangles that are slightly larger than sentences that represent important details. For example, note the following paragraph and the corresponding illustration (Figure 6–6).

FIGURE 6–6

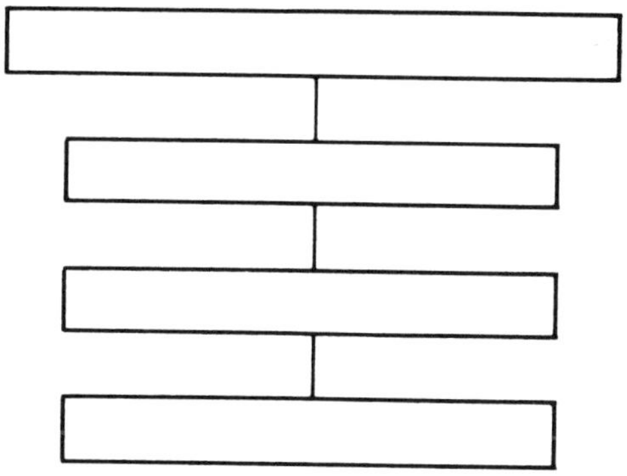

Meadowlarks are wonderful birds.
They sing pretty songs.
They are very beautiful.
And they destroy insects that would harm our gardens.

> The large rectangle at the top of Figure 6–6 represents the main idea sentence, i.e., "Meadowlarks are wonderful birds," and each of the three supporting detail sentences are illustrated below it.

* From: Ekwall, Eldon E., and Shanker, James L. *Diagnosis and Remediation of the Disabled Reader* (2nd ed.). Newton, MA: Allyn and Bacon, Inc., 1983. (Reprinted by permission.)

In using this system to teach paragraph structure you should start out by explaining that various-sized rectangles represent main ideas and important details, and then have students write their own paragraphs to fit various structural patterns. Students seem to find it easier in the beginning to write paragraphs of their own to fit a specific pattern than to analyze the structure of someone else's paragraph. This also has the added advantage of helping students to improve their ability to write well-structured paragraphs, and for some to understand what defines a paragraph. To use this as a method of instruction we would suggest the following procedure:

1. Introduce the idea as explained above.
2. Draw a simple structural form and have students work in small groups to write a paragraph to fit the form.
3. Change the structure by putting the main idea at the end and then have students rewrite their paragraphs to fit the new form.
4. Illustrate different forms, e.g., where there is a main idea sentence at the beginning, then several important detail sentences, and finally a summary sentence. (See Figure 6–7).
5. Provide students with well-written paragraphs that clearly show main idea and important detail sentences; have students illustrate them. Gradually increase the difficulty of the patterns.
6. When students are both writing their own and illustrating others' paragraphs, be sure to discuss their responses and allow them to justify what they write or draw. Be sure to accept reasonable alternatives. The important point is not necessarily that all students agree on how a paragraph form should be drawn, but it is important that students be able to justify their own illustrations.
7. As you work with differing forms, have students illustrate each new form and place it on a chart showing various forms. Use different colors to differentiate the main idea rectangles from the important detail rectangles on the permanent models.
8. Students also enjoy naming different forms; e.g., one group of students named the one shown in Figure 6–6 "the natural," and the one with a larger rectangle at both the beginning and the end (Figure 6–7) was called "the double natural."

FIGURE 6–7

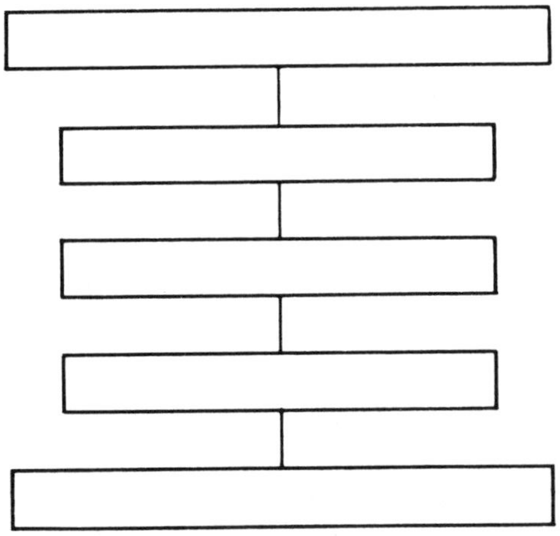

> In using this method of instruction you should remember that all paragraphs do not have a main idea sentence. It is very frustrating for students if they do not realize this in the early stages of looking for a structural pattern in paragraphs written by others. There are also paragraphs that have the main idea somewhere near the middle, and still others that have two main ideas with supporting detail sentences for only one of the two. (pp. 218–20)

Awareness of Signal Words

Many words serve as signals to the reader to inform him or her that the author is going to list a series of events or that a number of points will be covered. Help students to locate and become aware of these key words. Some key words and examples of how some of them are used follow:

first	finally	in the beginning
then	another	a further
last	and then	many more

> There are *a number of ways* that birds help us. *One way* they help us is by eating insects. *Sometimes* they furnish us with food. They *also* provide us with feathers which have been used in a great many ways. And, *finally,* they provide us with a great deal of pleasure with their beautiful songs.

Purpose Setting

Researchers have shown that when students are told to read something to try to find the answers to specific questions, they can usually do so but, at the same time, they often remember little if anything else. For this reason it is probably better to set a broad purpose for reading a passage or story rather than to focus on a few specific facts.

Teaching with the Cloze Procedure

Leave every seventh or eighth word out of a story and replace it with a blank. In the beginning you may wish to give the student several choices of words for each blank. At a later stage, you can simply ask them to fill in the blanks by using the context as well as they can. Also, in the beginning try to omit only words for which the surrounding words provide context clues. After students have completed the exercise, go through it sentence by sentence and ask for volunteers to tell what word or words might belong in each blank, why they believe one word might be more proper than another, and so forth.

Following Directions

There are many types of activities that can be used to help students learn to follow directions. Following are three examples:

Activity 1. Write out directions for drawing a certain design and have students draw the design and compare their illustrations. Then discuss what went wrong in some cases.

Activity 2. Have students write directions on how to get from their home to school, from their room at school to the playground, and so forth. Have one student follow one of these sets of directions to see whether he ends up in the right place.

Activity 3. Have some students write and others read and follow directions for paper folding to make such things as boats, hats, and so forth.

Critical Analysis of Editorials

Have students gather editorials and letters to the editor from newspapers. Read these and discuss whether the writer is biased, whether he or she is actually presenting the facts, and whether he or she uses words that make another appear bad (for example, "the militant leader," "the leftist group").

Matching Newspaper Articles with Headlines

Place a number of headlines from newspaper articles on cards and place the articles themselves on other cards. Have students try to match the headline with the proper article.

Paragraph Sequence

Cut a short article consisting of several paragraphs into separate paragraphs, and paste each one on a card. Place each article in a separate envelope. Distribute these envelopes to students and have them try to reconstruct the article by placing the paragraphs in the proper sequence. Number the back of each card so that when they are turned over they will be in the correct numerical order if the paragraphs were placed in the correct sequence.

Comic Strip Sequence

Do the same as described above, but use comic strips.

Matching Synonyms and Antonyms

Make sets of synonyms or antonyms on cards and place them in envelopes. Have students try to match each set of either synonyms or antonyms. This can also be made self-correctional by numbering each matching pair with the same number on the back of each card.

Matching Synonyms from Context

Place a number of sentences on paper or chalkboard as follows:

The man (rushed) ____________ to work.
Mary (answered) ____________ when she was asked the question.
Sam's face seemed to (shine) ____________ in the moonlight.
shouted—hurried—replied—glow—bright

Place a number of words under the sentences and have students try to find the proper synonym for each word in parenthesis.

Predicting the Outcome of a Story

Begin reading a story, but stop before the outcome is disclosed. Encourage students to predict the outcome. Discuss why one prediction is more logical than certain others, and so forth. Then read the conclusion and discuss why some answers were more logical than others.

Finding the Best Topic Sentence

Cut paragraphs out of books, newspapers, or magazines. Write several topic sentences for each paragraph, and make sure that one of the sentences is a more logical topic sentence than the others. Then have students read each paragraph and discuss which sentence from the choices would be the best topic sentence.

Learning to Recognize the Main Idea

Give students paragraphs that you have written, or paragraphs that you have cut from newspapers or magazines, that can easily be summarized in one sentence. Show these to students and ask them to write one sentence that tells what is in the whole paragraph. Have students read their answers and discuss which sentences really do summarize the paragraph and which do not.

Developing Visual Images

Read to the class, or have the class read, a short descriptive passage; then have them illustrate the scene that was described in the passage. After they have completed their drawings, discuss details that should have appeared in the pictures. Have various students show their pictures and discuss what is missing, things that were illustrated that some students might have missed, and so forth.

Highlighting Main Ideas in a Lesson

Many disabled readers have a great deal of difficulty in reading their social studies and science books. For these students, you may wish to take a highlighter pen and highlight only sentences that give the general meaning of the material written on each page. Place the disabled reader with another student who does read well and make sure that the disabled reader reads the material that has been highlighted or that the student who has been placed with him or her reads it to him or her. This way when the class discusses the subject matter in the textbook, the disabled reader will be able to enter into the discussion and thus build up his or her self-confidence.

Rewriting Stories for Disabled Readers

As an enrichment exercise for better readers, have them rewrite the chapters (they can take turns) in the science or social studies textbooks by using as few words as possible. Put these rewritten chapters in folders for disabled readers to use when it is time for them to read that material prior to discussing it in class.

Following Directions for Fact or Fiction

Give the students sentences that are either fact or fiction with directions such as those that follow:

Draw a blue box if chickens have feathers. ____________________
Draw a red ball if cows lay eggs. ____________________
Draw a purple house if foxes have fur. ____________________
Draw a green triangle if horses have two tails. ____________________

Following Directions and Finding Details

Give students slips of paper or place them in a box to be drawn out after they have read a short story. The slips should have directions on them such as the following:

1. Read the title of the story.
2. Read the part that tells why Paul wanted to go home.
3. Read the part that tells why Sam started to run.
4. Read the part that tells why Paul wanted Sam to go with him.

Who—What—When—Where—Why

Write or cut paragraphs or short stories from magazines or newspapers that generally tell who the subject matter is about, what it is about, when, where, and why it happened. Then have students read these paragraphs or stories and either write or discuss who it was about, what happened, when it happened, where it happened, and why it happened.

Arranging a Sequence of Events

Let students read a story or a set of directions for doing something. Then write a series of events on cards and have students arrange the cards in the same sequence as the events in the story or the directions for doing something. Number the back of the cards so that students can turn them over to see whether they are in the proper sequence. See the examples below:

Jim found his dog.	Jim went home.
Jim called his dog.	Jim asked mother if he could go for a walk in the woods.

Jim took his dog to the woods.	Jim heard his dog barking.

Semantic Mapping

Semantic mapping has been shown to be an effective method of improving reading comprehension and has also proven its worth with students with reading disabilities. The concept of semantic mapping was explained by Richard C. Sinatra, Josephine Stahl-Gemake, and David N. Berg (1984). They stated,

> A map or web is a graphic arrangement showing the major ideas and relationships in text or among word meanings. The map consists of "nodes" (drawn in circles, rectangles, or squares) containing key words or phrases, with connecting links (lines or arrows drawn between the nodes).
>
> Symbols common to flow charts may be used. For instance, a circle generally means program start or finish, a triangle means that a decision is to be made, while the rectangle holds the operations expressed in the program.

Classification map for "Our New Age-Old Foods"

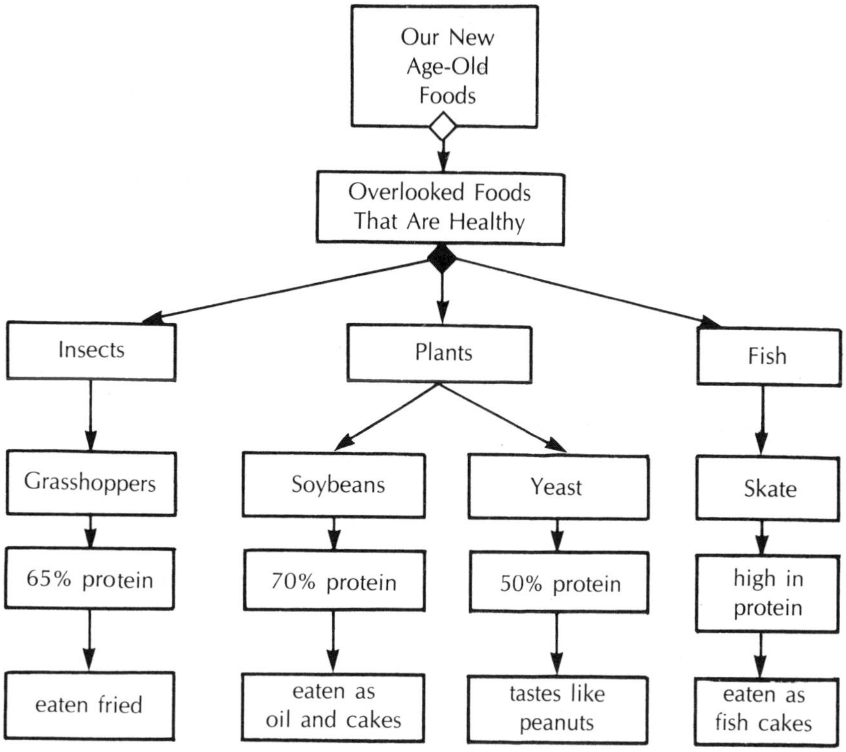

* Reprinted by permission of the International Reading Association.

> As an example, in a map for an episodic tale, the nodes are linked together by arrows showing the flow of events in the story. The title is written in the central node to focus attention to the story. Subsequent nodes show in sequence the story's main events or episodes. This web construction demonstrates evolving order of major story happenings, with minor events further webbed by added lines and nodes.
>
> The mapping procedure is appealing because of the practical, holistic way it generates schema theory with reading comprehension. Schema theory explains the essence of comprehension by proposing that what is understood during reading or listening is linked in some conceptual way with what existed in the mind of the learner beforehand. (pp. 22–23)

Sinatra, Stahl-Gemake, and Berg illustrated a classification map for "Our New Age-Old Foods." The authors noted that the class was not indicated clearly enough by the title so that it was necessary to use a separate node to illustrate the major concept, i.e., the rectangle that says, "Overlooked Foods That Are Healthy."

COMMONLY USED PROCEDURES FOR MEASURING STUDENTS' VOCABULARIES

Following are some of the most commonly used procedures for measuring students' vocabularies and some of the strongpoints and weaknesses of each method:

Group Standardized Achievement Tests

Teachers most frequently use group achievement tests in assessing students' vocabularies. Group standardized achievement tests are easy to administer, in terms of teacher time, and provide the teacher with a score for each student that will make it possible to compare that student's achievement with that of students of the same grade level. A common practice in the development of group standardized tests is to include a section under the heading of reading entitled *Reading Comprehension* and another entitled *Reading Vocabulary.* From this the user might infer that reading comprehension and reading vocabulary are somewhat unrelated. In actuality, reading vocabulary is the only subskill that we can accurately identify in the overall skill of reading comprehension. However, the separation of the two components as they are done on most tests does enable the teacher to make a general comparison between a student's overall ability to comprehend and a student's overall reading vocabulary. The user should, however, be cautioned that group standardized tests, while probably quite accurate for the measurement of a group's overall comprehension ability or overall vocabulary knowledge, may be somewhat inaccurate for the measurement of an individual student's vocabulary or a student's ability to comprehend.

The most common method of assessing a student's knowledge of vocabulary is to ask the student to select a word from a group of several words which he or she believes is a proper synonym for the word being tested. However, one of the major problems in the use of group standardized tests, when used with students in remedial reading, is that students are often lacking in word attack skills and, therefore, cannot accurately pronounce the word being tested or the various choices of synonyms. This then gives an inaccurate picture of the student's listening-speaking vocabulary. On the other hand, students who are reading considerably below grade level are forced to take a test designed for their grade level because of our norming procedures. When this occurs, a student, who in reality may read little or nothing at all, may score several grade levels beyond his or her actual grade level, in vocabulary, because the test allows the student to score well into the norms by simply guessing.

Because of the factors mentioned above, a teacher should probably not put a great deal of faith in an individual score for a disabled reader unless the student's score is at or above grade level, which would be highly unlikely.

Individual Intelligence Tests

Individual intelligence tests are probably one of the most accurate methods of assessing the vocabulary of a student with reading or other learning disabilities. The Wechsler Intelligence Scale for Children–Revised (WISC–R) is the test most used by psychologists and others responsible for placement of students in classes such as learning disabilities and remedial reading. One of the subtests of the WISC-R is called "Vocabulary." In this section the student is asked to define orally a number of words—the difficulty depending on the age of the student. The scoring is much more accurate than other types of vocabulary tests since the person administering the test is required to write a verbatim response given by the student being tested. The test administrator then has a number of responses with which he or she can compare the student's response to determine if the response should be counted as right or wrong. When a raw score is derived for the student, the test administrator may then look in a table of norms and find a standard score for the student. All subtests have a mean of ten and a standard deviation of three. Using this scoring system, and other tables, it is rather easy to convert the standard score to a percentile equivalent or even to an IQ score for that particular subtest.

Although most teachers of remedial reading or learning disabilities classes have not had the training to administer individual intelligence tests, these scores are often available and can serve as a most helpful piece of information in diagnosing students' vocabulary levels since they do not depend on the reading ability of the student. By comparing the scores made on a test such as the WISC-R and those made on a group standardized achievement test the teacher can easily see if there is a considerable discrepancy between the vocabulary score made by a student on a group standardized test and one made on the vocabulary section of a test such as the WISC-R. If the score made by the student on the WISC-R is considerably higher than the score made on the group standardized achievement test, then the teacher would, of course, know that the student probably did not possess the word attack skills to score up to his or her potential on the group standardized achievement test. One might assume that if the student was given considerable help with word attack skills, he or she would then have the potential to score considerably higher on a group standardized test.

Informal Reading Inventories

Most of the more popular commercial informal reading inventories require the student to read one or two passages, at a particular grade level. One is often read silently and the other is read orally. The tester than asks the students a number of questions on the subject matter of the passages. One or more of these questions is usually termed a "vocabulary" question. In the *Ekwall Reading Inventory* that appears in Appendix J of this text you will note that most passages have one "vocabulary" question over each passage. Since the student is to read one of the passages orally and one silently at each grade level, the student would be asked two vocabulary questions at each grade level while the student was reading. Questions over the vocabulary of the passage usually are somewhat like the following: What did the word XXXXXX mean in this reading passage? The student is then to define the word with some guidelines for scoring given by the person who designed the inventory.

The type of testing described above has the advantage of allowing the student to respond freely rather than having to respond in a more formal way as he or she would be required to do in a test such as a group standardized achievement test. It also allows the person administering the test to delve further by asking neutral questions if the student's first answer is found to be difficult to score. On the other hand, testing vocabulary knowledge by the use of informal reading inventories has some serious flaws. First of all, the developer of the inventory usually picks one or two words that appear in each passage that he or she believes would be appropriate for a student at that particular grade level. However, no attempt is usually made to make sure that the words selected are appropriate for that particular grade level, even though the passage, as a whole, may be written at the proper grade level. For example, an author of an informal reading inventory may ask a question over a particular word, in a fifth-grade passage, that, in reality, may be more appropriate for a fourth- or sixth-grade student. Another flaw in the use of informal reading inventories for assessing vocabulary knowledge is that only a very subjective judgment can be made since each question has not been normed. A third rather serious flaw is that the vocabulary words that are chosen are often used in a context that would allow any student, who is rather adept at using context clues, to figure out the meaning of the word from the context even though the student had no idea of the meaning of the word before reading the passage.

Oral Vocabulary Tests

Some of the tests often used in the diagnosis of students who are candidates for remedial reading or learning disabilities classes contain a subtest on oral vocabulary. For a teacher who has little or no other information on which to base the vocabulary development of a student these may be the easiest to administer and may also produce the most accurate information for the teacher. Most oral vocabulary tests allow the tester to orally present the student with a stimulus word and then give several alternative answers from which the student may attempt to pick a suitable synonym for the original stimulus. Norms are then usually provided for the subtest that will allow the tester to derive a grade equivalent for the student such as 4.3, 3.6, etc. The use of an oral vocabulary test will, of course, enable the teacher to determine quickly whether there is a considerable discrepancy between the student's score on a standardized achievement test and the oral vocabulary test. If the student did considerably better on the oral vocabulary test, then the teacher could assume that the student did not possess adequate word attack skills to score up to his or her potential on the group standardized test.

Picture Vocabulary Tests

Picture vocabulary tests are usually administered on a one-to-one basis in which the tester shows the student a picture and asks the student to tell what the picture represents. This type of test, as do individual intelligence tests and oral vocabulary tests, allows the tester to assess the student's vocabulary without the student being required to read. This would, of course, also be more fair for a disabled reader who was very poor in word attack skills and could not score up to his or her potential on a group standardized achievement test. The picture vocabulary test also usually provides norms so that a grade placement, or even an IQ score, can be derived from the raw score. The author of this text believes, however, that a student's cultural background can so heavily influence the outcome of this type of test that it may produce a score that is not really indicative of a student's speaking-listening vocabulary but only does what it says it does, i.e., test a student's knowledge of pictures which may not be realistic in terms of what one might expect of the student in a reading vocabulary test—even if the student could read the responses correctly. Perhaps this bias on the author's part comes from finding it not uncommon to see overall IQ differences of thirty to fifty points for a student in taking an oral vocabulary (IQ) test and the same student taking one of the more formal IQ tests such as the WISC-R.

STRATEGIES FOR INCREASING STUDENTS' VOCABULARIES

It is essential to remember that one important phase in the improvement of comprehension is the improvement of vocabulary. A student who does not know the meaning of a number of words in a reading passage cannot, of course, be expected to understand what he or she is reading. In the material that follows you will find a number of strategies or activities that will tend to improve the overall vocabularies of students.

Sustained Silent or Free Reading

The author believes that no activity can be more productive in quickly improving students' vocabularies than lots of sustained silent reading or free reading, as it is referred to by others. If you will stop and think how you learned the meaning of most words, whether it be words in your listening-speaking vocabulary or words in your reading vocabulary, you will quickly realize that most were learned either by hearing or reading them used in context. After encountering the word in context a number of times the reader or listener then continues to verify a particular meaning that he or she believed was correct for various words.

Word Awareness

In developing students' vocabularies one of the most important things you can do is teach students to become aware of new words. Most of us have the habit of simply ignoring words we do not know. Almost everyone has had the experience of looking up the meaning of a word in the dictionary and then becoming aware of that word appearing over and over again in the following weeks; in reality, the word had probably appeared many times before. You can develop word awareness in your students by continually calling new words to their attention through activities such as having a "New Word For The Day." To do this, you can, with the help of your students, select a new word every day, discuss it, and then put it on the bulletin board or in the upper corner of a chalkboard.

New Word Selection Committee

Before assigning a lesson in social studies and science, establish a set of rotating committees of students whose job is to scan the new material for any words that are unfamiliar to them. These words can then either be looked up and explained and discussed by members of the committee or by the teacher.

Picture Vocabulary File

For each unit in social studies, basal reader, or science books develop a picture file to illustrate key concepts and words. For example, in science when studying a unit on weather, the file might contain pictures of a hygrometer, anemometer, thermometer, and so forth. One important thing to remember is that most students develop new concepts by tying them to something in their past. If they do not have any past experiences with something very similar, the concept is difficult to grasp, and a picture is practically a necessity.

Context Awareness

Stress the fact that sometimes the meaning of new words can be derived through the use of meaningful context clues. Put sentences that present new words in meaningful contexts on the overhead projector and then hold a class discussion about the meaning of the new word and how students were able to derive its meaning from the context. Some examples of such sentences follow:

> There was a great *influx* of people into California when gold was discovered.
> Maria was such an *introvert* that she seldom said anything.

Vocabulary Card File

Give each student a shoebox and ask each to develop a file of new words by putting each new word acquired on a card and then filing it in the shoebox. Ask the students to write each word in the sentence in which it was first found, then write the meaning of the word after looking it up in the dictionary, and finally, write a new sentence that uses it in context. The cards can be reviewed during spare moments. Students can also work together and learn each other's words. One important advantage of this system is that students can actually see their vocabularies grow.

Bulletin Board Illustrations

On the bulletin board place a large picture that illustrates several new words. To the side of the picture write the new words on cards and then use different colors of yarn to connect the words on the cards to the objects in the picture. See illustration below:

Descriptive Cards

Write a number of new descriptive words on cards and place them in a pocket chart. By using either a picture or some object, have the class try to find the words on the cards that describe the picture or that tell what the object or thing in the picture can do.

Stump the Class

Have students look for new words that they think other members of the class will not know. They may find the words in newspapers or magazines at home. Each morning, let several students take turns writing a word on the chalkboard. After a word is written on the chalkboard, see whether any member of the class can guess its meaning. If no one can explain the meaning of the word, have the student give hints such as reading the sentence from which it was taken. You may wish to give points for each new word, each word that "stumped the class," or each person who knew the meaning of a word. Then give some small reward after a certain number of points are achieved.

Using New Words in a Paragraph or Story

After new words from a social studies or science unit or a basal reader story have been introduced and explained, have students try to write a paragraph or short story in which all of the words are used. After a few students read their paragraphs, discuss the correctness of the words as they appeared in the context of the stories.

Matching Words and Definitions

Place a number of words on cards in an envelope. In the same envelope write the definitions of each word on another set of cards. Distribute these envelopes to students and have them try to match the words with their definitions. The words and their definitions should be numbered on the back so that they match; for example, the letter *z* would appear on the back of one word card and also on the back of the card with the proper definition of that word. This, of course, makes the exercise self-correctional and students will eventually learn to match correctly all words with their proper definitions.

Firsthand Experiences and Audiovisual Aids

Many students cannot understand the meaning of words simply because they have had no firsthand experiences with the concepts they represent. Whenever it is feasible, the teacher should give students firsthand experiences with words, whether it be through students' actual experiences with the concepts represented by words or by the use of audiovisual aids.

The Use of the Cloze Procedure

The cloze procedure was originally developed to determine the "fit" between students and reading materials or for grade placement of students. Lyndon W. Seafross and John E. Readence (1985) have suggested several uses of the cloze procedure for the development of vocabulary skills. Some of their suggestions are as follows:

1. Use synonyms to replace words omitted instead of being concerned with the exact word that is omitted. When doing this, stress the variety of words that may be used in place of the omitted word.
2. In the normal or standard version of the cloze procedure every fifth word is usually omitted and replaced with a blank line. Seafross and Readence suggest lengthening the deletions to every seventh or tenth word so that students will be better able to use the context of the sentence in which the word was omitted.
3. These authors also suggest deleting every *nth* word such as verbs, nouns, adjectives, and adverbs. An example of a paragraph where every third noun is deleted is as follows:

> For the past few weeks, the child in my ________ have been using materials designed by a group of ________. These materials help children see more clearly that both ________ and men have an active, important part in making the ________ go round. These materials show women and ________ in equally active roles and aid children in thinking about the role ________ open to all people. (p. 198)

Seafross and Readence also suggest using the same format, however, omitting every *nth* preposition, every *nth* initial consonant, all vowels, and middle letters of words. Children may then be assigned to fill in the blanks either individually or in small groups.

REFERENCES

Babbs, Patricia J., and Moe, Alden. Metacognition: a key for independent learning from text. *The Reading Teacher,* January 1983, 36, 422–426.

Brozo, William G., Schmelzer, Ronald V., and Spires, Hiller A. The beneficial effect of chunking on good readers' comprehension of expository prose. *Journal of Reading,* February 1983, 26, 442–45.

Cohn, Marvin L. Structured comprehension. *The Reading Teacher,* February 1969, 22, 440–44+.

Ekwall, Eldon E., and Shanker, James L. *Diagnosis and remediation of the disabled reader.* 2d ed. Newton, MA: Allyn and Bacon, 1983.

Fowler, Gerald L. Developing comprehension skills in primary students through the use of story frames. *The Reading Teacher,* November 1982, 36, 176–79.

Hyman, Ronald T. Questioning for improved reading. *Educational Leadership,* January 1982, 39, 307–9.

Johnson, Marjorie, and Kress, Roy A. *Informal reading inventories.* Newark, Delaware: International Reading Association, 1965.

Manzo, Anthony V. The request procedure. *Journal of Reading,* November 1969, 13, 123–26+.

Rinehart, Steve D., and Platt, Jennifer M. *Forum for Reading,* Spring/Summer 1984, 15, 54–62.

Robinson, Francis P. *Effective study.* New York: Harper & Row, 1941.

Seafross, Lyndon W., and Readence, John E. *Helping children learn to read.* Englewood Cliffs, NJ: Prentice-Hall, 1985.

Sinatra, Richard C., Stahl-Gemake, Josephine, and Berg, David N. Improving reading comprehension of disabled readers through semantic mapping. *The Reading Teacher,* October 1984, 38, 22–29.

Spache, George D., and Spache, Evelyn B. *Reading in the elementary school.* Boston: Allyn and Bacon, 1977.

Stefferson, Margaret S., Joag-Dev, Chitra, and Anderson, Richard D. A cross-cultural perspective on reading comprehension. *Reading Research Quarterly,* 1979, 15, 10–29.

Stevens, Kathleen C. Chunking material as an aid to reading comprehension. *Journal of Reading,* November 1981, 25, 126–29.

Stewart, Oral, And Ebo, Tei. Some implications of metacognition for reading instruction. *Journal of Reading,* October 1983, 27, 36–43.

Strange, Michael. Instructional implications of a conceptual theory of reading comprehension. *The Reading Teacher,* January 1980, 33, 391–97.

7

Selection of Students and Operation of the Remedial Reading Program

COMMON PROBLEMS IN THE SELECTION PROCESS

Some of the most common problems the remedial reading teacher is likely to encounter, or questions the remedial reading teacher will have to answer are as follows:

1. What is the definition of a disabled or retarded reader?
2. To which age group of students should preference be given?
3. How should students be selected and who should be involved?
4. What tests should be administered in the screening process?
5. How many students can a remedial reading teacher handle and how often should classes meet?
6. From which classes or subjects should students be taken for remedial reading instruction?
7. How will students' progress be measured?
8. How long should students be kept in the program?

Every school system operates somewhat differently in answering the questions posed above. However, educational research suggests some very definite answers to most of these questions, which are discussed in the order in which they appear above.

What Is the Definition of a Disabled Reader?

In the past, one of the most commonly used definitions of a disabled or retarded reader was one who read two or more years below grade level. This is, however, a very unsatisfactory definition since a student in the beginning of the third grade and reading at a beginning first-grade level would be much worse off than one in the twelfth grade and reading at the tenth-grade level. The third grader would not be able to function at all, but the student reading at a tenth-grade level would probably encounter some difficulty but would at least be able to function in school.

Another approach in the selection of disabled readers has been to use a measure of their reading ability (grade level) versus their potential as measured by an IQ test. Those students who have the greatest discrepancy between their actual ability and potential are then considered to be the best candidates for remedial reading. One of the main problems with this approach is that, in spite of the fact that a student may have a high IQ and low reading ability, one never knows whether he or she will be able to learn to read any better than a student with a somewhat lower IQ. In reality, we only know whether a student has the ability to learn by trying to teach him or her. If students seem to learn rapidly, they are good candidates for remedial reading regardless of their intelligence levels.

It is also important to realize that unless a student has an IQ so low that he or she would be placed in a class for trainable students, then that student still must be educated and the IQ of the student should be of very little consequence. Perhaps it would also be more productive to give a student a learning rate test to determine if he or she is able to learn and retain information at a reasonable rate. This would have more direct bearing on the placement of the student than an IQ test.

This author feels that, regardless of grade level, perhaps the best definition of a student who belongs in remedial reading is one who cannot read his or her textbooks at the instructional level or one who reads his or her textbooks at the frustration reading level.

To Which Group of Students Should Preference Be Given

The research is very definite in indicating that preference should always be given to younger students. For example, one study as outlined by PREP (Putting Research Into Educational Practice) showed that when pupils who had reading problems were identified by the second grade, they had a ten times greater chance for successful remediation than did students who were not identified until the ninth grade. This study was done over a period of four years with some ten thousand students.

One of the reasons that remediation done with younger students is more successful than that done with older students is that they simply have less to learn in order to catch up. However, another major factor is that students who have been disabled in reading for a longer period of time have often developed poor self-concepts which, in turn, makes their problem considerably more difficult to deal with.

How Should Students Be Selected and Who Should Be Involved?

The enactment of Public Law 94–142 has made the traditional referral process for remedial reading somewhat more complicated in some cases; however, it has also done a great deal to ensure that handicapped students receive an equal education. A referral procedure such as that illustrated in Figure 7–1 is now mandated by law for some students. Among the provisions of Public Law 94–142 was a mandate that certain students who were found to be handicapped would be given a comprehensive assessment and that an individualized education program (IEP) would be developed for each student identified. P.L. 94–142 also stated that handicapped children must be educated, to the fullest extent possible, with children who are not handicapped. Children were to be placed in special classrooms, or special schools, only when the regular classroom or special school cannot provide satisfactory services.

A procedure for selection of students for remedial reading or learning disabilities classes such as that illustrated in the eleven-step procedure shown in Figure 7–1 might operate as follows:

Step 1: One of the provisions of P.L. 94–142 was that we should develop a public awareness of the problems of handicapped students. This public awareness was meant to encourage personnel from both inside and outside the school to make the problems of handicapped students known to school officials who are in a position to act on the problems of these students. Therefore, referrals may come to the school principal's office

FIGURE 7-1 *Educational Referral Process For Handicapped Students*

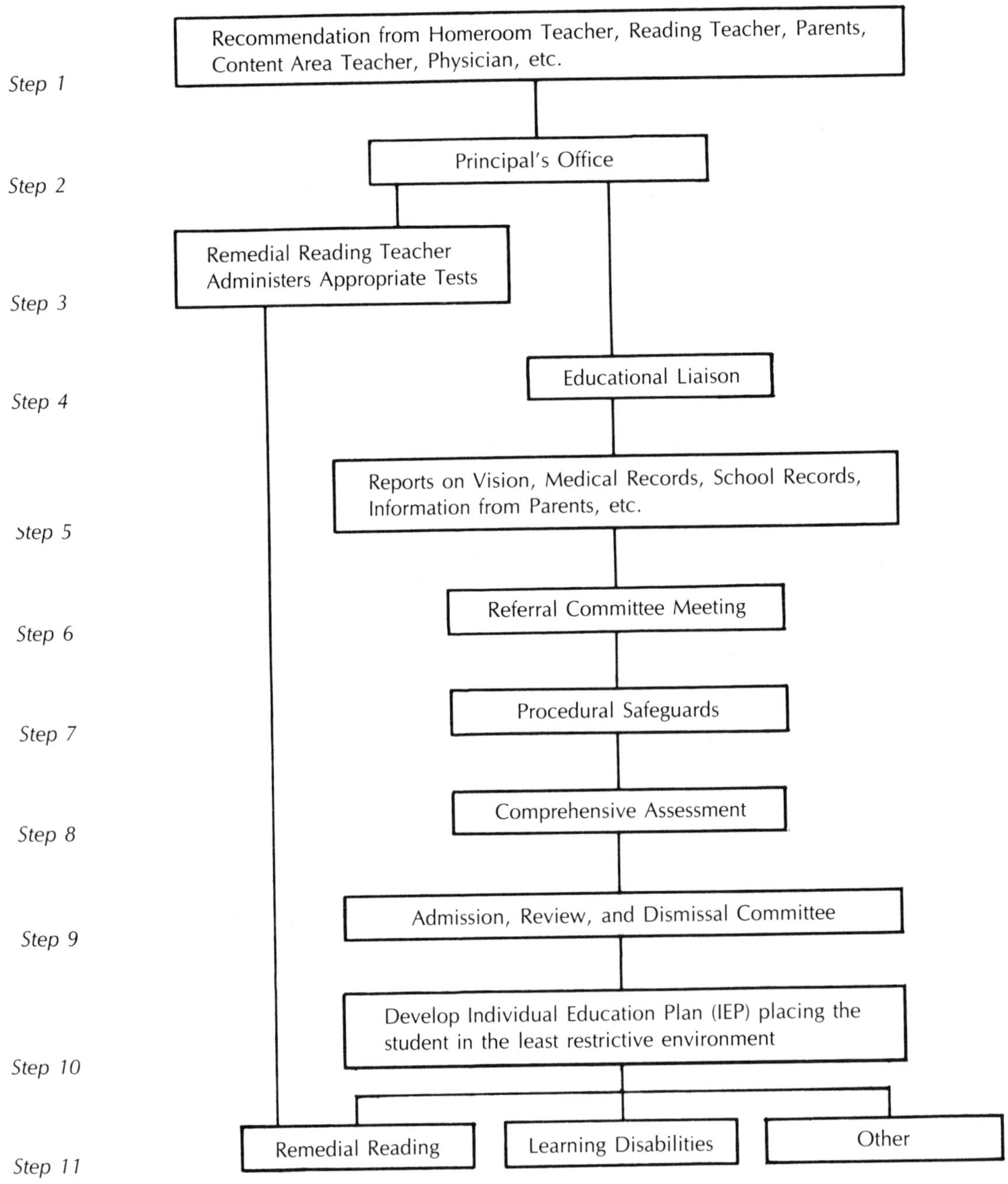
Step 1
Recommendation from Homeroom Teacher, Reading Teacher, Parents, Content Area Teacher, Physician, etc.
Step 2
Principal's Office
Step 3
Remedial Reading Teacher Administers Appropriate Tests
Step 4
Educational Liaison
Step 5
Reports on Vision, Medical Records, School Records, Information from Parents, etc.
Step 6
Referral Committee Meeting
Step 7
Procedural Safeguards
Step 8
Comprehensive Assessment
Step 9
Admission, Review, and Dismissal Committee
Step 10
Develop Individual Education Plan (IEP) placing the student in the least restrictive environment
Step 11
Remedial Reading
Learning Disabilities
Other

from such sources as a student's homeroom teacher, reading teacher, his or her parents, a physician, or any other person who is in a position that may enable them to become aware of a student's handicap.

Step 2 combined with *Step 3:* In this step the principal or assistant principal, after conferring with the Child Study Committee, and with permission from the parents of the student, might decide that the student had nothing more handicapping than a reading problem. In such a case the principal might proceed to *Step 3* and ask the remedial reading teacher to test the student and determine whether the student should simply be placed in a remedial reading classroom. If it was determined that the student needed nothing more than help with a reading problem, it is likely that the student would be placed in a remedial reading classroom with no further action necessary.

Step 2 combined with *Step 4:* In this situation the principal or assistant principal, in conference with the person making the referral and perhaps the student's homeroom teacher, may decide that the problem is more complex than that experienced by the student mentioned above. In this case the principal would be required by P.L. 94–142 to appoint an educational liaison as noted in *Step 4.* The educational liaison, in many schools, is a person trained in testing and may be known by a title such as Educational Diagnostician.

Step 5: The educational liaison would be responsible for gathering such data as the student's medical records (if indicated), information from parents, school records, and other sources of information—depending on the handicapping condition.

Step 6: A meeting would then be called of a committee to study the information provided by the educational liaison. This committee is sometimes called a Referral Committee or a Child Study Committee. It would include the parents of the student, unless they declined to attend, the educational liaison, the principal, and other school or non-school personnel with whom the educational liaison has consulted and who had information to contribute. This committee would decide if the information provided by the educational liaison would indicate that the student should have a comprehensive assessment that might include areas of development such as intellectual, emotional, physical, language, and various educational factors. It should be noted that parental consent is required for this testing.

Step 7: If it was decided that the student should receive a comprehensive assessment, then procedural safeguards would be taken. This would include written permission from the student's parents for the school to undertake individual assessment. The parents have a right to review individual assessment instruments and to have them explained. They also have the right to have their own individual assessment done if they wish.

Step 8: A comprehensive assessment is then done. This might include the testing of the student's intellectual functioning, his or her sociological maturity and functioning, language factors, physical factors, level of educational achievement, and learning competencies as indicated by criterion-referenced or standardized tests. This assessment may, for the most part, be done by the same person that was originally appointed as the educational liaison, who might be an educational diagnostician.

Step 9: A meeting is then called to analyze the data obtained in the comprehensive assessment and make appropriate recommendations for the placement of the student. This group of individuals must include, according to P.L. 94–142, at least three members representing the areas of administration, instruction, and assessment, and include at least one member from the field of special education, the educational liaison, and the parents of the student, unless they decline to attend. This group of individuals may be called the Admission, Review, and Dismissal Committee.

Step 10: P.L. 94–142 also requires that an individual education plan (IEP) be developed for each student identified as having a handicap. The following items must be included in an IEP:

1. A statement of the student's present level of performance
2. A statement of specific annual goals
3. A statement of short-term objectives
4. A list of educational services to be provided
5. A statement of the extent to which the student will participate in the regular classroom
6. A projected date for the initiation and duration of services
7. A statement of the criteria for evaluation procedures
8. A description of the schedule and procedures for review of the IEP (This must occur at least annually.)

An IEP can be thought of as having three levels:

1. Total service plan
2. Implementation of instructional plan
3. Annual review

A Total Service Plan contains:

1. A statement of the student's present level of achievement
2. The annual goals
3. The extent to which the student will participate in the regular classroom experiences
4. A recommendation for educational placement
5. A summary of the educational services to be provided
6. Recommendations concerning materials and methods of teaching
7. A projected date for the initiation and duration of services
8. A description of the evaluation criteria to be utilized

The Implementation–Instruction Plan contains:

1. A statement of specific program objectives
2. A list of specific instructional techniques
3. A statement of specific materials and resources
4. A list of criteria for the achievement of the implementation/instructional plan
5. A date on which the objectives are initiated and completed

The Annual Review consists of:

1. A review of the short-term objectives
2. A review of the annual goals
3. A review of overall educational program in relation to progress made by the student

(An example of an individual education plan is shown in Chapter 8.)

Step 11: Based on the Admission, Review, and Dismissal Committee's findings the student is then placed in the *least restrictive environment* which has come to be known as mainstreaming. The student may, as shown in Figure 7–1, be placed in a remedial reading classroom for only one period per day or may be referred to a learning disabilities teacher for one or more periods per day or may be placed in any number of other environments, according to his or her handicapping condition.

What Tests Should Be Administered in the Screening Process?

In Step 1, the remedial reading teacher might want to furnish the classroom teachers with some guidelines for making their recommendations of students who might benefit from the remedial reading program. The author has found that this can easily be accomplished in the following way:

First, to help classroom teachers determine students' sight word knowledge and word attack skills, give each teacher the list of words from the San Diego Quick Assessment List for each one's particular grade level only (for example, the second-grade teachers would be given the second-grade list, the third-grade teachers would get the third-grade list only, and so forth). Ask teachers simply to have each student read this list to them. Students who make three or more errors are automatically recommended for possible remedial reading instruction (three or more errors on a given list indicates a Frustration Level of reading).

Second, to help classroom teachers measure students' silent reading comprehension, give each teacher a graded passage from one of the commercial reading inventories listed in Appendix G or a passage from the *Ekwall Reading Inventory* which appears in Appendix J. Teachers need only one passage that corresponds to the grade level of the students they are teaching. In addition to the passage from the commercial reading inventory the remedial reading teacher may also want to use teacher-made commercial reading inventories made from the textbooks the students are using at their respective grade levels, or may wish to help teachers construct a cloze passage from the textbooks used at their respective grade levels. This entire procedure was explained in Chapter 6.

In Step 2, the remedial reading teacher may wish to give each of the students referred by classroom teachers an informal reading inventory to determine the extent of his or her reading retardation. The teacher may also wish to give the San Diego Quick Assessment prior to administering the informal reading inventory. By using these two instruments, the remedial reading teacher should obtain a fairly good idea of the student's knowledge of word attack skills, basic sight word knowledge, overall sight word knowledge, and ability to comprehend.

After the screening committee has made its selection of students to be placed in the program (Step 3), the remedial reading teacher will, of course, need to administer more specific tests as indicated by the student's performance on the initial screening tests.

How Many Students Can a Remedial Reading Teacher Handle and How Often Should the Classes Meet?

The number of students in the remedial reading class will vary according to the age-grade levels of the students and the similarity of the problems of students who could be scheduled to work with the remedial reading teacher at the same time. A few students will need such intensive training that it will be imperative that they receive individual help, especially in the beginning stages of their remediation.

The author would not recommend that a remedial reading teacher attempt to work with more than three to four students at a time, and only then if the students were grouped so that they had similar problems. This way they could be taught together, in some cases, and use materials such as games in which they could all participate for reinforcement. Any number of students beyond three or four tends to cause a situation where the students are no longer given the individual teaching, according to their unique problems, and thus would simply resemble a normal developmental reading classroom.

Most reading authorities also agree that a teacher's total case load should not exceed forty pupils. In many cases, depending on the severity of the cases, and the amount of consulting the teacher is expected to do, the maximum case load might be thirty.

Several research studies have been done in remedial and developmental reading classes to determine the effectiveness of differing lengths of class sessions as well as the effectiveness of the frequency of class sessions. As pointed out earlier in the chapter, younger students have the best chance of recovering from reading disabilities and of then maintaining these gains.

The research tends to indicate that at third grade, and probably below, students will benefit from two or three sessions per week, but they will gain and retain even more if they are given four to five sessions per week. On the other hand, students at fourth-grade level, and above, are simply not likely to gain and retain progress in a short-term program (one year or less) regardless of the number of sessions. There would, of course, be many exceptions to this rule. For example, in our own Reading Center we have seen one to two grade levels of improvement in students at fourth-grade level and above in remedial sessions held once per week for a period of one semester. In general, we might conclude that students in any grade can be helped, and the more often the sessions are held, the greater the chance for success. However, for those students at fourth grade or above the remedial process is likely to take much longer.

The length of class sessions will, in many cases, depend upon the administrative structure of the school. However, if possible, a remedial period of 20–30 minutes for second and third graders and 40–50 minutes for fourth graders and above is usually adequate to teach a good lesson and yet keep them from becoming overly restless. If possible, these time periods should be broken up into several activities. Among these activities should be a time set aside for the selection of books for students to read on their own outside the classroom situation. Although students often require some assistance in book selection, this time period also allows time for record keeping by the teacher.

From Which Classes or Subjects Should Students Be Taken for Remedial Reading Instruction?

One of the major problems faced by the remedial reading teacher and the principal is from which classes to take students for remedial reading training. The author suggests that, where possible, students be taken from either social studies or science classes to attend the remedial reading class. To begin with, much of the instruction in these classes is based on the reading of material from textbooks. Students who are candidates for remedial reading would, in most cases, not be able to benefit from that part of the instruction. Furthermore, we do not tend to have a national science or social studies curriculum such as we do in reading or mathematics. For this reason, overall school achievement test results are not adversely affected to any great extent if students miss a portion of these classes. In fact, most achievement tests only measure social studies and science vocabularies. And, the author's own studies, done while teaching remedial reading in Arizona, tended to show that students who were encouraged to read books about social studies and science in remedial reading gained as much, and in many cases more, in vocabulary knowledge as students in regular classes.

If possible, students should not be taken from their regular reading classes or from physical education, art, or music classes. Much can be gained from their own reading classes if the teachers of these students understand their problems. And, in the case of classes such as physical education, art, and music, the student is likely to miss a great opportunity to compete in a fun type of activity on an equal basis with other students.

Richard L. Allington (in press and personal correspondence) has found that students taken from their regular reading classes for instruction actually received less reading instruction than they would have had if they been left in their normal classroom situation. It would then seem imperative that time not be taken from the student's normal reading class. It should also be stressed that remedial work done outside the classroom should be coordinated, if possible, with that done with the student's developmental reading teacher.

How Will Students' Progress Be Measured?

A traditional method of measuring students' gain in remedial reading programs as well as in developmental reading programs has been through the use of standardized group achievement tests. In remedial reading, the use of group standardized tests is sometimes unsatisfactory because students can score fairly high by simply randomly marking their answer sheets.

When using a standardized test as one measure of achievement, you should keep several cautions in mind. First, you should make sure the norms of the test you select do not allow students to obtain a score at any grade level unless they score higher than they would by randomly marking the answer sheet. For example, if there are 100 questions on a test and four choices for each answer, then by the law of averages a student would be able to get 25 answers right even if he or she couldn't read. Thus, on such a test any raw score below 25 should be discounted.

A second caution in using group standardized tests would be to use them only for measuring group achievement—that is, how much all students gain in a certain period of time. One should not look at individual scores from a pretest period to a posttest period and attempt to draw any conclusions about the achievement of a particular student.

If you wish to use group standardized achievement tests for measuring overall class gain, you may wish to read the explanation given by Eldon E. Ekwall and James L. Shanker about the concept of *ratio-of-learning*. Using this method enables the remedial reading teacher to compare the student's rate of learning prior to entering the remedial reading program with his or her rate of learning in the program. It is not uncommon, when using this method, to find students learning two to five times faster in the remedial reading program than they did before entering the program.

Although most teachers and administrators are used to looking at grade-level scores in assessing student achievement, there are probably more meaningful ways of measuring progress in remedial reading. For example, the examination of pretest and posttest scores on diagnostic tests will often give a much more accurate picture of what a student has learned. Some illustrations of this follow:

Pretest (Administered when student entered the program)	**Posttest (Administered at the end of the year or remediation period)**
1. Number of basic sight words not known	Number of basic sight words learned.
2. Number of sounds not known on phonics test	Number of sounds learned
3. Student's attitude from "Attitude Inventory"	Improvement of attitude
4. Free, Instructional, and Frustration Levels from an IRI	Change in Free, Instructional, and Frustration Levels from an IRI

Still another method of assessing improvement is to examine the average number of books a student has read per month or year before entering the program versus the average number he or she reads per month or year after entering the program.

How Long Should Students Be Kept in the Program?

Ideally students should be terminated from the remedial reading program when they are again reading up to grade level. A number of studies have, however, shown that it is necessary to continue remediation on a less intensive basis to enable formerly disabled readers to maintain reading skills already learned as well as keep up with their normally achieving peers. From the research one might make the following general conclusions:

1. The earlier disabled readers are identified (grades 1–3) and placed in a remedial program the more likely they are to gain the competence needed for achieving on a level with their normal reading peers. Even then, some type of follow-up program should probably be provided for these students.
2. Older students (grade 4 and above) who are severely disabled in reading should be considered as chronic cases who will not only need long-term treatment, but should also receive some follow-up help after being discharged from the full-time, intensive remedial reading program.
3. Most students, and especially those at the third-grade level or below, should be referred to other specialists if they have not shown considerable gain after four to five months of instruction.

REFERENCES

Ekwall, Eldon E., and Shanker, James L. *Diagnosis and remediation of the disabled reader.* 2d ed. Newton, MA: Allyn and Bacon, 1983

8

Forms for Communication in a Remedial Reading Program

USING REPORTS AND RECORD KEEPING

The various lines of communication necessary for a successful remedial reading or learning disabilities program are illustrated below. In some cases the remedial reading teacher does all of the diagnosis; however, in others at least part of the work is done by a diagnostician or learning disabilities teacher. Therefore, in illustrating these lines of communication the author has referred, in some cases, to the teacher and/or diagnostician who may or may not be the same person.

1. Remedial Reading Teacher←——————→Classroom Teacher or Administrators
2. Remedial Reading Teacher←——————→Parents
3. Diagnostician←——————→Parents
4. Diagnostician←——————→Classroom Teacher or Administrators
5. Learning Disability Teacher←——————→Classroom Teacher or Administrators
6. Learning Disability Teacher←——————→Parents

In the pages that follow you will find twelve forms that are likely to be useful in communicating information in a remedial reading program. (Pages 125–149 contain master copies that can be removed for duplication.) A description of each of these forms and some brief information on the use of each one follows:

REMEDIAL READING REFERRAL (P. 125)

This form is to be used by classroom teachers when making referrals of students from the classroom to the remedial reading teacher.

TEACHER'S REPORT FOR REMEDIAL READING REFERRAL (PP. 125–127)

This is a form for the classroom teacher or learning disabilities teacher to use when more data are needed on individual students when the referral is made.

INDIVIDUAL READING DIAGNOSIS REPORT (P. 128)

This form can be used by the diagnostician or remedial reading teacher in reporting information derived in the initial diagnosis back to the classroom teacher. A form such as this is often helpful in providing guidance in placing students at the proper reading levels, in pinpointing specific weaknesses, and in determining whether students appear to be candidates for remedial reading instruction.

STUDENT PROGRESS REPORT (P. 129)

This form is designed to provide information for the classroom teacher from the remedial reading teacher after the initial diagnosis of a student's reading problem(s) has been completed and the remedial procedures have begun. This form may also be slightly modified and used by learning disabilities teachers for other subjects.

ASSIGNMENT SHEET (P. 130)

This form is used by the remedial reading teacher or learning disabilities teacher to communicate homework or out-of-class assignments to parents or to the classroom teacher.

PARENTAL PERMISSION FORM FOR REMEDIAL READING (P. 131)

This form is designed to be used by the remedial reading teacher to obtain parental permission to place students in remedial reading and to invite them to visit and become acquainted with the remedial reading program.

PROGRESS REPORT TO PARENTS (P. 132)

This form is designed to be sent to parents to report on the progress of students in a remedial reading program.

PERMISSION TO OBTAIN RECORDS (P. 133)

This form is to be used by the remedial reading teacher to obtain test results or records from other schools, psychological evaluation centers, and so forth. Note that it requires the signature of the student's parent.

APPLICATION FOR ADMISSION TO READING CENTER (PP. 134–138)

This form may be filled out by parents when requesting admission for a student to a college or public school reading center or clinic.

INITIAL CASE ANALYSIS (PP. 139–142)

This form is designed to be used by the remedial reading teacher to make an initial (and continual) diagnostic record of a student in remedial reading.

DAILY RECORD OF ACTIVITIES (P. 143)

This form is to be used at the close of each remedial session to make a record of the day's activities, to make a brief plan for the next session, and to note any diagnostic implications from the day's activities.

DAILY WORKSHEET (P. 144)

This form is designed to be used in planning daily activities for a period of a week for a group of students in remedial reading.

INDIVIDUALIZED EDUCATIONAL PLAN (PP. 145-149)

This is the form that the Admission, Review, and Dismissal Committee must prepare for any student who has been classified as handicapped.

REMEDIAL READING REFERRAL

TEACHER ______________________ SCHOOL ______________________

GRADE ______________________ DATE ______________________

Nothing is so valuable in determining which students need remedial help as the opinion of the classroom teacher. If you have, or have had, students you feel need special help in reading, would you please list them in the space provided below. Following is a partial list of common weaknesses. If you feel any of these apply to students you are referring, please list the corresponding numbers after their names. If there are other difficulties that you have noted, please explain these also.

1. Poor sight vocabulary
2. Inability to use context clues
3. Poor use of phonic analysis
5. Makes reversals (*saw* for *was*, etc.)
6. Cannot adjust speed to difficulty of material
7. Word-by-word reads
8. Makes insertions, omissions, etc.
9. Poor work and study habits
10. Poor concentration
11. Lacks confidence
12. Exhibits poor attitude
13. Poor comprehension
14. Phrases poorly
15. Other (please explain)

If you have additional information, please enter it in the "Remarks" blank.

Student ______________________

Remarks ______________________

Student ______________________

Remarks ______________________

Student ______________________

Remarks ______________________

Student ______________________

Remarks ______________________

Student ______________________

Remarks ______________________

If you have additional students needing remedial help, please list their names and weaknesses on the back of this sheet.

TEACHER'S REPORT FOR REMEDIAL READING REFERRAL

STUDENT'S NAME ______________________ TEACHER'S NAME ____________________

1. What do you think is the student's main problem(s) in reading? ______________

____

____

____

2. What is the student's reading level or what book is he/she presently using? ____

____

3. How is this student grouped for reading? ______________________________

____

4. How is this student grouped for other subjects, and what is provided for any special reading problems that he/she may have? ____________________________

____

____

5. What are some other weak points that you have observed in this student (other than in reading)? ____

____

____

6. What are some of this student's strong points? ___________________________

____

____

7. What are the student's reactions to reading (interests, attitude, etc.)? ________

____

____

8. What is the attitude of the student?

   Emotionally calm ____

   Apathetic ____

   Excitable ____

9. How does the student react to authority?

Resistant ____

Accepting ____

Overly dependent ____

10. Describe the student's relationships to other students. ____________________

____

____

11. Have you noted any unusual emotional behavior in this student? ____________

____

____

12. How does this student react to a difficult task?

Withdraws ____________________

Faces problem with little or no difficulty ____________________

Acts impulsively ____________________

13. How does the student act in the classroom?

Calm and quiet (if withdrawn, please explain) ____________________

Talkative ____________________

Normal ____________________

Other information that you feel is important: ____________________

____

____

____

____

____

____

INDIVIDUAL READING DIAGNOSIS REPORT

STUDENT ______________________ DATE TESTED ______________________

SCHOOL ______________________ DATE ______________________

STUDENT'S AGE AT TIME OF TESTING ________ STUDENT'S GRADE AT TIME OF TESTING ____

In accordance with your referral, the above-named student was tested and in my opinion does _____ does not _____ need to be in the remedial reading program.

Comprehension

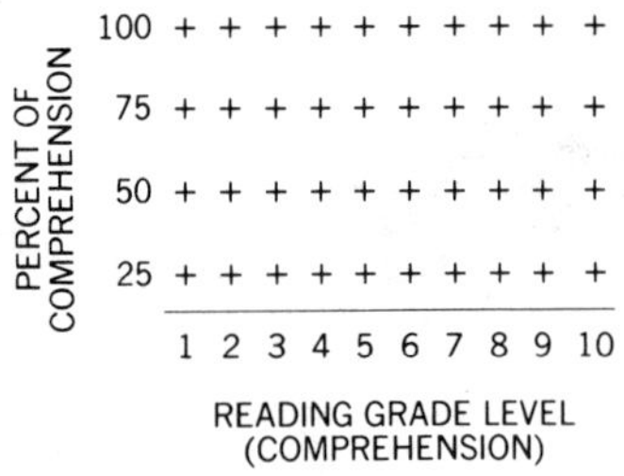

1. Independent Reading Level Grade _____
2. Instructional Grade Level Grade _____
3. Frustration Reading Level Grade _____

See below for explanation of these three reading levels.

Reading difficulties: ____

____

____

Physical or other difficulties noted: ____

____

Type of help or remediation recommended: ____

____

____

1. *Independent Reading Level* Reading level at which child can function adequately with no teacher help. Word recognition should be 99 percent accurate; comprehension of all types should average at least 90 percent.
2. *Instructional Reading Level* Reading level at which child can function adequately with teacher guidance and, at the same time, meet enough challenge to stimulate further growth. On a pretest at this level, word recognition should be 95 percent accurate and comprehension at least 75 percent.
3. *Frustration Level* Reading level at which the child's abilities to function break down. Word recognition falls to 90 percent or below; comprehension, to 50 percent or below. May also be indicated by presence of symptoms of difficulty, such as vocalization, tension movements, and so on.

STUDENT PROGRESS REPORT

FROM ______________________________ TO ______________________________

As you know ____________________ is receiving help in reading. This time amounts to approximately _____ minutes _____ times per week. That time is shared with several other students. In order to make the most of that time, I hope we can work together with this student to his/her maximum benefit. I will try to give you a report from time to time on what I am working on with this particular student, and what I have asked him/her to do between these sessions. If you have any questions, please feel free to contact me or write a note at the bottom of this page and ask the student to return it to me. Thank you.

Remedial reading teacher's diagnosis of the problem: ____________________

____

____

____

____

Work being carried on for correction of the above problem: ______________

____

____

____

____

Assignment for student: ____

____

____

____

Comments or questions: ____

____

____

____

ASSIGNMENT SHEET

NAME ______________________ DATE DUE ______________________

PURPOSE OF ASSIGNMENT ______________________

____

The following work has been assigned to be completed before the next meeting with the student's remedial reading instructor:

1. ______________________
2. ______________________
3. ______________________
4. ______________________
5. ______________________

Remedial Reading Teacher ______________________

____
(Signature of parent or teacher)

PARENTAL PERMISSION FORM FOR REMEDIAL READING

TO ______________________________

FROM ____________________________

DATE ____________________________

Your child ________________________ has been given a series of reading and diagnostic tests that have indicated that he/she should be given the kind of help provided in our remedial reading program. This is a class for children of normal intelligence who have some type of difficulty in reading.

I would like to extend the opportunity for you to visit with me concerning your child's reading problem and to visit the class in which we would like to enroll him/her.

If you would like to visit this class, it meets on ____________ from ____________

to ____________ in room ____________

Please feel free to visit at any time.

You have my permission to enroll ________________________ in the remedial reading program.

____

(Signature of parent or guardian)

Note: Please ask your child to return this to me at school or mail it to me at the following address:

PROGRESS REPORT TO PARENTS

DATE ______________________

TO ______________________ ☐ Remedial Reading Teacher

FROM ______________________ ☐ Learning Disabilities Teacher

As you know your child ______________ has been receiving help in reading in our remedial reading program. We feel that his/her primary need is:

____

____

In addition to the help that your child has been getting at school, it would also be beneficial if he/she could receive help from you in the following areas:

1. ____ Show interest in homework assignments that have been given and check to see that these are completed on the date they are due.

2. ____ Take your child to the public library and help him/her to find books that he/she would like to read.

3. ____ Help your child by being a good listener when he/she reads to you. Do not be overly concerned with the teaching of specific skills. We will try to do this in the remedial reading program.

4. ____ Try to set aside a certain period of time each day for pleasure reading. This seems to work better if a *specific time* is set aside rather than a certain *amount* of time. In other words, the amount of time is important—for example, 30–40 minutes—but it is more important that it be done at the same time each day if possible.

5. ____ Please comment in the "Remarks" space below whether you believe your child has taken an increased interest in reading on his/her own.

6. ____ Other ____

____

Remarks ____

____

____

PERMISSION TO OBTAIN RECORDS

TO ______________________________ DATE ______________________________

____

____

____

The following student ______________________________

who lives at ______________________________ is receiving remediation in our remedial reading program. In order to facilitate this remediation we would appreciate receiving any test results that you may have concerning this student.

Thank you.

____

____

* *

You have my permission to release any records or test results concerning my daughter ____ son____ other ____

______________________________ to the remedial reading
(student's name)

teacher in the ______________________________ school district.

Send to:

______________________________ ______________________________
(parent's or guardian's signature)

____

____

APPLICATION FOR ADMISSION TO READING CENTER
(to be filled out by parents or guardians of student)

NAME OF STUDENT ____
(Last) (First) (Middle)

ADDRESS ______________________ TELEPHONE ______________________

____
(City) (County) (State)

STUDENT'S BIRTHDATE ____________ AGE ____ SEX ____

SCHOOL ______________________________ GRADE LEVEL ____________
(if not in school, indicate occupation of applicant) (if not in school, last grade level reached)

Name of Parents or Guardians ______________________________________

Address of Parents or Guardians ______________________________________

Telephone Number of Parents or Guardians (Home) ____________ (Work) ____________

Occupations of Parents or Guardians ______________________________________

(A) Father ____________________ Employed by ____________________
(be specific)

(B) Mother ____________________ Employed by ____________________
(be specific)

Father's Place of Birth ____________ Birthdate ____________ Age ______

Mother's Place of Birth ____________ Birthdate ____________ Age ______

Father's Educational Level ____________ Mother's Educational Level ____________

Is this student adopted? ____ If so, student's age when acquired ____________

Does student know he/she is adopted? ____ Father deceased? ____

Mother deceased? ____ Cause of death? ____________

Are parents separated? ____ Divorced? ____

Has either parent remarried? ____ Has either parent been married before? ____

If yes, which one? ______________________________________

With whom does student live? ______________________________________

Reading Problem

1. Why is student being referred to the reading center? ______________________

____

____

____

____

____

____

____

Family History

1. List names, ages, and sexes of other children—oldest to youngest. ____________

____

2. Are the children all full brothers and/or sisters? Yes _____ No _____

   If no, please explain. ______________________________

   ____

3. Which of the above children are presently living at home? ______________

   ____

4. Has anyone else ever lived in the home? If yes, who? ______________

   ____

5. Has your family ever lived with anyone else? If yes, who? ______________

   ____

6. What languages are spoken in the home? ______________________

   ____

7. Do any other members of the family have a reading problem? ____________

   ____

8. How is the general health of other members of the family? ____________

Birth History

1. Was child born prematurely? ____ If so, how much? ____________

2. Was birth completely normal? If no, please explain. ____________

____

____

Developmental History

1. At what age did child say first words? ____________

2. At what age did child first walk? ____________

3. Did this child walk and speak words at an earlier or later age than other members of the family? (Please explain.) ____________

____

____

4. Has child ever had any serious illnesses? If yes, please explain. ____________

____

____

5. Has child ever had any serious accidents? If yes, please explain. ____________

____

____

6. Does child presently wear, or has child ever worn, glasses? ____________

If yes, who prescribed them? ____________

7. When did student have last examination by an eye doctor? What were the results? ____________

____

8. Has student ever had any ear infections? If yes, please explain. ____________

____

9. Has student's hearing ever been checked by a doctor? ____________________

____

10. Do *you* think the student hears well? ____________________

Socio-Educational Information

1. Any special schools attended? _____ Name of school, type, where, when, and how long in attendance. ____________________ ____________________

____

2. Has student ever had an intelligence or other mental test? ____________________

If so: what test(s), by whom given, where and when, and results (findings)? _____

____

____

3. Has child ever failed in school? _____ What grades? ____________________

4. Has the student ever missed school for any long periods of time? If yes, please explain. ____________________

____

5. Usual scholastic rating: __________ 6. Best subjects: ____________________

7. Worst subjects: ____________________

8. How does student get along with siblings? ____________________

Other children? ____________________ Parents? ____________________

9. Disposition? Happy ________ Affectionate ________ Dependable ________

Concentration ____________ Temper ____________ Fears____________

Other comments ____________________

10. Does student fatigue easily? ____________ Symptoms observed ____________

11. How much does student sleep? ______ At night ______ Daytime nap ______

12. Interests and abilities ____________________

13. What does student like to do in spare time? ______________________

14. Does student like to compete with others? Explain. ______________________

____

Referral Information

1. Who referred you to the reading center?

NAME ______________________

ADDRESS ______________________

____
(City) (State)

2. Full name and address of family physician or student's physician:

NAME ______________________

ADDRESS ______________________

____
(City) (State)

Case Record Information

Name of person who has completed this form ______________________

____
(Signature) (Date)

INITIAL CASE ANALYSIS

NAME ______________________ SEX __________________ GRADE ____________

SCHOOL ____________________ TEACHER ________________________________

I. Test Results (tests administered at clinic) (Informal Reading Inventory)

A. READING STATUS

1. Informal Reading Inventory

	ORAL	SILENT
Independent Level	_______	_______
Instructional Level	_______	_______
Frustration Level	_______	_______
Listening Comprehension Level	______________	

FIRST TRIAL	TYPES OF ERRORS (INDICATE NUMBER OF EACH TYPE)	SECOND TRIAL	PERCENT OF INCREASE (+) OR DECREASE (–)
	*Omissions		
	Insertions		
	Partial Mispronunciations		
	Gross Mispronunciations		
	Substitutions		
	Repetitions		
	Inversions		
	Aid		
	Self-corrected errors		

* When listing the number of omissions show two numbers. One should represent the number of purposeful omissions and the other the number of non-purposeful omissions. Thus eight omissions of which three were purposeful and five were non-purposeful would be indicated as follows: Omission 3=P, 5=N.

FIRST TRIAL	CHARACTERISTICS OF THE READER (INDICATE WITH CHECK MARK)	SECOND TRIAL
	Poor word anaylsis skills	
	Head movement	
	Finger pointing	
	Disregard for punctuation	
	Loss of place	
	Overuse of phonics	
	Does not read in natural voice tones	
	Poor enunciation	
	Word-by-word reading	
	Poor phrasing	
	Lack of expression	
	Pauses	

B. INTELLIGENCE

1. WISC.

   a. Verbal ____________

   b. Performance ____________

   c. Full scale ____________

2. Slosson Intelligence Test

   IQ____________

3. Stanford-Binet

   IQ____________

C. OTHER (Phonics, Basic Sight Words) (Be specific, i.e., exact words not known, which areas of phonics are weak, etc.)

D. SUMMARY OF TEST RESULTS FROM STUDENT'S SCHOOL RECORDS

II. Interpretation of Test Results

A. READING TESTS

1. Phonics

2. Structural Analysis

3. Comprehension

B. INTELLIGENCE TESTS

C. OTHER

D. PHYSICAL
  1. Vision
    a. Presently wears glasses. Yes _____ No _____

    b. Prescribed by whom ______________________________

       when ______________________________

    c. Results of visual screening test ______________________________

  2. Hearing
    a. Auditory discrimination test results

    b. History of hearing problems. Yes _____ No _____
       If yes, explain:

  3. Present General Health (level of energy, activity, sleep, diet)

  4. Health History (severe illnesses, operations, accidents, head and back injuries, allergies, etc.)

  5. Other

E. ENVIRONMENTAL AND PERSONALITY FACTORS
  1. Home (parents, siblings, general environment)

  2. Home and Family Adjustment (security, dependence-independence, affection, warmth, etc.)

  3. Attitude toward School (rebellious, submissive, indifferent, relations with teachers, etc.)

  4. Emotional Adjustment

III. Summary of Results (possible and/or probable causes of reading difficulty)

IV. Recommendations
   A. PLACE OF TREATMENT

   B. MATERIALS AND APPROACH

   C. PREDICTION OR CONCLUSION (regarding the course and termination of the reading problem)

   D. INSTRUCTIONAL PERIOD WITH STUDENT. (circle)

   Days: Monday—Tuesday—Wednesday—Thursday—Friday

   Hours ____________ to ____________

DAILY RECORD OF ACTIVITIES

STUDENT ______________________ MEETING NUMBER ______________________

DATE ______________________ TIME ______________________

Relevant conditions (if any) of meeting ______________________

____

Length of session ______________________

Summary of activities ______________________

____

____

____

____

Plan for next session ______________________

____

____

____

Diagnostic implications from today's activities ______________________

____

____

Teacher comments ______________________

____

____

____

DAILY WORKSHEET

DATE ____________ TO ____________ PERIOD ____________ GRADE ____________

Code	Name of Program*	Code	Name of Program

NAME	MONDAY	TUESDAY	WEDNESDAY	THURSDAY	FRIDAY

* The name of a program that you may wish to use would be the *SRA Pilot Library*. Therefore, you may wish to write *Pilot Library* under Name of Program and *PL* under Code. Thus you will have an easy way to keep track of what has been used on a daily basis.

INDIVIDUAL EDUCATIONAL PLAN

STUDENT'S NAME: ______________________ DATE OF BIRTH: ______________

SCHOOL DISTRICT: ____

SCHOOL: ______________________ GRADE OR LEVEL: ______________

Present Competencies

A. Academic/Developmental Abilities

B. Physical Abilities

C. Behavior

D. Pre-vocational/Vocational Skills

EDUCATIONAL SERVICES

A. Special Education

Curriculum Area	Amount of Time	Starting Date	End Date	Justification
____ None	____	____	____	____
____ Basic Living Skills	____	____	____	____
____ Cognition	____	____	____	____
____ Communication Skills	____	____	____	____
____ Independent Mobility	____	____	____	____
____ Leisure & Recreational Skills	____	____	____	____
____ Mathematics	____	____	____	____
____ Perceptual Training	____	____	____	____
____ Physical, Developmental, and Motor Skills	____	____	____	____
____ Pre-Vocational Skills	____	____	____	____
____ Reading	____	____	____	____
____ Science	____	____	____	____
____ Social-Emotional Development	____	____	____	____
____ Social Studies	____	____	____	____
____ Vocational Adjustment Class	____	____	____	____

Annual Goals: ____

B. Regular Education

Curriculum Area	Amount of Time	Starting Date	End Date	Justification
____ None	____	____	____	____
____ Language Arts	____	____	____	____
____ Reading	____	____	____	____
____ Spelling	____	____	____	____
____ Mathematics	____	____	____	____
____ Social Studies	____	____	____	____
____ Science	____	____	____	____
____ Foreign Language	____	____	____	____
____ Music	____	____	____	____
____ Art	____	____	____	____
____ Electives	____	____	____	____
____	____	____	____	____
____	____	____	____	____

Annual Goals: ____

C. Vocational

Curriculum Area	Amount of Time	Starting Date	End Date	Justification
____ None	____	____	____	____
____ Coordinated Vocational and Academic Education	____	____	____	____
____ Trades & Industry	____	____	____	____
____ Vocational Education for the Handicapped	____	____	____	____

Annual Goals:____________________

D. Physical Education

Curriculum Area	Amount of Time	Starting Date	End Date	Justification
____ Regular	____	____	____	____
____ Adaptive	____	____	____	____
____ Remedial	____	____	____	____

Annual Goals:____________________

E. Related Services

Curriculum Area	Anticipated Benefit	Amount of Time	Start Date	End Date	Justification
____ None	____	____	____	____	____
____ Speech Therapy	____	____	____	____	____
____ Physical Therapy	____	____	____	____	____
____ Transportation	____	____	____	____	____
____	____	____	____	____	____
____	____	____	____	____	____
____	____	____	____	____	____

Annual Goals:____________________

SHORT-TERM INSTRUCTIONAL OBJECTIVES
(One to be used for each area of Special Education)

Student Name: ______________________

Short-Term Objectives	Special Education Procedures	Measurement Procedures
Curricular Area: (Reading, etc.) ______________		
______________		
______________		

I have participated in all of the decisions detailed on the preceding pages on this date: ______________________________
and my signature appears below:

Agree	Disagree
______________________ Parent	______________________ Parent
______________________ Parent	______________________ Parent
______________________ School Administrator	______________________ School Administrator
______________________ Evaluator	______________________ Evaluator
______________________ Regular Teacher	______________________ Liaison
______________________ Liaison	______________________ Regular Teacher
______________________ Special Education Teacher	______________________ Special Education Teacher
______________________ Vocational Instructor	______________________ Vocational Instructor
______________________ Student	______________________ Student
______________________ Other (Title)	______________________ Other (Title)

9

Evaluating and Purchasing Materials for Remedial Reading

IMPORTANT QUESTIONS IN EVALUATING READING MATERIALS

How Is Material to Be Used?

An important point to keep in mind in using materials in remedial reading is that some materials are meant to teach, some are meant to reinforce concepts already learned, and others simply test students' ability in various areas of reading. Some reading teachers mistakenly use for teaching purposes materials that really only test students' ability to do a task. For example, some programmed textbooks teach by first asking a question (at this point they are testing) and by then providing an answer, in which case they are then teaching the right answer to the concept questioned. Many audiotape exercises actually teach as the lesson progresses. On the other hand, most workbook exercises provide reinforcement for material just taught. However, if this material has not just been taught, using the workbook exercises would merely test the student's ability in that subject.

What Are the Characteristics of the Material?

Some important characteristics to look for in evaluating materials for remedial reading may or may not be quite so important in purchasing materials for a developmental reading program. For example, remedial reading programs must be highly individualized. Because of this, materials must be of such a nature that they require little teacher direction once the teacher gets a student started on a lesson. The teacher will need to work on specific skills of each student and, therefore, with six to eight students in a class, is likely to have as many individual lessons in progress at one time.

A second important characteristic of materials for use in remedial reading is that they should be of such a nature that lessons can be located to teach, test, or reinforce a specific area of learning, such as knowledge of the two *oo* sounds or the *bl* blend. Or, for example, in a program that teaches basic sight words the program or material should be of such a nature that a few unknown basic sight words can be taught without the student being required to go through an entire program.

A third important consideration in purchasing materials for remedial reading is the cost of the material in relation to the number of students that can be serviced at one time. For example, some materials require the use of an expensive audio component that can be used by only one student at a time. On the other hand, less expensive materials may have several sets of materials for each skill or level that will allow many students to work with the material at the same time.

A fourth important consideration is the cost in relation to the life expectancy of the material. Some programs may appear rather expensive but, in reality, may be less expensive than materials that are consumable and thus have to be replaced on a yearly basis.

A fifth important consideration is the adequacy of the teacher's manual. For example, you should examine it to see whether it provides a list of the specific skills taught in the program as well as instructions on how to locate easily each lesson. It should be thorough, but it should not be burdensome.

Although there are other characteristics you should consider, the final important factor to be noted here is whether replacement booklets, cards, cassettes, and so forth can be ordered separately without having to purchase the whole program. Consideration should also be given to the availability of replacement parts in terms of the amount of time it would take to receive them after the order is placed and whether there is a local dealer who will furnish replacement parts and service equipment.

RECOMMENDED BOOKS FOR REMEDIAL READING

Many of the books sold by publishers are listed as having a readability level of, for example, third through sixth grade. What this may really mean is that the readability level varies so much that the publisher is hesitant to designate any one grade level. In such a case, the material might be appropriate for the very best readers in the third grade to the poor-to-good readers in the sixth grade. For students in remedial reading, books must be written at a reading level that is consistent throughout the book. Most of the books in the following list tend to be fairly consistent from page to page in their readability level.

Any given list of books will also tend to become outdated with the passage of time because publishers drop older books that no longer sell well and replace them with newer books. However, the books in the following list tend to be popular in remedial reading classrooms and are likely to be available for some time. A list of other materials and programs for use in remedial reading may be found in Appendix H.

Recommended High Interest-Low Vocabulary Books for Remedial Reading Programs

BENEFIC PRESS, 1250 SIXTH AVENUE, SAN DIEGO, CA 92101

Cowboy Sam Series, by Edna Walker Chandler. These exciting western-life adventures offer three levels of difficulty for each reading level. In each book, a section lists the reading skills covered.

Title	*Reading Level*	*Interest Level*
Cowboy Sam and Big Bill	pp[1]	pp-2
Cowboy Sam and Freckles	pp	pp-2
Cowboy Sam and Dandy	pp	pp-2
Cowboy Sam and Miss Lily	p[2]	p-3
Cowboy Sam and Porky	p	p-3
Cowboy Sam	p	p-3
Cowboy Sam and Flop	1	1-4
Cowboy Sam and Shorty	1	1-4
Cowboy Sam and Freddy	1	1-4

Cowboy Sam and Sally	2	2-5
Cowboy Sam and the Fair	2	2-5
Cowboy Sam and the Rodeo	2	2-5
Cowboy Sam and the Airplane	3	3-6
Cowboy Sam and the Indians	3	3-6
Cowboy Sam and the Rustlers	3	3-6
Teacher's Manual for Series		

Treat Truck Series, by Joy Treadway and Sandra Altheide. Stories in a modern environment provide humor and action. Vocabulary section lists words at and above reading level.

Title	*Reading Level*	*Interest Level*
Mike and the Treat Truck	pp	pp-2
Treat Truck and the Fire	pp	pp-2
Treat Truck and the Dog Show	p	p-2
Treat Truck and the Big Rain	p	p-2
Treat Truck and the Parade	1	1-2
Treat Truck and the Lucky Lion	1	1-2
Treat Truck and the Storm	2	2-4
Treat Truck and the Bank Robbery	3	3-5

[1] pp = pre-primer.
[2] p = primer.

Moonbeam Series, by Selma and Jack Wassermann. These realistic spaceage adventures afford reading practice to increase speed. They utilize the potential for critical thought.

Title	*Reading Level*	*Interest Level*
Moonbeam	pp	pp-3
Moonbeam Is Caught	pp	pp-3
Moonbeam and the Captain	pp	pp-3
Moonbeam Is Lost	p	p-3
Moonbeam and the Rocket Port	p	p-3
Moonbeam and the Big Jump	p	p-3
Moonbeam and the Rocket Ride	1	1-4
Moonbeam and the Dan Star	1	1-4
Moonbeam Finds a Moon Stone	2	2-5
Moonbeam and Sunny	3	3-6

Dan Frontier Series, by William J. Hurley. These adventure stories are about early frontier life in the Midwest. Dan, the main character, is a heroic frontiersman—not unlike Daniel Boone.

Title	*Reading Level*	*Interest Level*
Dan Frontier	pp	pp-2
Dan Frontier and the New House	pp	pp-2
Dan Frontier and the Big Cat	p	p-3

Dan Frontier Goes Hunting	p	p-3
Dan Frontier, Trapper	1	1-4
Dan Frontier with the Indians	1	1-4
Dan Frontier and the Wagon Train	2	2-5
Dan Frontier Scouts with the Army	2	2-5
Dan Frontier, Sheriff	3	3-6
Dan Frontier Goes Exploring	3	3-6
Dan Frontier Goes to Congress	4	4-7
Teacher's Manual for Series		

Tom Logan Series, by Edna Walker Chandler. Even slow readers are successful with the carefully controlled vocabulary in these stories about the Old West.

Title	*Reading Level*	*Interest Level*
Pony Rider	pp	pp-2
Talking Wire	pp	pp-2
Track Boss	p	p-3
Cattle Drive	p	p-3
Secret Tunnel	1	p-4
Gold Train	1	1-4
Gold Nugget	2	2-5
Cattle Cars	2	2-5
Stage Coach Driver	3	3-6
Circus Train	3	3-6

Butternut Bill Series, by Edith McCall. These high-interest, low-difficulty readers are about a boy named Butternut Bill and his life in the Ozark Mountain region.

Title	*Reading Level*	*Interest Level*
Butternut Bill	pp	pp-2
Butternut Bill and the Bee Tree	pp	pp-2
Butternut Bill and the Big Catfish	pp	pp-2
Butternut Bill and the Bear	p	p-3
Butternut Bill and the Little River	p	p-3
Butternut Bill and the Big Pumpkin	p	p-3
Butternut Bill and His Friends	1	1-3
Butternut Bill and the Train	1	1-4

Animal Adventure Readers, by Gene Darby. These are scientifically based animal adventure stories for primary children.

Title	*Reading Level*	*Interest Level*
Becky, the Rabbit	pp	1-3
Squeaky, the Squirrel	pp	1-3
Doc, the Dog	pp	1-3

Pat, the Parakeet	pp	1-3
Kate, the Cat	pp	1-3
Gomar, the Gosling	p	1-3
Skippy, the Skunk	p	1-3
Sandy, the Swallow	p	1-3
Sally, the Screech Owl	1	1-4
Pudgy, the Beaver	1	1-4
Hamilton, the Hamster	1	1-4
Horace, the Horse	1	1-4

Helicopter Adventure Series, by Selma and Jack Wassermann. This series features various ethnic groups and women in active roles. It offers controlled vocabulary and mature story content.

Title	*Reading Level*	*Interest Level*
Chopper Malone and the New Pilot	p	p-1
Chopper Malone and Susie	p	p-1
Chopper Malone and the Big Snow	1	1-2
Chopper Malone and Trouble at Sea	1	1-2
Chopper Malone and the Mountain Rescue	2	2-3
Chopper Malone and the Skylarks	3	3-4

Alley Alligator Series, by Athol B. Packer and Bill C. Cliett, Jr. These low-difficulty readers are about the adventures of three rangers and a baby alligator named Alley in the Florida Everglades.

Title	*Reading Level*	*Interest Level*
Alley Alligator	pp	1-3
Alley Alligator and the Fire	p	1-3
Alley Alligator and the Hurricane	1	1-4
Alley Alligator and the Big Race	2	2-5
Alley Alligator and the Hunters	3	3-6

Inner City Series, by Mike Neigoff. These stories deal with today's city life and how young people meet their problems with humor, imagination, and a determination to succeed.

Title	*Reading Level*	*Interest Level*
Beat the Gang	2	2-5
Tough Guy	3	3-6
Runaway	3	3-6
New in School	4	4-7
No Drop Out	4	4-7

Racing Wheel Readers, by Anabel Dean. Readers of this series are taken on the racing adventures of Woody Woods and his friends. Particularly appropriate for below-average readers, the stories are mature and contemporary, but they are written with a carefully controlled vocabulary.

Title	*Reading Level*	*Interest Level*
Hot Rod	2	4-12
Motorcycle Scramble	2	4-12
Motorcycle Racer	2	4-12
Drag Race	3	4-12
Destruction Derby	2	4-12
Stock Car Race	3	4-12
Baja 500	3	4-12
Safari Rally	3	4-12
Grand Prix Races	4	4-12
Le Mans Race	4	4-12
Road Race	4	4-12
Indy 500	4	4-12

Target Today Series, by Charles M. Brown, Dr. Helen Truher, and Dr. Phillip Weise. Each book in this series contains 100 short stories dealing with life today; the story characters are from many different ethnic and socioeconomic backgrounds.

Title	*Reading Level*	*Interest Level*
Here It Is	2	4-12
Action Now	2-3	4-12
Move Ahead	3-4	5-12
Lead On	4-6	5-12

Horses and Heroines Series, by Anabel Dean. This series features high-interest content with controlled vocabulary. Although the leading character is a girl, both boys and girls will identify with Mary Major.

Title	*Reading Level*	*Interest Level*
Saddle Up	2	2-5
Junior Rodeo	2	2-5
High Jumper	3	3-6
Harness Race	3	3-6
Ride the Winner	4	4-7
Steeplechase	4	4-7

Sports Mystery Series, by Alan and Evelyn Lunemann. These readers would be very appropriate in remedial reading programs ranging from sixth to ninth grades. These are stories about teenagers, their problems and how they solve them, and the excitement they find in sports activities.

Title	*Reading Level*	*Interest Level*
Luck of the Runner	2	4-12
Ten Feet Tall	2	4-12

No Turning Back	2	4-12
Gymnast Girl	3	4-12
Ski Mountain Mystery	3	4-12
Fairway Danger	3	4-12
Tip Off	3	4-12
Pitcher's Choice	3	4-12
Scuba Diving Adventure	4	4-12
Face Off	4	4-12
Swimmer's Mark	4	4-12
Tennis Champ	4	4-12

World of Adventure Series, by Henry A. Bamman. Each adventure-filled book contains a vocabulary listing, a story map, a news article, and a tall tale.

Title	*Reading Level*	*Interest Level*
Lost Uranium Mine	2	4-9
Flight to the South Pole	2	4-9
Hunting Grizzly Bears	3	4-9
Fire on the Mountain	3	4-9
City Beneath the Sea	4	4-9
The Search for Piranha	4	4-9
Sacred Well of Sacrifice	5	4-9
Viking Treasure	6	4-9

Space Science Fiction Series, by Henry A. Bamman. People of the future face danger in outer space on trips of exploration and negotiation. There are extension sections for enrichment reading at the back of each book.

Title	*Reading Level*	*Interest Level*
Space Pirate	2	4-12
Milky Way	2	4-12
Bone People	3	4-12
Planet of the Whistlers	4	4-12
Inviso Man	5	4-12
Ice-Men of Rime	6	4-12

Mystery Adventure Series, by Henry A. Bamman. These mystery stories take teenage boys and girls into situations that test their determination, courage, and deductive reasoning. This series is for intermediate and junior high students who are reading below grade level.

Title	*Reading Level*	*Interest Level*
Mystery Adventure of the Talking Statues	2	4-12
Mystery Adventure of the Jeweled Bell	2	4-12
Mystery Adventure at Cave Four	3	4-12
Mystery Adventure of the Indian Burial Ground	4	4-12

Mystery Adventure at Longcliff Inn	5	4-12
Mystery Adventure of the Smuggled Treasure	6	4-12

Houses of Books Series. Two sets of clothbound books on high-interest subjects that let the child become involved in the book.

Title	*Reading Level*	*Interest Level*
House of Reading Fun	2-3	1-3
House of Challenge	4-8	4-6

Ranger Don Series, by Robert Whitehead. These books feature Don, a park ranger, his friends Mary Ash and Toni Green, and his dog Red. These books have high interest and controlled vocabulary.

Title	*Reading Level*	*Interest Level*
Ranger Don	pp	1-2
Ranger Don and the Forest Fire	pp	1-2
Ranger Don and the Wolverine	p	1-3
Ranger Don and the Indian Cave	p	1-3
Ranger Don and the Ghost Town	1	1-4
Ranger Don and the Tree Thief	1	1-4
Ranger Don and the Cougar	2	2-5
Ranger Don and the Mountain Trail	3	3-6

Cowboys of Many Races Series. This series presents life in the early West with the action, excitement, and adventure experienced by many people of different races and backgrounds.

Title	*Reading Level*	*Interest Level*
Cowboy Without a Horse	pp	pp-3
Cowboy on the Mountain	p	p-4
Cowboy Matt and Belleza	1	1-4
Adam Bradford, Cowboy	2	2-5
Cowboy on the Trail	3	3-6
Cowboy Soldier	4	4-6
Cowboy Marshall	5	5-7

Emergency Series. A series with high interest and controlled vocabulary based on the activities of a paramedic team.

Title	*Reading Level*	*Interest Level*
Emergency Squad	2.0	2-5
Emergency Ambulance #10	2.6	2-5
Emergency Life Support Unit	3.0	3-7
Emergency Air Ambulance	3.4	3-7

Emergency Firefighters	4.0	4-9
Emergency Rescue Team	4.3	4-9

Intrigue Series. Tales of mystery and intrigue to interest the most reluctant reader. High-interest, low-vocabulary stories emphasize vocabulary development and comprehension.

Title	*Reading Level*	*Interest Level*
Escape from Willing House	2.0	4-12
Pearls of Maslan	2.0	4-12
Danger in the Deep	3.0	4-12
The Jade Horse	3.0	4-12
Hidden Gold	4.0	4-12
Cave of the Dead	4.0	4-12

BOWMAR-NOBLE PUBLISHERS, INC., P.O. BOX 25308, 1901 N. WALNUT STREET, OKLAHOMA CITY, OK 73125

Reading Incentive Program, by Ed and Ruth Radlauer. This series is appropriate for students from grade three through high school. Action photographs are combined with idiomatic language and humor in twenty books. The reading range is grades three to five based on the Spache Readability Formula.

Motorcycles
Horses
Dune Buggies
Snowmobiles
Custom Cars
Drag Racing
Karting
Minibikes
Slot Car Racing
Teen Fair
VW Bugs
Dune Buggy Racing
The Mighty Midgets
Surfing
Motorcycle Racing
Drag Racing—Funny Cars
Hot Air Balloons
Bicycles
Bicycle Racing
Dogs

Starting Line Series, by Ed and Ruth Radlauer. This four-book collection focuses on high-interest content and a controlled-vocabulary format while reteaching basic reading skills. The interest level range is from grades four to six.

Title	*Reading Level*
Cats!	pp
Racing!	pp-1
Wheels!	pp-1.5
Kickoff!	2

Sports Reading Series. These kits are high-interest reading programs for students in grades four to eight. The reading level ranges from 2 to 4.5 on the Fry Readability Formula.

Big League Baseball Reading Kit
Pro Basketball Reading Kit
NFL Reading Kit

Gold Dust Books. This high-interest novelette series deals with mystery, adventure, sports, science fiction, and character development. Written at 2.0 to 2.9 reading level on the Fry Readability Formula, these twelve stories appeal to children grades four to six.

Library I
Mystery at Beach Bay
No Place to Hide
The Big Find
Crazy Minnie
Ride to Win
Big Bad Ernie

Library II
Raging Rapids
The Full of the Moon
The Champion's Jacket
Nightmare Nine
Calling Earth
Escape from the Tower

The Double Play Reading Series, for grades four to eight with a reading level of 2.5 to 5.9.

The Triple Play Reading Series, for grades seven to nine with a reading level of 2.0 to 7.0.
These series involve students in reading and acting out plays.

Kit 1: *Falling Star and Other Plays*
Kit 2: *A Light in the Window and Other Plays*
Kit 3: *The Motocross Trial and Other Plays*
Kit 4: *Purple Power and Other Plays*
Kit 5: *Second Stringer and Other Plays*

Crosswinds One and Two. This is a series designed for seventh and eighth graders whose reading levels range from 3 to 6 on the Fry Readability Formula. The texts cover a wide range of timely subjects.

The Reading Comprehension Series. This is a series of high-interest stories for students in grades four to eight printed on 8½″ x 14″ cards. On the back of each is a comprehension check. The reading level is from 3.0 to 4.4 on the Fry scale.

Dogs
Marguerite Henry's Horses
Aviation
Cars and Cycles

Crime Fighters
Fads
Special People
Escape!

Quicksilver Books. This is a collection of high-interest reading/writing books for use in grades four to eight. The reading level is from 3.0 to 4.5 on the Fry scale.

CHILDREN'S PRESS, 1224 WEST VAN BUREN STREET, CHICAGO, IL 60607

Laura Brewster Mysteries, by Lisa Eisenberg. A series of exciting mysteries for reluctant readers. The series features insurance investigator Laura Brewster. Reading level is 3.0; interest level is grades four and up.

Falling Star
Fast-Food King
Golden Idol
House of Laughs
Killer Music
Tiger Rose

Space Police, by Leo P. Kelley. A series of action-packed stories of space-age cops and robbers. Reading level is 3.0; interest level is grade four and up.

Backward in Time
Death Sentence
Earth Two
Prison Satellite
Sunworld
Worlds Apart

Ready, Get Set, Go Books, by the Radlauers. A series of high-interest, low-vocabulary books presented on three levels of difficulty.

Ready Books: reading level is 1.1 to 1.5

Shark Mania
Skateboard Mania
Monster Mania
Roller Skate Mania
Dinosaur Mania
Flying Mania
Monkey Mania
Motorcycle Mania

Get Set Books: reading level is 1.9 to 2.5.

Minibike Racing
Trucks
Boats
CB Radio
Fast, Faster, Fastest
Model Trains
Racing Numbers
Wild Wheels

Go Books: reading level is 2.5 to 3.0

Dolls
Miniatures
Bicycle Motocross
Model Airplanes
Model Cars
Ready, Get Set, Whoa!
Soap Box Racing
Soccer

The Mania Books, by the Radlauers. A series of high-interest books written on the first-grade level. Contains many full-color photographs. Interest level is kingergarten to grade five.

Baseball Mania
Chopper Cycle Mania
Hot Rod Mania
Pet Mania

Gemini Books, by the Radlauers. These books are written on topics of high interest to today's readers. These contain many interesting facts and color photographs. Reading level is 2.5 to 4.0. Interest level is grades three to twelve.

Some Basics about Classic Cars
Some Basics about Hang Gliding

Some Basics about Windsurfing
Some Basics about Waterskiing
Some Basics about Women's Gymnastics
Some Basics about Bicycles
Some Basics about Motorcycles
Some Basics about Running
Some Basics about Skateboarding
Some Basics about Vans

Pacesetters. Through the controlled vocabulary of these books of fiction and fantasy the reader can be successful. Reading level is 1.0 to 4.0; interest level is grades four and up.

Pacesetters 1—Ten titles
Pacesetters 2—Ten titles

DELL PUBLISHING COMPANY, INC., EDUCATIONAL DEPARTMENT, ONE DAG HAMMARSKJOLD PLAZA, NEW YORK, NY 10017

Hi/Lo Paperbacks. A series of paperback books designed to motivate reluctant readers. Interest level is for ages ten and up.

Title	*Reading Level*
Brainstorm	2.1
Great Unsolved Cases	2.6
The Hotshot	3.9
Pele: The King of Soccer	2.7
The Plant People	4.6
Run For Your Life	2.2
Tennis Rebel	2.3
Toni's Crowd	2.5
The Weekend	2.5
A Wild Heart	1.9
City Cop	3.8
Dracula Go Home	2.4
Frauds, Hoaxes and Swindles	2.9
A Test of Love	2.3
World War II Resistance Stories	3.5

DOUBLEDAY & COMPANY, GARDEN CITY, NY 11530

Signal Books. These books are designed to stimulate, excite, and motivate reluctant readers. This series contains mysteries, tales of adventure, and biographies of people who have special meaning for today's young people. Reading level is grade four; interest level is grades seven to twelve.

THE ECONOMY COMPANY, 1901 NORTH WALNUT, OKLAHOMA CITY, OK 73125

Guidebook to Better Reading Series. A series of high-interest, low-vocabulary materials for use in grades five to twelve. The reading levels range from grades two to six.

FOLLET PUBLISHING COMPANY, 1010 WEST WASHINGTON BOULEVARD, CHICAGO, IL 60607

Beginning-to-Read and Just Beginning-to-Read Books. These low-level, high-interest books with their simple sentence structure are great for independent reading by primary children—as well as older children with difficulties in reading.

Pre-primer Level
The Birthday Car
Cinderella at the Ball
Circus Fun
Come Play with Me
The Cookie House
The Funny Baby
The Golden Goose
Happy Birthday, Dear Dragon
A House for Little Red
Little Puff
The Little Runaway
The Magic Beans
Play Ball
The Snow Baby
The Three Bears
The Three Goats
The Three Little Pigs
What Is It?
The Yellow Board

Level I
Big New School
Baby Bunny
The Ball Book
Away Go the Boats
City Fun
Four Good Friends
Follet Beginning-to-Read Picture Dictionary
Jiffy, Miss Boo and Mr. Boo
Little Red Hen
Nobody Listens to Andrew
The Wee Little Man
Have You Seen My Brother?
You Are What You Are
You Can Go Jump
Funny Ride
I Love You, Dear Dragon
I Like Things
It's Halloween, Dear Dragon
Happy Easter, Dear Dragon
Know When to Stop
Let's Go, Dear Dragon
Let's Have a Play
Little Red Riding Hood
Magic Little Ones
Magic Nutcracker

Level II
An Elephant in My Bed
The Boy Who Would Not Say His Name
Mabel the Whale
Barefoot Boy
The Dog Who Came to Dinner

Level III
Beginning-to-Read Poetry
Beginning-to-Read Riddles and Jokes
Ride, Willy, Ride
A Frog Sandwich: Riddles and Jokes

One Day Everything Went Wrong
Bears Who Went to the Seaside
Beginning Crafts for Beginning Readers
The No-Bark Dog
Making Toys That Crawl and Slide
Making Toys That Swim and Float
Gingerbread Children
The Ice Cream Cone
Look Who's Cooking
Our Statue of Liberty
The Strange Hotel: Five Ghost Stories
Bear, Wolf and Mouse
The Cookie Cookbook
The Dog That Took the Train
The First Thanksgiving
When the Wild Ducks Come

GARRARD PUBLISHING COMPANY, 1607 NORTH MARKET STREET, P.O. BOX A, CHAMPAIGN, IL 61820

The First Reading Books, by E. W. Dolch. Written with the very first sight words a reader learns, these books contain true and folklore tales about animals. These books are written on approximately a grade-one reading level; their interest level ranges from grades one to four.

Once There Was a Coyote
In the Woods
Monkey Friends
On the Farm
Tommy's Pets
Zoo Is Home
Once There was a Bear
Once There was a Cat
Once There was an Elephant
Once There was a Monkey
Once There was a Rabbit
Big, Bigger, Biggest
Dog Pals
Friendly Birds
I Like Cats
Some Are Small

The Basic Vocabulary Series, by E. W. Dolch. These true-life and folklore stories from all over the world are written almost entirely with the Dolch 220 Basic Sight Words and 95 Most Common Nouns. Their reading level is grade two, and their interest level ranges from grades one to six.

Folk Stories
Animal Stories
"Why" Stories
Pueblo Stories
Tepee Stories
Wigwam Stories
Lodge Stories
Horse Stories
Irish Stories
Navaho Stories
Dog Stories
More Dog Stories
Elephant Stories
Bear Stories
Lion and Tiger Stories
Circus Stories

Pleasure Reading Books, by E. W. Dolch. These old classics have been rewritten with a simple vocabulary so that even slow readers can derive pleasure from them. The reading level of these books is grade four; the interest level ranges from grades three and up.

Fairy Stories
Andersen Stories
Old World Stories
Far East Stories

Aesop's Stories
Famous Stories
Robin Hood Stories
Robinson Crusoe
Ivanhoe
Greek Stories
Gospel Stories
Bible Stories
Gulliver's Stories

Target Books. Garrard's most popular Discovery, Americans All, and Sports books have been reset in a format that is mature in design and approach. These series were created for poor readers in high school and for less-skilled readers in grades six to eight. However, their readability levels are grades three and four.

Adventures in Buckskin
Black Crusaders for Freedom
The Founding Fathers
Heroes of the Home Run
Indian Patriots of the Eastern Woodlands
Let's Hear It for America!
The Super Showmen
Three Jazz Greats
Women Who Dared to Be Different
The Game of Football
Susan B. Anthony
Louis Armstrong
Nellie Bly
Duke Ellington
Walt Disney
America the Beautiful
The Story of the United States Flag
Big League Pitchers and Catchers
Football Replay
Four Women of Courage
Hockey Hotshots
Indian Patriots of the Great West
Men of the Wild Frontier
They Loved the Land
Women in the White House
Women with a Cause
Pro Football's Greatest Upsets
Lou Gehrig
William C. Handy
Harry Houdini
Will Rogers
Sojourner Truth
The Statue of Liberty Comes to America

Folklore of the World Books. These high-interest books are written with the storyteller's vocabulary. They retell stories from every corner of the world. The reading level is grade three; the interest level ranges from grades two to eight.

Animal Stories from Alaska
Stories from Alaska
Stories from France
Stories from India
Stories from Japan
Stories from Old China
Stories from Old Russia
Stories from Africa
Stories from Canada
Stories from Hawaii
Stories from Italy
Stories from Mexico
Stories from Old Egypt
Stories from Spain

Young Animal Adventure Books. Easy reading books about baby animals. Reading level is grade two; interest level is grades one to four.

Doll: Bottle-Nosed Dolphin
Little Blue and Rusty: Red Kangaroos
Pen: Emperor Penguin

GLOBE BOOK COMPANY, 50 WEST 23 STREET, NEW YORK, NY 10010

A Better Reading Workshop. A series of four text workbooks for use in intermediate and senior high. Includes many different kinds of reading material. Reading level is grades four to six.

The World of Vocabulary Series. A series of five workbooks each containing short, nonfiction selections for building vocabulary and other skills. For use in intermediate and senior high with students reading on grade levels two through seven.

Stories of Surprise and Wonder. Eighteen "thrillers" written on a third-grade level. Good for intermediate and senior high.

Beyond Time and Space. Twenty-two science-fiction stories to help interest intermediate and senior high students in reading. Reading level is grades three to five.

Weird and Mysterious. A series of twenty-seven nonfiction stories and exercises with an emphasis on word analysis, comprehension, vocabulary development, grammar, and usage. For use in intermediate and senior high. Reading level is grades two to three.

Ghosts and Spirits	*Adventures into the Unknown*
Creatures: Real and Imagined	*The Power of Mind, Medicine and Magic*

HOLT, RINEHART & WINSTON, 383 MADISON AVENUE, NEW YORK, NY 10017

Impact on Reading. This series provides high-interest, high-quality literature for junior and senior high students. Each book contains literary selections in the different genres: short stories, poems, biographies, and novel excerpts.

Title	*Reading Level*
Circles	3.0–4.0
Mirrors and Windows	3.5–4.5
Blue Notes, Bright Notes	4.0–4.5
Searching	4.5–5.5
Conflict	5.0–6.0
Dreams and Dangers	5.5–6.9

HOUGHTON MIFFLIN COMPANY, ONE BEACON STREET, BOSTON, MA 02107

Vistas. Stories for reluctant readers that were chosen for their high interest and appeal. Interest level is grades seven to twelve and reading level is grades four to six.

Horizons
Summits
Tempos
Paces
Networks
Patterns

JAMESTOWN PUBLISHERS, P.O. BOX 6743, PROVIDENCE, RI 02940

The Adult Learner Series, by Judith Andrews Green. These books contain stories of very high interest to young adults. Yet they are written at the second-grade reading level, as established by the Fry Readability Formula.

Murder by Radio
The Man Who Stopped Time
The Man with the Scar

Attention-Span Stories. These stories consist of one-page episodes with three cliff-hangers at the bottom of each page. The principal characters are in their teens and late teens, making the interest level ideal for students in middle school through early high school. The reading levels of the stories are grades two and three, as determined by the Fry Formula.

Time Trip
Survival Trip
Sports Trip
Jungle Trip
Star Trip

Jamestown Classics. This program was developed by Walter Pauk. These classics are stories adapted from the world's greatest writers. Each forty-eight-page booklet contains an illustrated story written at grade five reading level. The interest level is from grades six to twelve.

From Jack London:
The Law of Life
Nam-Bok, the Liar
The Marriage of Lit-Lit
Diablo, a Dog

From Bret Harte:
Mliss
The Girl from Pike County
The Outcasts of Poker Flat
The Luck of Roaring Camp

From Arthur Conan Doyle's Sherlock Holmes:
The Musgrave Ritual
The Case of the Six Napoleons
The Red-Headed League
The Case of the Five Orange Pips

LESWING PRESS, P.O. BOX 3577, SAN RAFAEL, CA 94901

Star Knights Reading Series. This series is science fiction at its best with the Lambites, the Eaglepeople, and the Tortonians. The two vanguard books of this thirteen-book series are available now. The entire series is written at grades four to five reading level with an interest level geared all the way to young adults.

Star Magicians
Star Peril

Fast Wheels Reading Series, by Jerry Berg. Each book involves young people in fast-moving plots centered around cars, motorcycles, and the crucial problems that all young people face today—identity and social conflict. This series is designed for junior and senior high school students.

Title	*Reading Level*
Chevy V-8	3.4
Dirt-Track Racers	3.5
Camaro	3.6
Black-Powered Roadster	3.7

Learning to Read While Reading to Learn Series, by Dr. Jo Stanchfield and Dr. S. I. Hayakawa. Excitement, suspense, and action-filled experiences coupled with vivid photography and art work make older students want to read. Self-helps are included for decoding unknown words, for setting the stage, for motivation, and for analysis and interpretation.

Title	*Reading Level*
Set I	3.5–3.9
Behind the Scenes	3.5–3.9
A Place for Joe	3.5–3.9
Rescue on the Mountain	3.5–3.9
Dognappers	3.5–3.9
Viceroy's Daughter	3.5–3.9
Peculiar Lawn Mower	3.5–3.9
Operation Phoenix	3.5–3.9
Loud and Clear	3.5–3.9
Pedro's Secret	3.5–3.9
Set II	
The Bit Break	3.9–4.3
Deadline for Tim	3.9–4.3
Chilling Escape	3.9–4.3
The Big Wild	3.9–4.3
The Vanishing Pirate	3.9–4.3
Hundred-Milers	3.9–4.3
Racing the Salt	3.9–4.3
Athlete, Artist—Jerry	3.9–4.3
Danger along the Trail	3.9–4.3

Your Own Thing Reading Series. These books have fast-moving stories about kids of the "now generation." The settings, urban in nature, provide for an honest approach to life in inner-city surroundings. The reading levels range from grades 4.1 to 5.8. However, the series will appeal to teenagers and young adults.

Turn On	*Go-Go Sawyer*
On the Run	*The Bad Scene*
Battle of Jericho	*Reach for the Sky*
Where the Action Is	*Out of Sight*
Tell It Like It Is	*High Octane*
Walk Like a Man	*El Rey*
Baby, That's Love	

SCHOLASTIC BOOK SERVICES, 904 SYLVAN AVENUE, ENGLEWOOD CLIFFS, NJ 07632

Action and Double Action, developed by Mel Cebulash. These series are designed for students in grades seven to twelve. The programs develop basic word-attack, reading, and comprehension skills through reading, role playing, discussion, and writing.

Title	*Reading Level*
Action	*2.0–4.0*
Double Action	*3.0–5.0*
Action Library 1	*2.0–2.4*
Action Library 1A	*2.0–2.4*
Action Library 2	*2.5–2.9*
Action Library 2A	*2.5–2.9*
Action Library 3	*3.0–3.4*
Action Library 4	*3.5–3.9*

Scope Activity Kits. Written at grades four to six reading level for grades eight to twelve, the kits permit a student to explore a timeless theme at his or her own level of depth. They develop reading, reasoning, and language skills.

Human Behaviors	*Comedy*
Families	*Outsiders*
Science Fiction	*Poetry*
Do-It-Yourself Plays	*Monsters*
Survival	*Exploring the Unknown*
Advertising	*Television*
Radio	*The News*
Mystery	*Frauds and Hoaxes*
Sports	*Who Am I?*
Love	

SPRINT Libraries. Exciting, "grown-up" novels for students in grades four to six who have reading difficulties. These sets come in several ranges of difficulty.

Starter A, B	1.5–1.9
Library 1	2.0–2.4
Library 2	2.5–2.9
Library 3	3.0–3.4
Library 4	3.5–3.9

Reluctant Reader Libraries. Each library contains fifty paperbacks for use with children who read below grade level. All books are of high interest to young readers.

	Interest Level	*Reading Level*
Reluctant Reader	5	3, 4
	6	4, 5
	7	5, 6
	8	6, 7
	9	7, 8

SCIENCE RESEARCH ASSOCIATES, INC., 259 EAST ERIE STREET, CHICAGO, IL 60611

Science Research Associates Pilot Libraries. Pilot Library selections are unaltered excerpts from selected juvenile books. Each library contains seventy-two selections, from sixteen to thirty-two pages in length, of graded levels of difficulty. For each of the libraries the teacher is provided with a handbook that provides a synopsis of each book and questions for discussion. A student record book provides exercises for testing the student's comprehension.

Pilot Library Ic, Third Grade
Pilot Library IIa, Fourth Grade
Pilot Library IIb, Fifth Grade
Pilot Library IIc, Sixth Grade and Seventh Grade
Pilot Library IIIb, Eighth Grade

Super A, AA, B, and BB Kits. These kits are composed of comic book readers. They are high-interest stories with controlled vocabulary, based on the Harris-Jacobson word lists. They are suggested for grades four to eight, or even older.

Title	*Reading Level*
Kit A	2.0
Kit AA	3.0
Kit B	4.0
Kit BB	5.0

The Job Ahead: A Career Reading Series. This series contains high-interest stories at low reading levels that emphasize basic survival skills. The three texts have different reading levels (level 1: grade 3; level 2: grade 4; and level 3: grade 5), but look alike. Students in one class can read at different levels but share the same information. The Job Ahead is for grades seven to adult.

Getting It Together: 9–Adult. A series of books for use in remedial programs in grades nine through adult. These books contain the same material but are written on three levels of difficulty:

Level 1: grade three
Level 2: grade four
Level 3: grades five and six

A Mature Student's Guide to Reading and Composition. A series designed to help poor readers learn basic communications skills. The mature student is exposed to such everyday material as want ads, leases, contracts, and résumés written at a low reading level. Records and words cards are also available. Reading level is .0 to 4.0; interest level is grades seven to adult.

SUNBURST COMMUNICATIONS, P.O. BOX 40, WASHINGTON AVENUE, PLEASANTVILLE, NY 10570

Easy Reading Award Winners. Each of these titles is a proven winner with junior high school readers. The selection is broad enough to suit widely varied tastes and interests. Each paperback has been carefully checked in terms of reading level; they range from grades six to nine.

The Black Cauldron
The Contender
A Day No Pigs Would Die
Deathwatch
The Egypt Game
The House of Dies Drear
Hurry Home, Candy
Jazz Country
The King's Fifth
My Side of the Mountain
No Promises in the Wind
Old Yeller
Our Eddie
Quennie Peavy
Sing Down the Moon
Summer of my German Soldier
The Upstairs Room
To Be a Slave
Where the Lilies Bloom
Zeely

The Hi/Lo I, Hi/Lo II, and Hi/Lo High School have been carefully tested for readability with the Fry Readability Formula. Level 1 contains twenty-five titles with an average reading level of grade three. Level 2 averages grade four for its twenty-five titles. The high school program features twenty paperbacks, with reading levels grades four to six, that are popular with today's teens.

Reading for Every Day. This set of durable, colorfully illustrated cards helps the student learn and practice reading skills necessary for everyday life. It includes road maps, menus, and table of contents. Reading level is grade four; interest level is grades four to seven.

WEEKLY READER/SECONDARY UNIT BOOKS, 1250 FAIRWOOD AVENUE, P.O. BOX 16618, COLUMBUS, OH 43216

The Scrambler Series. This series provides short stories in comic book form on themes such as adventure, sports, wild tales, superstars, and superheroes. The interest level spans grades five and six. The reading level increases from grade 2.5 to 4.0

Cave-In and Other Stories about Rescue
The Night Walker and More Scary Tall Tales
Shark and Stories about Fighting to Win
The Rubber Sole Kid and Other Funny Superstars

Read It Right. Reading skills are strengthened through contact with materials used in real-life situations. These materials include newspapers, TV listings, menus, and train schedules. Reading level is 2.5–3.5; interest level is grades five to nine.

Reading Success Series. A high-interest series for problem readers ages ten to sixteen. Develops phonetic analysis, structural analysis, and word meaning skills. Reading level is 2.0 to 4.0; interest level is grades five to nine.

Reading All Around You. These three books are ideal for slow readers because of their real-life content. Reading level is 1.0 to 2.0; interest level is grades two to four.

10

Using Microcomputers in the Diagnosis and Remediation of the Disabled Reader

In this chapter you will first be advised of some cautions that should be observed in using the computer in conjunction with your program of remediation. Although the information in this section of the chapter is rather lengthy it should not be construed as meaning that the author of this test is anti-computer. In fact, the opposite is true. However, the author believes that the cautions mentioned are so important that they should appear first in the chapter. Following that section some information is presented on some of the most common uses of the computer in the teaching of reading. You will then be introduced to a section on the evaluation of computer software that should help you in making decisions when purchasing this *most important* part of your computer system. You will then be advised of some factors that you may wish to consider in the purchase of computer hardware. At the end of the chapter you will find some important sources of information for the computer user. These include the following: educational software directories from which you can obtain a wealth of information concerning programs that are available for use in your classroom, sources of software reviews, magazines with information about computers and computer software, a listing of some computer programs, along with their purpose, a list of companies that publish and/or distribute computer software, and, finally, a glossary of computer terminology which includes terms, in addition to those used in this chapter, that should be helpful to you in making decisions in developing a workable program for the diagnosis and remediation of reading difficulties.

SOME CAUTIONS TO BE OBSERVED

Perhaps the most important consideration of which administrators and teachers should be advised is that of determining what you wish to do with your computer after it is purchased. All too many boards of education, administrators, and teachers have made the mistake of purchasing one or more of a particular computer because they were able to "get a good deal at the time." They then find, in examining the advertisements and software directories, that very little, if any, software exists that is compatible with their computer. The teacher who is more familiar with the field will soon learn that, in the case just cited, the process of computer use has been reversed. That is, teachers should first consult the software directories (some of the best known are listed at the end of this chapter) and determine what software programs are available for the concepts they wish to teach or which software programs are available for using the computer in the manner in which they envisioned using it. Some programming can, of course, be done by the teacher; however, it is unlikely that the teacher will have the time or the inclination to develop his or her own software for nearly everything he or she wishes to teach. Therefore, before purchasing a computer you should first study the software directories and determine your computer needs in terms of the software that is available.

Do the Materials Teach, Test, or Reinforce?

The cautions that should be observed in purchasing computer software are much the same as those that one would use in the purchase of nearly any type of materials for the diagnosis and remediation of the disabled reader. One should, of course, first determine what it is that needs to be taught or what it is that you wish the computer to do. The teacher should then keep in mind that there are essentially three categories into which materials for use in reading education would logically fall. These are materials that *test,* those that *teach,* and those that *reinforce.* This is, of course, true whether it be software materials for use with the computer, books for use in the classroom, or various types of audiovisual materials which are in abundance in the field of reading education.

Some materials actually teach the student who is using them, just as the teacher would do in presenting a new concept. For example, if a teacher finds that a student does not know the /b/ sound when the student looks at a new word with the letter *b* at the beginning, then the teacher might be likely to write some words beginning with the /b/ sound on the chalkboard or overhead projector and ask the student to listen to the beginning sound in these words. The teacher might then proceed to pronounce such words as ball, bat, bit, bear, bite, or by, while he or she pointed to the letter *b* in each word as the word was being pronounced. The teacher might then ask the child to say these same words to reinforce the concept. The teacher might also ask the student simply to give the /b/ sound while he or she listened to the student say that sound. This, then, would be a situation where the teacher taught the sound to the student and then briefly tested the student to see if he or she had learned what had just been taught.

For a beginning or rather seriously disabled reader such as the one described above, it would be difficult to duplicate this same *teaching* procedure with the computer. It would be possible to add a voice synthesizer to a computer and, to some extent, give the student practice in hearing the /b/ sound. On the other hand, voice synthesizers at this time are still in their infancy in terms of accuracy in reproducing sounds. They are, however, improving rather rapidly and in the future will, no doubt, be able to do this task quite well. The second part of the teaching procedure, i.e., determining when the student has actually learned the sound well enough to reproduce it accurately would be much more difficult for the computer as a teacher. For example, the computer could be programmed so that it would show a series of pictures of various objects and then ask the student to respond by pressing the *Y* key if a picture represented an object, the name of which began with a /b/sound or the *N* key if it presented a picture the name of which did not begin with the /b/ sound. The problem that arises here, of course, is that a student may be able to identify objects that begin with the /b/ sound; however, that same student may be unable to reproduce the /b/ sound when he or she sees it in print.

Books also teach, providing the student is able to read them with an adequate degree of understanding. If the student is at this stage, then a computer can teach quite well and has the advantage of being able to interact with the student by giving him or her an immediate response to an answer as well as providing some type of reinforcement such as GOOD, BILL, YOU'RE DOING FINE! appearing on the screen with an occasional sound that is designed also to reinforce the response.

As already mentioned, audiovisual materials also teach, i.e., they are able to let the student see what is being taught and then provide an oral narration as needed in conjunction with the picture. Computers, in their present state of development, can be used with a tape recorder or voice synthesizer providing a narration and also providing a picture, although less clear than what one might see in a filmstrip or a picture on an audiovisual device such as an electronic card reader.

Computers can also test many concepts just as well as the teacher; however, at this time, they are unable to interpret an oral response with accuracy, which is often a necessary essential in teaching students to read, especially at the lower levels of difficulty. It would be unfair to say that students do not learn from a certain amount of testing. The computer, of course, has an distinct advantage over the usual paper-and-pencil test in that the student is able to get an immediate response which is often the difference between a test serving only a test purpose versus enabling the student also to learn from the test.

In reality, a larger proportion of the software now on the market most closely fits the description of materials that *reinforce.* The most common reinforcement device that teachers are used to is probably traditional workbook exercises. Although teachers often feel they are "teaching" when using a workbook, it should be kept in mind that, although reinforcement is a part of good teaching, the reinforcement device usually does not actually "teach." Workbooks only do what they are supposedly designed to do, i.e., reinforce what has already been learned. Several colleagues of the author have recently said that what they have seen, in terms of reading software for the teaching of word attack skills, are essentially "electronic workbooks."

Another caution that should be observed is that of purchasing software materials for teaching concepts that are not clearly defined or that have already been shown by the research to be less than worthwhile in terms of the remediation of reading disabilities. For example, several programs now exist that supposedly diagnose students' abilities in the area of reading comprehension. These programs are supposed to enable the teacher to decide whether a student is unable to determine the main idea of a passage or whether he or she can identify important details, etc. At this time the author knows of no definitive research that has proven that these skills even exist as separate entities, i.e., we cannot prove that there is a separate skill in the process of comprehension that could be called "the ability to get main ideas." If we cannot prove this with many years of the best research, then obviously a computer software program cannot do this, in spite of the claims made by the vendor of such programs.

Other examples of programs that would seem to be less than worthwhile are those that supposedly teach such skills as *visual discrimination.* Again, the author of this text knows of no definitive research that shows that working with students in the area of visual discrimination ultimately helps alleviate their reading disabilities.

Still another example of programs that seem less than worthwhile for students in remedial reading or learning disabilities programs are those that purport to increase reading speed. In such programs one is, of course, usually not concerned with reading speed per se. However, even if the teacher wanted to improve students' speed of reading, most of the studies that were done during the middle and late 1960s (when a great deal of federal money was available for the purchase of tachistoscopes and controlled reading devices) tended to show that simply having students pace their reading with their hand usually improved their speed more than the most expensive of the mechanical devices, which essentially did what is now being done with the computer.

Can the Computer Be Used in a Situation That Is Analogous to Reading?

It should be stressed that there is a considerable difference between the ability to encode (write) and the ability to decode (read). Many of the skills that must be tested in reading require an oral response from the student. For example, one of the most important purposes of having a student read orally is to determine areas of weakness. The teacher may wish to know if the student reads word by word which might be an indication that the student has not developed an adequate sight vocabulary. The teacher who listens to a student read aloud will also know if the student is making omissions, insertions, partial or gross mispronunciations. Knowledge of the student-error pattern then becomes a blueprint for instruction. The computer cannot perform this sort of task at this time. However, computer experts believe this will be possible in the near future.

One might assume that a student's knowledge of basic sight words could be tested by showing the student four or more words and then pronouncing one of them using a tape recorder or voice synthesizer in conjunction with the computer. The student might then be asked to place the cursor on the screen of the computer under the word that had been pronounced. The author has, however, found that asking students to pronounce a word when it is seen is a much more difficult task than identifying a word when it is pronounced by the teacher. In fact, in a study done by the author it was found that students at the third, fourth, and fifth grade levels missed nearly six times as many words in pronouncing a word when it was shown to them as when they were asked to identify one of four words pronounced by the teacher. With our present state of technology the teacher using the computer could gain only a small amount of knowledge about a student's sight vocabulary.

In testing for students' knowledge of most of the phonics skills an oral response is also the only way the teacher can be sure, with any degree of certainty, that a student knows the concept being tested. For example, if the teacher wants to know if a student knows the sound represented by a certain grapheme such as the /ch/ sound, the teacher could show a student four pictures and ask which of the four stood for a picture the name of which started with the /ch/ sound. If the student could move the cursor under the proper picture or select a letter such as a choice between A, B, C, or D representing the picture, the teacher would know that the student could probably identify the picture as that which stood for the /ch/ sound; however, the teacher could not be sure that the student could give the pronunciation of the /ch/ sound when it was used in conjunction with a phonogram, such as *ill* to form a word such as *chill.* Admittedly, a student who could identify a picture beginning with the /ch/ sound would be more likely to be able to pronounce the /ch/ sound; however, the teacher could not be assured of this.

One of the most common uses of the computer today is in the teaching of comprehension. In most of these exercises the student is asked to read a paragraph and then respond to a question, in some manner, pertaining to the paragraph just read. This is a typical workbook exercise in which the computer has an advantage over the workbook in that it can give the student an immediate response, and perhaps even tell the student why a particular answer is not correct. It should, however, be remembered that simply giving a student material to read and then asking questions over the subject matter of that material is not actually "teaching" but is simply testing. Although, if done enough, we know that most students improve through this method, it should be stressed that there are much more efficient ways of improving a student's comprehension—such as those described in Chapter 6.

In summary, then, the teacher who wishes to use the computer should constantly be asking such questions about computers and computer software as: Am I using the computer to teach? And, if so, does the material being used teach a new concept not known, or is it only reviewing what is already known? Am I using the computer to test? If I am using the computer to test, will the results be accurate enough for prescriptive teaching or will they only tell me that the student is weak in a certain broad area (that I may have already known)? Does the material test the student over skills that he or she will need to know in actually using those skills or are they only similar? At a minimum, the teacher should recognize whether materials being used are testing when they are supposed to teach. And the teacher should recognize materials that only test or reinforce when, in reality, they are represented as teaching materials.

PRESENT STATUS OF MICROCOMPUTERS IN THE DIAGNOSIS AND REMEDIATION OF DISABLED READERS

Following are some of the most common uses for microcomputers in the diagnosis and remediation of disabled readers. Since the use of microcomputers is a rapidly changing field, it should be remembered that this information is constantly changing as new programs are added and improved in the field of reading education. At the end of this chapter you will find a listing of the various kinds of programs described below. Along with a description of the programs you will find the name of the company that publishes or distributes each program.

Word Processing and Creative Writing

Perhaps the most important use to which computers have been put in the reading and language arts classroom is for word processing. Several word processing packages are available that are meant for use by students in grades one through eight. Others are, of course, available for students above those grade levels and could be mastered, in most cases, by students in the elementary school grades.

Also several programs are available that are highly motivational for students in doing various kinds of writing. For example, one such program covers persuasion techniques and is designed to develop analytical skills. Another teaches sentence combining that has been found to be an extremely useful technique in the improvement of students' writing skills whether it be with the computer or in normal paper-and-pencil writing exercises. Still another permits the use of branching techniques to encourage creative writing. Some programs are designed to teach students the mechanics of writing sentences and paragraphs while others emphasize the proper use of various kinds of punctuation marks as well as proofreading skills.

Readability Formulae

The use of the microcomputer has enabled the reading teacher to use various readability formulae with considerably more ease than in the past. The most burdensome part of using some of the most popular readability formulae was going through each of the words in a passage to determine if it was on a list of "easy words" that accompany those readability formulae. For example, one program that is now available allows the teacher simply to type approximately 100 (or less) words of the material on the computer screen. The teacher may then request complete information on the readability of the formula on the screen of the computer or it may be printed for a permanent record. The program will search such rather long word lists as the Dale List to determine which words in the passage are not in that list in order to determine a score on the Dale-Chall Readability Formula. It will then give complete information as to grade level using that formula—meant to be used in grades 4–adult. It will also enable the user to do an examination of readability formulae. Complete statistics on a passage may also be printed giving the user such information as the number of sentences, number of characters, the number of characters per word, number of words with two syllables, the number of syllables, number of words, number of words per sentence, number of syllables per word, number of syllables per 100 words, and number of sentences per 100 words. Having such information as the number of syllables per 100 words and the number of sentences per 100 words will enable the user to obtain quickly an estimate of the readability of the passage, using the Fry Graph. The program will also quickly give the user an alphabetized list of all of the words in the passage. Using this type of program on the computer does, however, enable the user to see quickly the inadequacies of some of our most commonly used readability formulae since it is not uncommon to see disagreement among the formulae of two to three years on a passage that is obviously written at the pre-primer or primer level.

Use as a Record-Keeping System

Several programs are available that provide the teacher with a complete record-keeping system for grades. These programs will enable the teacher quickly and easily to keep up-to-date records of students' grades on a weekly, monthly, quarterly, or semester basis. They will write progress reports and keep track of missing grades as well as enable the teacher to curve total grades.

Some systems for teaching various word attack and other reading skills also provide their own record-keeping system. These systems enable the teacher to call up a student's name and information will be presented on the lessons that each student has completed, and, in addition, the student's performance on each lesson may be monitored. For this type of activity the computer works extremely well; however, it is very difficult to provide meaningful lessons on word attack and the lower-level reading skills if the student is unable to read directions. The problem of accurately monitoring the student's achievement is also somewhat difficult since many of the lower-level skills require the monitoring of an oral rather than a written response by the student.

Testing for Knowledge of Basic Sight Words

Most diagnosticians would agree that students' knowledge of basic sight words can best be tested when each of the words is given a flash presentation to the student. This has been a difficult task since most people who wanted to present the basic sight words in this manner were forced to use flash cards. Attempting to manipulate the cards and mark a score sheet at the same time can be a very difficult task. The computer can be used for presenting a flash presentation of basic sight words to each student. With a little programming experience each word can be programmed to flash at a rate determined by the programmer. In our Reading Center at the University of Texas at El Paso we use the Radio Shack Pocket Computer (PC-2) for this purpose. It is programmed to present a word every 1-¾ seconds. This gives the person doing the testing an opportunity to record correct responses with a plus (+) mark and write incorrect responses in the blanks. Studying students' incorrect responses can often be helpful in analyzing their reading problem. It is important to use a computer that displays the words in lower case when testing for students' knowledge of basic sight words. The user should keep this point in mind when shopping for a pocket computer for this purpose.

The Development of Comprehension

Numerous programs are now available for the so-called "teaching" of comprehension. Most of these, however, do what teachers have done for so long, i.e., present a reading passage and then ask a number of questions over that passage on the pretext of "teaching comprehension." It should be remembered, however, that simply presenting information and then asking questions about it is not *teaching* comprehension but is simply *testing* it. We do, however, know that enough of this type of activity will improve students' comprehension by simply providing a great deal of practice. Other programs, in spite of the traditional format, present material in such a way that it is considerably more motivating than the same materials presented in the traditional workbook form.

The Use of the Cloze Procedure

The use of the cloze procedure for the development of comprehension as well as vocabulary development is also becoming a popular type of activity in using the computer. In the cloze procedure a word is omitted that the student is required to fill in or choose from several words presented by the computer. The interaction provided by the computer makes this activity considerably more attractive to students than the traditional format.

The use of the cloze procedure as a device for determining the proper match between students and the materials they are to read will, no doubt, come into its own more in the future. In using the cloze procedure for this purpose the teacher deletes every fifth word and replaces the words with blanks of equal length. The student then attempts to fill in the blanks using exactly the same words as were omitted from the original selection. A percentage of correct responses is then computed. A score of 43 percent, or less, is usually considered to be equivalent to the student's frustration level. A score of 44 through 56 percent is considered to be at the students' instructional level, and a score of 57 percent or more is considered to be at the students' independent level. A much more thorough explanation of the cloze procedure to match students with the proper level of materials is presented in Chapter 6.

The Development of Word Attack Skills

A number of programs are also available for improving students' word attack skills. Since the use of the computer requires some ability to read, it is much more difficult to provide meaningful types of activities than with some of the higher-level reading skills. The reader is cautioned to be extra careful in selecting these materials and to consider the purpose for which they are to be used, i.e., for *testing, teaching,* or for *reinforcement* of previously taught skills.

The Neurological Impress Method

The use of the neurological impress method has been thoroughly explained in Chapter 3 of this text. It can be extremely helpful in expanding students' sight vocabularies; however, it requires a great deal of the teacher's time. In using the neurological impress method the teacher sits beside the student and points to words from material to be read. The student is to read words as the teacher points to them. As the teacher reads, the student is also to read words immediately after the teacher pronounces them. The teacher is to read slightly more loudly than usual and is to sit so that he or she reads directly into the student's ear. The reason for the success of the neurological impress method is, apparently, that it presents the student with numerous exposures to many words in a short time. Various researchers have attempted to duplicate the success of the one-on-one teaching situation using a tape recorder and asking the student to follow along in a reading passage as it is read via the tape recorder.

This however, has not produced results comparable to those obtained when the teacher performs the activity personally with the student. It is this writer's belief that the inability of the tape recorder to produce the same results as those obtained by a one-on-one teaching situation is that when the student reads in conjunction with a tape recorder the teacher cannot be assured that the student is actually looking at the word being pronounced. That is to say, the student may be looking ahead of, or behind, the word as it is being pronounced by the tape recorder and the student. As voice synthesizers continue to improve, the neurological impress method will, no doubt, become more widely used in this application, since it will be possible to ensure that the word being pronounced by the voice synthesizer is the same one at which the student is looking while pronouncing it. This can be done with the computer by underlining or highlighting the word on the computer screen as it is being pronounced by the voice synthesizer.

Spelling

In the teaching of spelling considerable success is being experienced using the computer. Some programs review and teach students various spelling rules and generalizations and emphasize the spelling of the most common prefixes and suffixes. Others teach the proper spelling of various contractions, homonyms, synonyms, and antonyms. Spelling programs are also available that adjust to the difficulty level of the student and allow the teacher constantly to monitor students' progress. Still others allow the teachers to use their own word lists and use the format developed for that program.

Life Skills

For students with various learning disabilities a number of programs are also available that teach students various life skills such as how to read labels, classified ads, and telephone directories, how to bank, information needed for travel, and the like. Others teach students important information such as learning to budget, learning how to fill out commonly used forms for employment, financing, etc. A program is also available for teaching students to budget their time—even allowing them to print out their own schedule. Another program teaches students how to count money through simulating a shopping trip.

THE EVALUATION OF COMPUTER SOFTWARE*

You are likely to want the same features in computer software that you would want in any good program for locating and correcting reading difficulties. However, in order to make an intelligent decision, it is necessary

* From: Ekwall, Eldon E. *Locating and correcting reading difficulties,* 4th ed. Columbus, Ohio: Charles E. Merrill, 1985. (Reprinted by permission)

to know some of the capabilities of a computer in relation to traditional reading materials. The information that follows should help you to understand some of the capabilities and limitations of the computer in relation to the teaching of reading.

Computer software could logically be divided into three categories—(*1*) for management or record keeping, (*2*) as a supplement to the regular reading program, or (*3*) as the main reading program. Remember that there are essentially three main kinds of reading materials—those that teach, those that test, and those that reinforce. In evaluating computer software, you should first decide whether you are considering the purchase of the materials for managing your reading program, for supplementing it, or for using it as a main curriculum (which will be doubtful, in the case of locating and correcting reading difficulties). In reading the description of the materials, or more likely in evaluating materials as you use them on a computer, you should decide how you might use them—to *teach,* to *test,* or to *reinforce.*

Following are some characteristics you may wish to consider, as well as questions you may wish to ask in evaluating reading software.

Purchasing of Software

1. The cost of the materials is, of course, an important factor. If the materials are quite expensive, then one would perhaps want to spend more time in evaluating them just as you would spend more time evaluating what kind of new automobile to buy than you would spend on which dinner to have at a restaurant. However, regardless of cost, an inexpensive program that is of little value should never be considered as an alternative to a more expensive program that meets all or most of the characteristics of an excellent teaching program.
2. In addition to the cost, you should consider whether or not the distributor will allow you to return materials that you do not deem worthwhile.
3. A number of writers suggest that most programs that you purchase (especially the more expensive ones) should have been on the market for at least a year or more.
4. It is best to purchase from software companies that are well known and that have been in business for a considerable length of time.
5. When purchasing a major program, make sure the dealer will allow you to return older versions of the program for newer or updated ones as they become available.
6. Purchase only programs that have been tested and have proven worthwhile.
7. Purchase only materials for which you can make a back-up copy.
8. Was the material developed by someone well known in the field of reading or was the material developed by a team of reading and computer consultants? Since most programmers do not have adequate knowledge in the field of reading and many people in reading do not have adequate experience in programming, using the

skills of a programmer, a reading expert, and an instructional expert would be the ideal combination.

Teacher's Manual or Directions

1. Are the objectives for the program listed, so you will know exactly what is to be covered?
2. Is information given on the entry level of the student in terms of grade level or previous skills that student should have acquired?
3. Are some sample frames shown, so that you will have some idea of the general format?
4. Are the directions for use of the materials clear and understandable?
5. Is information provided on minimum and maximum times that students will need to complete various lessons?
6. Are the directions for the student clear and at a reading level appropriate for the grade level of the skills taught? (This refers to any written materials that accompany the program. This same question should be asked of the material that appears on the screen—see Program Characteristics)

Program Characteristics

1. If the program is linear, is the material in proper sequence? Most programs currently on the market are programmed in a linear sequence. In this type of programming, a student must go through a certain sequence of lessons or steps regardless of how well he performs on each step.
2. If the program is of the branching type, does it provide for a number of options? (For example, a program that is of the branching type should allow the student to move ahead into more difficult material or move back into easier material as needed.)
3. If some type of written material is necessary as a follow-up, are they provided with the program?
4. Does the lesson provide prompts or hints for answers with which the student is experiencing difficulty?
5. Are the contents free of any racial or sexual bias?
6. Is this program a more effective way of presenting the information than other materials that may be less costly and more easily obtained?
7. Can the student load (boot) the program without having an extensive knowledge of the use of microcomputers?

User Control

1. Can the student determine the entry point, in terms of difficulty, of the materials being presented?
2. If the student cannot determine the entry point, can the teacher realistically determine the proper entry point?
3. Can the student skip over material that he already knows or increase the rate at which it is presented? (Keep in mind that this

option exists with a book and that this, along with the ability of the computer to interact with the student, should be two of the most important features of a computer.)

4. Can the student exit the program and reenter at another time?
5. Can the student review the directions if necessary?

Feedback Characteristics

1. Feedback should be designed so that the student knows whether he has made the right or wrong response; and if it would be helpful, depending upon the concept being taught, the student should be told why a certain response is wrong.
2. Feedback should be positive; i.e., the student should be given praise for right answers but should not be scolded for those answers that are not right.
3. Praise or reinforcement should come only periodically for best results. If the student is praised after each correct response, it will become somewhat meaningless.
4. Is the type of feedback appropriate for the age-grade level of the student?

User Friendliness

1. Can the student easily understand the directions on the screen?
2. Can the student move from one part of a program to another without going through long elaborate directions? (For example, a user friendly program might ask the student, "Do you wish to go to an easier question?" At this point the prompt *Y/N* might appear. If the student had been answering a number of questions wrong, he might then go to an easier part of the program by pressing the *Y* key for *yes*.

Graphics

1. Do the graphics add to or detract from the presentation of the material being taught?
2. Are the graphics in color?
3. Are the graphics appropriate for the grade level of the student?
4. Graphics *should not be* such that a wrong response will bring forth a more colorful or interesting display than a correct response.
5. Is the program free from violence or imitation of violent games used in arcades? (It should be.)

Evaluation System

1. Does the program have its own evaluation system?
2. Is there a record of student performance that will be useful to the teacher?
3. Does the program collect and store data and then prescribe appropriate lessons based on the student's performance.

4. What are the criteria for successfully completing the material?
5. Can the teacher transfer certain information to other programs to keep an overall record of a student's performance?
6. Can a particular student's record of performance be printed?

Compatibility

1. Will the software operate on your computer?
2. Does your computer have sufficient memory for the program? (A program designed for a 64K computer will not run on a computer with less memory.)
3. Does the program run on a computer using the same language as yours?

Peripheral Requirements

1. Does the program require a printer?
2. Does the program require a voice synthesizer?
3. Does it require one or two disk drives? (Some computers use a cassette to store information. Information stored on a cassette is more difficult to retrieve than information stored on a disk because of the tape recorder's slow speed; therefore, it is highly recommended that cassettes not be considered for serious instructional programs in the school setting.)

THE EVALUATION OF COMPUTER HARDWARE*

Probably the worst mistake a user can make is to purchase a computer and then find that there is very little computer software available for that computer. For this reason the author would emphasize that before considering the purchase of a computer, you should look at one of the more comprehensive software directories listed under *Educational Software Directories* to see what software is available for whatever you wish to teach. It will take only a minute or so to decide that most of the educational software that is available is for use on only a few brands of computers. After deciding what software you would like to use, you should then consider some of the following factors in choosing a computer:

1. Is the dealer reputable and how long has the company been in business?
2. Does the dealer have a service plan?
3. What is the memory capacity of the computer? Will it handle all of the programs that you are likely to use?
4. Do you need one disk drive or two disk drives? Many programs require two disk drives and, in many cases, it would be impossible to duplicate disks without two disk drives.
5. What languages does the computer use, or in what languages can it be programmed?

* From: Ekwall, Eldon E. *Locating and correcting reading difficulties,* 4th ed. Columbus, Ohio: Charles E. Merrill, 1985. (Reprinted by permission)

6. What peripherals are available for each computer, and which are you likely to need?
7. How large is the screen display? Most computers range in width from twenty to eighty characters, and the length of the display tends to run from sixteen to thirty-two lines. However, on word processors the screen display length may be up to fifty-four lines or more.
8. Do you need a color monitor? If most of the programs you will run will be in color, you will need a color monitor. However, if most of the programs will be in black and white, you may actually get a better quality of image with a black and white monitor.
9. What is the quality of the graphics on the monitor? The greater the number of dots on the monitor screeen, the better your image will be.
10. Does the computer have built-in sound or music available? On some programs this is a necessity.
11. What is the cost of the computer in relation to comparable models?

After looking at numerous computers, you may wish to make an evaluation sheet for each computer to help you make your decision. Different factors will be worth different weights, depending upon which factors you think are most important. Using the factors listed above, your evaluation sheet for a particular computer might appear as follows.

Computer Evaluation Sheet

Brand of Computer ________ Dealer ________ Date ________

Factors	Factor Number†	×	Computer Rating*	=	Weighted Score
1. Dealer reputation	3		2		6
2. Dealer service plan	4		4		16
3. Memory capacity	5		5		25
4. Number of drives	5		5		25
5. Languages	3		2		6
6. Peripherals available	4		2		8
7. Screen display	3		1		3
8. Color monitor	3		3		9
9. Graphics	2		1		2
10. Sound/Music	3		3		9
11. Cost	5		3		15
			Final Score		124

† The factor number used in this case was arbitrarily picked between one and five with five being extremely important and numbers less than five being of less importance. The factor number would have to be derived by the user depending upon his needs.

* The computer rating is your rating based on what you can determine about each of the eleven factors listed. Again, a rating scale of 1–5 was used with five being an excellent or superior rating and one being the lowest possible rating.

In evaluating the final score you may find that two or three brands of computers have nearly the same score. On the other hand, you may find that others vary by twenty to thirty points. If the final scores are within a very close range (perhaps 2–6 or slightly more), you may wish to reexamine various factors in relation to the numbers assigned to them as well as the computer rating and the numbers assigned to this category. Your ultimate decision will, of course, need to be made on the basis of the factors and computer ratings that you feel are most important in your own teaching situation.

GUIDELINES OF THE INTERNATIONAL READING ASSOCIATION

The International Reading Association (1984) has also developed an excellent set of guidelines for educators using computers in the schools. These are as follows:*

The Computer Technology and Reading Committee of the International Reading Association has compiled the following guidelines in an effort to encourage the effective use of technology in reading classrooms. The guidelines are designed to highlight important issues and provide guidance to educators as they work to make the best possible use of the many new technologies which are rapidly finding their way into schools and classrooms everywhere.

1. ABOUT SOFTWARE

Curricular needs should be primary in the selection of reading instructional software. Above all, software designed for use in the reading classroom must be consistent with what research and practice have shown to be important in the process of learning to read or of reading to learn. The IRA believes that high quality instructional software should incorporate the following elements:

- clearly stated and implemented instructional objectives.
- learning to read and reading to learn activities which are consistent with established reading theory and practice.
- lesson activities which are most effectively and efficiently done through the application of computer technology and are not merely replications of activities which could be better done with traditional means.
- prompts and screen instructions to the student which are simple, direct and easier than the learning activity to be done.
- prompts, screen instructions and reading texts which are at a readability level appropriate to the needs of the learner.
- documentation and instructions which are clear and unambig-

* Reprinted by permission of the International Reading Association. (The author would like to extend his thanks to the Computer and Technology Committee.)

uous, assuming a minimum of prior knowledge about computers for use.
- screen displays which have clear and legible print with appropriate margins and between-line spacing.
- documentation and screen displays which are grammatically correct, factually correct, and which have been thoroughly proofed for spelling errors.
- a record keeping or information management element for the benefit of both the teacher and the learner, where appropriate.
- provisions for effective involvement and participation by the learner, coupled with rapid and extensive feedback, where appropriate.
- wherever appropriate, a learning pace which is modified by the actions of the learner or which can be adjusted by the teacher based on diagnosed needs.
- a fair, reasonable and clearly stated publisher's policy governing the replacement of defective or damaged program media such as tapes, diskettes, ROM cartridges and the like.
- a publisher's preview policy which provides pre-purchase samples or copies for review and which encourages a well-informed software acquisition process by reading educators.

2. ABOUT HARDWARE

Hardware should be durable, capable of producing highly legible text displays, and safe for use in a classroom situation. Hardware should be chosen that conforms to established classroom needs. Some characteristics to be aware of include, but are not limited to, the following:

- compatibility with classroom software appropriate to the curriculum.
- proven durability in classroom situations.
- clear, unambiguous instruction manuals appropriate for use by persons having a minimum of technical experience with computers.
- sufficient memory (RAM) capability to satisfy anticipated instructional software applications.
- availability of disk, tape, ROM cartridge or other efficient and reliable data storage devices.
- screen displays which produce legible print, minimize glare, and which have the lowest possible screen radiation levels.
- a functional keyboard and the availability of other appropriate types of input devices.
- proven, accessible and reasonably priced technical support from the manufacturer or distributor.

3. ABOUT STAFF DEVELOPMENT AND TRAINING

Staff development programs should be available which encourage teachers to become intelligent users of technology in the reading classroom. Factors to consider include, but are not limited to, the following:

- study and practice with various applications of computer technology in the reading and language arts classroom.
- training which encourages thoughtful and informed evaluation, selection and integration of effective and appropriate teaching software into the reading and language arts classroom.

4. ABOUT EQUITY

All persons, regardless of sex, ethnic group, socioeconomic status, or ability, must have equality of access to the challenges and benefits of computer technology. Computer technology should be integrated into all classrooms and not be limited to scientific or mathematical applications.

5. ABOUT RESEARCH

Research which assesses the impact of computer technology on all aspects of learning to read and reading to learn is essential. Public and private funding should be made available in support of such research. Issues which need to be part of national and international research agendas include, but are not limited to:

- the educational efficacy of computer technology in the reading and language arts classroom.
- the affective dimensions of introducing computer technology into the schools.
- the cognitive dimensions of introducing computer technology into the reading classroom.
- the application of concepts of artificial intelligence to computer software which address issues of reading diagnosis, developmental reading, remedial reading, and instructional management.
- the impact of new technology on students, reading teachers, schools, curricula, parents, and the community.

6. ABOUT NETWORKING AND SHARING INFORMATION

Local area and national networks or information services should be established and supported which can be accessed through the use of computers. Such services should be designed to provide an information resource on reading related topics. Such services could also be used to provide linkage and information exchange among many institutions, including professional associations such as the IRA.

7. ABOUT INAPPROPRIATE USES OF TECHNOLOGY

Computers should be used in meaningful and productive ways which relate clearly to instructional needs of students in the reading classroom. Educators must capitalize on the potential of this technology by insisting on its appropriate and meaningful use.

8. ABOUT LEGAL ISSUES

Unauthorized duplication and use of copyrighted computer software must not be allowed. Developers and publishers of educational software have a right to be protected from financial losses due to the unauthorized use of their products. Consumers of educational software have a concomitant right to expect fair prices, quality products and reasonable publishers' policies regarding licensing for multiple copies, replacement of damaged program media, network applications and the like. Without mutual trust and cooperation on this important issue both parties will suffer and, ultimately, so will the learner.

1983–84 Computer Technology and Reading Committee:
Alan E. Farstrup, Chair, Ossi Ahvenainen, Isabel Beck, Darlene Bolig, Jayne DeLawter, Shirley Feldmann, Peter Joyce, Michael Kamil, Gerald J. Kochinski, George E. Mason, Harry B. Miller, Jane D. Smith, Art Willer, Carmelita K. Williams, Linda Roberts, Consultant

SUMMARY

There is little doubt that the computer as a tool for the diagnosis and remediation of reading disabilities is here to stay. As better programs are developed and as the technology for the improvement of voice synthesizers as well as the ability of the computer to interpret oral responses improves, the computer will become an even more important tool for the teaching of students with reading and other kinds of learning disabilities.

SOFTWARE DIRECTORIES*

Software directories provide the teacher with a listing of various programs that are available by subject matter. They also describe each progam, including the type of microcomputer for which the software is designed. Included in the descriptions you will usually find the capacity of the microcomputer needed to run the program as well as the necessary hardware accessories.

Addison-Wesley Book of Apple Computer Software
Addison-Wesley Publishing Co., Inc.
Applications Software Division
Jacob Way
Reading, MA 01867

Best of Educational Software for Apple II Computers
SYBEX Computer Books
2344 6th Street
Berkeley, CA 94710

The Book of Apple Software
&
The Book of IBM Software
Arrays, Inc./Book Division
11223 South Hindry Ave.
Los Angeles, CA 90045

EISI Computer Courseware
2225 Grant Road, Suite 3
Los Altos, CA 94022

Guide to Free Computer Materials
Educators Progress Service, Inc.
214 Center Street
Randolph, WI 53956

INSTRUCTOR
Fall Computer Directory for Schools
545 Fifth Avenue
New York, NY 10017

Parent/Teacher's Microcomputing Sourcebook for Children
R. R. Bowker Company
205 East Forty-second Street
New York, NY 10017

* From: Ekwall, Eldon E. *Locating and Correcting Reading Difficulties.* (4th ed.). Columbus, Ohio: Charles E. Merrill, 1985 (pp. 188–189). (Reprinted by permission of Charles E. Merrill)

PC Telemart/Vanloves Apple
Software Directory
R. R. Bowker Company
205 East Forty-second Street
New York, NY 10017

School Microware Directory
Dresden Associates
Department CCN
P.O. Box 246
Dresden, ME 04343

Skarbek Software Directory
Skarbek Corporation, Inc.
1531 Sugargrove Ct.
St. Louis, MO 63141

Swift's Directory of Educational
Software for the IBM-PC
Sterling-Swift Publishing Co.
7901 South IH-35
Austin, TX 78744

TRS Educational Software
Sourcebook
Radio Shack
Education Division
1400 One Tandy Center
Fort Worth, TX 76102

Wallace User's Guide to Apple
Computers
Wallace Micro-Mart, Inc.
3010 North Sterling Ave.
Peoria, IL 61604

Where to Find Free Programs For
Your TRS-80, Apple, or IBM Microcomputer
Mother Goose Distributing
512 Winston Ave.
Pasadena, CA 91107

Whole Earth Software Catalog
Quantum Press/Doubleday
Garden City, NY 11530

SOURCES OF SOFTWARE REVIEWS*

AEDS Bulletin
Association for Educational Data Systems
1201 Sixteenth Street, N.W.
Washington, DC

Apple Journal of Courseware Review
P.O. Box 28426
San Jose, CA 95159

Classroom Computer News
P.O. Box 266
Cambridge, MA 92138

Computers, Reading and Language Arts
P.O. Box 13247
Oakland, CA 94661

Courseware Report Card
150 West Carob St.
Compton, CA 90200

Electronic Education
1311 Executive Center Drive, Suite 220
Tallahassee, FL 32301

Electronic Learning
902 Sylvan Avenue
Englewood Cliffs, NJ 07632

EPIE Micro-Courseware PRO/FILES
EPIE & Consumers' Union
Box 620
Stony Brook, NY 11790

InfoWORLD
375 Cochituate Road
P.O. Box 880
Framingham, MA 01701

MicroSIFT Reviews
Northwest Regional Educational Laboratory
300 S.W. Sixth Avenue
Portland, OR 97204

Popular Computing
70 Main Street
Peterborough, NH 03458

School Microware Reviews
Dresden Associates
P.O. Box 246
Dresden, ME 04342

The Computing Teacher
Dept. of Computer Science
University of Oregon
Eugene, OR 97403

* Reprinted by permission of *Computers, Reading and Language Arts.*
From: Ekwall, Eldon E. *Locating and Correcting Reading Difficulties.* (4th ed.). Columbus, Ohio: Charles E. Merrill, 1985 (pp. 184–185). (Reprinted by permission of Charles E. Merrill)

MAGAZINES WITH INFORMATION ABOUT COMPUTERS AND COMPUTER SOFTWARE*

ANALOG COMPUTING
P.O. Box 615
Holmes, PA 19043

BYTE
BYTE Subscriptions
P.O. Box 590
Martinsville, NJ 08836

Cider
Subscription Department
P.O. Box 911
Farmingdale, NY 11737

CLOSING THE GAP
P.O. Box 68
Henderson, MN 56004

COMPUTE
Compute Publications, Inc.
P.O. Box 5406
Greensboro, NC 27403

COMPUTERS, READING AND LANGUAGE ARTS
P.O. Box 13247
Oakland, CA 94661

COMPUTER WORLD
375 Cochituate Road, Rte. 30
Framingham, MA 01701

CREATIVE COMPUTING
MICROSYSTEMS
PC
SYNC
COMPUTERS & ELECTRONICS
Ziff Davis Publications
Customer Service Group
39 East Hanover Ave.
Morris Plains, NJ 07950

EDUCOM
(Newsletter)
Computer Literacy Project
P.O. Box 364
Princeton, NJ 08540

ELECTRONIC EDUCATION
902 Sylvan Avenue
Englewood Cliffs, NJ 07632

ELECTRONIC LEARNING
902 Sylvan Avenue
Englewood Cliffs, NJ 07632

INSIDER
P.O. Box 911
Farmingdale, NY 11737

INSTRUCTOR
Computer Directory for Schools
Instructor
757 Third Avenue
New York, NY 10017

MICROCOMPUTERS IN EDUCATION
Queue, Inc.
5 Chapel Hill Drive
Fairfield, CT 06432

PEACHWARE QUARTERLY
3445 Peachtree Road, N.E.
Atlanta, GA 30326

POPULAR COMPUTING
70 Main Street
Peterborough, NH 03458

SCHOOL MICROWARE REVIEWS
P.O. Box 246
Dresden, ME 04343

SOFTALK
Softalk Curriculum
P.O. Box 60
North Hollywood, Ca 91603

THE COMPUTING TEACHER
Department of Computer
& Information Science
University of Oregon
Eugene, OR 97403

* From: Ekwall, Eldon E. *Locating and Correcting Reading Difficulties.* (4th ed.). Columbus, Ohio: Charles E. Merrill, 1985 (pp. 187–188). (Reprinted by permission of Charles E. Merrill)

Alphabet

Name of Program	Skills Taught	Computer Requirements	Grade Level	Publisher/Distributor
Stickybear ABC	Introduce alphabet	Apple II/II+/IIe (48k)	K–2	Scholastic
Alphabet Circus	Alphabet sequence	Apple II/II+/IIe (48k)	K–2	Scholastic
Alphabet Zoo	Relationshp between sound and letters	Apple II/II+/IIe (48k) Atari 400.800, & (48k) 1200 (cassette)	K–3	Scholastic
Alpha-Betizing	Alphabet skills	PET or Commodore 64 (cassette) (8k)	1–6	Scholastic
Letter Recognition & Alphabetization	Letter discrimination alphabetical sequence of letters	Apple II+/IIe (48k)	1–8	Milliken
Working With the Alphabet	Introduction to the Alphabet	Apple II+/IIe (48k) Pet, 2001, 2016, (16k) 2032, 4001, 4016, 4032 Commodore 64 (with emulator) TRS-80 I, III (requires dual drives (16k) Atari 400, 800, 1200 (16k for cassettes and 24k for diskettes)	K–4	Orange Cherry Media
Alphabet Song	Alphabet recognition	Commodore 64, Pet (8k)	Kinder	Micrograms Inc.

Content Area Reading

Name of Program	Skills Taught	Computer Requirements	Grade Level	Publisher/Distributor
How to Read in the Content Areas	Content Area science, social studies, literature, mathematics, spotlighting vocabulary building, surveying to determine the information given in a particular reading, detecting main ideas, inferences, recalling important facts, ideas and details, utilizing and applying these skills to content areas	Apple II+/IIe, TRS-80 I, III, IV, Pet, Commodore 64 with emulator, 64, or Atari (diskette or cassette)	5–6 remedial, 7–8	Educational Activities, Inc.
Science Content Area Reading	Context clues, syntactic clues, signal words, pronoun referents, prediction clues	Apple II+/IIe, TRS 80 I, III, IV, Pet, Commodore 64 with emulator, 64, or Atari (diskette or cassette)	Jr.–Sr. High School	Educational Activities, Inc.

Comprehension

Name of Program	Skills Taught	Computer Requirements	Grade Level	Publisher/Distributor
Comprehension Power	Comprehension	Apple II+/IIe (48k)	4–12	Milliken
Cloze-Plus	Comprehension and/or Vocabulary Development	Apple II+/IIe (48k)	3–8	Milliken
Reading Drills Program	Speed and Comprehension	Apple II/II+/IIc/IIe (48k)	4–College	Jamestown
Reading Comprehension Games	Fact/Opinion, Context clues, Getting the main ideas	Apple II with Applesoft & DOS 3.3, or Apple IIe (48k)	2–5	The Micro Center
Reading for Comprehension	Word attack, vocabulary, literal comprehension, interpretive comprehension, work-study skill, and paragraphs	Sony SMC-70 Microcomputer	3.0–6.9	Computer Curriculum Corporation
PAL (Comprehension)	Classify words, details, best title, real/make-believe, sequence sentences, pronouns, who is talking, and inference	Apple II with Applesoft RAM (48k)	second	Universal Systems for Education Inc.
PAL (Comprehension)	Details, main idea, story sequence, real/make believe, character traits, story endings, similarities/differences, inference, why questions (story), past, present, future, conversation meaning, and pronoun referent	Apple II with Applesoft RAM (48k)	third	Universal Systems for Education, Inc.
PAL (Comprehension)	Details, main idea, story setting, character role, outcomes, drawing conclusions, inference, sequencing events, cause, effect, similarities/differences, fact, fiction, persuasion, and simile	Apple II with Applesoft RAM (48k)	fourth	Universal Systems for Education, Inc.

PAL (Comprehension)	Commas for meaning, details, main idea, simile/metaphor, idioms, personification, comparatives, sequence, story ending, cause/effect, pronoun referent, inference, characterization, fact/opinion, story setting, similarities/differences, persuasion, drawing conclusions, meaning of quotations	Apple II with Applesoft RAM (48k)	fifth	Universal Systems for Education, Inc.
PAL (Comprehension)	Details, main idea, inference, story climax, story outcome, fact/opinion, fact/fiction, inferred story setting, character traits, similarities/differences, drawing conclusions, cause/effect, figurative language, persuasion, analogies, slanted reporting, and generalization	Apple II with Applesoft RAM (48k)	sixth	Univeral Systems for Education, Inc.
Who, What, Where, When, Why	Discriminating between who, what, where, when & why	Apple II & IIe (48k)	1–4	Hartley Courseware, Inc.
Fact and Opinion	Discriminating between fact and opinion	Apple II & IIe (48k)	3–6	Hartley Courseware, Inc.
Our Weird and Wacky World	Literal comprehension, and critical reading	Apple II+/IIe, TRS-80 I, III, IV, Pet, Commodore 64 with emulator, 64, or Atari (diskette or cassette)	3–4 remedial, intermediate	Educational Activities, Inc.

Comprehension

Name of Program	Skills Taught	Computer Requirements	Grade Level	Publisher/Distributor
Our Wild and Crazy World	Literal comprehension, and critical reading	Apple II+/IIe, TRS-80 I, III, IV, Pet, Commodore 64 with emulator, 64, or Atari (diskette or cassette)	4–5	Educational Activities, Inc.
The Cloze Technique for Developing Comprehension	Comprehension through the use of cloze	Apple II+/IIe (48k) Pet, Commodore 64 with emulator (16k) TRS-80 I, III, (16k) III requires dual drives Atari, 400, 600, and 1200 (16k for cassettes and 24k for diskettes)	3–5	Orange Cherry Media

Critical reading

Name of Program	Skills Taught	Computer Requirements	Grade Level	Publisher/Distributor
Critical Reading Skills	Critical reading	Sony SMC-70 Microcomputer	7–up	Computer Curriculum Corporation

Placement tests

Name of Program	Skills Tested	Computer Requirements	Grade Level	Publisher/Distributor
Descriptive Reading	Word and passage comprehension	Apple II+/IIe, TRS-80 II, Pet, Commodore 64 Atari (cassette or diskette)	Inst. level 1–8 Remed. level 4–6	Educational Activities, Inc.
The O'Brien Vocabulary Placement Test	Independent reading level	Apple II+/IIe, TRS-80 I, III, IV, Pet, Commodore 64 with emulator, 64, or Atari	1–7	Educational Activities, Inc.
Informal Reading Comprehension Placement Test	Word comprehension, passage comprehension	Apple II+/IIe, TRS-80 I, III, IV, Pet, Commodore 64 with emulator, 64, or Atari (diskette or cassette)	Inst. level 1–8 Remed. level secondary	Educational Activities, Inc.
Descriptive I	Main idea, details, vocabulary, sequence, and inference	Apple II+/IIe, TRS-80 I, III, IV, Pet, Commodore 64 with emulator, 64, or Atari (diskette or cassette)	1.5–5.5	Educational Activities, Inc.
Descriptive II	Main idea, details, fact/opinion, vocabulary, sequence, and inference	Apple II+/IIe, TRS-80 I, III, IV, Pet, Commodore 64 with emulator, 64, or Atari (diskette or cassette)	3–8	Educational Activities, Inc.

Spelling

Name of Program	Skills Taught	Computer Requirements	Grade Level	Publisher/Distributor
Pop 'R Spell	Spelling	Apple II+/IIe (48k) Atari (32k) IBM PC (64k)	3–8	Milliken
Pop 'R Spell Challenge	Advanced Spelling Vocabulary Development	Apple II+/IIe (48k) Atari (32k) IBM PC (64k)	9 & up	Milliken
Instant Words Program	Sight Word/Spelling	Apple II/II+/IIc/IIe (48k)	1–4, remedial, ESL, & Adult Basic Ed.	Jamestown
Fry Word Drills Program	Spelling and Word Recognition	Apple II/II+/IIc/IIe (48k)	3–8, remedial	Jamestown
Spelling Wiz	Learning to spell commonly misspelled words	Apple II/II+/IIe (48k)	3–6	Scholastic
Flash-Spell-Helicopter	Spelling skills	Pet or Commodore 64 (cassette) (16k)	1–6	Scholastic
U-Spell	Audiovisual recognition: spelling skills	TRS-80 III/4 (16k)	1–8	Scholastic
Language Skills	Spelling Skills	TRS-80 III/4 (16k) (cassette)	4–7	Scholastic
The Spelling Machine	Spelling Skills	Apple II/II+/IIe (32k)	K–6	Scholastic
Language Arts Elementary Volume 2	Spelling Skills	Apple II/II+/IIe (32k)	2–6	Scholastic
Spelltronics	Vowel patterns, Long vowel patterns, Consonant patterns, Word endings, useful Words, unexpected Spellings	Apple II+/IIe/, TRS-80 Models I/II/IV, Pet, Commodore 64 with Emulator, 64, Atari	4th remedial all levels	Educational Activities, Inc.
Spelling Volume I	Spelling skills	Apple II Basic (48k)	1–6	Minnesota Educational Computing Consortium
Spelling Volume II	Spelling skills	Apple II Basic (48k)	Jr. Hi–Adult	Minnesota Educational Computing Consortium
Spelling Demons, Computer Spell Down	Spelling mastery	Apple II+/IIe DOS 3.3 (48k) TRS-80 III (48k) TRS-80 I, III (16k) (cassette)	2–6	Random House School Division

Fundamental Spelling Words in Context	Spelling skills	Apple II+/IIe DOS 3.3 (48k) TRS-80 III (48k) TRS-80 I, III (16k) (cassette)	3–8	Random House School Division
The Spelling System	Vowel spellings, Consonant spellings, Special vowel spellings, & Word building	Apple II+/IIe (48k)	4–8	Milliken
Spelling 1. See and Spell 2. The Spelling Bee	Commonly misspelled words and spelling drill	Apple II+/IIe (48k) Pet, 2001, 2016, (16k) 2032, 4001, 4016, 4032 Commodore 64 (with emulator) TRS-80 I, III (requires dual drives) (16k) Atari 400, 800, 1200 (16k for cassettes and 24k for diskettes)	2–4	Orange Cherry Media

Study Skills

Name of Program	Skills Taught	Computer Requirements	Grade Level	Publisher/Distributor
PAL	ABC order, dictionary order, table of contents	Apple II with Applesoft RAM (48k)	Second	Universal Systems for Education, Inc.
PAL	ABC order, table of contents, title page, best reference, guide words, using the dictionary	Apple II with Applesoft RAM (48k)	Third	Universal Systems for Education, Inc.
PAL	Alphabetical order, index, glossary, dictionary-location, dictionary-meaning, outline, best reference	Apple II with Applesoft RAM (48k)	Fourth	Universal Systems for Education, Inc.
PAL	Dictionary, best reference, index, card catalog, outlining, parts of a book	Apple II with Applesoft RAM (48k)	Fifth	Universal Systems for Education, Inc.
PAL	Outline headings, table of contents, using the dictionary, best reference, newspaper reading, timetables and schedules, reading ads, bibliography	Apple II with Applesoft RAM (48k)	Sixth	Universal Systems for Education, Inc.

Vocabulary

Name of Program	Skills Taught	Computer Requirements	Grade Level	Publisher/Distributor
Vocabulary Builders	Recognizing homonyms, synonyms, antonyms, meanings through context building clues	Apple II+/IIe (48k) Pet, Commodore (16k) 64, (with emulator) TRS-80 I, III, (16k) (III requires dual drives) Atari 400, 800, 1200 (16k for cassettes & 24k for diskettes)	3–8	Orange Cherry Media
Vocabulary Builder	Definitions	Commodore 64, Pet (8k)	2–3	Micrograms Inc.
Vocabulary Expander	Word drill	Commodore 64, Pet (16k)	disks available: 9–11 & Up	Micrograms Inc.
Homonyms	Distinguishing between homonyms in the context of a sentence	Apple II/II+/IIe (48k)	1–6	Scholastic Inc.
Antonyms/Synonyms	Selecting correct antonyms and synonyms	Apple II/II+/IIe (48k)	3–8	Scholastic Inc.
PAL	Prefixes, suffixes, root or base words, abbreviations, contractions, compound words, plurals, synonyms, antonyms, homonyms, word families, word meaning in context	Apple II with Applesoft RAM (48k)	Second	Universal Systems for Education, Inc.

Vocabulary

Name of Program	Skills Taught	Computer Requirements	Grade Level	Publisher/Distributor
PAL	Prefixes, suffixes, root or base words, abbreviations, contractions, ownership words, plurals, synonyms, antonyms, homonyms, word families, context clues/sentences, multiple meaning words, incomplete sentences	Apple II with Applesoft RAM (48k)	Third	Universal Systems for Education, Inc.
PAL	Root or base words, affixes, prefix meaning, suffix meaning, synonyms, antonyms, irregular plurals, abbreviations, pronoun meaning, contractions, possessives, multiple meaning words, conversation shift, context clues	Apple II with Applesoft RAM (48k)	Fourth	Universal Systems for Education, Inc.
PAL	Prefix/suffix, root words, possessives, synonyms, antonyms, prefix/suffix meaning, Word meaning/sentences	Apple II with Applesoft RAM (48k)	Fifth	Universal Systems for Education, Inc.
PAL	Alphabetical order, index, glossary, dictionary–location, dictionary–meaning, outline, best reference	Apple II with Applesoft RAM (48k)	Sixth	Universal Systems for Education, Inc.
Homonyms	Recognizing and using words that sound the same	Apple II/II+/IIe (48k) Applesoft Basic DOS 3.3	1–6	Scholastic Inc.

Language Arts Elementary Volume 2	Vocabulary and spelling skills	Apple II/II+/IIe Applesoft Basic DOS 3.3	(48k)	2–6	Scholastic Inc.
Language Arts Elementary Volume 5	Prefixes	Apple II/II+/IIe Applesoft Basic DOS 3.3	(48k)	2–6	Scholastic Inc.
Word Master	Identify word pairs that are synonyms, antonyms	Apple II/II+/IIe Applesoft Basic DOS 3.3	(48k)	3–6	Scholastic Inc.
Antonyms/Synonyms	Identify and correctly select antonyms and synonyms	Apple II/II+/IIe Applesoft Basic DOS 3.3	(48k)	3–8	Scholastic Inc.
Homonyms in Context	Recognize homonyms in context	Apple II+/IIe Applesoft DOS 3.3 TRS-80 III TRS-80 I, III Cassettes	(48k) (48k) (16k)	3–6	Random House, Inc.
Word Focus II Prefixes and Suffixes	High frequency words with prefixes and suffixes	TRS-80 III	(48k)	4–9	Random House, Inc.
Vocabulary-Dolch	Dolch vocabulary lists, drill	Apple II/IIe Requires cassette control device (CCD)	(48k)	PP-3	Hartley Courseware, Inc.
Vocabulary-Elementary	Sight-say words drill	Apple II/IIe (Requires CCD)	(48k)	1–3	Hartley Courseware, Inc.
Vocabulary-Controlled	Short vowel sounds, double vowel sounds, long (glided) vowel sounds	Apple II/IIe (Requires CCD)	(48k)	K-3	Hartley Courseware, Inc.
Create-Vocabulary	Create list to correlate with basal	Apple II/IIe (Requires CCD)	(48k)		

Word attack

Name of Program	Skills Taught	Computer Requirements	Grade Level	Publisher/Distributor
Word Man	Long and short vowel patterns	Apple II/II+/IIe (48k)	3–6	Scholastic
Long/Short Vowel Spaceships	Mastery of vowels	TRS–80 III/4 (16k) (cassette)	2–4	Scholastic
Word Families	Make new words by replacing a letter	Apple II/II+/IIe (48k)	1–4	Scholastic
Using Phonics in Context	Initial Consonants, final Consonants, digraphs, blends, short Vowels, Long vowel patterns (CVe), long vowel patterns (CVVC), Irregular vowel patterns, Vowel plus "r" combinations	Apple II+/IIe, TRS-80, Models I, III, IV, Pet, Commodore 64, Atari	2–4	Educational Activities, Inc.
Fundamental Phonics and Word Attack	Visual discrimination, letter recognition, sight words, beginning consonant sounds, ending consonant sounds, vowel sounds, phonetic generalizations, and syllabication	TRS-80 III (48k) TRS-80 I, III (16k) (cassette)	1–4	Random House School Division
Phonics	Initial and final consonants, short and long vowels, initial and final consonant blends, consonant and vowel digraphs, and silent letters	Atari 800 (32k)	primary	Science Research Associates, Inc.

Beginning/Ending Sounds	Make new words by replacing a letter	TRS-80 (32k) for cassette (16k)	1–2	Little Bee Educational Programs
Mr Long/Mr Short	Distinguishing between long and short vowels	TRS-80 (32k) for cassette (16k)	Kinder–1	Little Bee Educational Programs
Blending Blends	Matching beginning blends with word endings	TRS-80 (32k) for cassette (16k)	1–2	Little Bee Educational Programs
Word Sound Juggler	Selecting the correct vowel for a word in context	TRS-80 (32k) for cassette (16k)	1–2	Little Bee Educational Programs
PAL	Single consonants, consonant blends, consonant digraphs, silent letters, short vowels, long vowels, dipthongs, "vowel plus R" words, vowel pairs, rhyming words	Apple II with Applesoft RAM (48k)	Second	Universal Systems for Education, Inc.
PAL	Sounds of "C," sounds of "G," consonant blends, consonant digraphs, silent letters, short vowels, long vowels, "Y" as vowel, vowel pairs, "vowel plus R" words	Apple II with Applesoft RAM (48k)	Third	Universal Systems for Education, Inc.
Word Families	Make new words by replacing a letter	Apple II & IIe (48k)	1–3	Hartley Courseware, Inc.

Word Attack

Name of Program	Skills Taught	Computer Requirements	Grade Level	Publisher/Distributor
Vowels Tutorial (three-disk program)		Apple II & IIe (48k) (requires a Cassette Control Device)	1–3	Hartley Courseware, Inc.
1. Short Vowels	Discriminate between short vowels in words with regular and irregular spellings			
2. Long Vowels #1	Discriminate between long and short vowels and type long vowel sounds			
3. Long Vowels #2	Type vowels that make long vowel sounds in words with regular spellings			
Vowels	Long vowels, short vowels, double vowels, dipthongs, r-controlled, shwa, and others	Apple II & IIe (48k)	1–3	Hartley Courseware, Inc.
Consonants	Initial and final consonants and blends	Apple II & IIe (48k)	1–4	Hartley Courseware, Inc.
Beginning Sounds	Identifying beginning sounds of pictured objects	Commodore 64, Pet (16k)	K–1	Micrograms Inc.
Ending Sounds	Identifying ending sounds of pictured objects	Commodore 64, Pet (16k)	K–1	Micrograms Inc.
Using Phonics In Context	Initial consonants, final consonants, digraphs, blends, short vowels, long vowel patterns (VCe), long vowel patterns (CVVC), irregular vowel patterns, vowel plus R combinations	Apple II+/IIe, TRS-80 I, III, IV, Pet, Commodore 64 with emulator, 64, & Atari	2–4	Educational Activities, Inc.

Writing

Name of Program	Skills Taught	Computer Requirements	Grade Level	Publisher/Distributor
Kidwriter	Communication skills through writing	Apple II/II+/IIe (48k)	2–4	Scholastic
The Bank Street Writer	Word processing	Apple II+ (48k, 64k) Atari (48k) Commodore 64 (64k) Expanded Apple IIe/IIc (64k, 128k) IBM PC/jr (64k)	4–8	Scholastic
The Bank Street Speller	Proofreader	Apple II+/IIe/IIc (48k)	4–up	Scholastic
Story Tree	Creative Writing	Apple II+/IIe/IIc (64k) IBM PC/PCjr (64k) Commodore 64 (64k)	4–12	Scholastic
Story Maker	Creative writing	Apple II+/IIe/IIc (48k) Commodore 64 (64k)	2–up	Scholastic
Writing Competency Program	Letter writing, Report organization, & Persuasion	Apple II+/IIe, TRS-80, Pet, Commodore 64 with emulator/64, Atari	Jr–Sr High	Educational Activities, Inc.
Processing Words	Word processing	Apple II, Basic (48k)	6–9	Minnesota Educational Computing Consortium
Writing A Narrative	Creative writing	Apple II, Basic (48k)	7–9	Minnesota Educational Computing Consortium
Writing A Character Sketch	Creative writing	Apple II, Basic (48k)	9–12	Minnesota Educational Computing Consortium
Fundamental Punctuation Practice	Punctuation skills	Apple II+/IIe 3.3 DOS (48k) TRS-80 III (48k) TRS-80 I, III (16k)	3–8	Random House School Division

Writing

Name of Program	Skills Taught	Computer Requirements	Grade Level	Publisher/Distributor
Fundamental Punctuation Practice Courseware PLUS	Punctuation skills	Apple II+/IIe 3.3 DOS (48k) TRS-80 III (48k)	2–8	Random House School Division
Fundamental Capitalization Practice	Capitalization skills	Apple II+/IIe 3.3 DOS (48k)	3–8	Random House School Division
Story Starter	Creative writing	TRS-80 III (48k) TRS-80 I, III (16k)	2–4	Random House School Division
Story Builder	Creative writing	Atari 400, 800 (48k) TRS-80 III (48k) TRS-80 I, III (16k)	3–6	Random House School Division
Capitalization	First word in sentence, I, proper personal names, days of the week, months, holidays, A.M., P.M., proper place names, titles, misc. including capitalization of mom, dad, etc.	Apple II & IIe (48k)	2–6	Hartley Courseware, Inc.

COMPANIES THAT PUBLISH OR DISTRIBUTE SOFTWARE MATERIALS FOR USE IN READING EDUCATION*

Adventure International
Box 3435
Longwood, FL 32750

Apple Computer, Inc.
Customer Relations, MS 18-F
20525 Mariani Ave.
Cupertino, CA 95014
(General Information)

Apple Educators' Newsletter
9525 Lucerne
Ventura, CA 93004

Atari, Inc.
2110 Powers Ferry Road, Suite 303
Atlanta, GA 30339

A/V Concepts Corp.
30 Montauk Blvd.
Oakdale, NY 11769

Borg-Warner Educational Systems
600 West University Drive
Arlington Heights, IL 60004

BrainBank, Inc.
Suite 408
220 Fifth Ave.
New York, NY 10001

Compress
P.O. Box 102
Wentworth, NH 03282

Computer Curriculum Corporation
1701 W. Euless Boulevard, Suite 139
Euless, TX 76039

Creative Curriculum, Inc.
15632 Producer Lane
Huntington Beach, CA 92649

Creative Publications
3977 East Bashore Road
P.O. Box 10328
Palo Alto, CA 94303

Dale Seymour Publications
P.O. Box 10888
Palo Alto, CA 94303

Dormac, Inc.
P.O. Box 752
Beaverton, OR 97075

Dorsett Educational Systems, Inc.
Golsby Airport
P.O. Box 1226
Norman, OK 73070

Educational Activities, Inc.
P.O. Box 392
Freeport, NY 11520

Educational Industrial Sales, Inc.
2225 Grant Rd., Suite 3
Los Altos, CA 94022

Educational Teaching Aids
159 West Kinzie Street
Chicago, IL 60610

Edutek Corporation
415 Cambridge #4
Palo Alto, CA 94306

EMC Publishing
300 York Avenue
St. Paul, MN 55101

George Earl
1302 So. General McMullen
San Antonio, TX 78237

Ginn & Company
1250 Fairwood Avenue
Columbus, OH 43216

Hartley Courseware, Inc.
123 Bride St.
Box 419
Dimondale, MI 48821

Holt, Rinehart & Winston
383 Madison Ave.
New York, NY 10017

I/CT-Instructional/Communications
Technology, Inc.
10 Stepar Place
Huntington Station, NY 11746

* From: Ekwall, Eldon E. *Locating and Correcting Reading Difficulties.* (4th ed.). Columbus, Ohio: Charles E. Merrill, 1985 (pp. 185–187). (Reprinted by permission of Charles E. Merrill)

Ideal School Supply, Co.
11000 S. Lavergne Ave.
Oak Lawn, IL 60453

Krell Software Corp.
1320 Stony Brook Road
Stony Brook, NY 11790

Kress Software Corporation
1320 Stony Brook Road
Stony Brook, NY 11790

Learning Well
Dept. 21
200 South Service Road
Roslyn Heights, NY 11577

Little Bee Educational Programs
P.O. Box 262
Massillon, OH. 44648

The Micro Center
Department MK 28
P.O. Box 6
Pleasantville, NY 10570

Microcomputer Workshops Course-ware
225 Westchester Ave.
Port Chester, NY 10573

Mic-Ed Incorporated
8108 Eden Road
Eden Prairie, MN 55344

Micro Learningware
Highway 66 South Box 307
Mankato, MN 56002

Micromatics, Inc.
181 N. 200 W., Suite 5
Bountiful, UT 84010

Microphys
1737 West 2nd Street
Brooklyn, NY 11223

Micrograms, Inc.
P.O. Box 2146
Loves Park, IL 61130

Micro Power & Light Co.
12820 Hillcrest Road, Suite 219
Dallas, TX 75230

Milliken Publishing Company
1100 Research Blvd.
St. Louis, MO 63132

Milton Bradley Company
Springfield, MA 01101

Minnesota Educational Computing Consortium
3490 Lexington Ave. North
St. Paul, MN 55112

Orange Cherry Media
7 Delano Drive
Bedford Falls, NY 10507

Peachtree Software by Eduware
3445 Peachtree Road, N.E.
8th Floor
Atlanta, GA 30326

Powersoft, Inc.
P.O. Box 157
Pitman, NJ 08071

Program Design, Inc.
95 East Putnam Ave.
Greenwich, CT 06830

The Psychological Corporation
4640 Harry Hines Blvd.
Dallas, TX 75235

Queqe
5 Chapel Hill Drive
Fairfield, CT 06432

Radio Shack
Education Division
1400 One Tandy Center
Fort Worth, TX 76102

Random House, Inc.
2970 Brandywine Rd., Suite 201
Atlanta, GA 30341

Reader's Digest Services, Inc.
Educational Division
Pleasantville, NY 10570

Right On Programs
P.O. Box 977
Huntington, NY 11743

Scholastic Book Services
P.O. Box 1068
Jefferson City, MO 65102

Scholastic, Inc.
P.O. Box 7501
2931 E. McCarty Street
Jefferson City, MO 65102

Science Research Associates, Inc.
155 North Wacker Drive
Chicago, IL 60606

Skillcorp Software, Inc.
3741 Old Conejo Road
Newbury Park, CA 91320

Sliwa Enterprises, Inc.
2360-J George Washington Highway
Yorktown, VA 23692

Society for Visual Education, Inc.
Department LX
1345 Diversey Parkway
Chicago, IL 60614

Softside
10 Northern Boulevard
Amherst, NH 03031

Speco Educational Systems
3208 Daniels, Suite #6
Dallas, TX 75205

Sterling Swift Publishing Co.
7901 South IH 35
Austin, TX 78744

Sunburst Communications
Rm. Y 4747
39 Washington Avenue
Pleasantville, NY 01570

Tamarack Software
P.O. Box 247
Darby, MT 59829

TIEs
1925 West Country Road B2
St. Paul, MN 55113

Tycom Associates
68 Velma Ave.
Pittsfield, MA 01201

Unicom
297 Elmwood Ave.
Providence, RI 02907

Universal Systems for Education, Inc.
14901 East Hampden Ave., Suite 250
Aurora, CO 80014

COMPUTER TERMINOLOGY*

Access Time The time required to retrieve a word from memory.

Add-On A device for coupling a computer with a telephone for the transmission of data.

Applications Software Computer programs written to perform actual tasks such as inventory, mail list, accounts payable/receivable.

Audio Device Any computer device that accepts sound or produces sound. Examples include voice recognition and music or speech synthesis devices.

Auxiliary Storage A storage device in addition to the "core" or main storage of the computer. Auxiliary storage is the permanent storage for information. It includes magnetic tapes, cassette tapes, cartridge tapes, hard disks, floppy disks. Auxiliary storage can't be accessed as fast as main storage.

BASIC Beginner's All-Purpose Symbolic Instruction Code; a type of computer programming language.

Baud Bits Per Second. Actually binary units of information per second. Teletypes transmit at 110 baud. Each character is 11 bits, and the teletype transmits at 10 characters per sound.

Back Up Duplicate data files, redundant equipment, or procedures used in the event of failure of a component or storage media.

Binary Number Representation of a number in the binary system, using a series of zeros and ones.

Bit The contraction of Binary Digit. A bit always has the value of zero or one. Bits are universally used in electronic systems to encode information, orders (instructions), and data. Bits are usually grouped in nybbles (four), bytes (eight), or larger units.

* This selected glossary of terminology is reprinted with permission of the R. R. Bowker Company from a compilation by Advanced Software Technology, Inc. Copyright © 1983.

Byte A set of eight bits. A byte is universally used to represent a character. Microcomputer instructions require one, two, or three bytes. One byte includes two nybbles.

CAI Computer Assisted Instruction

Cassette A small plastic cartridge that contains two spools of 1.8″ magnetic tape, and which has recently been applied to mass storage requirements of microcomputers and minicomputers.

Character Any letter, number, symbol or punctuation mark that can be transmitted as output by the computer.

Character Printer A printer that transfers a fully formed letter, number, or symbol with each impression stroke. The characters are generally more legible than those created by a dot matrix printer.

COBOL Common Business Oriented Language A high-level computer language using commands that resemble English. Cobol was designed specifically for business use.

Coding The entering of a program or data into a computer, usually by means of a keyboard.

Command An order to the computer in the form of words and numbers typed on a keyboard, words spoken into a microphone, positions of a game or joystick, etc.

Compile To translate high-level language into a set of binary instructions.

Compiler System software that produces a machine-code version of a program originally written in a high-level language such as Cobol, PL/1, etc.

Computer A general purpose electrical system designed for the manipulation of information and incorporating a central processing unit (CPU), memory, input/output (I/O) facilities, power supply, and cabinet.

Computer Time Sharing Permits one computer to serve several terminals in remote locating simultaneously and allows the cost of the computer to be divided among the users.

CP/M Control Program/Monitor. One of the more common computer operating systems on which many computers are based and much software written.

CPU Central Processing Unit. The computer module in charge of fetching, decoding, and executing instructions.

CRT Cathode Ray Tube. The television tube used to display pictures or characters. Also the computer terminal made from a CRT.

Daisywheel A style of printer or typewriter printing element in the shape of a disk. Each character is located at the end of a "petal" connected at the center of the disk, hence the name.

Data Information stored or processed by the computer.

Database Systematic organization of data files for easy access, retrieval, and update.

Dedicated If a computer or a piece of hardware is assigned exclusively to one task, it is said to be a dedicated system.

Disk A flat, circular object that resembles a phonograph record. A record "stores" music; a disk stores information. The disk is inserted into a disk drive that rotates at a high speed. The drive writes new information onto the disk and reads information that is already stored on the disk. There are two major types of disks found on small computers, flexible floppy disks and hard disks.

Diskette Floppy disk. A circular mylar substrate coated with a magnetic oxide, rotating inside a special jacket that internally cleans the surface.

Display Screen Same as CRT.

Dot Matrix The type of printer in which characters are formed from multiple dots, much as a TV picture is created.

Dual Density A reference to storage disks and disk drives that are capable of storing and reading twice the number of information tracks (80) per disk as the early standard (35–40).

Error Message A one-sentence statement by the computer to the operator that something has been done incorrectly, e.g., "Does not compute."

External Memory Used to store programs and information that would otherwise be lost if the computer was turned off. Cassette tapes, disks, bubble memory, and CCD (charge coupled devices) are also known as mass memory and removable memory.

File A logical block of information, designated by name, and considered as a unit by a user. A file may be physically divided into smaller records.

Fixed Disk A device in which the disk pack is sealed and cannot be removed. Being sealed it cannot be exposed to dust and dirt and, therefore, can be operated at higher speeds than removable units, with greater reliability.

Flexible Disk Recent mass-storage device using a soft (floppy) disk to record information. The disk rotates in a cardboard jacket. Cutout holes provide access for the moving head (which must be applied against the disk in order to read and write) and for index information.

FORTRAN FORmula TRANSlator. Early high-level language devised for numerical computations. Although complex, it is most frequently one of the programming languages used in scientific environments. Requires a compiler (by contrast, BASIC, derived from Fortran can be interpreted).

Grid A method of dividing the computer screen into evenly spaced horizontal and vertical lines. Used for locating points on the screen. These points are expressed as row and column coordinates.

Hard Copy Computer output on paper.

Hard Disk A data storage medium encompassing a permanently mounted disk and drive with a storage capacity 10 to 30 times that of the removable floppy disk.

Hardware The bolts, nuts, boards, chips, wires, transformers, etc., in a computer. The physically existing components of a sytem.

Input Any information coming into the computer.

Input Device Any machine that allows you to enter commands or information into the computer's main (RAM) memory. An input device could be a typewriter keyboard, an organ keyboard, a tape drive, a disk drive, a microphone, a light pen, a digitizer, or electronic sensors.

Keyboard A group of push buttons used for entering information into a computer system.

Kilo A prefix meaning "1000."

Kilobyte Term meaning "1000 bytes" (precisely, 1024 bytes).

Language In relation to computers, any unified, related set of commands or instructions that the computer can accept. Low-level languages are difficult to use but closely resemble the fundamental operations of the computer. High-level languages resemble English.

LCD Liquid Crystal Display.

LED Light Emitting Diode.

Light Pen An input device for a CRT. It records the emission of light at the point of contact with the screen. The timing relationship to the beginning of a scan determines the approximate position on the screen.

Letter Quality Printer One that forms whole characters and provides output much like a standard office typewriter in quality.

Line Printer A device that prints information from the computer at a high speed; produces a hard copy.

LOGO A computer language, developed by scientists at MIT's Artificial Intelligence Laboratory, that has been used experimentally over the last several years in a children's learning laboratory as a tool to help youngsters master concepts in mathematics, art, and science.

Loop A group of instructions that may be executed more than once.

Main Memory The internal memory of the computer contained in its circuitry, as opposed to peripheral memory (tapes, disks).

Mainframe The box that houses the computer's main memory and logic components—it's CPU, RAM, ROM, interface input/output (I/O) circuitry, and so on. The word is also to distinguish the very large computer from the minicomputer or microcomputer.

Matrix Printer A matrix printer prints using a grid of dots usually 5 by 7. Characters are formed by striking certain dots in the grid.

Master File A file that contains the main, permanent information used in a system. Other files are transaction files or files used as temporary work areas.

Menu A list of programs or applications that are available by making a selection. For example, a small home computer might display the following menu: "Do you want to 1. Balance checkbook? 2. See appointments for May? 3. See a recipe? Type number desired.

Microcomputer A small but complete computer system, including CPU, memory, input/output (I/O) interfaces, and power supply.

Minicomputer A small computer, intermediate in size between a microcomputer and a large computer.

Mini-Floppy A 5¼″ diskette.

Modem Modulator-demodulator. A device that transforms a computer's electrical pulses into audible tones for transmission over a phone line to another computer. A modem also receives incoming tones and transforms them into electrical signals that can be processed and stored by the computer.

Natural Language A spoken, human language such as English, Spanish, Arabic, or Chinese. In the future, small computers will probably be fast enough and have large enough vocabularies to enable you to talk to them using your natural language. Yet there will still be a need for special computer languages that are more efficient than natural languages for handling certain kinds of tasks.

Network A group of small computers communicating over telephone lines or by use of radio microwaves.

Nybble Usually four bits, or half a bite.

Off Line Equipment or information that is not currently part of an operating computer system.

On Line Directly connected to the computer system and in performance-ready condition.

Operating System Software required to manage the hardware and logical resources of a system, including scheduling and file (OS) management.

Output Any processed information coming out of a computer, via any medium; print, CRT, etc.

Packaged Program A program designed for a specific application of broad, general usage, unadapted to any particular installation.

Permanent Storage Storage of computer data on a disk or magnetic tape.

Password A code word or group of characters a computer system might require to allow that operator to perform certain functions. An operator's password might allow him to update payroll hours, but not run checks.

Pascal A high-level programming language.

Peripheral A human interface device connected to a computer.

Plotter A mechanical device for drawing lines under computer control.

Program A sequence of instructions that results in the execution of an algorithm. Programs are essentially written at three levels: (1) binary (can be directly executed by the MPU), (2) assembly language (symbolic representation of the binary), (3) high-level language (such as BASIC), requiring a compiler or interpreter.

Programming Language A set of rules and conventions used to prepare the source program for translation by the computer. Each language has its own rules. Examples of programming languages are BASIC, COBOL, and RPG.

RAM Random Access Memory The portion of computer memory generally available to execute programs and store data. Memory locations can both be read from and written to at high speeds.

Random Access An access method where each word can be retrieved directly by its address.

Retrieval The reading of data from a permanent storage device and its transfer into memory.

ROM Read Only Memory. A portion of computer memory where information is permanently stored. This information can be read at high speed but can never be altered. It is not available to execute programs or to store data.

Run Execute a program.

Screen Same as CRT.

Sign-Off The disconnect procedure that severs interactions between a user and a computer.

Sign-On The connect procedure that establishes contact between a user and a computer.

Software The programs (contrasted to hardware). Any set of coded instructions causing the computer to perform a task.

System A set of programs, a set of hardware, or a set of programs and hardware that work together for some specific purpose.

Synthesizer Any device that produces something that is based on digital signals stored in the computer. A voice synthesizer produces sounds that closely resemble a person talking. A music synthesizer makes music.

Terminal Usually a work station remote from the main computer allowing keyboard input and CRT and/or printer output.

Time Sharing Occurs when a single computer has multiple users who are each getting a "slice" of each second of the computer's processing time.

User Friendly Descriptive of both hardware and software that are designed to assist the user by being scaled to human dimensions, self-instructing, error proof, etc.

Video Monitor A computer picture screen.

Word A logical unit of information. It may have any number of bits, but it is usually four, eight, or sixteen for microcomputers.

REFERENCES

International Reading Association. *The Reading Teacher,* October 1984, 18, 80–82.

Appendices

A

Preparing and Using the Materials for Testing Letter Knowledge

PREPARATION OF MATERIALS FOR THE TEST

The author suggests that you remove p. 226 (LETTER KNOWLEDGE ANSWER SHEET) and make multiple copies of it for use in testing students in the future. You may also wish to remove the sheet entitled DIRECTIONS FOR LETTER KNOWLEDGE SHEET (p. 227) and duplicate it on the back side of the LETTER KNOWLEDGE ANSWER SHEET. If this is done, the directions for administering the letter knowledge test will always be available on the back of the LETTER KNOWLEDGE ANSWER SHEET. It is also suggested that p. 225 (LETTER STIMULUS SHEET) be removed and put in a three-ring notebook. Before placing it in the notebook you may wish to rubber cement it to a piece of oaktag or tagboard and then laminate it so that it will not become soiled from use since the LETTER STIMULUS SHEET will be handled by students as you test them for letter knowledge.

DIRECTIONS FOR TESTING LETTER KNOWLEDGE

Have your LETTER KNOWLEDGE ANSWER SHEET available and hand the student a copy of the LETTER STIMULUS SHEET. Full directions for the testing of letter knowledge are contained on a separate sheet labeled DIRECTIONS FOR LETTER KNOWLEDGE ANSWER SHEET.

FURTHER INFORMATION ON TESTING LETTER KNOWLEDGE

It should be kept in mind that there are various levels of skills involved in the testing of letter knowledge. For example, a student may be able to recite the alphabet but that same student may not be able to identify all the letters when they are shown to him or her. It is important to read the DIRECTIONS FOR LETTER KNOWLEDGE SHEET very carefully so that you will know about all aspects of the student's abilities in this area.

LETTER STIMULUS SHEET

1.	e	n	i	p	c	
2.	v	x	a	j	z	
3.	b	o	s	u	q	
4.	k	y	f	l	d	
5.	g	t	m	r	h	w

6.	C	J	P	H	K	
7.	O	G	N	Q	D	
8.	L	R	B	Z	Y	
9.	A	S	F	M	V	
10.	I	W	T	X	U	E

---

11. b m g d r p m b g r p d m o

LETTER KNOWLEDGE ANSWER SHEET

STUDENT'S NAME ______________________ SCHOOL ______________________

DATE ______________________

TESTER ______________________

Directions: See next page.

1. e______ n______ i______ p______ c______
2. v______ x______ a______ j______ z______
3. b______ o______ s______ u______ q______
4. k______ y______ f______ l______ d______
5. g______ t______ m______ r______ h______ w______
6. C______ J______ P______ H______ K______
7. O______ G______ N______ Q______ D______
8. L______ R______ B______ Z______ Y______
9. A______ S______ F______ M______ V______
10. I______ W______ T______ X______ U______ E______

TASK 1: ____Student can write all lower case letters correctly

____Student can write all upper case letters correctly

Exceptions noted: ______________________

____

TASK 2: ____Student can name all lower case letters correctly

____Student can name all upper case letters correctly

TASK 3: ____Student can identify all lower case letters when named

____Student can identify all upper case letters when named

____Student cannot identify all lower case letters when named

____Student cannot identify all upper case letters when named

Exceptions noted: ______________________

____

TASK 4: ____Student can match all upper and lower case letters

____Student cannot match all upper and lower case letters

Exceptions noted: ______________________

____

TASK 5: ____Student can match a letter with another one that is exactly the same

____Student cannot match letters that are exactly the same

Exceptions noted: ______________________

____

DIRECTIONS FOR LETTER KNOWLEDGE ANSWER SHEET

Before beginning this test you may first wish to have the student write all of the letters in both upper and lower case. If this is done correctly, then place a plus (+) mark in the blank by TASK #1 on the opposite side of this sheet. If they are not all done correctly, you may wish to note exceptions. (Optional)

A. Give the student the LETTER STIMULUS SHEET and ask him or her to read each of the letters in row 1, then row 2, row 3, etc. Mark them as plus (+) if they are answered correctly or you may simply wish to place a plus (+) mark in the blank beside TASK #2 (opposite side of this sheet) to indicate that they were all given correctly. If they are not answered correctly, then write the answer given by the student in each blank. If the student can do this task, stop the test. If he or she cannot name all of the letters, continue with the tasks listed below:

B. Show the student the LETTER STIMULUS SHEET and ask him or her to point to letters as you name them. Do them in random order from the lower case letters and then do them in random order from the upper case letters. Be sure to do all of them or do enough of them so that you are certain the student can identify all letters when they are named. If the student can do this, then place a plus (+) mark by TASK #3 (opposite side of this sheet) and discontinue the testing. If the student cannot do this task, then note that on TASK #3 and continue with the tasks listed below:

C. Show the student the LETTER STIMULUS SHEET and ask him or her to match upper case letters with lower case letters, e.g., point to the *n* in the lower case letters and ask the student to point to the *N* from the letters in the upper case group. You may wish to alternate by first pointing to a letter in the lower case and having the student match it with the corresponding letter from the upper case group; then point to a letter in the upper case and have the student match it with the corresponding letter in the lower case group. Be sure to do all of them or do enough of them so that you are certain the student can match all letters. If the student can do this, then place a plus (+) mark by TASK #4 (opposite side of this sheet) and discontinue the testing. If the student cannot do this task, then note that on TASK #4 and continue with the task listed below:

D. Show the student the LETTER STIMULUS SHEET and point to a letter from row #11 and ask the student to point to another letter that is exactly the same as that letter. Do this with all of the letters, i.e., first *b* then *m*, etc., until all pairs have been matched. If the student can do this, then place a plus (+) mark by TASK #5. If the student cannot do this task, then note that on TASK #5.

B

Preparing and Using the Materials for Testing Basic Sight Words

PREPARATION OF MATERIALS FOR THE TEST

The author suggests that you remove pp. 233–234 (EKWALL BASIC SIGHT WORD LIST—ANSWER SHEET) and make multiple copies of it for use in testing students in the future. It is also suggested that pp. 231–232 be removed and put in a three-ring notebook. Before placing these pages in the notebook you make wish to rubber cement them to oaktag or tagboard and then laminate them so that they will not become soiled from use since they will be handled by students as you test them for their knowledge of basic sight words.

DIRECTIONS FOR TESTING BASIC SIGHT WORDS

Have the EKWALL BASIC SIGHT WORD ANSWER SHEET available and hand the student a copy of the EKWALL BASIC SIGHT WORD LIST—STIMULUS SHEET. Ask the student to read the words on the stimulus sheet beginning with number one, then number two, etc. Mark a plus (+) in the corresponding blanks for answers that are correct and a minus (−) in the corresponding blanks for answers that are incorrect. If time permits, write the wrong pronunciation of words in the blanks. If the student says, "I don't know," or makes no response after a period of time, then write "dk" for "Don't know."

FURTHER INFORMATION ON TESTING STUDENT'S KNOWLEDGE OF BASIC SIGHT WORDS

Testing students using a list has some advantages as well as some disadvantages. If the student being tested knows the words very well, he or she is likely to read them more rapidly than they could be flashed using flash cards or some other method of presenting the words such as with the use of the Radio Shack TRS Model 80 Pocket Computer. This will result in time saved in the overall testing. On the other hand, using a stimulus sheet such as the one suggested for use here, allows the student time to stop and use word analysis skills if the word is not instantly known. This is the reason the author has suggested that words for which the student pauses for slightly longer than others be counted as incorrect. After finishing testing the student, you may wish to go back over the words the student has missed and give him or her a flash presentation of the word using a flash card or some other method to make sure the student does not have instant recognition of the word(s).

EKWALL BASIC SIGHT WORD LIST STIMULUS SHEET

1. a
2. did
3. have
4. know
5. one
6. to
7. and
8. do
9. her
10. like
11. play
12. too
13. are
14. down
15. here
16. little
17. put
18. two
19. away
20. eat
21. him
22. look
23. run
24. water
25. be
26. for
27. his
28. make
29. said
30. we
31. big
32. get
33. house
34. my
35. the
36. what
37. but
38. go
39. I
40. no
41. then
42. where
43. can
44. good
45. in
46. not
47. this
48. who
49. come
50. has
51. it
52. of
53. three
54. will
55. oh
56. you
57. your
58. about
59. call
60. had
61. mother
62. see
63. time
64. after
65. came
66. he
67. now
68. she
69. tree
70. all
71. could
72. help
73. old
74. so
75. up
76. am
77. day
78. how
79. on
80. some
81. us
82. an
83. find
84. is
85. other
86. something
87. very
88. around
89. fly
90. jump
91. over
92. stop
93. want
94. as
95. from
96. let
97. ran
98. take
99. was
100. back
101. funny
102. man
103. red
104. that
105. way
106. blue
107. give
108. may
109. ride
110. them
111. went
112. by
113. green
114. me
115. sat
116. there
117. when
118. saw
119. they
120. would
121. yes
122. again
123. boy
124. fun
125. long
126. or
127. soon
128. well
129. any
130. brown
131. girl
132. Mr.
133. out
134. stand
135. were
136. ask
137. buy
138. got
139. Mrs.
140. please
141. tell
142. white
143. at
144. children
145. high
146. more
147. party
148. than
149. why
150. ate
151. cold
152. happy
153. morning
154. pretty
155. thank
156. with
157. ball
158. color
159. if
160. much
161. pull
162. their
163. work
164. been
165. cry
166. into
167. must
168. rabbit
169. these
170. yellow
171. before
172. dog

EKWALL BASIC SIGHT WORD LIST (Page 2) STIMULUS SHEET

173. just
174. name
175. read
176. think
177. began
178. door
179. laugh
180. never
181. shall
182. thought
183. better
184. far
185. light
186. new
187. side
188. took
189. black
190. fast
191. night
192. sleep
193. under
194. father
195. walk
196. five
197. four
198. always
199. does
200. going
201. live
202. pick
203. sure
204. another
205. each
206. grow
207. made
208. place
209. ten
210. because
211. end
212. hand
213. many
214. right
215. thing
216. best
217. enough
218. hard
219. men
220. round
221. those
222. book
223. even
224. head
225. near
226. say
227. together
228. both
229. every
230. hold
231. next
232. school
233. told
234. box
235. eye
236. home
237. once
238. should
239. until
240. bring
241. fall
242. hot
243. only
244. show
245. wait
246. carry
247. first
248. hurt
249. open
250. sit
251. warm
252. clean
253. found
254. keep
255. our
256. six
257. which
258. cut
259. friend
260. kind
261. own
262. start
263. while
264. full
265. last
266. still
267. wish
268. gave
269. left
270. year
271. dear
272. seem
273. today
274. done
275. seven
276. try
277. drink
278. sing
279. turn
280. off
281. small
282. use
283. most
284. such
285. wash
286. people
287. write
288. present
289. also
290. don't
291. draw
292. eight
293. goes
294. its
295. king
296. leave
297. myself
298. upon
299. grand

EKWALL BASIC SIGHT WORD ANSWER SHEET

NAME ______________________ DATE __________

SCHOOL __________ TESTER ________

Directions: As the student reads the words from the stimulus sheet mark those read correctly with a plus (+). Mark those read incorrectly with a minus (–) or write the word substituted. Use a question mark (?) to indicate that the student says he or she does not know the answer. If a student hesitates longer than approximately one second before pronouncing a word, then count it wrong.

Pre-Primer

1. a ____
2. did ____
3. have ____
4. know ____
5. one ____
6. to ____
7. and ____
8. do ____
9. her ____
10. like ____
11. play ____
12. too ____
13. are ____
14. down ____
15. here ____
16. little ____
17. put ____
18. two ____
19. away ____
20. eat ____
21. him ____
22. look ____
23. run ____
24. water ____
25. be ____
26. for ____
27. his ____
28. make ____
29. said ____
30. we ____
31. big ____
32. get ____
33. house ____
34. my ____
35. the ____
36. what ____
37. but ____
38. go ____
39. I ____
40. no ____
41. then ____
42. where ____
43. can ____
44. good ____
45. in ____
46. not ____
47. this ____
48. who ____
49. come ____
50. has ____
51. it ____
52. of ____
53. three ____
54. will ____
55. oh ____
56. you ____
57. your ____

Primer

58. about ____
59. call ____
61. had ____
61. mother ____
62. see ____
63. time ____
64. after ____
65. came ____
66. he ____
67. now ____
68. she ____
69. tree ____
70. all ____
71. could ____
72. help ____
73. old ____
74. so ____
75. up ____
76. am ____
77. day ____
78. how ____
79. on ____
80. some ____
81. us ____
82. an ____
83. find ____
84. is ____
85. other ____
86. something ____
87. very ____
88. around ____
89. fly ____
90. jump ____
91. over ____
92. stop ____
93. want ____
94. as ____
95. from ____
96. let ____
97. ran ____
98. take ____
99. was ____
100. back ____
101. funny ____
102. man ____
103. red ____
104. that ____
105. way ____
106. blue ____
107. give ____
108. may ____
109. ride ____
110. them ____
111. went ____
112. by ____
113. green ____
114. me ____
115. sat ____
116. there ____
117. when ____
118. saw ____
119. they ____
120. would ____
121. yes ____

First Reader

122. again ____
123. boy ____
124. fun ____
125. long ____

126. or _____
127. soon _____
128. well _____
129. any _____
130. brown _____
131. girl _____
132. Mr. _____
133. out _____
134. stand _____
135. were _____
136. ask _____
137. buy _____
138. got _____
139. Mrs. _____
140. please _____
141. tell _____
142. white _____
143. at _____
144. children _____
145. high _____
146. more _____
147. party _____
148. than _____
149. why _____
150. ate _____
151. cold _____
152. happy _____
153. morning _____
154. pretty _____
155. thank _____
156. with _____
157. ball _____
158. color _____
159. if _____
160. much _____
161. pull _____
162. their _____
163. work _____
164. been _____
165. cry _____
166. into _____
167. must _____
168. rabbit _____
169. these _____
170. yellow _____
171. before _____
172. dog _____
173. just _____
174. name _____
175. read _____
176. think _____
177. began _____
178. door _____
179. laugh _____
180. never _____
181. shall _____
182. thought _____
183. better _____
184. far _____
185. light _____
186. new _____
187. side _____
188. took _____
189. black _____
190. fast _____
191. night _____
192. sleep _____
193. under _____
194. father _____
195. walk _____
196. five _____
197. four _____

2-1 Reader

198. always _____
199. does _____
200. going _____
201. live _____
202. pick _____
203. sure _____
204. another _____
205. each _____
206. grow _____
207. made _____
208. place _____
209. ten _____
210. because _____
211. end _____
212. hand _____
213. many _____
214. right _____
215. thing _____
216. best _____
217. enough _____
218. hard _____
219. men _____
220. round _____
221. those _____
222. book _____
223. even _____
224. head _____
225. near _____
226. say _____
227. together _____
228. both _____
229. every _____
230. hold _____
231. next _____
232. school _____
233. told _____
234. box _____
235. eye _____
236. home _____
237. once _____
238. should _____
239. until _____
240. bring _____
241. fall _____
242. hot _____
243. only _____
244. show _____
245. wait _____
246. carry _____
247. first _____
248. hurt _____
249. open _____
250. sit _____
251. warm _____
252. clean _____
253. found _____
254. keep _____
255. our _____
256. six _____
257. which _____
258. cut _____
259. friend _____
260. kind _____
261. own _____
262. start _____
263. while _____
264. full _____
265. last _____
266. still _____
267. wish _____
268. gave _____
269. left _____
270. year _____

2-2 Reader

271. dear _____
272. seem _____
273. today _____
274. done _____
275. seven _____
276. try _____
277. drink _____
278. sing _____
279. turn _____
280. off _____
281. small _____
282. use _____
283. most _____
284. such _____
285. wash _____
286. people _____
287. write _____
288. present _____

3-2 Reader

289. also _____
290. don't _____
291. draw _____
292. eight _____
293. goes _____
294. its _____
295. king _____
296. leave _____
297. myself _____
298. upon _____
299. grand _____

C

Preparing and Using the Materials for Testing Context Clues

PREPARATION OF MATERIALS FOR THE TEST

The author suggests that you remove pp. 238–243 which are the stimulus sheets for the student as well as the materials for you to look at while the student is reading his or her side of the materials. As an example, take the material on p. 238, duplicate it, and then cut the duplicate copy into two pieces so that it is composed of two halves. One half will be the material between the top and middle line and the other half will be the material between the middle and bottom line. It is suggested that you then rubber cement the material so that the material on the top half of the line is on one side of a 5″ x 8″ card and the material on the bottom half is on the other side. In cementing the materials to the card make sure that they are in a position so that when you are holding the card so the student can look at it and read what is written on his or her half, the other half is in a position so that you can read and check on the accuracy of the material at the same time. The material with the directions and underlined words will, of course, be the side you will be looking at while the student is reading the material on the opposite side which shows only the passage with words omitted and replaced with lines of equal length. It is also suggested that after cementing the materials on a 5″ x 8″ card you then laminate the cards and punch them so that they can be kept in a three-ring notebook binder.

DIRECTIONS FOR TESTING STUDENT'S KNOWLEDGE OF CONTEXT CLUES

Begin testing at a level that you are relatively sure would be the student's independent or easy instructional reading level. Hold the card so that the student can easily read the material on his or her side while you are still able to read the material on the side with the directions. Read the directions to the student. As the student reads the materials, note whether each of the six words that have been omitted are read correctly as noted on your side of the card. Also note whether a word is substituted that would make sense in the context of the sentence. If a word is substituted that makes sense in terms of both semantic and syntactic content, then count it as correct. No standard norms exist for any context clues text with which the author is familiar. However, the author suggests that you use the following general scale for judging the ability of each student:

No error	Excellent
One error	Good
Two errors	Fair
Three or more errors	Poor

FURTHER INFORMATION ON TESTING STUDENT'S KNOWLEDGE OF CONTEXT CLUES

It is extremely important to make sure that students are reading at a level that is not too difficult for them when being tested for their knowledge of the use of context clues. Materials should be no more difficult than the student's independent or easy instructional reading level. If the student is asked to read materials more difficult than this, the student is not likely to do well even if he or she is able to use context clues effectively. If you do not know the meaning of the terms independent and instructional reading levels, more information on them can be found in Chapter 6 on pp. 72–73.

Here is a story with some words left out. Each time a word is left out it has been replaced with a line. As you read and come to a line, try to figure out what word should go where the line is. Ready, begin.*

Jan has a cat.
The cat's *name* is Tab.
Tab does not *like* dogs.
One day *a* dog ran after Tab.
Tab ran up a tree.
The dog could not go *up* the tree.
Then *the* dog went away.

Grade 1 reading level (If the student gives a response that is obviously as good as the original, count it as correct.)

Jan has a cat.
The cat's ______ is Tab.
Tab does not ______ dogs.
One day ______ dog ran after Tab.
______ ran up a tree.
The dog could not go ______ the tree.
Then ______ dog went away.

* From: Ekwall, Eldon E. *Locating and correcting reading difficulties*, 4th ed. Columbus, Ohio: Charles E. Merrill, 1985. (Reprinted by permission of Charles E. Merrill)

Here is a story with some words left out. Each time a word is left out it has been replaced with a line. As you read and come to a line, try to figure out what word should go where the line is. Ready, begin.

One day Sam was going to school
He was riding with *his* father in their car.
He looked out of the window and *saw* an elephant
He said, "Look, father, *there* goes an elephant."
Sam's *father* did not even look because they were in a large city. That day *Sam's* father heard that an elephant had escaped from a circus.
That evening Sam's father said, "I'm sorry, Sam, you did *see* an elephant this morning."

Grade 2 reading level (If the student gives a response that is obviously as good as the original, count it as correct.)

One day Sam was going to school.
He was riding with ______ father in their car.
He looked out of the window and ______ an elephant.
He said, "Look father, ______ goes an elephant."
Sam's ______ did not even look because they were in a large city. That day ______ father heard that an elephant had escaped from a circus. That evening Sam's father said, "I'm sorry, Sam, you did ______ an elephant this morning."

Here is a story with some words left out. Each time a word is left out it has been replaced with a line. As you read and come to a line, try to figure out what word should go where the line is. Ready, begin.

Ann and her brother Mike like to play basketball in a park that is far from their home. When they *want* to play they usually take a bus to get *to* the park. There are other boys and girls *that* play there too. Sometimes when they *go* to the park their father and *mother* go with them. Their father and mother like to take some food and *have* a picnic while they are at the park.

Grade 3 reading level (If the student gives a response that is obviously as good as the original, count it as correct.)

Ann and her brother Mike like to play basketball in a park that is far from their home. When they ______ to play they usually take a bus to get ______ the park. There are other boys and girls ______ play there too. Sometimes when they ______ to the park their father and ______ go with them. Their father and mother like to take some food and ______ a picnic while they are at the park.

Here is a story with some words left out. Each time a word is left out it has been replaced with a line. As you read and come to a line, try to figure out what word should go where the line is. Ready, begin.

Most kinds of dogs make excellent pets. They *can* learn fast *and* they also *have* an excellent memory. An intelligent *dog* can learn *to* respond to many commands. Many dogs that have been taught well may learn more *than* 100 words and phrases.

Grade 4 reading level (If the student gives a response that is obviously as good as the original, count it as correct.)

Most kinds of dogs make excellent pets. They _______ learn fast and they also _______ an excellent memory. An intelligent _______ can learn _______ respond to many commands. Many dogs that have been taught well may learn more _______ 100 words and phrases.

Here is a story with some words left out. Each time a word is left out it has been replaced with a line. As you read and come to a line, try to figure out what word should go where the line is. Ready, begin.

Fire is very important to all of us today. Wherever ruins of early man have *been* found there has always been evidence *of* fire in that civilization. It is thought *that* early man may *have* first found fire when lightning struck trees and caused *them* to burn. Some people think that man might have been able *to* start fires by getting them from active volcanoes.

Grade 5 reading level (If the student gives a response that is obviously as good as the original, count it as correct.)

Fire is very important to all of us today. Wherever ruins of early man have ______ found there has always been evidence ______ fire in that civilization. It is thought ______ early man may ______ first found fire when lightning struck trees and caused ______ to burn. Some people think that man might have been able ______ start fires by getting them from active volcanoes.

Here is a story with some words left out. Each time a word is left out it has been replaced with a line. As you read and come to a line, try to figure out what word should go where the line is. Ready, begin.

One of the most famous eagles in the entire world is not the one we see on stamps or coins. It was *an* eagle caught by an Indian named Blue Sky *who* lived in Wisconsin. Blue Sky sold *the* eagle to a man that sold him to a soldier *in* the Civil War who named him Old Abe. Before the eagle died *he* had been through four years *of* war and had survived twenty-two battles.

Grade 6 reading level (If the student gives a response that is obviously as good as the original, count it as correct.)

One of the most famous eagles in the entire world is not the one we see on stamps or coins. It was _______ eagle caught by an Indian named Blue Sky _______ lived in Wisconsin. Blue Sky sold _______ eagle to a man that sold him to a soldier _______ the Civil War who named him Old Abe. Before the eagle died _______ had been through four years _______ war and had survived twenty-two battles.

D

Preparing and Using the *Quick Survey Word List* and the *El Paso Phonics Survey*

PREPARATION OF THE *QUICK SURVEY WORD LIST*

The author suggests that you cover the top of page 247 and then photocopy the *QUICK SURVEY WORD LIST* and place it in a three-ring notebook. Before placing it in the notebook you may wish to laminate it as it will be handled by students and in the process of usage may become soiled if not laminated.

DIRECTIONS FOR ADMINISTERING THE *QUICK SURVEY WORD LIST*

The *Quick Survey Word List* is designed to enable the tester to determine quickly if a student has the necessary word attack skills to read successfully material written at an adult level. It may be given to students at approximately the fourth-grade level, or above, to determine whether it is necessary to administer the *El Paso Phonics Survey.* The student is simply given the word list and asked to pronounce each word. The student should be told, however, that the words that he or she is about to attempt to pronounce are nonsense words or words that are not real. The student should also be told that the words are very difficult, but that you would like to know if he or she is able to pronounce them anyhow. If the student can pronounce each of the words correctly it would not be necessary to administer the *El Paso Phonics Survey,* since the ultimate purpose of learning sound-symbol correspondence is to enable the student to attack new words. On the other hand, if it becomes apparent, after one or two words, that the student is not able to pronounce the words on the *Quick Survey Word List,* then it should be discontinued and the *El Paso Phonics Survey* should be administered.

The correct pronunciation of the words on the *Quick Survey Word List* is shown on p. 248. This key shows the correct pronunciation as well as the part of each word that should be stressed. It should be remembered, however, that accent rules or generalizations pertaining to the English language are not consistent; therefore, if the words are pronounced correctly except for the accent or stress shown on certain syllables, they should be considered as correct.

FURTHER INFORMATION ON THE USE OF THE *QUICK SURVEY WORD LIST*

The *Quick Survey Word List* is also designed to test a student's knowledge of such word attack skills as syllabication, vowel rules, rules for *C, G,* and *Y,* and accent generalizations. It should, however, be stressed that students who do not do well on the list should be stopped after the first two or three words. *Only if the student is able to pronounce all of the words correctly* (except for accent) *would you continue through the entire list.* Having a student attempt to pronounce the words when he or she is not able to do so without difficulty will only tend to discourage the student. If the student does not do well on the first one or two words, then you should simply say, "Let's stop, these words are usually meant for adults and you would not be expected to be able to read them."

The correct pronounciation of the words is shown on p. 248. It should be kept in mind that there can be slight variances from the pronunciation shown, as with many words in the English language.

QUICK SURVEY WORD LIST

wratbeling

dawsnite

pramminciling

whetsplitter

gincule

cringale

slatrungle

twayfrall

spreanplit

goanbate

streegran

glammertickly

grantellean

aipcid

PRONUNCIATION OF QUICK SURVEY WORDS

răt′-bĕl-ĭng

däs′-nīt

prăm′-mĭn-cĭl-ĭng

hwĕt′-splĭt-tər

jĭn′-kyo͞ol

crĭn′-gāl

slăt′-rŭn-gəl

twā′-fräl

sprēn′-plĭt

gōn′-bāt

strē′-grăn

glăm′-mər-tĭck-ly

grăn′-tĕl-lēn

āp′-sĭd

PRONUNCIATION KEY

l — litt<u>le</u>

ə — <u>a</u>bout

ä — f<u>a</u>ther

ə — tamp<u>e</u>r

hw — <u>wh</u>at

kyo͞o — <u>cu</u>te

PREPARATION OF THE *EL PASO PHONICS SURVEY*

The author suggests that you remove pp. 253 to 255 (*El Paso Phonics Survey: General Directions* and *El Paso Phonics Survey: Special Directions*) and place them in a three-ring notebook for future reference in administering the *El Paso Phonics Survey.* You should also remove pp. 256 to 257 (*El Paso Phonics Survey: Answer Sheet*) and make multiple copies of this material to be used with students when administering the *El Paso Phonics Survey.* These pages should also be placed in a three-ring notebook so that they will be available for use in duplicating more copies of the answer sheet when more are needed. You should also remove pp. 259 to 260 and laminate them. These pages are the stimulus sheets for the *El Paso Phonics Survey* and they will be handled by students and, if not laminated, will become soiled. It is suggested that these pages also be kept in a three-ring notebook.

DIRECTIONS FOR ADMINISTERING THE *EL PASO PHONICS SURVEY*

As you will note, there are two sets of directions for administering the *El Paso Phonics Survey*—the *General Directions* and the *Special Directions.* The *General Directions* give overall instructions for administering the *El Paso Phonics Survey* and should be read thoroughly before attempting to give it for the first time. The *Special Directions* give information on specific items that should be helpful for teachers' aides and others not trained in phonics. They should, however, be read by anyone who is administering the *El Paso Phonics Survey* for the first time.

FURTHER INFORMATION ON THE *EL PASO PHONICS SURVEY*

In the pages preceding the *El Paso Phonics Survey* you will find a section entitled Advantages of the El Paso Phonics Survey. Knowing this information will ensure that in evaluating phonics tests you will not be "learning for obsolescence" as newer instruments are developed for use in phonics testing.

Advantages of the El Paso Phonics Survey

The El Paso Phonics Survey tests those initial consonants, consonant digraphs, consonant blends, vowels, diphthongs, and *r-, l-,* and *w*-controlled vowels of high utility. It also tests for knowledge of several commonly used vowel rules. Recent phonics research has shown that some commonly tested letter combinations are of such low utility, or appear in so few words, that learning their corresponding sounds is of little value to a reader. Furthermore, certain vowel combinations may represent so many variations of sounds that a student should not be expected to associate any one sound with these combinations. For example, the rule "when two vowels are together, then the first one is long and the second one is silent" has been shown to hold true less than 50 percent of the time. However, for the vowel combinations *ee, ea, ai, ay,* and *oa* this rule is generally applicable. Therefore, these and certain other combinations of high utility are tested.

The El Paso Phonics Survey must be administered individually. Most teachers would probably prefer to administer a group test. Our research at the Reading Center at the University of Texas at El Paso, however, has shown that it is doubtful that you can give a group test for phonics knowledge and obtain accurate results. Following are five commonly used methods of testing for phonics knowledge and what has been found to be wrong with each of them:

Method 1. Children are shown letters (*a, b, c,* and so forth) and are told to give the sounds of these letters.

First of all, although perhaps a minor point, the letters don't "have" sounds; they represent sounds, and we should ask the child to tell us the sound that these letters stand for. One of the major problems with this method, however, is in determining whether a certain sound given is correct. In playing tape recordings of children taking this type of test in our classes, we found that the agreement among the scores is so low that this method, although appearing somewhat valid, cannot in reality be at all valid since it is not even reliable—that is, the scorers do not agree on which answers are right and which are wrong. This type of test, then, lacks interscorer reliability. The main problem among the scorers is that they do not "hear" the same thing. For example, they cannot agree on whether they hear *er* or *ruh* for the *r* sound. Another problem with this method is that some children who know their sounds in the context of a word do not know the sounds in isolation. Testing sounds in isolation would yield irrelevant information in such cases.

Method 2. Children are given a piece of paper on which four letters, blends, and so forth appear beside each number. They are told to circle or underline the letter or blend that begins or ends, or has the same middle sound, as a word pronounced by the tester.

The problem with this type of test is that hearing a word and circling a sound heard in it is not the same as actual reading. Furthermore, it would be possible for the student to get one-fourth of the answers right on such a test even if he or she didn't know any of the answers (if there were four possible choices). There is a fairly high correlation between being able to do this and actually attacking a new word, and thus those children who are good at this task will probably be good at attacking words and vice versa. However, this type of test, as shown by our research, is simply not accurate enough for prescriptive teaching purposes.

Method 3. Children are given a sheet of paper with a blank beside each number. They are then instructed to write down the beginning sound, beginning blend, vowel sound, and so forth heard in a word pronounced by the tester.

This method has the same weaknesses as those described in Method 2—that is, it is not analogous to actual word attack in reading. It is perhaps a more appropriate test for spelling rather than reading knowledge.

Method 4. Children are shown nonsense words that contain the initial consonants, blends, vowels, and so forth to be tested. For example, in testing for knowledge of the *p* sound a child may be given the nonsense word "pide."

For some children this is a major problem. In order to pronounce the nonsense word "pide," they would have to know the following:

(a) The long and/or short vowel sound for *i;*
(b) The *d* sound;
(c) The vowel rule stating that when we have a vowel-consonant-final *e,* the first vowel is usually long and the *e* is silent.

As you can see, all of the knowledge included in this list is equal to, or more difficult than, simple knowledge of the *p* sound. Therefore, if the child doesn't respond, you would not really know whether it was because he or she did not know the *p* sound or whether, in reality, he or she had no knowledge of one, two, or all three areas listed above. It should also be kept in mind that vowel sounds and/or vowel rules are usually taught somewhat later than initial consonant sounds. Therefore, many children having difficulty with initial consonant sounds are likely to experience even more problems with vowel sounds and/or vowel rules.

Method 5. Children are given a list of real words each beginning with a specific initial consonant, blend, and so forth to be tested.

The problem here, of course, is that if the words are already in the child's sight vocabulary, this method does not provide a test of phonic word attack skills at all. And, if the words are not in the child's sight vocabulary, the same problems encountered in using nonsense words are also encountered here.

The El Paso Phonics Survey requires prior testing to make sure that the student knows three "stimulus words." "These words are *in, up,* and *am.* These words are almost always known by students near the end of the first grade and above. If they are not known, they must be taught to the student before he or she is tested. Each letter sound, blend, and so forth is then placed with one of these stimulus words as follows:

1. p	am	pam
2. n	up	nup

The student is asked to say the *name* of the letter (not its sound), the stimulus word, and then the nonsense word formed by putting the two together.

Administering a test of this nature is not difficult and the results are gratifying. You will also find this type of test to be highly reliable. Some of the reasons for, and advantages, of using this type of test are as follows:

1. It places the testing in a situation that is similar to actually reading—that is, the student has to react as he or she would in reading or "decode" words rather than "encode" as one does in spelling. Also sounds are not tested in isolation when this method is used.
2. Although nonsense words are used, you can feel assured that the student will know all of the word but the element being tested.

This way, if he or she fails to respond properly, you can be reasonably sure it is because he or she does not know the element being tested and not some other part of the word. In a few instances, students will fail to respond because they do not know how to blend. If you find that a student does not respond, then you can easily check to see whether blending is a problem by having him or her give the sounds in isolation. If he or she can give them in isolation, you can assume that blending is a problem. If he or she cannot do that, you can assume that he or she does not know the letter sounds.

3. The student is not being tested on words that may already be in his or her sight vocabulary; therefore, if he or she responds correctly, you are assured that he or she does not know the element being tested.
4. When the student responds, it is not at all difficult to determine whether the response is correct or incorrect. The author has often demonstrated this with fifty or more teachers in actual testing situations and has been able to get 100 percent agreement on all answers. When testing sounds in isolation, one seldom gets 100 percent agreement from fifty teachers on any answer.

A EL PASO PHONICS SURVEY: GENERAL DIRECTIONS

1. Before beginning the test, make sure the student has instant recognition of the test words that appear in the box at the top of the first page of the survey. These words should be known instantly by the student. If they are not, reschedule the test at a later date, after the words have been taught and the student has learned them.
2. Give the student the El Paso Phonics Survey stimulus sheet pages (D).
3. Point to the letter in the first column and have the student say the name of that letter (not the sound it represents). Then point to the word in the middle column and have the student pronounce it. Then point to the nonsense word in the third column and have the student pronounce it.
4. If the student can give the name of the letter, the word in the middle column, and the nonsense word in the third column, mark the answer sheet with a plus (+). If he or she cannot pronounce the nonsense word after giving the name of the letter and the word in the middle column, mark the answer sheet with a minus (−), or you may wish to write the word phonetically as the student pronounced it.
5. If the student can tell you the name of the letter and the small word in the middle column but cannot pronounce the nonsense word, you may wish to have him or her give the letter sound in isolation. If he or she can give the sound in isolation, either the student is unable to "blend" or does not know the letter well enough to give its sound and blend it at the same time.
6. Whenever a superior letter appears on the answer sheet, you may wish to refer to the Special Directions sheet (B).
7. To the right of each answer blank on the answer sheet, you will note a grade-level designation under the heading "PEK." This number represents the point at which most basal reading series would have already taught that sound. Therefore, at that point, you should expect it to be known. The designation 1.9 means the ninth month of the first year, and so forth.
8. When the student comes to two- or three-letter consonant digraphs or blends, as with *qu* in number 22, he or she is to say *"q-u"* as with the single letters. *Remember:* the student never gives letter sounds in isolation when engaged in actual reading.
9. When the student comes to the vowels (number 59), he or she is to say "short *a,*" and so forth, and then the nonsense word in column two. If the student does not know that the beve (˘) over the vowels means short *a, e,* and so forth, then explain this. Do the same with the long vowels where the macron (¯) appears.
10. All vowels and vowel combinations are put with only one or two of the first eight consonants. If any of these first eight consonants are not known, they should be taught before you attempt to test for vowel knowledge.
11. You will note that words appear to the right of some of the blanks on the answer sheet. These words illustrate the correct consonant or vowel sound that should be heard when the student responds.
12. Only phonic elements have been included that have a high enough utility to make them worthwhile learning. For example, the vowel pair *ui* appears very seldom, and when it does it may stand for the short *i* sound as in "build," the long *oo* sound as in "fruit," or the short *u* sound as in "luck." Therefore, there is really no reason to teach it as a sound. However, some letters, such as *oe,* may stand for several sounds but most often stand for one particular sound. In the case of *oe,* the long *o* sound should be used. In cases such as this, the most common sound is illustrated by a word to the right of the blank on the answer

sheet. If the student gives another correct sound for the letter(s), then say, "Yes, but what is another way that we could say this nonsense word?" The student must then say it as illustrated in the small word to the right of the blank on the answer sheet. Otherwise, count the answer as wrong.

13. Stop the test after five consecutive misses or if the student appears frustrated from missing a number of items even though he or she has not missed five consecutive items.

B EL PASO PHONICS SURVEY: SPECIAL DIRECTIONS

[a]3. If the student uses another *s* sound as in "sugar" (*sh*) in saying the nonsense word "sup," ask, "What is another *s* sound?" The student must use the *s* as in "sack."

[b]15. If the student uses the soft *c* sound as in "cigar" in saying the nonsense word "cam," ask, "What is another *c* sound?" The student must use the hard *c* sound as in "coat."

[c]16. If the student uses the soft *g* sound as in "gentle" in saying the nonsense word "gup," ask, "What is another *g* sound?" The student must use the hard *g* sound as in "gate."

[d]17. Ask, "What is the *y* sound when it comes at the beginning of a word?"

[e]23. The student must use the *ks* sound of *x*, and the nonsense word "mox" must rhyme with "box."

[f]33. If the student uses the *th* sound heard in "that," ask, "What is another *th* sound?" The student must use the *th* sound heard in "thing."

[g]34. If the student uses the *hoo* sound of *wh* in saying the nonsense word "whup," ask, "What is another *wh* sound?" The student must use the *wh* sound as in "when."

[h]69. The student may give either the *oo* sound heard in "moon" or the *oo* sound heard in "book." Be sure to note which one is used.

[i]70. If the same *oo* sound is given this time as was given for item 69, say, "Yes, that's right, but what is another way we could pronounce this nonsense word?" Whichever sound was *not* used in item 69 must be used here; otherwise, it is incorrect.

[j]71. The student may give either the *ea* sound heard in "head" or the *ea* sound heard in "meat." Be sure to note which one is used.

[k]72. If the same *ea* sound is given this time as was given for item 71, say "Yes, that's right, but what is another way we could pronounce this nonsense word?" Whichever sound was *not* used in item 71 must be used here; otherwise, it is incorrect.

[l]78. The student may give either the *ow* sound heard in "cow" or the *ow* sound heard in "crow." Be sure to note which one is used.

[m]79. If the same *ow* sound is given this time as was given for item 78, say, "Yes, that's right, but what is another way we could pronounce this nonsense word?" Whichever sound was not used in item 78 must be used here; otherwise, it is incorrect.

EL PASO PHONICS SURVEY: ANSWER SHEET*

NAME ____________________ SEX ________ DATE ____________________

SCHOOL ____________________ EXAMINER ____________________

Mark Answers as Follows

PEK *Point at which phonic element is expected to be known*

Pass +
Fail – (or write word as pronounced)

			Answers	PEK
Initial Consonant Sounds				
1.	p	pam	______	1.9
2.	n	nup	______	1.9
[a]3.	s	sup	______	1.9
4.	t	tup	______	1.9
5.	r	rin	______	1.9
6.	m	min	______	1.9
7.	b	bup	______	1.9
8.	d	dup	______	1.9
9.	w	wam	______	1.9
10.	h	hup	______	1.9
11.	f	fin	______	1.9
12.	j	jin	______	1.9
13.	k	kam	______	1.9
14.	l	lin	______	1.9
[b]15.	c	cam	______	1.9
[c]16.	g	gup	______	1.9
[d]17.	y	yin	______	1.9
18.	v	vam	______	1.9
19.	z	zin	______	1.9
20.	c	cin	______	2.5(sin)
21.	g	gin	______	2.9(jin)
22.	qu	quam	______	1.9
Ending Consonant X				
[e]23.	x	mox	______	1.9
Initial Consonant Clusters				
24.	pl	plup	______	1.9
25.	fr	frin	______	1.9
26.	fl	flam	______	1.9
27.	st	stup	______	1.9
28.	bl	blin	______	1.9
29.	tr	trin	______	1.9
30.	gr	grup	______	1.9

			Answers	PEK
31.	br	brin	______	1.9
32.	sh	shup	______	1.9
[f]33.	th	thup	______	1.9(thing)
[g]34.	wh	whup	______	1.9(when)
35.	ch	cham	______	2.5(church)
36.	dr	drup	______	2.5
37.	pr	pram	______	2.5
38.	sl	slup	______	2.5
39.	cl	clin	______	2.5
40.	gl	glam	______	2.5
41.	sm	smin	______	2.5
42.	sk	skam	______	2.5
43.	cr	crin	______	2.5
44.	tw	twam	______	2.5
45.	sn	snup	______	2.5
46.	sch	scham	______	2.5
47.	sp	spam	______	2.9
48.	sc	scup	______	2.9
49.	str	stram	______	2.9
50.	thr	thrup	______	2.9
51.	shr	shrup	______	2.9
52.	squ	squam	______	2.9
53.	sw	swup	______	3.5
54.	spr	spram	______	3.5
55.	spl	splin	______	3.5
56.	wr	wrin	______	4.5
57.	dw	dwin	______	4.5
58.	scr	scrup	______	4.5
Vowels, Vowel Teams, and Special Letter Combinations				
59.	ă	tam	______	1.9
60.	ĭ	rit	______	1.9
61.	ĕ	nep	______	1.9
62.	ŏ	sot	______	1.9

			Answers	PEK
63.	ŭ	tum	______	1.9
64.	ĭ	tipe	______	2.5
65.	ē	rete	______	2.5
66.	ā	sape	______	2.5
67.	ū	pune	______	2.5
68.	ō	sote	______	2.5
[h]69.	oo	oot	______	2.5(moon or book)
[i]70.	oo	oot	______	2.5(moon or book)
[j]71.	ea	eap	______	2.5(head or meat
[k]72.	ea	eam	______	2.5(head or meat)
73.	ai	ait	______	2.5(ape)
74.	ay	tay	______	2.5(hay)
75.	oe	poe	______	2.5(hoe)

			Answers	PEK
76.	oa	oan	______	2.5(soap)
77.	ee	eem	______	2.5(heed)
[l]78.	ow	owd	______	2.5(cow or crow)
[m]79.	ow	fow	______	2.5(cow or crow)
80.	or	orm	______	2.5(corn)
81.	ir	irt	______	2.5(hurt)
82.	ur	urd	______	2.5(hurt)
83.	aw	awp	______	2.9(paw)
84.	oi	doi	______	2.9(boy)
85.	ou	tou	______	2.9(cow)
86.	ar	arb	______	2.9(harp)
87.	oy	moy	______	2.9(boy)
88.	er	ert	______	2.9(her)
89.	ew	bew	______	2.9(few)
90.	au	dau	______	2.9(paw)

* Superior letters indicate notes listed in El Paso Phonics Survey: Special Directions.

EL PASO PHONICS SURVEY*

Test Words	in	up	am

1.	p	am	pam
2.	n	up	nup
3.	s	up	sup
4.	t	up	tup
5.	r	in	rin
6.	m	in	min
7.	b	up	bup
8.	d	up	dup
9.	w	am	wam
10.	h	up	hup
11.	f	in	fin
12.	j	in	jin
13.	k	am	kam
14.	l	in	lin
15.	c	am	cam
16.	g	up	gup
17.	y	in	yin
18.	v	am	vam
19.	z	in	zin
20.	c	in	cin
21.	g	in	gin
22.	qu	am	quam
23.	m	ox	mox
24.	pl	up	plup
25.	fr	in	frin
26.	fl	am	flam
27.	st	up	stup
28.	bl	in	blin
29.	tr	in	trin
30.	gr	up	grup
31.	br	in	brin
32.	sh	up	shup
33.	th	up	thup
34.	wh	up	whup
35.	ch	am	cham
36.	dr	up	drup
37.	pr	am	pram
38.	sl	up	slup
39.	cl	in	clin
40.	gl	am	glam
41.	sm	in	smin
42.	sk	am	skam
43.	cr	in	crin
44.	tw	am	twam
45.	sn	up	snup
46.	sch	am	scham
47.	sp	am	spam
48.	sc	up	scup
49.	str	am	stram
50.	thr	up	thrup
51.	shr	up	shrup
52.	squ	am	squam

EL PASO PHONICS SURVEY*

Test Words	in	up	am

53.	sw	up	swup
54.	spr	am	spram
55.	spl	in	splin
56.	wr	in	wrin
57.	dw	in	dwin
58.	scr	up	scrup
59.	ă	tam	
60.	ĭ	rit	
61.	ĕ	nep	
62.	ŏ	sot	
63.	ŭ	tum	
64.	ī	tipe	
65.	ē	rete	
66.	ā	sape	
67.	ū	pune	
68.	ō	sote	
69.	oo	oot	
70.	oo	oot	
71.	ea	eap	

72.	ea	eam
73.	ai	ait
74.	ay	tay
75.	oe	poe
76.	oa	oan
77.	ee	eem
78.	ow	owd
79.	ow	fow
80.	or	orm
81.	ir	irt
82.	ur	urd
83.	aw	awp
84.	oi	doi
85.	ou	tou
86.	ar	arb
87.	oy	moy
88.	er	ert
89.	ew	bew
90.	au	dau

E

Preparation and Use of Materials for Testing Knowledge of Vowel Rules and Syllable Principles

PREPARING FOR THE TEST

The materials on pp. 266–270 should first be photocopied. You will note that there are eighteen rectangles, each with something printed on it. These are meant to be cut out and rubber cemented or taped to 3″ x 5″ cards. They should then be laminated. You will note that the cards are numbered from 1 to 15; however, there is a 1–B, a 7–B, and a 14–B. The 1–B should be cemented to the back of number 1, 7–B should be cemented to the back of number 7, and 14–B should be cemented to the back of number 14. In cementing the materials to the backs of these three cards, make sure that the material on both sides of the cards is placed so that you can read the material on the back of the card while someone is reading the material on the front of the card. When you have finished laminating each card, place them in order, face up on the table so that they are numbered from 1–15. You may wish to use a rubber band to keep them in this order when not being used.

You will also note that on pp. 264–265 there is an answer sheet for each of the vowel rules and syllable principles. These should be removed from the text and duplicated so that you will have a copy for each student being tested.

SPECIFIC DIRECTIONS FOR TESTING VOWEL RULES AND SYLLABLE PRINCIPLES

Have your answer sheet in front of you, so you can mark it easily as the student responds. Show the student the first card that says *Syllable Principles* on the front. At this time read the material on the back of this card to the student. After reading the directions on the back of this card, show the student the first card with words on it (#2). Take the card marked #1 and put it on the back of the deck and continue in this order. Ask the student to read each of the nonsense words. If the student reads all of the words correctly, then mark syllable principle number 1 as correct with a plus (+) or if it is wrong mark it with a minus (−). Continue in this manner until you have tested all of the syllable principles. The testing of the vowel rules is done by the same procedure as the testing of the syllable principles.

IMPORTANT POINTS TO REMEMBER

When testing for knowledge of vowel rules and syllable principles, remember that the ultimate goal is to enable the student to *use,* not just to *recite* the rule or principle that applies to each word.

Phonics research in the past two decades has not always been used to the best advantage; too many outdated rules appear in textbooks and teacher's manuals even today. The material on the following pages is designed to test the student's knowledge of phonics rules in terms of using the rules and principles, rather than reciting them.*

* From: Ekwall, Eldon E. *Locating and correcting reading difficulties,* 4th ed. Columbus, Ohio: Charles E. Merrill, 1985. (Reprinted by permission of Charles E. Merrill)

ANSWER SHEET FOR VOWEL RULES AND SYLLABLE PRINCIPLES TEST

NAME OF STUDENT____
(Last) (First) (Middle Initial)

GRADE IN SCHOOL__________ SEX_____ DATE TESTED________________________________

Syllable Principles

Instructions: Make a plus (+) on the line following the number of the syllable principle if the answer is correct. Make a minus (–) on the line following the number of the syllable principle if the answer is incorrect.*

1. _____ Divide wherever there are two consonants surrounded by vowels providing there are no consonant clusters between the vowels. al/pil, op/por, bot/nap, and cur/ron
2. _____ When a word ends in consonant-*le,* the consonant preceding the *le* is included in the syllable with *le.* na/ple, fra/ble, da/ple, and sa/ple
3. _____ Divide between compound words and normal places in the words making up the compound words, cow/per/son, dog/leg, and cow/lick
4. _____ Do not divide between consonant digraphs or blends (consonant clusters). In this case treat the cluster as though it were a single consonant and divide the word so that the "cluster" goes with the second vowel as in #5 below, or as you would in #1 above. ba/chop, ba/shil, and da/phod
5. _____ In vowel-consonant-vowel situations "VCV" first try dividing so that the consonant goes with the second vowel. mo/nan, fa/dop, and da/lop

Vowel Rules

Instructions: Mark vowel rules the same as the syllable principles above using a (+) or a (–).

1. _____ Single syllable words with only one vowel at the end should usually be pronounced so that the vowel stands for its long sound. ra, de, and po
2. _____ A single vowel at the end of a syllable in a multisyllable word should be given the long sound first. molo, game, and ralo
3. _____ A single vowel in a closed syllable usually stands for the short sound of the vowel. loc, pid, and dap
4. _____ Whenever "r" follows a vowel, providing it is in the same syllable, it usually changes the sound of the vowel. (They may be grouped as follows: *er, ur, ir* sound as *ur* in *fur; ar* sounds like the *ar* in *car;* and *or* sounds like *or* in *corn.*) der, bir, cur, par, and por
5. _____ The letters *w* and *l* influence the vowel sound preceding them making the vowel neither long nor short. This is true more of the time when there is a double *l.* kaw, rall, baw, and kall
6. _____ When a vowel-consonant-final *e* appears at the end of a word, the first vowel will usually stand for its long sound. Although this is not true an extremely large percentage of the time, it is more true than not. nide, lode, and pake

* The student should get all of the responses correct within each rule for that rule to be considered as mastered.

7. _____ A *y* at the end of a single syllable word, preceded by a consonant, usually stands for the long *i* sound. (Note that in this rule the *y* must be preceded by a consonant.) bly and cly
8. _____ A *y* at the end of a multisyllable word preceded by a consonant usually stands for the long *e* sound. (Note in this rule the *y* must be preceded by a consonant and not a vowel.) noply and dalry
9. _____ A *y* at the beginning of a word usually has the *y* consonant sound as in the word *yard.* yamp and yorp

Syllable Principles

1

Syllable Principles

Say, "Here are some nonsense words. In other words they are not real words. Tell me where you would divide them into syllables if they were real words."

Optional

Why?

1–B

alpil
oppor
botnap
curron

2

naple
frable
daple
saple

3

cowperson dogleg cowlick 4	bachop bashil daphod 5
monan fadop dalop 6	Vowel Rules 7

Vowel Rules

Say, "I'm going to show you some nonsense words again. This time tell me how you would pronounce each word."

Optional

Why?

7–B

ra
de
po

8

molo
gamo
ralo

9

loc
pid
dap

10

der
bir
cur
par
por

11

kaw
rall
baw
kall

12

nide
lode
pake

13

Rules for "Y"

14

Rules for "Y"

Say, "Here are some more nonsense words. They will help me know if you know how to pronounce the 'Y' sound."

Optional

Why?

14–B

bly
cly
noply
dalry
yamp
yorp

15

F

Preparation and Use of Materials for Testing Knowledge of Contractions

PREPARING FOR THE TEST

Before administering the test it is suggested that you remove p. 273 (KNOWLEDGE OF CONTRACTIONS ANSWER SHEET) and duplicate it so that you will have multiple copies to use as answer sheets for testing each student. Be sure to place this sheet back into your three-ring notebook so that you will have it for duplicating more answer sheets as they are needed. Also remove p. 274 (KNOWLEDGE OF CONTRACTIONS TESTING SHEET) and rubber cement or tape it to a piece of oaktag or tagboard. It is also suggested that it be laminated as you will be giving it to students to handle and with time it will become soiled if it is not laminated.

SPECIFIC DIRECTIONS FOR TESTING FOR KNOWLEDGE OF CONTRACTIONS

Have your KNOWLEDGE OF CONTRACTIONS ANSWER SHEET ready (p. 273) and give the student the stimulus sheet. Then read the directions that appear on the answer sheet.

IMPORTANT POINTS TO REMEMBER

A rather high percentage of students have occasional problems with the pronunciation of contractions; however, you are likely to find a greater percentage who do not know what two words each of the various contractions stand for. It should be kept in mind that pronunciation is more important for reading purposes, but students will not use a contraction, in their writing, until they know the two words for which each contraction stands.

KNOWLEDGE OF CONTRACTIONS ANSWER SHEET

NAME ______________________ DATE ______________________

SCHOOL ______________________ TESTER ______________________

Directions: Say, "Here is a list of contractions. I want you to begin with number one and say the contraction and then tell me what two words it stands for." Following each contraction are two lines. If the student is able to pronounce the contraction correctly, put a plus (+) in the first block. If he or she can then tell you what two words it stands for, put a plus (+) in the second blank. Mark wrong answers with a minus (−). The grade-level designation following each blank stands for the point at which the contraction should be known.

1. let's	____	____	2.9
2. didn't	____	____	2.9
3. it's	____	____	2.9
4. won't	____	____	2.9
5. that's	____	____	2.9
6. can't	____	____	2.9
7. wasn't	____	____	2.9
8. isn't	____	____	2.9
9. hadn't	____	____	2.9
10. don't	____	____	3.5
11. I'll	____	____	3.5
12. we'll	____	____	3.5
13. I've	____	____	3.5
14. he'll	____	____	3.5
15. hasn't	____	____	3.5
16. haven't	____	____	3.5
17. aren't	____	____	3.5
18. I'm	____	____	3.5
19. he's	____	____	3.5
20. we're	____	____	3.5
21. you're	____	____	3.5
22. what's	____	____	3.5
23. there's	____	____	3.5
24. she's	____	____	3.5
25. wouldn't	____	____	3.5
26. she'll	____	____	3.5
27. here's	____	____	3.5
28. ain't	____	____	3.9
29. couldn't	____	____	3.9
30. they're	____	____	3.9
31. they'd	____	____	3.9
32. you'll	____	____	4.5
33. she'd	____	____	4.5
34. weren't	____	____	4.5
35. I'd	____	____	4.5
36. you've	____	____	4.5
37. you'd	____	____	4.5
38. we'd	____	____	4.5
39. anybody'd	____	____	4.5
40. there'll	____	____	4.5
41. we've	____	____	4.5
42. who'll	____	____	4.5
43. he'd	____	____	4.5
44. who'd'	____	____	4.5
45. doesn't	____	____	4.5
46. where's	____	____	4.5
47. they've	____	____	4.5
48. they'll	____	____	4.5

KNOWLEDGE OF CONTRACTIONS TESTING SHEET

1. let's
2. didn't
3. it's
4. won't
5. that's
6. can't
7. wasn't
8. isn't
9. hadn't
10. don't
11. I'll
12. we'll
13. I've
14. he'll
15. hasn't
16. haven't
17. aren't
18. I'm
19. he's
20. we're
21. you're
22. what's
23. there's
24. she's
25. wouldn't
26. she'll
27. here's
28. ain't
29. couldn't
30. they're
31. they'd
32. you'll
33. she'd
34. weren't
35. I'd
36. you've
37. you'd
38. we'd
39. anybody'd
40. there'll
41. we've
42. who'll
43. he'd
44. who'd
45. doesn't
46. where's
47. they've
48. they'll

G

Tests Useful in Diagnosing and Remediation of Disabled Readers

*Auditory Discrimination Tests**

Name and date of test	Vocabulary	Comprehension	Word attack	Speed	Listening	Other	Time for administration	Number of forms	Grade level	Group (G) or individual (I)	Publisher*
	Skills or Areas Measured										
Goldman-Fristoe-Woodcock Test of Auditory Discrimination (no date given)					X	Measures speech-sound discrimination	10–15 min.	1	Ages 4 and over	I	American Guidance Service
Wepman Auditory Discrimination Test (1973)					X	Recognize the sound differences between minimal pairs	15–20 min.	2	K–3	I	Language Research Associates

*Addresses of test publishers appear in the back of this appendix.

Basic Sight Word Inventories

Name and date of test	Skills or Areas Measured: Vocabulary	Comprehension	Word attack	Speed	Listening	Other	Time for administration	Number of forms	Grade level	Group (G) or individual (I)	Publisher*
Dolch Basic Sight Word Test (1942)						Tests recognition of 220 high-utility words	Varies	1	All levels	G	Garrard Press
The Group Instant Words Recognition Test (no date given)						Sight recognition of 600 most common words	Varies	2	All levels	G&I	Jamestown Publishers
Harris-Jacobson List (1980)						Tests recognition of 335 high-utility words	Varies	1	All levels	I	Harris, Albert J., and Sipay, Edward R. *How to Increase Reading Ability*. New York: Longman, 1980, pp. 372–373.

Basic Sight Word Inventories (continued)

Name and date of test	Skills or Areas Measured: Vocabulary	Comprehension	Word attack	Speed	Listening	Other	Time for administration	Number of forms	Grade level	Group (G) or individual (I)	Publisher
The Instant Words Criterion Test (1981)						Sight recognition of 300 most common words	Varies	1	All levels	I	Jamestown Publishers
Johnson Basic Sight Vocabulary Test (1973)						Tests recognition of 300 high-utility words	Varies	2	1–3	I	Personal (University of Wisconsin, Madison, Wisconsin)

Commercial Informal Reading Inventories (see also Chapter 3, Commercially Developed Informal Reading Inventories)

Name and date of test	Skills or Areas Measured: Vocabulary	Comprehension	Word attack	Speed	Listening	Other	Time for administration	Number of forms	Grade level	Group (G) or individual (I)	Publisher
Analytical Reading Inventory (1981)	X	X			X	Graded word lists	Varies	3	2–9	I	Charles E. Merrill
Bader Reading & Language Inventory		X	X			Spelling, Graded Word Lists	Varies	3	pp–12	I	Macmillan
Basic Reading Inventory (1978)	X	X				Graded word lists	Varies	3	Pre-primer–8	I	Kendall/Hunt
The Classroom Reading Inventory (1982)	X	X				Graded word lists, graded spelling survey	12 min.	4	All levels	I	William C. Brown
The Contemporary Classroom Reading Inventory (1980)	X	X				Group cloze tests, graded word lists	Varies	3	2–9	I	Gorsuch Scarisbrick

Commercial Informal Reading Inventories (*see also* Chapter 3, *Commercially Developed Informal Reading Inventories*) (continued)

Name and date of test	Skills or Areas Measured: **Vocabulary**	**Comprehension**	**Word attack**	**Speed**	**Listening**	**Other**	**Time for administration**	**Number of forms**	**Grade level**	**Group (G) or individual (I)**	**Publisher**
Diagnostic Reading Inventory (1979)	X	X			X	Graded word lists, phrase list	Varies	1	3–8	I	Kendall/Hunt
Ekwall Reading Inventory (1986)	X	X	X	X	X	Graded word list, El Paso Phonics Survey	21–30 min. depending on level	4	Pre-primer–9	I	Allyn and Bacon
Informal Reading Assessment (1980)	X	X		X	X	Graded word lists		4	Pre-primer–12	I	Rand McNally
Sucher-Allred Reading Placement Inventory (1981)	X	X				Word recognition test, oral reading test	20 min.	1	Primer–9	I	Economy

Content-Area Inventories

Name and date of test	Skills or Areas Measured: Vocabulary	Comprehension	Word attack	Speed	Listening	Other	Time for administration	Number of forms	Grade level	Group (G) or individual (I)	Publisher
Content Inventories: English, Social Studies, Science (1979)	X	X				Cloze tests, study skills	Varies	1	4–12; English, 7–12	G	Kendall/Hunt

Decoding Inventories

Name and date of test	Skills or Areas Measured: Vocabulary	Comprehension	Word attack	Speed	Listening	Other	Time for administration	Number of forms	Grade level	Group (G) or individual (I)	Publisher
Decoding Inventory, 3 levels (1979)			X			Auditory and visual discrimination, context clues	Varies	1	Pre-primer–4 and above	I	Kendall/Hunt

Intelligence Tests

Name and date of test	Skills or Areas Measured: Vocabulary	Comprehension	Word attack	Speed	Listening	Other	Time for administration	Number of forms	Grade level	Group (G) or individual (I)	Publisher
McCarthy Scales of Children's Abilities (1972)						Assess motor and intellectual development	45 min. for age 5 and under; 1 hour for older children	1	Ages 2½–8½	I	Psychological Corporation
Peabody Picture Vocabulary Test—Revised (PPVT-R) (1981)						For testing verbal intelligence through pictures	15 min. or less	1	Ages 2½–40	I	American Guidance Service
Slosson Intelligence Test (1981)						A measure of intelligence	10–30 min.	1	Age 1–adult	I	Slosson Educational Publications
Stanford-Binet Intelligence Scale, Form LM (1972 Norms)	X	X				A measure of overall intelligence	45–90 min.	1	2–12 and sometimes older	I	Houghton Mifflin

Wechsler Adult Intelligence Scale—Revised (WAIS-R) (1980)	X	X				A measure of intelligence using subtests	1 hr.	1	Ages 16–74	I	Psychological Corporation
Wechsler Intelligence Scale for Children—Revised (WISC-R) (1974)	X	X				A measure of intelligence using subtests	1 hr.	1	Ages 6.0–16.11	I	Psychological Corporation
Wechsler Preschool and Primary Scale of Intelligence (WPPSI) (1967)	X	X				A measure of intelligence using subtests	50–70 min.	1	Ages 4–6½	I	Psychological Corporation

Language Dominance and/or Assessment Tests

Name and date of test	Vocabulary	Comprehension	Word attack	Speed	Listening	Other	Time for administration	Number of forms	Grade level	Group (G) or individual (I)	Publisher
	Skills or Areas Measured										
Ambiguous Word Language Dominance Test (1978)						Spanish/ English language dominance	30 min.	1	Age 10 and above	I	Publishers Test Service, McGraw-Hill
Flexibility Language Dominance Test (1978)						Spanish/ English language dominance	30 min.	1	Age 10 and above	G	Publishers Test Service, McGraw-Hill
Houston Test for Language Development (1978)	X	X	X		X	Also nonverbal communication	20–40 min. depending on age	2	Infancy–6 yrs.	I	Stoelting
Language Assessment Battery (LAB) (1977)					X	Subtests in reading, writing, speaking				K–2, I; 3–12, G&I	Riverside Publishing
English Edition							41 min.	1	K–12		
Spanish Edition							41 min.	1	K–12		

Readiness Tests (Including Bilingual)

Name and date of test	Skills or Areas Measured						Time for administration	Number of forms	Grade level	Group (G) or individual (I)	Publisher
	Vocabulary	Comprehension	Word attack	Speed	Listening	Other					
Comprehensive Tests of Basic Skills, Readiness Test (1977)					X	Letter names, letter forms, phonics	2 hrs. 39 min.	1	K–1.3	G	CTB/ McGraw-Hill
Cooperative Preschool Inventory						Knowledge of self, ability to follow directions, verbal expression, number concepts					Addison-Wesley
English Edition (1970)							Approx. 15 min.	1	Preschool	I	
Spanish Edition (1974)							Approx. 30 min	1	Preschool	I	
Metropolitan Readiness Tests, 2 levels (1976)		X			X	Auditory and visual discrimination, phonics, math	Level 1, 90 min.; Level 2, 3 hrs.	2	K–1	G	Psychological Corporation

	Skills or Areas Measured										
Name and date of test	**Vocabulary**	**Comprehension**	**Word attack**	**Speed**	**Listening**	**Other**	**Time for administration**	**Number of forms**	**Grade level**	**Group (G) or individual (I)**	**Publisher**
Assessment of Reading Growth (1981)											Jamestown Publishers
Level 9		X					50 min.	1	2–4	G	
Level 13		X					50 min.	1	6–8	G	
Level 17		X					42 min.	1	10–12	G	
Botel Reading Inventory (1978)						Used to find the student's highest instructional level	Varies		All levels	I	Follett
Spelling Placement Test								1			
Word Recognition Test	X					Estimate of oral reading fluency		2			
Word Opposites Test		X						2			
Decoding Test			X					1			

California Achievement Tests, C & D (Reading) (1977)	X	X					45–60 min.	2	K–12	G	CTB/McGraw-Hill
Comprehensive Tests of Basic Skills, Español (Reading) (1978)	X	X				Based on *CTBS S & T*	45–60 min.	1	K–8	G	CTB/McGraw-Hill
Comprehensive Tests of Basic Skills, S & T (Reading) (1973)	X	X					45–60 min.	2	K–12	G	CTB/McGraw-Hill
Comprehensive Tests of Basic Skills U & V (Reading) (1981)	X	X	X				45–70 min.	2	K–12	G	CTB/McGraw-Hill
Diagnostic Reading Scales (1981)	X	X	X		X	Graded word lists, reading passages, word-analysis tests	Varies	1	1–8 and above	I	McGraw-Hill
Doren Diagnostic Reading Test of Word Recognition Skills (1973)			X			Spelling and sight words	1–3 hrs.	1	1–6	G	American Guidance Service

Name and date of test	Vocabulary	Comprehension	Word attack	Speed	Listening	Other	Time for administration	Number of forms	Grade level	Group (G) or individual (I)	Publisher
	Skills or Areas Measured										
Durrell Analysis of Reading Difficulty—Revised (1980)	X	X	X	X	X	Spelling, visual, and auditory discrimination	Untimed: approx. 30–40 min.	1	1–6	I	Psychological Corporation
Gates-MacGinitie Reading Tests (1978)							65 min.	2			Riverside Publishing
Basic R	X	X							1.0–1.9	G	
A	X	X							1.5–1.9	G	
B	X	X							2	G	
C	X	X							3	G	
D	X	X							4–6	G	
E	X	X							7–9	G	
F	X	X							10–12	G	
Gates-McKillop-Horowitz (1981)			X			Spelling, auditory discrimination	Untimed	1	1–6	I	Teachers College Press
Iowa Silent Reading Tests, 3 levels (1973)	X	X		X		Study skills	56 min.–1½ hrs. depending on level	2	6–12, college	G	Psychological Corporation

Iowa Tests of Basic Skills (1982)											Riverside Publishing
Early Primary Battery	X	X	X		X	Also subtests in language, mathematics	2 hrs.–2 hrs. 40 min.	1	K–1.9	G	
Primary Battery	X	X	X		X	Same as above plus work-study skills	3 hrs. 55 min.	1	1.7–3.5	G	
Multilevel Battery	X	X				Language, math, work-study skills	4 hrs. 4 min.	2	3–8	G	
Iowa Tests of Educational Development (1978)	X	X				Language arts and mathematics	2¼ hrs.	2	9–12	G	SRA
McCarthy Individualized Diagnostic Reading Inventory (1976)	X	X	X			Study skills	Part 1, 35 min.–1 hr.; Part 2, 34 min.	1	2–12	I	Stoelting
Metropolitan Achievement Tests (Reading) (1978)		X					30–50 min. depending on level	2	K–12	G	Psychological Corporation
Nelson-Denny Reading Test (1981)	X	X		X			35 min.	2	9–12, college, adult	G	Riverside Publishing

Reading Tests (continued)

	Skills or Areas Measured										
Name and date of test	**Vocabulary**	**Comprehension**	**Word attack**	**Speed**	**Listening**	**Other**	**Time for administration**	**Number of forms**	**Grade level**	**Group (G) or individual (I)**	**Publisher**
Nelson Reading Skills Test (1977)		X				Word meaning	33 min.	2	3–9	G	Houghton Mifflin
Oral Reading Criterion Test (no date given)			X			To determine independent and instructional levels	Varies	1	1–7	I	Jamestown Publishers
Peabody Individual Achievement Test (no date given)		X	X			Spelling, math, general information	30–40 min.	1	K–adult	I	American Guidance Service
Performance Assessment in Reading (PAIR) (1978)	X	X				Study skills	Varies	1	Jr. high	G	CTB/McGraw-Hill
Pressey Diagnostic Reading Tests (no date given)	X	X		X			25 min. per section (3)	2	3–9	G	Bobbs-Merrill

School and College Ability Tests (SCAT) Series III (1979)	X	X					20 min.	2	3.5–12.9	G	Addison-Wesley
Sequential Tests of Educational Progress (STEP III)											Addison-Wesley
Primary Levels A–D (1974)		X	X		X		Untimed: 30–40 min. (approx.)	2	Pre-primary–3.5	G	
Intermediate and Advanced E–J (1979)	X	X			X		40 min.	2	3.5–12.9	G	
Sipay Word Analysis Test (SWAT) (1974)			X			Tests word analysis in detail	Varies	1	All levels	I	Stoelting
Skills Monitoring System—Reading (1977)	X	X					Untimed	1	3–5	I	Psychological Corporation
Slosson Oral Reading Test (1977)			X				3 min.	1	Pre-school–high school	I	Slosson Educational Publications

Reading Tests (continued)

Name and date of test	Skills or Areas Measured: Vocabulary	Comprehension	Word attack	Speed	Listening	Other	Time for administration	Number of forms	Grade level	Group (G) or individual (I)	Publisher
SRA Achievement Series (1978)						Reading, math, language arts					SRA
Primary Levels (Levels A–D)	X	X	X		X	Auditory discrimination	2½–3 hrs. depending on level	2	K–3	G	
Upper Levels (3rd edition) (Levels E–H)	X	X					3 hrs.	2	4–12	G	
Stanford Achievement Test (1973)	X	X	X		X	Spelling	75–150 min. depending on level	2	1.5–9.9	G	Psychological Corporation
Stanford Diagnostic Reading Test (1978)	X	X	X	X		Auditory discrimination	96–145 min. depending on level	2	1.6–13	G	Harcourt Brace Jovanovich
Stanford Test of Academic Skills (TASK) (1973)		X					40 min.	2	8–13	G	Psychological Corporation

Tests of Achievement and Proficiency (1982)		X				Subtests in study skills and other subject areas	4 hrs.	1	9–12	G	Riverside Publishing
Tests of Adult Basic Education, 3 levels of difficulty (1978)	X	X				Also language, math for vocational-bound persons	1½–2½ hrs. depending on level	1	Adult	G	CTB/McGraw-Hill
Test of Reading Comprehension (1978)	X	X					Varies	1	2–12	G	Pro-Ed
The 3-Rs Test (1982)						Subtests in reading, math, language	130 min.	2	K–12	G	Riverside Publishing
Wide Range Achievement Tests (*WRAT*) (1978)			X			Also, spelling and math	15–30 min.	1	Ages 5–adult	I	Stoelting
Woodcock Reading Mastery Test (1974)		X	X			Letter identification	20–30 min.	2	K–12	I	American Guidance Service

Other

Name and date of test	Skills or Areas Measured: Vocabulary	Comprehension	Word attack	Speed	Listening	Other	Time for administration	Number of forms	Grade level	Group (G) or individual (I)	Publisher
Basic Achievement Skills Individual Screener (BASIS) (1983)		X				Spelling Mathematics Writing exercise	Untimed (Under 1 hr.)	2	Readiness to 8th	I	Psychological Corporation
Test of Written Language (1983)						Thematic maturity Spelling Vocabulary	None given	1	Ages 7–0 to 18–11	G	Pro-Ed

ADDRESSES OF TEST PUBLISHERS

Addison-Wesley Publishing Company
Jacob Way
Reading, MA 01867

Allyn and Bacon, Inc.
7 Wells Ave.
Newton, MA 02159

American Guidance Service
Publishers Building
Circle Pines, MN 55014

Bobbs-Merrill Educational Publishing
4300 West 62nd Street
Indianapolis, IN 46206

Charles E. Merrill
1300 Alum Creek Drive
Columbus, OH 43216

CTB/McGraw-Hill
Del Monte Research Park
Monterey, CA 93940

The Economy Company
Box 25308
1901 West Walnut Street
Oklahoma City, OK 73125

Follett Publishing Company
Dept. D. M.
1010 West Washington Blvd.
Chicago, IL 60607

Garrard Publishing Company
1607 North Market Street
Champaign, IL 61820

Gorsuch Scarisbrick Publishers
576 Central
Dubuque, IA 52001

Harcourt Brace Jovanovich
757 Third Ave
New York, NY 10017

The Houghton Mifflin Company
1 Beacon Street
Boston, MA 02107

Jamestown Publishers
P.O. Box 6743
Providence, RI 02940

Kendall/Hunt Publishing Company
2460 Kerper Blvd.
Dubuque, IA 52803

Language Research Associates, Inc.
P.O. Drawer 2085
Palm Springs, CA 92262

The Macmillan Company
Front and Brown Streets
Riverside, NJ 08370

Pro-Ed
5341 Industrial Oaks Blvd.
Austin, TX 78735

The Psychological Corporation
757 Third Avenue
New York, NY 10017

Publishers Test Service
2500 Garden Road
Monterey, CA 93940

Rand McNally and Company
Box 7600
Chicago, IL 60680

Riverside Publishing Company
P.O. Box 1970
Iowa City, IA 52244

Science Research Associates
155 North Wacker Drive
Chicago, IL 60606

Slosson Educational Publications
P.O. Box 280
East Aurora, NY 14052

Stoelting Company
1350 South Kostner Ave.
Chicago, IL 60623

Teacher's College Press
Teacher's College
Columbia University
1234 Amsterdam Ave.
New York, NY 10027

William C. Brown Company
2460 Kerper Blvd.
Dubuque, IA 52001

H

Materials for Teaching Reading Skills in a Remedial Reading Center

Program	Reading skills	Level of difficulty
American Guidance Services, Inc. Department RT-L Circle Pines, MN 55014		
GOLDMAN-LYNCH SOUNDS AND SYMBOLS DEVELOPMENT KIT There are sixty-four activities to stimulate production of the English speech sounds and recognition of their associated symbols. This kit contains puppet, tape cassettes, posters, picture cards, magnetic symbols and adventure story books.	Word-analysis skills (specifically phonetic analysis)	Primary-intermediate junior high
Barnell Loft, Ltd. 958 Church Street Baldwin, NY 11510		
AUDITORY READINESS SKILLS The *Auditory Readiness Series* offers instruction in the basic auditory skills. They are presented with an enjoyable gamelike technique that captures the students' interest. Suggested related classroom activities are included for reinforcement.	Auditory skills	Primary
CAPITALIZATION & PUNCTUATION This program develops ninety-four key capitalization and punctuation concepts. The program may be used for individual or group instruction. Duplicating masters are included.	Capitalization and punctuation	Grades 1–9
INSTRUCTIONAL AID PACKS Each *Instructional Aid Pack* contains twenty-five to thirty-three cards, instructions to the teacher, a pretest, a posttest, and a class record. Each kit develops a specific skill. Examples are as follows:	Decoding skills Vocabulary development	Primary-junior high
Matching Letters and Words;		K–1
Matching Consonants;		K–1
Initial Blends;		Grade 2
Final Blends;		Grade 2
Vowels;		Grade 2
Compounds;		Grades 1–6
Prefixes;		Grades 4–9
Suffixes.		Grades 2–9
MULTIPLE SKILLS SERIES This is a comprehensive program designed to teach all of the basic reading skills from basic sight words to comprehension. Teachers may purchase these kits according to skills or grade level desired. Each multilevel set in-	All	Primary-senior high

Program	Reading skills	Level of difficulty
cludes forty-eight booklets, a teacher's manual, duplicating masters for worksheets, and a class record sheet. This series also comes in a Spanish edition.		
PICTO-CABULARY SERIES This program consists of two sets that are used to stimulate pupils' interest in words and to enlarge their own vocabularies. Each set is of equal difficulty. Each is made up of two copies of each of six different titles for a total of twelve booklets. Worksheets and teacher's manual are included with each set.	Vocabulary development (sight and meaning)	Intermediate-senior high
SPECIFIC SKILL SERIES This program gives students specific and concentrated experiences in reading for different purposes. It provides practice material for pupils on a number of different reading levels. It is a structured reading program with all the advantages of programmed learning. Learners get additional drill in areas of need. Each booklet is concerned with the development of one reading skill on one reading level.	Basic sight words Vocabulary development Word-analysis skills Dictionary skills Comprehension skills Study skills	Primary-adult
SUPPORTIVE READING SKILLS This is a diagnostic and prescriptive reading program that supplements the *Specific Skills Series.*	All	Grades 1–9
WE STUDY WORD SHAPES These are reading readiness workbooks designed to help kindergartners and first graders make use of word shapes and word parts so that they will be prepared for the visual scrutiny necessary in the reading act. Children are taught to combine reliance on word shapes with letter clues at the beginning of words and to develop a sensitivity to specific visual qualities, such as shape, size, length, and peculiar characteristics.	Recognizing word shapes	Preschool-primary
Bell and Howell Company 7100 McCormick Road Chicago, IL 60645		
LANGUAGE MASTER The language master is a card teacher. The student inserts a card, watches and listens, records, and then immediately compares his or her responses to the information on the instructor track. The programs include a phonics program, alphabet mastery program, vocabulary-builder program, word-picture program, and a language-stimulation program. This program employs sight, speech, touch, and hearing in coordinated, effective instruction. The system includes a compact, portable	Vocabulary development Word-analysis skills (specifically structural analysis and phonetic analysis)	Primary-adult

Program	Reading skills	Level of difficulty
unit that provides complete, self-contained, dual track recording and playback capability. The unit is used with sets of cards containing visual material and a strip of magnetic recording tape.		
THE READING GAME	Sight-vocabulary program	Primary and elementary
VOCABULARY MASTERY PROGRAM	Vocabulary development	Level 5–7 (supplementary) Level 8–9 (remedial)
WORD-PICTURE PROGRAM	Vocabulary development	Grades 1–6
STAR PROGRAM	Comprehension development	Grades 4–8
Benefic Press 1250 Sixth Avenue San Diego, CA 92101		
COMPREHENSION—CRITICAL READING KITS This kit is designed to develop reading comprehension skills. The high-interest reading selections include content in language arts, social studies, and science.	Comprehension	Primary–junior high
COMPREHENSION AND CRITICAL READING WORKBOOKS This workbook series is also designed to develop comprehension skills. These workbooks provide instruction and practice in four areas of reading comprehension: (1) Identifying main ideas, (2) Understanding details, (3) Seeing relationships, (4) Thinking critically.	Comprehension	3–8
VOCABULARY MASTERY The *Vocabulary Mastery Series* consists of duplicating master books designed to improve vocabulary. Activities include: (1) Matching word and meaning, (2) Word categories, (3) Dictionary use, (4) Meaning from context, (5) Games and puzzles.	Vocabulary development	3–8
Bowmar/Noble Publishers, Inc. 4563 Colorado Blvd. Los Angeles, CA 90039		
BOMAR NOBLE SKILLS SERIES This is a workbook program designed to teach the skills shown.	Vocabulary development Dictionary skills Map-reading skills Spelling skills Library and reference skills	Grades 3–6

Program	Reading skills	Level of difficulty
DOUBLE PLAY READING SERIES TRIPLE PLAY SERIES These kits are for motivating reluctant readers to read. Students listen and participate in plays of drama, comedy, and adventure. There are worksheets to evaluate comprehension. A teacher's guide is included.	Comprehension development	Grades 4–8
LETTER SOUNDS ALL AROUND This is a program to teach beginning students the alphabet. Included are filmstrips, cassettes, workbooks, and a teacher's guide.	Consonant and vowel recognition	Primary
PRIMARY READING SERIES This kit consists of high-interest story cards written at the interest level of younger readers. On the back of each card are questions to teach and evaluate basic comprehension skills. Also included is a teacher's guide.	Word recognition Comprehension development Vocabulary development	Interest: K–3 Reading: 1.3–2.5
READING COMPREHENSION SERIES This kit consists of high-interest story cards. On the back of each card are questions designed to teach and evaluate basic comprehension skills. Also included is a teacher's guide.	Comprehension development	Middle elementary–junior high
READING INCENTIVE PROGRAM—STARTING LINE This kit consists of high-interest filmstrips designed to motivate students to read. There are matching books, workbooks to evaluate comprehension skills, duplicating masters, and a teacher's guide.	Vocabulary development Comprehension development	Grades 3–12
READING ZINGO In this program the children listen to letters or words from a record, then mark the appropriate place on their cards, much like bingo.	Vocabulary development Word-recognition skills (specifically consonant blends and contractions)	Grades 3–6
SPORTS READING SERIES This kit consists of high-interest story cards about professional sports. On the back of each card are questions designed to teach and evaluate comprehension skills. Also included is a teacher's manual.	Comprehension development	Middle elementary-junior high
College Skills Center 1250 Broadway New York, NY 10001		
88 PASSAGES TO DEVELOP READING COMPREHENSION	Comprehension development	Intermediate-senior high

Program	Reading skills	Level of difficulty
These passages are to teach and evaluate comprehension skills. Selections range over the fields of literature, sports, hobbies, mythology, historical oddities, the arts and sciences, and current-day happenings. Each passage has a comprehension check and can be graded on a progress chart for speed and comprehension.		
A PHONICS CHART FOR DECODING ENGLISH This chart organizes forty-four basic sounds into an easy-to-teach, easy-to-learn sequence. The chart features silent letters and common deviations from normal rules of phonics. The Continental Press, Inc. 520 E. Bainbridge St. Elizabethtown, PA 17022	Decoding skills	Primary-intermediate
CONTINENTAL PRESS MATERIALS Workbooks and liquid duplicating material to teach and emphasize fundamental and individualized instruction in reading skills. The Economy Company P.O. Box 25308 1901 North Walnut Street Oklahoma City, OK 73125	Basic sight words Vocabulary development Word-analysis skills Dictionary skills Comprehension skills Study skills Oral reading skills	Primary-adult
GUIDEBOOK TO BETTER READING SERIES This is a remedial reading program for students reading below grade level. All selections are written at a high-interest, low-vocabulary level. The program includes diagnostic exercises, evaluative exercises, review exercises, and recreational reading.	All	Grades 5–adult
READER'S THEATER This program is designed primarily to develop oral reading skills, build confidence, and encourage student participation. *Reader's Theater* offers students active involvement through reading scripts in a reader's-theater situation. EMC Corporation 180 East Sixth Street St. Paul, MN 55101	Oral reading skills Vocabulary development Comprehension development	Grades 1–6
PROGRAM BREAKAWAY This program consists of twelve readers, workbooks, and teacher's editions, all of which are designed to teach comprehension skills in the content areas. Globe Book Company, Inc. 50 West 23rd Street New York, NY 10010	Comprehension development	Grades 1–6

Materials for Teaching Reading Skills in a Remedial Reading Center

Program	Reading skills	Level of difficulty
A BETTER READING WORKSHOP This is a set of four workbooks.	Comprehension development Study skills	Intermediate-junior high
A NEED TO READ This is a flexible, multitext approach to teaching reading comprehension. It is a sequential program including seventy-two books and a teaching guide. The basic skill areas concentrated on are: finding the main idea, building vocabulary, understanding details, and sequence.	Comprehension development	Intermediate-junior high
READING POWER THROUGH CLOZE This is a set of workbooks that utilize the cloze procedure. Each lesson focuses on different kinds of words: verbs in one lesson; homophones in another; nouns, adjectives, adverbs, etc. There are follow-up activities and competency tests for each lesson.	Word analysis Vocabulary development Comprehension development	Intermediate-senior high
Harper & Row Publishers, Inc. Keystone Industrial Park Scranton, PA 18512		
READING WITH PHONICS *Reading with Phonics* presents forty-four basic speech sounds in an organized, logical order. The program may be used either as a developmental or as a remedial program. Included are three texts/workbooks and a teacher's edition for each level.	Word-analysis skills (phonics)	Grades 1–4
SOUNDS AND SIGNALS A–E These five workbooks provide activities to reteach or reinforce phonetic-analysis skills taught at the primary levels. There are mastery tests at the end of each book as well as an instructor's manual.	Word-analysis skills (phonics)	Grades 1–3
Hayes School Publishing Co., Inc. 321 Pennwood Avenue Wilkinsburg, PA 15221		
HAYES COMPANY MATERIALS Workbooks and liquid duplicating material to teach and emphasize fundamental and individualized instruction in all reading skills.	Word-analysis skills Dictionary skills Vocabulary development Study skills Oral reading skills	Primary-senior high
Incentives for Learning, Inc. 600 West Van Buren Chicago, IL 60607		
SPREAD READING PROGRAM This is an individualized, self-paced program designed to teach word-attack skills. Each lesson	Word-analysis skills	Primary-intermediate

Program	Reading skills	Level of difficulty
consists of task cards that stress different skills. In both programs (primary and intermediate) a mastery test is provided at the end of each section for review purposes.		
Jamestown Publishers P.O. Box 6743 Providence, RI 02940		
COMPREHENSION CROSSROADS These are crossword puzzles designed to stimulate interest at the student's specific level. The puzzles are carefully restricted to the noted reading levels. Duplicating masters are included.	Vocabulary development Comprehension development	Reading: 3–12 Interest: 6–12
COMPREHENSION SKILLS SERIES Each booklet of this series is designed to develop a specific comprehension skill. There is a description of the skill, a lesson teaching the accurate use of the skill, and exercises to evaluate students' progress.	Comprehension development	Reading level: 4–12 Interest level: 6–adult
GRAPHICAL COMPREHENSION *Graphical Comprehension* is a text workbook designed to teach students how to read graphs as well as how to make their own graphs based on what they read. Each drill contains a lesson about one type of graph, followed by practical exercises that enable the student to practice the skill just learned.	How to read and make graphs	Reading level: 7–10 Instructional level: 9–college
READING DRILLS These texts/workbooks contain thirty timed passages, each followed by comprehension questions, cloze tests, and a vocabulary exercise. The middle level is designed for students in elementary and junior high school. The advanced level is for high school and above.	Vocabulary development Comprehension development	Reading level: 4–10 Interest level: 4–adult
3000 INSTANT WORDS *3000 Instant Words* contains the most common words in the English language ranked in order of frequency. A diagnostic test is included for placement and measuring individual progress.	Vocabulary development	Primary–junior high
King Features Education Division Department 134 235 East 45th Street New York, NY 10017		
BASIC SKILLS READING PROGRAM This is a self-checking program for teaching the basic reading skills. The heart of the program consists of card matching, which the student does according to cassette-tape stories.	Sequence Main idea Following directions Classification Noting details Word recognition	Lower elementary-intermediate

Program	Reading skills	Level of difficulty
CAREER AWARENESS PROGRAM This is a thirty-two book set that covers fifteen career clusters. Students learn about training and education requirements, job conditions, etc., in popular comic-book form.	Learning about various careers	Upper elementary-junior high
COMICS READING PROGRAM This program includes high-interest stories involving famous comic-strip characters, workbooks with puzzles and games, duplicating masters, and a teacher's guide. It is intended to motivate young students to master basic reading skills. Little Brown Bear Learning Associates, Inc. P.O. Box 56116 Miami, FL 33156	All	Grades 3–6
PHONICS LEARNING GAMES This company markets many games for teaching phonics. Some games have specific series for remedial instruction. Some of the games are as follows: *Easy Word Puzzle, Easy Decoding for Vowels, Easy Decoding for Consonants,* and *Easy Decoding for Syllables.* The Macmillan Company 866 Third Avenue New York, NY 10022	Phonics	Primary-intermediate
MACMILLAN READING SPECTRUM This program consists of the spectrum of skills that are word-analysis level 1–6, vocabulary development level 1–6, comprehension level 1–6. The books are self-directing, self-correcting, and nonconsumable. There are eighteen booklets providing sequential instruction in word analysis, vocabulary development, and reading comprehension. The spectrum of books offers two classroom sets of children's books that have been carefully selected, a set A for grades 2–6 and a set B for grades 3–8. Each set contains many books so that every child can choose what he or she wants to read. In every book there is a synopsis, a cast of characters, excerpts for "flavor," and comprehension and interpretation questions.	Basic sight words Vocabulary development Word-analysis skills Dictionary skills Comprehension skills Study skills Oral reading skills	Intermediate-senior high
HIP READER PROGRAM This is a beginning reading program for teenage and adult nonreaders. The mature interest of these readers provides motivation to learn how to read. Mafex Associates, Inc. 90 Cherry Street P.O. Box 519 Johnstown, PA 15907	Word-analysis skills	Grades 1–4

Program	Reading skills	Level of difficulty
PHONIC WORD BUILDER This is a general word list arranged by phonic element in increasing order of conceptual difficulty. There are two sections. The first is composed of single vowels. The second is composed of vowel teams.	Word-analysis skills	All
Charles E. Merrill 1300 Alum Creek Drive Columbus, OH 43216		
MERRILL READING SKILL TEXT SERIES This program is a logically planned, developmental reading-skills program designed to develop essential reading and learning skills through carefully devised sequential exercises. Some of the titles are *Bibs; Nicky; Uncle Bunny; Ben, the Traveler; Tom, the Reporter;* and *Pat, the Pilot*	Vocabulary development Word-analysis skills Comprehension skills Study skills	Primary-senior high
NEW PHONICS SKILL TEXT SERIES This program contains books A–D and teacher's editions for A–D. It is designed to teach accuracy and independence in word recognition and comprehension through recognition of the sound and structure of words. The series may be used independently or with any basal or individualized reading program.	Word-analysis skills (specifically phonetic analysis)	Primary-junior high
Milliken Publishing Company 1100 Research Blvd. St. Louis, MO 63132		
K–1 READING READINESS PROGRAM These are duplicating masters and task cards that teach word-analysis skills such as initial consonants, final consonants, long and short vowels, vowel teams, etc.	Word-analysis skills	Preschool-primary
Phonovisual Products, Inc. Box 5625 Washington, DC 20016		
PHONOVISUAL: PHONICS PROGRAM This is a program for teaching phonics and structural analysis.	Word-analysis skills (specifically phonics and structural analysis)	Primary-junior high
READING TUTORIAL PROGRAM This is a sequential reading program. The kit contains nine readers, one teacher's manual, and award materials to help motivate the students.	All	Pre-primer–grade 6
VOWELS AND STORIES *Vowels and Stories* is a set of exercises designed to provide extensive practice in vowel sounds while building basic elementary reading skills.	Word-analysis skills (specifically vowel sounds)	Grades 2–6

Program	Reading skills	Level of difficulty
This is intended primarily as a remedial program for use with the reader above the first grade. The program consists of twenty-four units, each devoted to a particular vowel sound.		
Raintree Educational 205 West Highland Ave. Milwaukee, WI 53202		
LIFE CYCLE CLIPPERS These books present the step-by-step growth process of familiar animals. Attention has been paid to vocabulary control in order to understand facts of animal life. Consists of read-along books, cassettes, and skills cards. 8 full-color books and 8 read-along cassettes, 8 book jackets with cassette holders, 8 student skills cards, and 1 teacher's guide.	Science vocabulary, comprehension skills, recall, animal classification, and observation of writing	Grades 1 & 2
FAIRY TALE CLIPPERS An educational program of interesting books, read-along cassettes, and skills cards that provide practice with vocabulary. They consist of 8 full-color hardcover books, 8 read-along cassettes, 8 vinyl book jackets with cassette holders, 8 student skills cards, and 1 teacher's guide.	Practice with vocabulary, recall, comprehension, observation, and writing.	Grades 2 & 3
LIFE CYCLE POSTER BOOKS Each book presents solid, easy-to-understand information about the cycles of life for various high-interest animals and plants. Set One contains 8 titles on the beaver, butterfly, frog, oak tree, black swan, dandelion, honeybee, and salmon. Set Two contains 8 titles on the crocodile, gorilla, penguin, whale, elephant, kangaroo, tiger, and wolf.	Practice with comprehension, including making inferences, and putting things in sequence. Also provides practice in writing	Grades 1 & 2
FACT Strategies for initiating fluent reading behavior, activities that develop and enhance fluency, and a system for charting fluency progress.	Development of fluency, attitude comprehension, taste	Grades Mid–3 to 6
Rand-McNally & Company (School Dept.) P.O. Box 7600 Chicago, IL 60680		
COMPREHENSION WE USE PROGRAM This is a basic workbook program for teaching and evaluating comprehension skills.	Comprehension development	Grades 1–6
DISCOVER PHONICS WE USE Appealing one-page lessons incorporate a variety of teaching strategies: letter substitution, rhyming words, riddles, crossword puzzles, and word games. There are optional filmstrip/cassette sets as well as various combinations of levels and materials for flexibility.	Word-analysis skills	Grades 1–6

Program	Reading skills	Level of difficulty
Reader's Digest Services, Inc. Educational Division Pleasantville, NY 10570		
COMPREHENSION AUDIO LESSONS Each audio lesson helps to develop a specific reading skill—such as recognizing main ideas or noting sequence of events. Teachers can use this program with pupils on an individual, small group, or class basis. In each lesson a narrator first introduces the story; actors then portray roles in the dramatization while music and other sound effects heighten pupil interest, reinforce reading skills, improve aural comprehension and oral reading, help diagnose a pupil's ability to comprehend ideas, and demonstrate correct pronunciation and intonation, especially for bilingual students.	Oral reading skills Comprehension skills	Primary–adult
NEW SERIES READING SKILL BUILDERS Each skill builder in the program helps to develop a specific reading skill, such as recognizing main ideas and noting sequence of events. There are cones with duplicating masters for each level and reading skill. Use it to spark the interest of both the good and reluctant readers, reinforce reading skills, improve aural comprehension and oral reading, help diagnose a pupil's ability to comprehend ideas, and demonstrate correct pronunciation and intonation. It may serve as a model for class dramatization.	Vocabulary development Comprehension development Study skills Oral reading skills	Primary-adult
ORIGINAL SERIES READING SKILL BUILDERS Each skill builder in the program helps to develop a specific reading skill such as recognizing main ideas, noting sequence of events, etc. This program is designed to spark the interest of both good and reluctant readers, reinforce reading skills, improve aural comprehension and oral reading, help diagnose a pupil's ability to comprehend ideas, demonstrate correct pronunciation and intonation, and serve as models for class dramatizations.	Vocabulary development Comprehension skills Study skills Oral reading skills	Primary-adult
RD 2000 LABS OR READING CENTER This is a comprehensive reading program in colorfully illustrated, high-interest magazine form. There are also accompanying audio lessons, activity books, and a teacher's edition. Each lesson highlights a specific reading skill.	Comprehension development Vocabulary development Word recognition Oral reading skills	Primary-junior high
READER'S DIGEST ADVANCED SKILL BUILDERS The advanced skill builders continue to refine the skills introduced in the original skill build-	Vocabulary development Comprehension development	Grades 7–9

Program	Reading skills	Level of difficulty
ers series. It is directed to the high school students who possess basic reading skills. Each kit contains readers, matching cassette tapes, workbooks, and a teacher's manual.	Study skills Oral reading skills	
READER'S DIGEST READING SKILL PRACTICE PADS These are high-utility workbooks that extend basic reading, writing, vocabulary, and word-study skills.	Vocabulary development Word-analysis skills Comprehension development Study skills	Grades 1–6
READERS' WORKSHOP This is a program for all reading skills. The stories are of high interest, colorfully illustrated, and have easy-to-read type. It is an individually paced, self-checking program in which the student can monitor his or her own progress.	Vocabulary development Work-analysis skills Comprehension development Oral reading skills	Grades 3–9
READING SKILLS LIBRARY This is a reading and listening resource unit that will aid in building critical reading skills. It offers material to meet the reading needs of all the pupils in a class or school through use of books and cassettes.	Comprehension development Study skills	Primary–adult
READING TUTORS This program is a compact reading and listening comprehension unit that offers "private reading lessons" for pupils in a classroom. It offers self-contained learning materials. Pupils can learn at their own speed while the teacher moves from group to group or helps pupils with other activities.	Comprehension development Study skills	Primary–adult
VOCABULARY AUDIO SKILLS LESSON This program extends the audio program with dramatizations from thirty additional skill-builder stories. There are six vocabulary lessons on three cassettes at each level from 1–6. The program concentrates on developing word-study or word-analysis skills, such as mastering words by matching words and definitions, using key words correctly, identifiying words with sensory appeal, identifying the correct word, using context clues to identify meanings, and using context clues to identify special meaning.	Vocabulary development Word-analysis skills	Primary–junior high
Scholastic Book Service 904 Sylvan Avenue Englewood Cliffs, NJ 07632		
INDIVIDUALIZED READING FROM SCHOLASTIC This material helps a student to develop his or her own reading program by choosing what he	Basic sight words Vocabulary development Word-analysis skills	Primary-junior high

Program	Reading skills	Level of difficulty
or she wants to read from a wide range of children's literature in paperback. Students can progress at their own pace and sharpen important skills while becoming successful and independent readers. The titles of the program are: *Reaching Out, Reaching Up, Reaching Higher, Reaching Forward, Reaching Ahead,* and *Reaching Beyond.*	Dictionary skills Comprehension development Study skills Oral reading skills	
SCHOLASTIC LITERATURE UNITS This program contains titles such as *Animals, High Adventure, Small World, Courage, Family, Frontiers, Moments of Decision, Mirrors, The Lighter Side, Survival, Success,* and *Personal Code.* The students usually become interested when the subject matter of the course stems from their own most serious concerns. This program focuses on themes of vital interest, provides for individual differences, emphasizes major literary forms, integrates literature and reading skills, and develops good reading habits.	Vocabulary development Comprehension skills Study skills	Junior high-senior high
Science Research Associates, Inc. 155 North Wacker Chicgo, IL 60606		
THE DIMENSIONS SERIES Each kit offers 120 reading selections in multilevel format, centered around a single broad theme. Skill cards provide comprehension checks and extension activities. *Our Story: Women of Today and Yesterday* (reading levels 3.0–8.9): selections illustrate accomplishments of women through the ages. *We Are Black* (reading levels 2.0–6.0) fills a gap by portraying persons and events often neglected in traditional textbooks. *How America Began* (reading level 3.0–8.9): American history from Columbus through the Civil War. *As America Grew* (reading level 3.0–8.9): American history from post-Civil War reconstruction to the Kennedy administration. *Countries and Cultures* (reading level: 4.5–9.5): fascinating glimpses of life as it is lived in foreign places.	Comprehension development	Grades 4–12
GETTING IT TOGETHER: A READING SERIES ABOUT PEOPLE This program consists of a text, a student resource book, a student resource-book answer key, and a teacher's guide. The text contains stories about concerns of adolescents (family, school, dating, etc.). The student resource book has three sections. The first contains comprehension questions, the second informa-	Comprehension development	Grade 3–senior high

Program	Reading skills	Level of difficulty
tion and exercises to help solve problems related to the story, the third suggests additional projects and research.		
INDIVIDUALIZED READING SKILLS PROGRAM This program consists of four pupil books and a teacher's guide. Each book emphasizes a different vowel-skill program (short vowels, long vowels, variant vowels). The books are filled with high-interest reading selections and exercises to develop and evaluate new skills.	Phonics Structural analysis Vocabulary development	Grades 2–6
MARK II READING LABORATORY SERIES These kits each have ten levels. This allows the students to start at their present reading level and progress at their own rate, independent of the other students. Students check their own work and chart their own progress. Built-in mechanisms tell them when given skills need extra practice. Each kit contains 150 power-builder cards, 150 rate-builder cards, 150 skill-development cards—each with a key card. Teacher's handbook and duplicating masters included.	Word study Comprehension Study skills Vocabulary development Listening Rate improvement Dictionary skills Study skills	Kit 2A: reading 2.0–7.0 Kit 2B: reading 2.5–8.0 Kit 2C: reading 3.0–9.0
THE MATURE STUDENT'S GUIDE TO READING AND COMPOSITION The 107 lessons use a phonics and sight-word approach. Students move through recognition of vowels into material written at a 4.0 reading level. Each lesson concentrates on the learning of a specific skill. After basic skills are properly developed, composition skills are introduced.	All	Grade 7–adult
THE PHONOGAMES SERIES This series contains three kits of phonics skill games. *The Readiness Stage* (grades K–1): this kit requires no reading. Thirty-six games on six levels help students discriminate and recognize initial and final sounds. Method of play involves two students in a simple form of tic-tac-toe. *The Phonics Explorer* (grades K–3): this kit emphasizes consonants, consonant blends, and consonant digraphs. Forty games and eighty stories provide practice with sounds and vocabulary. Reading activity sheets extend learning. *The Phonics Express* (grades 1–3): this kit emphasizes vowels and vowel digraphs. Thirty-six games and seventy-two stories provide practice with sounds, vocabulary, and reading. Activity sheets extend learning.	Word-analysis skills Phonics	K–3

Program	Reading skills	Level of difficulty
READING LABORATORY I: WORD GAMES This kit includes phonics and structural analysis exercises for grades 1–3 and games that help students match their reading vocabulary to their listening vocabulary. This kit may be used independently or with reading laboratory kits IA, IB, and IC.	Phonics Structural analysis	Grades 1–3
SCHOOLHOUSE READING KITS All three of these schoolhouse kits contain activity cards with duplicates, plastic response overlays, markers, pupil progress sheets, and teacher's guides. *Word Attack Skills Kit* (grades 1–3): this kit is organized into ten units, covering auditory discrimination; initial consonants; final, medial, and variant consonants; consonant combinations; vowels; compound words; contractions; variant endings; and affixes. *Word Attack 1-C* (grades 3–4): extends coverage of word-attack skills. Contains six units, covering phonics, structural analysis, syllables, word meanings, and dictionary skills. *Comprehension Patterns* (grades 3–8): this program focuses on the basic unit of comprehension, the sentence. Ten units include: simple sentence combining, rearranging sentence parts, modifiers of nouns, indirect objects, punctuation, pronouns and function words, ambiguity, and more.	Phonics Structural analysis Syllabication Word meaning Dictionary skills Sentence patterns Use of modifiers Punctuation Use of clauses	Grades 1–8
SRA BASIC READING SERIES This program contains an alphabet book for the readiness level, readers from A to F, workbooks from A to F, teacher's manual, teacher's handbook, test from A to F, cumulative tests from A to F, and teacher's test guide. This program concentrates on developing children's decoding skills through controlled exposure to sequenced sound-spelling patterns in stories, poems, and teacher-directed activities.	Basic sight words Vocabulary development Word-analysis skills Comprehension skills	Primary–junior high
SRA LUNCHBOX LIBRARIES This is a recreational reading series of short books to motivate young readers. Each kit contains two copies each of thirty-two selections. There are two levels in each kit, written a level *below* the level at which children are working in their basals to ensure that beginners can succeed independently. Simple comprehension questions are at the end of each volume. *SRA Lunchbox Library: Pre-primer* (grades K–1), *SRA Lunchbox Library 1A* (grades 1–2), and *SRA Lunchbox Library 1B* (grades 1–2).	Word recognition Vocabulary development Comprehension skills	Grades 1–3

Program	Reading skills	Level of difficulty
SRA PILOT LIBRARIES This program contains five levels of reading—1c, 2a, 2b, 2c, and 3b—with student record books, teacher's handbook, and key booklet. This program is designed to bridge the gap between reading training and independent reading by using short excerpts, complete in themselves, from full-length books. Each pilot library kit contains seventy-two selections called pilot books to whet a young reader's appetite and lead the reader to the original work. The books are sixteen to thirty-two pages long and are chosen for their interest, appeal, and reading level.	Comprehension skills	Grades 3–7
SRA READING FOR UNDERSTANDING This program is a set of four hundred reading comprehension exercises designed to aid each student in improving his or her ability to get meaning from reading.	Comprehension skills	R.F.U. 1: Grades 1–3 R.F.U. 2: Grades 3–adult
SRA READING LABORATORIES This program contains reading labs from 1a to 1c, 2a to 2c, 3a to 3b, and 4a, pupil booklets for labs, and is an individualized reading system based on the principle that learning is most effective if the student starts at his or her own level of reading, where the student is assured success. It allows the student to proceed as fast as his or her learning rate permits.	Basic sight words Vocabulary development Word-analysis skills Dictionary skills Comprehension skills Study skills	Grades 3–9
SRA SKILLS SERIES There are three basic skills sets to this series. Each kit contains forty-eight independent teaching units with instruction and practice for specific skills. A lesson plan for small-group or class instruction and a cassette tape for independent students are included in each kit. *Phonics Kit* (grades 1–3): this kit includes practice in initial consonants, final consonants, blends, consonant digraphs, vowel sounds, rhyming words, and other basic skills. *Structural Analysis Kit* (grades 3–7): this kit covers forty-eight essential skills, including prefixes, suffixes, possessives, contractions, syllabication, and stress. *Comprehension Skills Kit:* this kit covers forty-eight skills in three major comprehension areas: literal, inferential, and critical. This kit includes such skills as main ideas, supporting details, cause and effect, fact vs. opinion, and more.	Phonics Structural analysis Comprehension skills	Grades 1–8
SUPER KITS This is a high-interest, controlled-vocabulary, comic-book series designed for reluctant read-	Vocabulary development Oral reading skills	Grades 4–8

Program	Reading skills	Level of difficulty
ers with limited word-attack and comprehension skills. The series features well-known characters such as Batman, Superman, and Wonderwoman. Each kit contains ten readers, forty duplicator masters for activity sheets, forty-eight task cards, and a teacher's manual.	Phonics Comprehension skills	
VOCABULARY 3 PROGRAM This kit contains twenty explora-wheels that show the elements of word structure such as prefixes, roots, and suffixes. Also included are 150 vocabulary builders that contain stories, articles, exercises, and activities in ten different interest areas. Sunburst Communications RM U23 39 Washington Ave. Pleasantville, NY 10570	Vocabulary development	Grades 5–junior college
HI-LO READING ACTIVITY CARD PROGRAMS This is a remedial reading program for improving reading comprehension. The program consists of high-interest books, activity cards for each book, and a teacher's guide for each set of activity cards.	Comprehension development	Both levels: 4–12 and 3–7
READING FOR EVERY DAY: SURVIVAL SKILLS Students develop reading competency by applying reading skills to everyday experiences. Examples include road maps, menus, and want ads. Teaching Resources Corporation 50 Pond Park Road Hingham, MA 02043	Survival reading skills	Grades 4–7
GAMES This company markets many games useful for teaching the most basic reading skills. Some examples of games are: *Phonics Puzzles and Games, Phonics Wheel, Word Family Picture Cards, Pictures for Sound Posters, Sound Puzzles* (initial sounds, final sounds).	Word-analysis skills	Primary-intermediate
ESSENTIAL SIGHT WORDS PROGRAM This is a program to teach 200 basic sight words considered essential to mature reading. It contains many low-imagery words that may be difficult for students to learn. The program consists of two levels. Each level contains a pretest, worksheets, mastery sheets, books, and a posttest. Webster Division McGraw-Hill Book Company Manchester Road Manchester, MO 63011	Basic sight words	Grades 1–3

Program	Reading skills	Level of difficulty
WEBSTER WORD WHEELS This program contains sixty-three wheels, seventeen beginning blends, twenty prefix wheels, eighteen suffix wheels, eight two-letter consonant wheels, and a file box. The purpose of this program is to teach students the basic phonetic and structural-analysis skills needed for reading readiness, vocabulary development, and basic sight word development on an individualized basis. Xerox Education Publications Education Center Columbus, OH 43216	Word-analysis skills (specifically structural analysis and phonetic analysis)	Primary-senior high
DICTIONARY SKILLS AND USING THE DIK*SHUH*NEHR*EE This program contains four books: book A is about a merry magician who teaches his tricks for alphabetizing; book B helps strengthen pronunciation and definition skills; book C works on root words, abbreviations, and parts of speech; book D reviews previous skills and stresses vowel and consonant sounds.	Dictionary skills	Primary-junior high
FIRST STEP TO READING *First Step* teaches left-to-right progression by coloring, cutting, pasting, and painting. The pictures tell the youngsters which tools to use for each activity—such as pencil, crayon, scissors, paste, or paint.	Basic sight words Vocabulary development	Primary-intermediate
GRAPHS AND SURVEYS This program is an introduction to interpreting and preparing graphs and surveys and assembling, evaluating, organizing, and translating information into graphic form.	Study skills	Junior high-adult
LIBRARY SKILLS AND LEARNING TO USE THE LIBRARY This program contains four books: book A works with book parts; book B works with "cracking the code" of the Dewey decimal system; book C works with learning how to use the Reader's Guide; and book D works with using different reference books and using tools such as tapes, filmstrips, earphones, recordings, etc.	Study skills	Primary-senior high
MAP SKILLS FOR TODAY AND READINESS FOR MAP SKILLS This program consists of five books that help the students use maps as learning tools by providing a thorough guide in map terminology, symbols, and other map skills.	Study skills	Primary-senior high

Program	Reading skills	Level of difficulty
PHONICS AND WORD POWER This program consists of books 1, 2, and 3; each book consists of three levels—A, B, and C—which help children review, maintain, and build the skills to turn printed symbols into units of meaning. Program 2 is for recognizing words, developing vocabulary and phonetic and structural-analysis skills. Program 3 is for multiple approaches to word-analysis skills.	Basic sight words Vocabulary development Word-analysis skills (specifically phonetic analysis)	Primary-junior high
READING SUCCESS SERIES This program uses a mature format, high-interest content, and stimulating illustrations. This series plots a sequence of skills based on what discouraged youngsters do know. There are six different thirty-two page books, numbered by skill steps and sequenced.	Vocabulary development Word-analysis skills Dictionary skills	Primary-senior high
READ–STUDY–THINK This is a series of practice books designed to improve reading comprehension. These skills are reading for literal and concrete facts, interpreting meaning and drawing generalizations, and organizing information.	Comprehension development	Primary-senior high
SPECTRUM OF SKILLS A series of books containing lessons and information designed to teach the skills noted.	Vocabulary development Comprehension development Word-attack skills	Intermediate and upper grades
TABLE AND GRAPH SKILLS This program contains four books. Book A teaches students to learn terms, symbols, and basic procedures that enable them to solve problems represented by tables and graphs. Book B introduces interpretive reading of tables and graphs. Books C and D introduce different kinds of graphs by pictures, box, bar, line, and circle, and emphasize critical and creative reading.	Study skills	Primary-junior high
SOME PUBLISHERS OF GAMES Barnell-Loft, Ltd. and Dexter and Westbrook, Ltd. 958 Church Street Baldwin, NY 11510 Garrard Publishing Company Champaign, IL 61820 Ideal School Supply Company Oak Lawn, IL 60453 Kenworthy Educational Service, Inc. 138 Allen Street Buffalo, NY 14205	Basic sight words Vocabulary development (sight and meaning) Word-analysis skills Dictionary skills Comprehension skills Study skills Oral reading skills	Primary Intermediate Junior high Senior high Adult

Program	Reading skills	Level of difficulty
Lyons and Carnahan Educational Publishers 407 East 25th Street Chicago, IL 60616		
Science Research Associates, Inc. 259 East Erie Street Chicago, IL 60611		

I

Companies That Publish Materials in Reading

The A. N. Palmer Co.
1720 West Irving Park Road
Schaumburg, IL 60193

ARO Publishing, Inc.
P.O. Box 193
Provo, UT 84601

A-V Concepts Corp.
30 Montauk Boulevard
Oakdale, NY 11769

Abingdon Press
201 Eighth Ave. South
Nashville, TN 37202

Abrahams Magazine Service
56 East 13 Street
New York, NY 10003

Academic Press
111 Fifth Avenue
New York, NY 10003

Academic Therapy Publications
20 Commercial Blvd.
Novatio, CA 94947

Acropolis Books, Ltd.
2400 17th Street N.W.
Washington, DC 20009

Addison-Wesley Publishing Co., Inc.
Jacob Way
Reading, MA 01867

Addison-Wesley Testing Services
2725 Sand Hill Rd.
Menlo Park, CA 94025

Allied Educational Press
P.O. Box 337
Niles, MI 49120

Allyn and Bacon, Inc.
7 Wells Ave.
Newton, MA 02159

American Council on Education
One Dupont Circle
Washington, DC 20036

American Guidance Service
Publishers' Building
Circle Pines, MN 55014

American Library Association
50 East Huron Street
Chicago, IL 60611

American Printing House for the Blind
P.O. Box 6085
Louisville, KY 40206

Ann Arbor Publishers, Inc.
P.O. Box 7249
Naples, FL 33940

Educational Div.
Avista Corp.
2 Park Ave.
New York, NY 10016

Association for Childhood Education International
3615 Wisconsin Avenue N.W.
Washington, DC 20016

Audio-Visual Research
1317 Eighth Street S.E.
Waseca, MN 56093

Avon Books
959 8th Ave.
New York, NY 10019

Baker & Taylor Co.
1515 Broadway
New York, NY 10036

Bantam Books, Inc.
School and College Marketing Division
666 Fifth Avenue
New York, NY 10019

Barnell Loft, Ltd.
958 Church Street
Baldwin, NY 11510

Barnes & Noble Books
10 E. 53 St.
New York, NY 10022

Clarence L. Barnhart, Inc.
P.O. Box 250—1 Stone Place
Bronxville, NY 10708

Basic Skills Program
Office of Basic Skills Improvement
400 Maryland Avenue, S.W.
Room 1167-Donohoe Building
Washington, DC 20202

Bell & Howell Co.
Audio-Visual Products Division
7100 N. McCormick Rd.
Chicago, IL 60645

Benefic Press
1250 Sixth Ave.
San Diego, CA 92101

Bobbs-Merrill Educational Publishing
4300 West 62nd Street
P.O. Box 7080
Indianapolis, IN 46206

Borg-Warner Educational Systems
600 West University Drive
Arlington Heights, IL 60004

R. R. Bowker Co.
1180 Avenue of the Americas
New York, NY 10036

Bowmar Noble Publishers, Inc.
4563 Colorado Blvd.
Los Angeles, CA 90039

William C. Brown Co., Publishers
2460 Kerper Boulevard
Dubuque, IA 52001

Burgess Publishing Co.
7108 Ohms Lane
Minneapolis, MN 55435

C B H Publishing, Inc.
P.O. Box 236
Glencoe, IL 60022

C. C. Publications, Inc.
P.O. Box 23699
Tigard, OR 97223

CTB/McGraw-Hill
Del Monte Research Park
Monterey, CA 93940

Carlson-Dellosa Publishing
1946 S. Arlington Road
Akron, OH 44306

Center for Applied Research in Education, Inc.
P.O. Box 130
West Nyack, NY 10995

Centurion Industries, Inc.
167 Constitution Dr.
Menlo Park, CA 94025

Chicago Tribune
435 North Michigan Avenue
Chicago, IL 60611

The Children's Book Council
67 Irving Place
New York, NY 10003

Children's Press
1224 West Van Buren Street
Chicago, IL 60607

Clarion Books
52 Vanderbilt Ave.
New York, NY 10017

College Skills Center
320 West 29th Street
Baltimore, MD 21211

Communacad
Box 541
Wilton, CT 06897

Consulting Psychologists Press, Inc.
577 College Ave.
Palo Alto, CA 94306

Contemporary Books, Inc.
180 North Michigan Avenue
Chicago, IL 60601

Continental Press, Inc.
Elizabeth Town, PA 17022

Coronado Publishers, Inc.
1250 Sixth Avenue
San Diego, CA 92101

Coronet—Perspective Films
65 East South Water Street
Chicago, IL 60601

Council for Exceptional Children
1920 Association Drive
Reston, VA 22091

Creative Curriculum, Inc.
15681 Commerce Lane
Huntington Beach, CA 92649

Creative Publications
P.O. Box 10328
Palo Alto, CA 94303

Crestwood House
P.O. Box 3427
Mankato, MN 56001

Crown Publishers, Inc.
1 Park Avenue
New York, NY 10016

Curriculum Associates, Inc.
6620 Robin Willow Ct.
Dallas, TX 75248

Curriculum Innovations, Inc.
3500 Western Avenue
Highland Park, IL 60035

Curriculum Review
517 S. Jefferson Street
Chicago, IL 60607

C. Lucas Dalton
5720 Caruth Haven
Suite 130
Dallas, TX 75206

DES Educational Publications
25 South Fifth Avenue
Post Office Box 1291
Highland Park, NJ 08904

Dale Seymour Publications
P.O. Box 10888
Palo Alto, CA 94303

A. B. Dick Co.
5700 Touhy Avenue
Chicago, IL 60648

Delacorte Press
One Dag Hammarskjold Plaza
New York, NY 10017

Dell Publishing Co.
Education Dept.
245 East 47th St.
New York, NY 10017

Department of Defense
Office of Dependent Schools
2461 Eisenhower Avenue
Alexandria, VA 22331

Developmental Learning Materials
P.O. Box 4000
1 Alm Park
Allen, TX 75002

Dormac, Inc.
P.O. Box 1699
Beaverton, OR 97075

Doubleday & Co., Inc.
245 Park Ave.
New York, NY 10167

Dreier Educational Systems
25 South Fifth Avenue
(P.O. Box 1291)
Highland Park, NJ 08904

EBSCO Curriculum Materials
P.O. Box 11521
Birmingham, AL 35202

EDITS
P.O. Box 7234
San Diego, CA 92107

EDL/McGraw-Hill Inc.
1221 Avenue of the Americas
New York, NY 10020

EDUCAT Publishers, Inc.
P.O. Box 2158
Berkeley, CA 94702

E. M. Hale and Company
Harvey House Publishers
128 West River Street
Chippewa Falls, WI 54729

E & R Development Co.
Vandalia Road
Jacksonville, FL 62650

ERIC Clearinghouse on Reading and Communication Skills
National Council of Teachers of English
1111 Kenyon Road
Urbana, IL 61801

ESP, Inc.
1201 E. Johnson Ave.
P.O. Drawer 5037
Jonesboro, AR 72401

ETA (Educational Teaching Aids)
159 West Kinzie Street
Chicago, IL 60610

Companies That Publish Materials in Reading

Econoclad Books
2101 N. Topeka Blvd.
(P.O. Box 1777)
Topeka, KS 66601

The Economy Company
P.O. Box 25308
1901 North Walnut Street
Oklahoma City, OK 73125

The Education Center
1411 Mill Street
P.O. Box 9753
Greensboro, NC 27408

Educational Activities, Inc.
P.O. Box 392
Freeport, NY 11520

Educational Development Corp.
8141 East 44th
P.O. Box 45663
Tulsa, OK 74145

Educational Progress
Division of: Educational Development Corp.
P.O. Box 45663
Tulsa, OK 74145

Educational Service, Inc.
P.O. Box 219—5060 St. Joe Rd.
Stevensville, MI 49127

Educational Testing Service
P.O. Box 999
Princeton, NJ 08540

Educators Publishing Service
75 Moulton Street
Cambridge, MA 02138

Educulture
1 Dubuque Plaza, Suite 150
Dubuque, IA 52001

El Paso Center of the Deaf, Inc.
1005 East Yandell
El Paso, TX 79902

Elsevier-Dutton Publishing Co., Inc.
2 Park Avenue
New York, NY 10016

Encyclopedia Britannica Educational Corp.
425 North Michigan Ave.
Chicago, IL 60134

Essay Press, Inc.
P.O. Box 2323
La Jolla, CA 92037

Farrar, Straus, & Giroux, Inc.
19 Union Square West
New York, NY 10003

Fawcett Books Group
Educational Marketing Dept.
1515 Broadway
New York, NY 10036

Fearon-Pitman Publishers, Inc.
6 Davis Drive
Belmont, CA 94002

Follett Publishing Co.
Dept. D.M.
1010 West Washington Blvd.
Chicago, IL 60607

Gamco Industries, Inc.
Box 1911
Big Spring, TX 79720

Garrard Publishing Co.
1607 North Market Street
Champaign, IL 61820

Ginn & Co.
9888 Monroe Drive
Dallas, TX 75220

Globe Book Co.
50 West 23 Street
New York, NY 10010

Good Apple, Inc.
Box 299
Carthage, IL 62321

Greenhaven Press, Inc.
577 Shoreview Park Road
St. Paul, MN 55112

Grosset & Dunlap Inc.
Education Division
51 Madison Avenue
New York, NY 10010

Grove Press, Inc.
196 West Houston Street
New York, NY 10014

Hammond Inc.
515 Valley Street
Maplewood, NJ 07040

Hampden Publications, Inc.
P.O. Box 4873
Baltimore, MD 21211

Harcourt Brace Jovanovich, Inc.
1250 Sixth Avenue
San Diego, CA 92101

Harper & Row, Inc.
10 East 53 Street
New York, NY 10022

Harper & Row, Publishers, Inc.
c/o Order Dept.
Keystone Industrial Park
Scranton, PA 18512

Hayden Book Co., Inc.
10 Mulholland Dr.
Hasbrouck Heights, NJ 07662

D.C. Heath & Co.
125 Spring Street
Lexington, MA 02173

Heinemann Educational Books, Inc.
70 Court St.
Portsmouth, NH 03801

Hertzberg-New Method-Perma-Bound Co.
617-E Vandalia Road
Jacksonville, IL 62650

Highlights for Children
2300 West Fifth Avenue
P.O. Box 269
Columbus, OH 43216

The Highsmith Co., Inc.
P.O. Box 800 A, Highway 106 East
Fort Atkinson, WI 53538

Holiday House, Inc.
18 East 53 St.
New York, NY 10022

Holt, Rinehart & Winston
CBS Inc.
383 Madison Avenue
New York, NY 10017

Houghton Mifflin Co.
1 Beacon Street
Boston, MA 02107

Hutchinson Books, Inc.
Chestnut Street
Lewiston, ME 04240

I/CT-Instructional/Communications Technology, Inc.
10 Stepar Place
Huntington Station, NY 11746

ITA
A Non-Profit Educational Foundation
Hofstra University
Hempstead, NY 11550

Ideal School Supply Co.
11000 South Lavergne Ave.
Oak Lawn, IL 60453

Imperial International Learning Corporation
P.O. Box 548
Kankakee, IL 60901

Incentive Publications
3835 Cleghorn Ave.
Nashville, TN 37215

Incentives for Learning Inc.
600 West Van Buren Street
Chicago, IL 60607

Innovative Sciences, Inc.
300 Broad Street
Stamford, CT 06901

Instructional Fair
P.O. Box 1650
Grand Rapids, MI 49501

The Instructor Publications, Inc.
757 Third Ave.
New York, NY 10017

International Reading Association
800 Barksdale Road
Newark, DE 19714

Jamestown Publishers
P.O. Box 6743
Providence, RI 02940

Jane Ward Co.
Dept. 4
1642 South Beech St.
Lakewood, CO 80208

Janus Book Publishers
2501 Industrial Pkwy. West
Hayward, CA 94545

Kenworthy Educational Service, Inc.
Box 60, 138 Allen Street
Buffalo, NY 14205

Keystone View
Division of Mast Development Co.
2212 East 12th Street
Davenport, IA 52803

Kimbo Educational
P.O. Box 477
Long Branch, NJ 07740

King Features
235 East 45th Street
New York, NY 10017

The Kingsbury Center
2138 Bancroft Place, N.W.
Washington, DC 20008

The Klamath Printery
628 Oak Street
Klamath Falls, OR 97601

Knowledge Industry Publications, Inc.
701 Westchester Ave.
White Plains, NY 10604

Kraus-Thomson Organization Ltd.
Rte 100
Millwood, NY 10546

Laidlaw Brothers
Thatcher & Madison Sts.
River Forest, IL 60305

Language Research Associates, Inc.
P.O. Drawer 2085
Palm Springs, CA 92262

Lansford Publishing Co.
1088 Lincoln Avenue
P.O. Box 8711
San Jose, CA 95155

Learning Arts
P.O. Box 179
Wichita, KS 67201

Learning Associates, Inc.
P.O. Box 561167
Miami, FL 33156

The Learning Line
P.O. Box 1200
Palo Alto, CA 94302

Learning Periodicals Group
19 Darvis Drive
Belmont, CA 94002

Learning Resources Corporation
8517 Production Avenue
San Diego, CA 92121

Learning Systems Co.
60 Connolly Parkway
Hamden, CT 06514

Learning Tree Publishing Inc.
7108 South Alton Way
Englewood, CO 80112

Learning Well
200 South Service Road
Roslyn Heights, NY 11577

Lerner Publications Co.
241 First Avenue N.
Minneapolis, MN 55401

Leswing Press
P.O. Box 3577
San Rafael, CA 94903

Listening Library, Inc.
1 Park Avenue
P.O. Box L
Old Greenwich, CT 06870

Little, Brown & Co.
College Division
34 Beacon Street
Boston, MA 02106

Litton Educational Publishing, Inc.
7625 Empire Drive
Florence, KY 41042

Longman Inc.
19 West 44 Street
New York, NY 10036

Longwood Division
Allyn & Bacon Inc.
Link Drive
Rockleigh, NJ 07647

McCormick-Mathers Publishing Company
Div. of Litton Education Publishing Inc.
7625 Empire Drive
Florence, KY 41042

McDonald Publishing Co.
925 Demun Avenue
St. Louis, MO 63105

McDougal, Littell & Co.
P.O. Box 1667-C
Evanston, IL 60204

McGraw-Hill Book Co.
8271 Redwood Highway
Novato, CA 94947

McGraw-Hill Ryerson L.
330 Progress Avenue
Scarbrough, Ontario, Canada
MLP 2Z5

Macmillan Inc.
Front and Brown Streets
Riverside, NJ 08370

Macmillan Educational Company
Houndmills, Basingstoke,
Hampshire
RG212XS

Mafex Associates, Inc.
90 Cherry St.
Johnstown, PA 15902

Mast Development Co.
2212 East 12th Street
Davenport, IA 52803

Mastery Education Corp.
85 Main Street
Watertown, MA 02172

Media Basics
Larchmont Plaza
Larchmont, NY 10538

Media Material, Inc.
Department MDR
2936 Remington Avenue
Baltimore, MD 21211

Media-Pak/82
P.O. Box 541
Wilton, CT 06897

Melody House Publishing Co.
819 N.W. 92nd Street
Oklahoma City, OK 73114

G. & C. Merriam Company
Merriam-Webster Reference Books
47 Federal Street
Springfield, MA 01101

Charles E. Merrill Publishing Co.
1300 Alum Creek Drive
Columbus, OH 43216

Julian Messner
1230 Avenue of the Americas
New York, NY 10020

Midwest Publications
P.O. Box 448
Pacific Grove, CA 93950

Milton Bradley Co.
Springfield, MA 01101

The Morgan Co.
4510 N. Ravenswood Avenue
Chicago, IL 60640

William Morrow & Co., Inc.
105 Madison Avenue
New York, NY 10016

NCS/Educational Systems Division
4401 West 76th Street
Minneapolis, MN 55435

National Association for the Deaf
814 Thayer Avenue
Silver Springs, MD 20910

National Council of Teachers of English
1111 Kenyon Road
Urbana, IL 61801

National Library Service for the Blind and Physically Handicapped
Library of Congress
1291 Taylor Street N.W.
Washington, DC 20542

National Public Radio
2025 M Street, N.W.
Washington, DC 20036

National Textbook Company
8259 Niles Center Road
Skokie, IL 60077

The New American Library, Inc.
1633 Broadway
New York, NY 10019

Newsweek
The Newsweek Building
Livingston, NJ 07039

W. W. Norton & Company, Inc.
500 Fifth Avenue
New York, NY 10036

Nystrom 333
3333 Elston Avenue
Chicago, IL 60618

Oceana Educational Communcations
75 Main Street
Dobbs Ferry, NY 10522

Optimal Corporation
Open Court Publishing Company
La Salle, IL 61301

The. A. N. Palmer Co.
1720 West Irving Park Road
Schaumburg, Il 60193

Pendulum Press, Inc.
The Academic Building
Saw Mill Road
West Haven, CT 06516

Penguin Books
299 Murray Hill Parkway
East Rutherford, NJ 07073

Phonovisual Products, Inc.
12216 Parklawn Drive
P.O. Box 2007
Rockville, MD 20852

PIRT c/o Tact
P.O. Box 1052
Doylestown, PA 18901

Pitman Learning Inc.
19 Davis Drive
Belmont, CA 94002

Plays Inc.
8 Arlington Street
Boston, MA 02116

Pleasantville Media
Suite E-61
P.O. Box 415
Pleasantville, NY 10570

Pocket Books
1230 Avenue of the Americas
New York, NY 10020

Educational Book Div.
Prentice-Hall Inc.
Englewood Cliffs,
NJ 07632

Pro-Ed
5341 Industrial Oaks Blvd.
Austin, TX 78735

Programs for Achievement in Reading, Inc.
Abbott Park Place
Providence, RI 02903

Pruett Publishing Co.
3235 Prairie Avenue
Boulder, CO 80301

The Psychological Corp.
757 Third Avenue or
304 E. 45 Street
New York, NY 10017

Psychological Test Specialists
P.O. Box 9229
Missoula, MT 59807

Publishers Test Service
2500 Garden Road
Monterey, CA 93940

G.P. Putnam's Sons
Coward McCann & Georghegan, Inc.
200 Madison Avenue
New York, NY 10016

Radio Shack
Publicity Dept.
300 One Tandy Center
Fort Worth, TX 76102

Raintree Publishers Inc.
205 West Highland Ave.
Milwaukee, WI 53203

Rand McNally & Co.
P.O. Box 7600
Chicago, IL 60680

Random House, Inc.
400 Hahn Road
Westminster, MD 21157

Readers Digest Services, Inc.
Educational Division
Pleasantville, N.Y. 10570

The Reading Laboratory
P.O. Box 681
S. Norwalk, CT 06854

Reflections & Images
6607 Northridge Drive
San Jose, CA 95120

Regents Publishing Co., Inc.
2 Park Avenue
New York, NY 10016

Resources
Instructional Communication Technology, Inc.
Huntington Station, NY 11746

Resources for the Gifted
P.O. Box 15050
Phoenix, AZ 85060

Richard C. Owen Publishers
P.O. Box 14007
Chicago, IL 60614

Frank E. Richards Publishing Co., Inc.
P.O. Box 66
Phoenix, NY 13135

Riverside Publishing Co.
P.O. Box 1970
Iowa City, IA 52244

Rourke Publishing Group
P.O. Box 711
Windermere, FL 32786

William H. Sadler, Inc.
11 Park Place
New York, NY 10007

Santillana Publishing Co.
575 Lexington Avenue
New York, NY 10022

Scarecrow Press, Inc.
52 Liberty Street
P.O. Box 656
Metuchen, NJ 08840

Frank Schaffer Publications
1028 Via Mirabel, Dept. 34
Palos Verdes Estates, CA 90274

Scholastic Book Service
904 Sylvan Avenue
Englewood Cliffs, NJ 07632

Science Research Associates, Inc.
155 North Wacker Drive
Chicago, IL 60606

Science Research Associates, Inc.
College Division
1540 Page Mill Road
P.O. Box 10021
Palo Alto, CA 94303

Scott, Foresman & Co.
11310 Gemini Lane
Dallas, TX 75229

Silver Burdett Co.
8301 Ambassador Row
Dallas, TX 75247

Simon & Schuster Inc.
1230 Avenue of the Americas
New York, NY 10020

Sirs
P.O. Box 2507
Boca Raton, FL 33442

Skillcorp Publishers, Inc.
P.O. Box 712
Columbus, OH 43216

Slosson Educational Publications
P.O. Box 280
East Aurora, NY 14052

Smithsonian Institution Press
475 L'Enfant Plaza
Suite 4800
Washington, DC 20560

Society for Visual Education
Dept. LX
1345 Diversey Parkway
Chicago, IL 60614

SVE Teacher's Choice
2750 North Wayne Avenue
Chicago, IL 60614

South-Western Publishing Co.
5101 Madison Road
Cincinnati, OH 45227

Special Learning Corporation
42 Boston Post Rd.
P.O. Box 306
Guilford, CT 06437

Steck-Vaughn Co.
P.O. Box 2028
807 Brazos St.
Austin, TX 78767

Stemmer House
2627 Caves Road
Owings Mills, MD 21117

Step Inc.
P.O. Box 887
Mukilteo, WA 98275

Stoelting Co.
1350 S. Kostner Avenue
Chicago, IL 60623

Story House Corp.
Charlotteville, NY 12036

Strine Publishing Co.
P.O. Box 149
York, PA 17405

Sunburst Communications
Room U 23 or VR-6
39 Washington Avenue
Pleasantville, NY 10570

Sundance
Newtown Road
Littleton, MA 01460

T S C
A Houghton Mifflin Co.
Dept. 70
P.O. Box 683
Hanover, NH 03755

Teachers & Writers Collaborative
84 Fifth Avenue
New York, NY 10011

Teaching Resources Corporation
50 Pond Park Road
Hingham, MA 02043

Thinking Skills
P.O. Box 448
Pacific Grove, CA 93950

Thurman Publishing Co.
1428 Harvard Ave.
Seattle, WA 98122

Trend Enterprises, Inc.
P.O. Box 43073
St. Paul, MN 55164

Troll Associates
320 Rte. 17
Mahwah, NJ 07430

United Learning
6636 West Howard Street
Niles, IL 60648

United States Government Printing Office
Washington, DC 20402

University of Chicago Press
5801 Ellis Avenue
Chicago, IL 60637
or
Journals Dept.
11030 South Langley Ave.
Chicago, IL 60628

University of Illinois Press
Box 5081
Urbana, IL 61601

University of Michigan Press
P.O. Box 1104
Ann Arbor, MI 48106

University of Nebraska Press
318 Nebraska Hall
901 North 17th Street
Lincoln, NE 68588

Viking Penguin Inc.
625 Madison Avenue
New York, NY 10022

Visual Materials, Inc.
4170 Grove Avenue
Gurnee, IL 60031

Franklin Watts, Inc.
730 Fifth Ave.
New York, NY 10019

J. Weston Walch, Publisher
321 Valley St.
Portland, ME 04104

Webster Division of McGraw-Hill Book Company
1221 Avenue of the Americas
New York, NY 10020

Weekly Reader
Long Hill Road
Middletown, CT 06457

Weekly Reader/Secondary Unit Books
1250 Fairwood Avenue
P.O. Box 16618
Columbus, OH 43216

Western Psychological Services
12031 Wilshire Blvd.
Los Angeles, CA 90025

Weston Woods Studios
Weston, CT 06883

E. H. White and Co.
Suite 710
1025 Vermont Avenue, N.W.
Washington, DC 20005

Albert Whitman & Co.
5747 West Howard Street
Niles, IL 60648

H. W. Wilson Co.
950 University Avenue
Bronx, NY 10452

The World Almanac
Education Division
1278 West Ninth Street
Cleveland, OH 44113

World Book-Childcraft International, Inc.
Merchandise Mart Plaza
Chicago, IL 60654

Xerox Education Publications
1250 Fairwood Avenue
Columbus, OH 43216

Youngheart Records
P.O. Box 27784
Los Angeles, CA 90027

Zaner-Bloser
2500 West Fifth Ave.
P.O. Box 16764
Columbus, OH 43216

Zweig Associates
1711 McGraw Ave.
Irvine, CA 92714

J

Ekwall Reading Inventory

Eldon E. Ekwall
University of Texas at El Paso

Allyn and Bacon, Inc.
Boston • London • Sydney • Toronto

Contents

Preface ERI v
Acknowledgments ERI vii
What Is the Ekwall Reading Inventory? ERI 1
Who Should Use the Ekwall Reading Inventory? ERI 2
Reading Levels Measured by the Ekwall Reading Inventory ERI 2
Preparation for Administering the Ekwall Reading Inventory ERI 5
Procedure for Administering the Ekwall Reading Inventory ERI 6
Procedure for Scoring the Graded Word List ERI 10
Procedure for Scoring the Graded Reading Passages ERI 10
Procedure for Scoring the Comprehension Questions ERI 13
Summarizing the Results of the Ekwall Reading Inventory ERI 13
Teacher Judgment in Scoring the Ekwall Reading Inventory ERI 15
Directions for Quick Administration of the Ekwall Reading Inventory ERI 17
How Long Does It Take to Administer the Ekwall Reading Inventory? ERI 17
The Development of the Ekwall Reading Inventory ERI 18
Reliability of the Ekwall Reading Inventory ERI 20
Analysis of a Completed Summary Sheet ERI 21
Diagnostic Flow Chart Sequence ERI 25
Student Reading Passages: Forms A and B ERI 41
Student Reading Passages: Forms C and D ERI 63
Passages to Be Duplicated for Teacher Use: Forms A and B ERI 85
Passages to Be Duplicated for Teacher Use: Forms C and D ERI 111

Preface

The *Ekwall Reading Inventory* represents an attempt to construct a reading inventory to measure students' oral and silent reading levels. The second edition of the *Ekwall Reading Inventory* also contains a diagnostic flow chart to help the diagnostician determine what to do with the information once the testing has been completed. The diagnostic flow chart should also help the diagnostician become more efficient in the diagnostic process.

The author has attempted to create interesting passages that would not appear childish to students regardless of grade level. All passages but those at pre-primer level contain ten questions that enhance the reliability of the inventory. The scoring procedure is based upon the most commonly accepted criteria for scoring informal reading inventories and upon research by the author.

All passages were written at specific levels based upon widely accepted readability formulae. However, the user should realize that there is less difference between a seventh versus an eighth grade passage than between a first versus a second grade passage. Consequently, at the upper grade levels, factors such as interest and knowledge of subject matter read may sometimes be more important in determining when a student can adequately read a passage than the designated grade level of the passage. This is simply a fact and the examiner should not become overly concerned about always obtaining a perfect sequence of independent, instructional, and frustration levels on the higher level reading passages.

E. E. E.

Acknowledgments

I would like to express my thanks to Kathy Billingsley, Woody Duree, Skip Holmes, Emily Ramey, Leticia Mulhauser, Sandra Rogers, Wedge Johnson, and Christine Johnson who as teaching assistants have helped in many ways in the development of the ERI. My thanks is also extended to principals Dennis Miller and Higino Peña, and Betty Wilkenson, reading consultant, in the Canutillo Independent School District who extended their help by providing students and facilities for the author and others to do the initial testing of the instrument. I would also like to thank the administrators and teachers of the El Paso Independent School District, the administrators and teachers of the Carlsbad New Mexico Public Schools as well as the administrators and teachers of the Canutillo Independent School District for their cooperation in reading rate studies done on the second edition of this instrument. My appreciation is also extended to Heidi Bleckman, Nancy Bryant, Lou Ann Peer, Marjorie Townsley, Charlotte Rasco, Cheryl Schwartz, Betty Emmons, Bill Fannin, and Leticia Ochoa for their help in studies of time factors for individual passages, and for administration times, as well as their help in the study of the reliability of the forms. A note of appreciation is also extended to Lilia Lavender and Sylva Trujillo for their help in the typing and retyping of the various revisions of the manuscript. Finally, I would like to express my appreciation to the many graduate students who administered the ERI as well as the many elementary and secondary students to whom it was administered.

WHAT IS THE EKWALL READING INVENTORY?

The Ekwall Reading Inventory is a set of reading passages ranging from pre-primer through ninth grade level in difficulty. It also contains instruments for assessing students' letter knowledge, and knowledge of phonics, basic sight words, vowel rules, syllable principles, and contractions. The reading passages are designed to measure students' oral and silent independent, instructional, and frustration reading levels. It may also be used to determine students' listening comprehension level. As in the administration of any informal reading inventory, students' use of word analysis skills, as well as their ability to comprehend, are taken into consideration in the scoring procedure.

The inventory contains four reading passages at each level as follows:

Preprimer-A	Preprimer-B	Preprimer-C	Preprimer-D
First Grade-A	First Grade-B	First Grade-C	First Grade-D
Second Grade-A	Second Grade-B	Second Grade-C	Second Grade-D
Third Grade-A	Third Grade-B	Third Grade-C	Third Grade-D
Fourth Grade-A	Fourth Grade-B	Fourth grade-C	Fourth Grade-D
Fifth Grade-A	Fifth Grade-B	Fifth Grade-C	Fifth Grade-D
Sixth Grade-A	Sixth Grade-B	Sixth Grade-C	Sixth Grade-D
Seventh Grade-A	Seventh Grade-B	Seventh Grade-C	Seventh Grade-D
Eighth Grade-A	Eighth Grade-B	Eighth Grade-C	Eighth Grade-D
Ninth Grade-A	Ninth Grade-B	Ninth Grade-C	Ninth Grade-D

The "A" passages are designed for the student to read orally on the first administration, and the "B" passages to read silently. The "C" and "D" passages may be used for a second administration at a later date, or as supplementary passages to confirm the results of the first administration. As with the "A" and "B" passages, the "C" passages are to be read orally and the "D" passages silently. Either the "C" or "D" passages may also be used to determine the student's listening comprehension level.

The Ekwall Reading Inventory also contains a graded word list, which has often been termed the *San Diego Quick Assessment.* This word list is a series of ten words at each level from the pre-primer through the ninth grade level. It is designed as a quick check of a student's word knowledge and word analysis skills and is normally used to make a rapid determination of the student's independent, instructional, and frustration reading grade levels before administering the oral and silent reading passages. The main purpose, however, in administering the graded word list is to determine, as closely as possible, the student's independent reading level. This list then serves as an entry level for beginning the oral and silent reading passages. It should be remembered that such a word list does not measure a student's ability to comprehend and is, by itself, an inadequate measure of a student's overall reading ability.

WHO SHOULD USE THE EKWALL READING INVENTORY?

The Ekwall Reading Inventory was designed for use by classroom teachers, remedial reading teachers, reading diagnosticians, and school psychologists, and for the training of prospective and in-service teachers. Most reading specialists readily agree that the reading grade level of a student can be determined more accurately by the use of a reading inventory of this nature than by the use of standardized achievement tests or other commonly used methods. Furthermore, while administering an inventory such as this a great deal of diagnostic information can be gathered to serve as a blueprint for instruction.

READING LEVELS MEASURED BY THE EKWALL READING INVENTORY

As stated previously, three reading levels are measured by the Ekwall Reading Inventory or by any informal reading inventory. These are the *independent level* (sometimes called "free" reading level), the *instructional level,* and the *frustration level.* A fourth level—listening ability—may also be determined by reading to the student. This is usually termed the student's *listening comprehension level.* A description of the *independent, instructional, frustration,* and *listening comprehension* levels follows:

Independent Reading Level

The independent reading level is the level at which a student should be able to read without any help of any kind from the teacher. This is the level at which one would normally expect the student to be reading when he or she reads a library or trade book selected voluntarily. The student should know at least 99 percent of the words and should comprehend at least 90 percent of the material.

Instructional Level

The instructional reading level is the level at which a student would normally be reading when required to read a social studies or science textbook or a basal reader without having had a chance to read it previously. The student should know at least 95 percent of the words and should comprehend at least 60 percent of the material.

It should be emphasized that although the student would approach initial reading at the instructional level, he or she should *not* be required to read at this level other than for testing purposes. If a student is reading at this level, the material is too difficult to read independently. Therefore, the teacher should discuss the material with the student and build up his or her background of experiences for improving both vocabulary and overall comprehension. Any new words should also be discussed so the student will be able to use word attack skills correctly when he or she encounters them. Consequently, in preparing the student for reading an instructional passage what essentially happens is that the teacher changes the student's reading level from instructional to independent.

Frustration Reading Level

The frustration reading level is the point at which reading material simply becomes too difficult for the student to read. It is the point at which the student knows 90 percent or less of the words and comprehends 50 percent or less of the material read.

Listening Comprehension Level

The listening comprehension level is usually considered to be the highest level at which the student can listen to a passage and comprehend 70–75 percent of the material. Since there are ten questions on the ERI, the lower percentage of 70 is used for easy scoring.

If you wish to determine the student's listening comprehension level you should read passages to the student and ask questions over those passages. Since you will not know, in advance, whether the student's listening comprehension level is above or below his or her frustration reading level, you are advised to start at the student's highest instructional level. Since you will be measuring listening ability, only the student's ability to comprehend will be taken into consideration. You will find directions for determining the student's listening comprehension level on page ERI 9.

The purpose for finding a student's listening comprehension level is to determine whether there is a discrepancy between the level at which the student can read and comprehend and between that at which the student can listen and comprehend. If the student can listen and comprehend at a grade level or several grade levels beyond what that same student can read and comprehend, then it is an indication that the student has more potential for comprehension than he or she is showing on the reading passages. This would indicate that with the remediation of problems with word attack or word analysis skills or with help in comprehending (depending on the nature of the student's problem) the student would be likely to improve in comprehension. It should, however, be kept in mind that some students' ability to listen and comprehend may not be as good as their ability to read and comprehend.

The scoring criteria for the independent, instructional, frustration, and listening comprehension levels could then be summarized as follows:

	Word Recognition	*Comprehension*
Independent level	99% or more	90% or more
Instructional level	95% or more	60% or more*
Frustration level	90% or less	50% or less

* This figure differs some from the 75 percent that is often used as the minimum for comprehension at the instructional level. However, research done by the author and Judy English indicated that students, in most cases, do not show signs of frustration until they fall below 60 percent if their word recognition errors are not excessive. This research may be found in Eldon E. Ekwall and Judy English, "Use of the Polygraph to Determine Elementary School Students' Frustration Level," Final Report-United States Department of Health, Education, and Welfare, Project No. 0G078, 1971.

In determining a student's oral reading level, you should take both word recognition and comprehension into consideration. Since you will not know how many words the student recognizes in silent reading, you will have to consider only the comprehension factor in scoring the silent reading pasages.

In scoring the Ekwall Reading Inventory, or any informal reading inventory, the ultimate decision on grade placement is usually based on the percentages previously mentioned. However, Johnson and Kress* have listed certain behavioral characteristics commonly observed in students at their independent, instructional, and frustration reading levels. These related behavioral characteristics are as follows:

INDEPENDENT AND INSTRUCTIONAL LEVELS

Rhythmical, expressive oral reading
Accurate observation of punctuation
Acceptable reading posture
Silent reading more rapid than oral
Response to questions in language equivalent to that of author
No evidence of
- lip movement
- finger pointing
- head movement
- vocalization
- subvocalization
- anxiety about performance (p. 6)

FRUSTRATION READING LEVEL

Abnormally loud or soft voice
Arhythmical or word-by-word oral reading
Lack of expression in oral reading
Inaccurate observation of punctuation
Finger pointing (at margin or every word)
Lip movement-head movement-subvocalization
Frequent requests for examiner help
Non-interest in the selection
Yawning or obvious fatigue
Refusal to continue (p. 10)

In examining the scoring criteria for the independent, instructional, and frustration levels shown on page ERI 3, you will note that the criteria for the instructional level are as follows:

	Word Recognition	*Comprehension*
Instructional level	95% or more	60% or more

On the other hand, the criteria for the frustration level are listed as follows:

* Marjorie S. Johnson and Roy A. Kress, *Informal Reading Inventories.* Newark, Delaware: International Reading Association, 1965.

	Word Recognition	Comprehension
Frustration level	90% or less	50% or less

In examining this, one might logically ask, What happens if a student's word recognition level falls between 91 through 94 percent or when the comprehension level falls between 51 through 59 percent? That is to say, these percentages have not been accounted for since the criterion for word recognition at the instructional level is 95% *or more* and the criterion for comprehension is 60% *or more;* whereas the word recognition for the frustration level is 90% *or less* and for comprehension is 60% *or less.* For a thorough explanation of this apparent discrepancy see the section entitled Teacher Judgment in Scoring the Ekwall Reading Inventory.

PREPARATION FOR ADMINISTERING THE EKWALL READING INVENTORY

All materials for administering the Ekwall Reading Inventory are contained in this book on pages ERI 41–135. However, before you begin testing, it will be necessary to duplicate the summary sheets or cover sheets for the inventory and the materials upon which you will be marking while the student is reading. Therefore, you should duplicate the following materials:

1. The summary sheets for the inventory (found on pp. ERI 86–88 and ERI 112–113).
2. The score sheet for the *San Diego Quick Assessment* or *Graded Word List* (found on pp. ERI 90 and ERI 114).
3. One set of oral and silent reading passages.
   "A" and "B" passages (found on pp. ERI 43–62).
   "C" and "D" passages (found on pp. ERI 65–84).

These materials should then be collated and stapled together in the following order:

1. Summary sheets.
2. The score sheet for *San Diego Quick Assessment* or *Graded Word List.*
3. The oral and silent reading passages beginning with pre-primer-A, then pre-primer-B, then first grade-A, first grade-B, etc., up to ninth grade-A and ninth grade-B. If you wish to use the "C" and "D" forms you would, of course, use pre-primer-C, then pre-primer-D, etc., up to ninth grade-C and ninth grade-D. (If you are testing younger students or disabled readers, you may wish to include passages up to only the fourth or fifth grade level.)

Learn to code students' oral reading errors. In order to do this it will be necessary to learn the code for marking in oral diagnosis. This code is shown on pp. ERI 10–11. If you already know a code that is somewhat similar, it will not be necessary to learn this one; however, you should learn to code the types of errors counted in scoring the Ekwall Reading Inventory. You should also learn to code "self-corrected errors," "disregard for punctuation," and "pauses" even though these are not counted as word recognition errors in the final computation of the student's reading level.

PROCEDURE FOR ADMINISTERING THE EKWALL READING INVENTORY

1. Find a place where the student can read to you without being heard or without bothering the rest of the class. Other students should not be able to hear the questions being asked the student who is taking the reading inventory. Have the student sit to one side of your desk or a table, facing you (as in the illustration).
2. Have your score sheets (copied from pp. ERI 89–90 or pp. 114–115) ready for marking the Graded Word List. Give the student the manual opened to either page ERI 42 or page ERI 64 and say, *"Here are some words I would like you to read aloud. Try to read all of them even if you are not sure what some of the words are. Let's begin by reading the words in this list"* (pointing to the list in which the student is to start). When testing students whom you believe to be reading up to grade level, have them begin with a list that is two years below their present grade placement. Record words pronounced correctly with a plus (+) on your answer sheet and write down all incorrect responses. You may wish to use diacritical marks on your answer sheet. For example, "thank" might be read "think" or "several" might be read as "sever'al." If the student misses any words in the first list, drop down to a lower level list until he or she makes no more than one error from these words.

If it is obvious that a student can read all of the words quite rapidly, you may not wish to put a plus (+) mark in front of each word as the student reads but wait until the student has completed that list and then place a plus on number one and draw a vertical line downward quickly through the rest of the blanks to indicate that all were read correctly as was the first. See the following example:

PP +

see ____

play ____

me ____

at ____

run ____

go ____

and ____

look ____

can ____

here ____

Have the student continue reading consecutively higher level lists until he or she misses three or more words.

The reading levels of the lists are designated as follows:

pp = Preprimer
| = First grade
L = Second grade
⊔ = Third grade
□ = Fourth grade
□ | = Fifth grade
□ L = Sixth grade
□ ⊔ = Seventh grade
□□ = Eighth grade
□□ | = Ninth grade

You will note that in grade levels one through nine there is one line for each number or level. For example, level two has two lines (L), level three has three lines (⊔), level six has four + two (□L), level seven has four + three (□ ⊔), level eight has four + four (□□), and level nine has four + four + one (□□ |). The grade levels are coded in this manner so that the student will not know at which level he or she is reading. These symbols designate the reading levels of the oral and silent reading passages that the student reads from the manual.

After administering the graded word list, have the student begin with the oral reading passage corresponding to his or her independent reading level as derived from the word list. This is the highest level list in which no more than one word was missed. Begin by saying to the student, *"I have some passages for you to read. Read the first one aloud as you would to your teacher or to the other students in your class. If you find a hard word, try to read it as best you can and continue reading. Try to remember what you read so that you can answer some questions about the passage when you are through."* At this point hand the manual to the student and say, *"Ready, begin."* If you are using the "A" and "B" passages, you will begin with the "A" passage that corresponds to the student's independent reading level on the graded word list (where no more than one word was missed). If you are using the "C" and "D" passages, then you will begin with the appropriate "C" passage.

You will note that times are given for the silent reading passages. These times are presented in terms of slow, average, and fast. You will also note that a mean (average) and a median (the point at which one-half the students read faster and one-half of them read slower than this time) are presented for each silent reading passage. If you wish to determine the time it takes the student to read the passage, you should have a stopwatch or a watch with a second hand or digital readout of seconds available. When you say, "Get ready to read, begin," and the student begins to read, start the stopwatch or note the time in seconds. When the student has finished the passage, again note the time (in seconds) it took to read the passages and write that time on the answer sheet where you see Time:______beside the small table that shows time factors.

There are several reasons why you may wish to make note of a student's reading speed for the silent reading passages. One of the most important of these is to see if the student is an extremely slow reader. If it is found that a student falls into the slow category, then it could be assumed that the student would be likely to do poorly on a group standardized reading achievement test regardless of the ability of the student to attack new words or regardless of a high level of reading comprehension. This is, of course, true since group reading achievement tests are timed; therefore, if a student could not begin to finish the test, then he or she would not be able to achieve a reasonably high score.

Another reason you may wish to check a student's silent reading speed is so that you can compare that student's reading speed with that of other students of a comparable grade level.

While the student is reading you should be coding his or her oral reading errors on your copy of the inventory forms that were duplicated and assembled as explained on p. ERI 5 of the manual. Do not give any further help to the student such as saying, "Try to sound that word out." However, if a student hesitates on a word, wait five seconds and then simply say the word yourself.

When the student has completed reading the passage, take the manual back from him or her and hold it up in front of your copy of the inventory answer sheet. Do this in a casual manner so the student does not get the feeling you are hiding the answer sheet. Then ask the student the questions as shown on your answer sheet. Mark correct answers with a plus (+) and incorrect answers with a minus (−). You may repeat the questions, if necessary, or if an answer seems incomplete you may question further by saying, "Tell me more" or "Can you tell me a little more about that?" However, do not rephrase the question to make it easier. For example, if a question was, "What color was the pony?" then *do not* ask, "Was it brown and white?"

After completing the questions on the first oral reading passage, say to the student, *"Here is another passage. Read this one to yourself and try to remember what you read so that you can answer some questions about it when you finish."* Then hand the manual to the student opened to the appropriate "B" passage corresponding to the "A" passage that he or she has just finished reading (or the "D" passage if the student has just read the corresponding "C" passage). When the student has finished reading the passage silently, then again take back the manual from him or her and ask the questions based on that passage.

After giving the first oral and silent reading passages it will be necessary to determine whether the student has been able to read them at the independent level. If both the oral and silent passages were at the student's independent reading level, then you would continue giving the next higher oral passage, then the corresponding silent passage, etc., until the student's frustration level is reached. In many cases a student may reach his or her frustration level on either oral or silent reading but not on both. In these instances continue giving only the passages (either silent or oral) until the student reaches frustration level on both oral and silent reading. For example, a student might reach frustration level at fifth grade level on oral reading because of difficulty with word recognition skills but may still comprehend adequately. In this case continue giving silent reading passages only until he or she reaches frustration level because of a lack of comprehension.

If, after giving the first oral and silent reading passages, the student is not reading at the independent level on either of the two or both, give the next easier oral and/or silent passages until both oral and silent independent reading levels have been established. Then continue upward until both the oral and silent frustration levels are reached.

Finding the Student's Listening Comprehension Level

After the student's frustration level has been reached on both oral and silent reading, you may then wish to find the student's listening comprehension level. In this case, the author suggests that you begin reading to the student beginning with the highest level at which the student comprehended (instructional level) adequately in either silent or oral reading. Explain that you are going to read a passage aloud and that the student is to listen carefully and be ready to answer some questions about the passage when you have finished reading. After reading the passage to the student, then ask the questions over that passage. If the student comprehends 70 percent or more, then continue upward with the more difficult passages until the student is unable to comprehend at least 70 percent of the questions. Should you find that the student cannot comprehend at the 70 percent level on the first passage, you would then begin with the reading passage at the next lower level and continue in this manner until the student reached a level where at least 70 percent of the questions could be answered. The student's listening comprehension level is the highest level at which he or she could comprehend 70 percent or more of the questions. In determining the student's listening comprehension level it is suggested that you use a different form of the test than the one you have been using. For example, if you have been testing the student using the "A" and "B" forms of the test then you may wish to use either the "C" or "D" forms to test for the student's listening comprehension level.

PROCEDURE FOR SCORING THE GRADED WORD LIST

The summary sheet for the Ekwall Reading Inventory contains a space for writing in the student's independent, instructional, and frustration levels. Fill in the following information:

1. The highest level list in which the student misses no more than one word is the independent reading level.
2. The list in which the student misses two words is the instructional level. There may be some instances where a student will not miss exactly two words in any one list. For example, he or she may miss one or no words in one list and then miss three or more words in the list at the next higher level. In this case, simply do not mark anything in the blank opposite the student's instructional level or mark "ND" for "Not Determined."
3. The list in which the student misses three or more words is the frustration reading level.

PROCEDURE FOR SCORING THE GRADED READING PASSAGES

In scoring the oral graded reading passages in the Ekwall Reading Inventory or in any informal reading inventory, two main factors are used in determining a student's reading level. These two factors are *word recognition* and *comprehension.* In scoring the silent graded passages only comprehension is taken into consideration.

In marking word recognition errors in oral reading, the following code should be learned:

CODE FOR MARKING IN ORAL DIAGNOSIS, TO BE SCORED AS ERRORS IN MARKING INFORMAL READING INVENTORIES

1. Encircle omissions.
2. Mark all insertions with a caret (^).
3. Draw a line through words for which substitutions or mispronunciations were made and write the substitutions or mispronunciations above the words. Determine later whether the words missed were substitutions or mispronunciations.
4. If the student reads too fast for you to write in all mispronunciations, draw a line through each word and write a "P" for partial mispronunciation or a "G" for gross mispronunciation.
5. Mark inversions the same way as substitutions and determine later whether the mistakes were really inversions or substitutions. Examples of inversions are "no" for "on," "ont" for "not," "saw" for "was," etc.
6. Use parentheses ( ) to enclose words for which aid was given.
7. Underline repetitions with a wavy line.

NOT TO BE SCORED AS ERRORS IN MARKING INFORMAL READING INVENTORIES

8. Put a check mark (√) over words that were self-corrected.
9. Use an arched line to connect words wherever there was a disregard for punctuation.
10. Draw two vertical lines (||) to indicate a pause before words.*

EXAMPLE OF A CODED READING PASSAGE

Jan has a brown and white kitten. The kitten was very little when she got it. Now the kitten is big. It likes to run and play. It is named Tab.

Procedure for Scoring Oral Reading Passages

1. Count the total number of errors as outlined in numbers 1 through 7 above (CODE FOR MARKING IN ORAL DIAGNOSIS). Write the total number of errors in the right-hand margin in your scoring booklet. Note that omissions, insertions, substitutions, mispronunciations, inversions, aid, and repetitions are all counted as errors. Words that are self-corrected, disregard for punctuation, and pauses of less than five seconds are *not* counted as errors.
2. In counting repetitions use the following guidelines:

Count all repetitions even though they may all be repetitions of the same word.†

Consecutively repeated words are counted as one repetition. For example, if a student repeats four words in a row, then it is considered as one error.

If a word is repeated more than one time, it is still only counted as one error. (See "has" in the sentence below.)

Jan has a brown and white kitten.

If some words in a series are repeated more than other words, then count one repetition for each different length of wavy line used to indicate repetitions. In the example above, in the words "and white kitten" there are three repetitions.

A word is not counted as a repetition unless it is repeated correctly in its entirety more than one time. For example, if a student said, "cough" and corrected it and said, "caught," then it would simply be a self-corrected error. Or, if a student did not finish a word and then began over and said the first part again, it would not be considered a repetition.

3. Following the questions for each oral passage in your scoring

* From: Ekwall, Eldon E. & Shanker, James L. *Diagnosis and remediation of the disabled reader,* 2d. ed. Newton, MA: Allyn & Bacon, Inc. 1983, p. 372.

† Research done by the author showed that if all repetitions are not counted as errors then students will become physiologically frustrated before their scores reach frustration level. (See Eldon E. Ekwall, "Should Repetitions Be Counted As Errors?" *The Reading Teacher,* Vol. 27 (January 1974), pp. 365–67.)

sheets you will note there is a table. Across the top of the table is a series of numbers that denote the number of word recognition errors. In the column on the left-hand side of the table is a series of numbers that denote the number of questions missed. Locate the number of word recognition errors made by the student in that passage, across the top of the table. Then locate the number of questions missed in the column on the left-hand side of the table. Find the point where the column showing the number of word recognition errors intersects with the row showing the number of questions missed. In that rectangle you will note one of the following symbols: The (+) means the student is reading at his or her independent level; the (*) means the student is reading at his or her instructional level, and the (x) means the student is reading at his or her frustration level.

For example, in the table shown below, if the student had made seven (7) word recognition errors and had missed two (2) questions, one would go across the table to the column marked 6-8 and follow the row in which the two (2) is shown for number of questions missed. These two figures intersect in a rectangle marked with an asterisk (*). This means that the student is reading at his or her instructional level. You should then make a check mark in the box opposite instructional level, as shown in the example below.

Number of Questions Missed	Number of Word Recognition Errors: 0–2	3–5	6–8	9–11	12–14	15+	Reading Level	
0	+	*	*	*	*	×	⊞ Independent	☐
1	+	*	*	*	×	×	[*] Instructional	☑
2	*	*	*	×	×	×	⊠ Frustration	☐
3	*	*	×	×	×	×		
4	*	×	×	×	×	×		
5+	×	×	×	×	×	×		

Procedure for Scoring Silent Reading Passages

1. Determine the number of comprehension errors from the ten questions that were asked of the student (except for the preprimer passages, which have only five questions). Following the questions under each passage to be read silently you will see the following:

Number of Questions Missed	Reading Level	
0–1 = Independent	Independent	☐
2–4 = Instructional	Instructional	☑
5+ = Frustration	Frustration	☐

Simply look to see at which level the student is reading depending on the number of questions missed. In the sample above the student missed three (3) questions; this corresponds to the instructional level (2-4) and the box corresponding to instructional level should be checked.

PROCEDURE FOR SCORING THE COMPREHENSION QUESTIONS

In scoring the comprehension questions on both the oral and silent reading passages the following guidelines should apply:

1. The student need not give the exact answer shown on the scoring sheet as long as it is a reasonable answer that means the same thing as the written answer; for example, "Dad" for "Father." If, however, the student gives an answer that is unclear or seems impossible to score, you should then ask a neutral question such as, "Can you tell me a little more about that?" or simply say, "Tell me more." If the answer that is then given is obviously incorrect, it should be counted as wrong.
2. In some cases the student must give two answers to a question in order to receive full credit; for example, the student may be asked what kinds of animals were on the farm. If the answer calls for at least two kinds to be named and the student responds with only one, then you should ask, "Can you tell me more?" If the student can not tell more but has given one of the two that were asked for, then give one-half credit for the answer. After completing the questions about a passage there may be two questions for which one-half credit was given. In this case you would, of course, give the student credit for one complete question. If there is only one question for which one-half credit was given, then the student should not be given credit for the question, since giving credit would possibly place him or her at a higher level than actual capability warrants.

SUMMARIZING THE RESULTS OF THE EKWALL READING INVENTORY

1. Fill in the student's name, the date, the grade in school, and the name of the examiner at the top of the summary sheet.
2. Fill in the student's independent, instructional, and frustration reading levels as derived from the graded word list according to the criteria on the summary sheet or those listed on page ERI 7.
3. Fill in the student's independent, instructional, and frustration reading levels for both oral and silent reading as derived from the reading passages. Also fill in the student's listening comprehension level if it was determined. The following guidelines may be helpful:

List the highest level passage at which the student read on an independent level when reading orally and the highest level passage at which the student read on an independent level when reading silently. Therefore, only one level will appear under each of the "Oral" and "Silent" headings at the independent reading level. One would take it for granted that any level below these would also be at the student's independent reading level.

List the *lowest* level at which the student read orally at his or her instructional level and also the *highest* level at which he or she read orally at the instructional level. Do the same for the student's silent instructional level. In some cases a student may have read at the instructional level at only one grade level. However, in some cases the student's instructional level may span several grade levels. In that case the numbers, such as "2-3," might appear under "Oral" at the student's instructional reading level. Likewise, the numbers "2-4" might appear under "Silent" at the student's instructional level. This would mean that the student's instructional level spanned grades two and three in oral reading and two through four in silent reading.

List the lowest level passages at which the student read at a frustration level orally and the lowest level passage at which he or she read at a frustration level silently. As in the case of the independent level, only one level would appear under "Oral" and only one level under "Silent." One would take it for granted that any level above these would also be at the student's frustration reading level.

Under listening comprehension level, list the highest level at which the student comprehended at least 70–75 percent of the questions asked by the tester. Again, one would take it for granted that anything below that level would also be at the listening comprehension level and anything above that level would be above the listening comprehension level.

4. Although filling in the remainder of the summary sheet is optional, you may wish to do so. Doing this will give you a much better picture of the student's word analysis skills, comprehension abilities, sight vocabulary, types of oral reading errors, rate of reading, and semantic-syntactic abilities.

To show the total number of each type of error, count the total number of omissions, insertions, repetitions, etc., in all passages read orally and enter the total number of each type of error in the boxes to the left of each type listed. Doing this will give you a better overall picture of the principal types of errors made by the reader. If the same passages are again administered to the reader at a later date, after a period of remediation, and the errors are again analyzed, you will be able to see how much progress has been made.

In counting mispronunciations you should consider words that barely resemble the pronunciation of the original words to be *gross* mispronunications. On the other hand, *partial* mispronunciations are instances where a wrong word beginning or ending was used—such as "milked" for "milks," or "run" for "runs"—or where only part of a word was mispronounced, such as "dekided" for "decided."

You may also want to check the blanks to the left of the various characteristics of the reader. Doing this will help you to analyze various faults the reader may possess and will enable you to determine if these weaknesses improve after a period of time.

An example of a student's summary sheet is shown on pp. ERI 24–25.

TEACHER JUDGMENT IN SCORING THE EKWALL READING INVENTORY

In examining the scoring criteria for the independent, instructional, and frustration levels shown on page ERI 3 you will note that the criteria for the instructional level are as follows:

	Word Recognition	*Comprehension*
Instructional level	95% or more	60% or more

On the other hand, the criteria for the frustration level are listed as follows:

	Word Recognition	*Comprehension*
Frustration level	90% or less	50% or less

In examining this, one might logically ask, What happens if a student's word recognition level falls between 91 through 94 percent or when the comprehension level falls between 51 through 59 percent? That is to say, these percentages have not been accounted for since the criterion for word recognition at the instructional level is 95% *or more* and the criterion for comprehension is 60% *or more;* whereas the word recognition for the frustration level is 90% *or less* and for comprehension is 60% *or less.* These levels were apparently designed this way so as to give the teacher a chance to make a judgment as to whether the student should be placed at the higher of the two levels (instructional) or the lower of the two levels (frustration) based on his or her performance during the testing. For example, a student might score at the 94% level on word recognition, which is near the minimum of 95% or more for the instructional level. This same student may then score at the 100% level on comprehension. If this was the case, the teacher would probably want to look at the types of errors the student made in word recognition. If it was noted that most of the student's word recognition errors were less serious ones, such as repetitions, then the student would probably be given the benefit of the doubt and placed at the higher (instructional) level. On the other hand if a student scored at the 91% level on word recognition and was near the minimum, in comprehension, for the instructional level (60%), then the teacher would probably choose to place the student at the lower (frustration) level. In using the *Ekwall Reading Inventory* you will find a table on the answer sheet, for each oral reading passage, showing the recommended level when both the student's oral reading errors and comprehension are taken into consideration.

Number of Word Recognition Errors

Number of Questions Missed	0–2	3–5	6–8	9–11	12–14	15+
0	+	(*)	*	*	(*)	(×)
1	+	(*)	*	(*)	(×)	×
2	(*)	*	(*)	(×)	×	×
3	*	*	(×)	×	×	×
4	(*)	×	×	×	×	×
5+	×	×	×	×	×	×

Reading Level

⊞	Independent	☐
⊡	Instructional	☑
☒	Frustration	☐

This table makes it easy to quickly determine the student's reading level regardless of where the two scores fall in terms of percentages since the calculations have already been done for you. However, when a student's score falls in an area just bordering another, such as between the independent and instructional levels or between the instructional and frustration levels as indicated by the circled plus marks (+), the circled asterisks, and the circled x's, then you may wish to exercise somewhat more judgment in deciding exactly which level would be appropriate for the student. For example, a repetition may, for some students, actually indicate that they were aware of an error and thus cause them to go back and correct it—making a repetition error in the process. The research referred to on page ERI 3 indicated that when using the percentages commonly given for scoring informal inventories, *repetitions should be counted as errors.* If they are not, the student may physiologically reach the frustration level even though there would not be a high enough percentage of errors to place him or her at that level if repetitions were not counted as errors. In using the *Ekwall Reading Inventory,* however, the experienced teacher should use some judgment in the scoring procedure. For example, if a student makes one or two repetition errors in a relatively short passage and comprehends nearly perfectly, he or she would probably be placed at the instructional level instead of at the independent level. In such a case one might want to give the student the benefit of the doubt and consider the performance to be at the independent level. Likewise, making a meaningful substitution is not as serious as making a nonmeaningful one. If a single error such as this makes the student drop from independent to instructional level or from instructional to frustration level, then the teacher may want to disregard the error. However, the teacher should keep in mind that this type of disregarding should not be overdone, or the student will ultimately be placed at too difficult a reading level.

A certain amount of teacher judgment should also be used in counting errors that are obviously a result of syntax. For example, in certain families or in certain parts of the country it might be common for a student to say, as in passage 3A, "Kathy had always wanted to go for a ride *in* an airplane," rather than "Kathy had always wanted to go for a ride *on* an airplane." If the student obviously knows all of the basic sight words and does not continuously make other substitutions that change the meaning of the passage, then you may wish to ignore such minor errors.

In recording the student's reading rate on the silent reading passages it should also be remembered that a student who reads in the "average" category, but who is near the "fast" end of the "average" reads considerably faster than the average student. For this reason you should keep in mind that the student, in reality, reads at a "high average" rate. The same is, of course, true for a student who reads on the low end of the "average" category, i.e., the student should, in reality, be considered as reading at a "low average" rate.

DIRECTIONS FOR QUICK ADMINISTRATION OF THE EKWALL READING INVENTORY

When administering the Ekwall Reading Inventory it may, in some cases, be desirable to use only the oral or silent passages rather than both. For example, with younger students (grades one to four) you may wish to have them read only the oral passages ("A" or "C"). Conversely, in testing older students (fourth grade and above) you may wish to use only the silent passages ("B" and "D"). In either case you should follow the same procedure as recommended when giving both the oral and silent passages, except that one or the other is simply omitted.

HOW LONG DOES IT TAKE TO ADMINISTER THE EKWALL READING INVENTORY?

The time it takes to administer the graded word list and the reading passages will depend upon the ability of the examiner to assess the starting point or the point at which the student reads at the independent reading level. It will also depend upon the reading ability of the student, since some students are very slow readers and will require more time to read as well as to answer the questions about each passage. However, some expected time guidelines, based on the administration of the ERI to approximately twenty children at each grade level, are shown below.

Grade Level	Average Time in Minutes	Range in Minutes	Grade Level	Average Time in Minutes	Range in Minutes
1	21	13–26	6	23	14–30
2	26	11–36	7	18	18–47
3	28	18–47	8	25	15–45
4	24	17–31	9	30	26–34
5	33	21–53			

The time for administering the phonics inventory will also depend upon the grade level and ability of the student. Some expected times for the administration of this part of the inventory are as follows:

Grade	*Expected Time for Administration*
1–4	7–18 Minutes
5+	10–25 Minutes

THE DEVELOPMENT OF THE EKWALL READING INVENTORY

The Graded Word List

The graded word list used in the Ekwall Reading Inventory was developed by Margaret La Pray and Ramon Ross at San Diego State University. This list was published in the *Journal of Reading* in January 1969. The author and his students have experimented with this and other published word lists for a number of years. From his experimentation the author believes that this list, more accurately than any other, is likely to place a student at the correct independent, instructional, and frustration reading grade levels based on his or her sight vocabulary and word attack skills. However, it should be stressed that grade levels determined from this list are based solely on word knowledge and word analysis; therefore, the examiner should not use the levels obtained as anything more than a guide for a starting point in administering the oral and silent reading passages in the Ekwall Reading Inventory and as a rough guide to the level of a student's word recognition and word analysis skills.

A preliminary study, using forty students from grades one through nine, was done to determine the accuracy with which the graded word list predicted the correct entry level (the same independent reading level) in the graded reading passages.

The results from this study were that the graded word list predicted the exact independent (entry) level of the student for reading passages 18 percent of the time, within one grade level 28 percent of the time, and within two grade levels 72 percent of the time.

The Graded Reading Passages

All of the passages in the Ekwall Reading Inventory were written by the author, who attempted to create passages that, according to research, would be of interest to students. The author also attempted to control the subject matter so that questions about the content of each passage could not be answered without the student having read that passage. All of the passages contain ten sentences, except the pre-primer passages. Usually there is one question about each sentence. The first question, in most cases, is rather easy and is designed to give the student confidence in his or her ability to answer the rest of the questions.

In all of the passages above the second grade level one question is designed to test the student's vocabulary. This question can often be answered by the student if he or she makes good use of meaning context. In all passages above the first grade level one question is designed to test the student's abilitity to make inferences. Most of the answers to the inference questions can be inferred from the passage itself. Any student with a good ability to reason should be able to answer these questions even though the answers are not directly stated. The author does not believe it is fair to expect a student to answer inference questions based strictly on background experiences, since some students with rich backgrounds would likely have an advantage over those with more meager backgrounds.

The initials "F," and "I," and "V" appear beside each blank on the comprehension questions on the teacher's answer sheet. These initials designate the type of questions being asked. The initial "F" stands for "factual," "I" stands for "inference," and "V" stands for "vocabulary."

In some cases the tester may feel it would be desirable to have more inference-type questions. However, the author did not include more inference questions because research has shown that most teachers use very few inference questions in their teaching. Research in the area of reading comprehension has also shown that it is difficult, if not impossible, to design questions accurately other than those sampling vocabulary knowledge and factual information. Furthermore, inference questions are less passage-dependent than literal-type questions. For this reason students would be unduly penalized if more than 10 percent of the questions were of the inference type.

The grade levels of the reading passages for pre-primer through grade eight were determined by using the Harris-Jacobson Readability Formula.* This is a formula based on a great deal of research done by Albert Harris and Milton Jacobson. The formula is based on the percentage of hard words in the passage (words not on the Harris-Jacobson List) and average sentence length. In writing the passages the author adjusted the average sentence length and the percentage of hard words so as to derive a score that would place the reading difficulty of each passage near the midpoint of each grade level.

The grade levels of the reading passages for ninth grade were determined by using the revised version by Powers et al.† of the original Dale-Chall‡ Readability Formula.

After the initial writing of the passages and the questions about them were completed, the author and several assistants administered the inventory to approximately fifty students. These administrations were tape-recorded and later analyzed to determine whether certain questions were consistently missed by nearly all students due to faulty wordings. Following this analysis, certain adjustments were made. The inventory was then reviewed by four professors of reading education. Based on these reviews, certain adjustments were again made. The inventory was then

* The Harris-Jacobson Readability Formula appears in Albert A. Harris and Edward R. Sipay, *How to Increase Reading Ability,* 6th Ed. New York: David McKay Co., Inc., 1980, Appendix D.

† R. B. Powers, W. A. Sumner, and B. E. Kearl, "A Recalculation of Readability Formulas," *Journal of Educational Psychology, 49* (1958), pp. 99–105.

‡ Edgar Dale and Jeanne Chall, "A Formula for Predicting Readability," *Educational Research Bulletin* (January 1948), pp. 11–20, 28.

administered to approximately sixty students of various ages, and further minor revisions were made in the content of the passages and the questions about them until it was determined that the questions and the levels of the passages were satisfactory.

The initial version of the inventory contained primer as well as pre-primer and first grade passages. It was found that although it is possible to differentiate between pre-primer and primer passages using a readability formula, it is not practical to include both pre-primer and primer passages. The reason is that there is simply not enough difference between the reading levels of pre-primer and primer passages to assess the difference accurately for most students. Therefore, only pre-primer and first grade level passages appear in the Ekwall Reading Inventory. The pre-primer passages represent the lowest level at which a student can be said to read, and the first grade passages represent a medium-to-high first grade level.

The Time Factors for the Silent Reading Passages.

The time factors for the silent reading passages are listed as *slow, medium,* and *fast,* and a *median* (the point at which half the students read slower and the other half read faster) and *mean* (average) are given in the second edition of the *Ekwall Reading Inventory.* These were developed by administering the inventory to approximately 170 students at each grade level. Care was taken to select students from schools and classrooms from various socioeconomic levels from three school districts. The districts from which students were selected were the Carlsbad New Mexico Public Schools, the El Paso, Texas, Independent School District, and the Canutillo, Texas, Independent School District. The times are for students who comprehended at 70 percent or higher. You may note that passages, even at the same grade level, tended to take a shorter amount of time to read, in terms of words per minute, when the passages were longer. Most studies of the reading speeds of children tend to vary a great deal. One of the factors that obviously accounts for this is passage length, and other time factors, of course, such as interest, prior knowledge, and distractions, among others.

The times given for the pre-primer level are for students in the first grade during the month of November and the times for the first grade and all other grade levels are for the months of late March, February, and early April.

RELIABILITY OF THE EKWALL READING INVENTORY

A preliminary study was done in which forty students were administered the "A" and "B" forms and "C" and "D" forms in order to study the reliability of the two forms. Two examiners tested forty students from grades one through nine. Half of the students were given the "A" and "B" forms first and the other half were given the "C" and "D" forms first. All students were given the second forms (not previously taken) within a period of one week, or less, after the administration of the first forms. A product-moment coefficient was calculated between the "A" and "C" (oral) forms and found to be .82. The same calculations between the "B" and "D" (silent) forms produced a correlation coefficient of .79. One examiner administered forms "A" and "B" and forms "C" and "D" in grades one through four, while the other examiner administered the same forms in grades five through nine. The correlation coefficients of .82 and .79 must, then, be considered as a measure of intrascorer reliability.

ANALYSIS OF A COMPLETED SUMMARY SHEET

On the two summary pages that follow, pp. ERI 23 and 24, is a sample of a completed summary sheet for a student who had taken the Ekwall Reading Inventory. This summary sheet contains the following information:

1. On the graded word list the student missed either one or no words at the pre-primer level. Therefore, his independent reading level was at pre-primer. He missed two words from each of the lists at the pre-primer and first grade levels. Therefore, his instructional level on word pronunciation placed him at pre-primer through first grade level. This student missed three or more words at the second grade level, which placed his frustration level at second grade on word pronunciation.
2. When the student read orally, he was at his independent level at pre-primer, at his instructional level at grade levels one and two, and at his frustration level at grade three. He did slightly better in reading silently. Here, his independent level was first grade. His instructional level was at grades two and three and his frustration level was at grade four. His listening comprehension level was also at grade four.

A pattern such as this usually indicates that the student has a low sight vocabulary and/or poor word analysis skills. However, it does indicate that he or she has good comprehension and that word attack and/or sight vocabulary are not so bad that they seriously hinder comprehension. The pattern of poor word analysis skills is further substantiated by the fact that the examiner indicated that this particular student needed improvement in his use of context clues, vowel sounds, vowel rules, syllable division, knowledge of contractions, and ability to blend.

The examiner indicated that his comprehension was adequate for his grade level, which is substantiated by his ability to score up to grade level on silent reading. The examiner did, however, indicate that he had difficulty with inference questions.

The examiner also indicated that he seemed to comprehend approximately the same on oral and silent reading. The student also lacks knowledge of immediate recognition of some basic sight words (common words of high utility) as well as some other sight words, in general, that should have been instantly recognized by third grade level.

The student's lack of knowledge of vowel sounds accounted for the high number of partial mispronunciations. His lack of knowledge of sight words and basic sight words tended to make him a word-by-word reader, resulting in poor phrasing and lack of expression. The pauses also indicated that he lacks instant knowledge of a number of sight words, thus contributing to his slow rate of reading.

This student also substituted one word for another in several cases, as indicated under Semantic-Syntactic Abilities. In these instances the student substituted words that he felt would belong in certain sentences based on his own background of experiences. For example, in passage 3-C he said, "Then a pilot came and told them he would take them for a ride on a large airplane" rather than the correct reading, which is: "Then a pilot came and told them he would take them on a large airplane."

As indicated by the student's listening comprehension score, he can comprehend at least one grade level above his own grade placement when material is read to him.

EKWALL READING INVENTORY
Summary Sheet • Forms C & D

STUDENT'S NAME: Jamie Morrow DATE: 11/16/8-

GRADE IN SCHOOL: 3rd EXAMINER: Jeff Brand

Results of Graded Word List:

Independent Reading Level	Grade pp	(Highest level at which one or no words were missed)
Instructional Reading Level	Grade p-1	(Two words missed)
Frustration Reading Level	Grade 2	(Lowest level at which three or more words were missed)

Results of Reading Passages:

		Oral	*Silent*
Independent Reading Level	Grade	pp	1
Instructional Reading Level	Grade	1-2	2-3
Frustration Reading Level	Grade	3	4
Listening Comprehension Level	Grade	4	

Word Analysis Skills

- ___ Adequate in all areas
- ___ Use of context clues adequate
- ✓ Aware of context clues but needs improvement
- ___ Little or no use of context clues
- ✓ Guesses at words by first letter only
- ___ Attempts to sound letter by letter
- ___ Lacks knowledge of consonants
- ___ Lacks knowledge of consonant clusters
- ✓ Lacks knowledge of vowel sounds
- ___ Lacks knowledge of common phonograms (Word families)
- ✓ Unable to blend adequately
- ✓ Appears unaware of common syllable division
- ✓ Appears unaware of common vowel rules (VCE, CV, CVC)
- ___ Unaware of configuration
- ___ Guesses by general configuration only
- ___ Calls words without association of any word attack skills (context, configuration, morphology, phonics)
- ✓ Some contractions not known

Comprehension

- ✓ Adequate for grade level
- ___ Below grade level
- ___ Difficulty with factual (F) questions
- ___ Difficulty with vocabulary (V) questions
- ✓ Difficulty with inference (I) questions

Oral Versus Silent Reading

_____ Comprehends *better* in *oral* reading
_____ Comprehends *better* in *silent* reading
✓ Comprehends approximately the *same* in *oral* and *silent* reading

Sight Vocabulary

Basic Sight Words
(Words of high utility)

_____ No difficulty with Basic Sight Words
✓ *Some* Basic Sight Words not known
_____ *Many* Basic Sight Words not known
_____ *Few* or *no* Basic Sight Words known

Sight Words in General

_____ No difficulty with sight words at or below grade level
✓ *Some* sight words not known
_____ *Many* sight words not known
_____ *Few* or *no* sight words known

Oral Reading Errors

2 Omissions
1 Insertions
10 Partial Mispronunciations
2 Gross Mispronunciations
3 Substitutions
6 Repetitions
3 Self-corrected errors
0 Inversions

Characteristics of the Reader

_____ Head movement
✓ Finger pointing
✓ Disregard for punctuation
_____ Loss of place
_____ Does not read in natural voice tones
✓ Word-by-word reading
✓ Poor phrasing
✓ Lack of expression
✓ Pauses
✓ Voicing or lip movement

Rate of Reading

_____ Silent rate fast for grade level
_____ Silent rate high average for grade level
_____ Silent rate average for grade level
_____ Silent rate low average for grade level
✓ Silent rate slow for grade level
_____ Oral rate fast
_____ Oral rate adequate
✓ Oral rate slow
_____ High rate at expense of accuracy

Semantic-Syntactic Abilities

✓ Made meaningful substitutions
_____ Made nonmeaningful substitutions
_____ Meaningful substitutions reflected student's dialect

Listening Comprehension

_____ Understanding of material heard is *below* grade level
✓ Understanding of material heard is *at* or *above* grade level

DIAGNOSTIC FLOW CHART SEQUENCE

3853 Words

Perhaps the most important information that a diagnostician will derive from the *Ekwall Reading Inventory,* or any good informal reading inventory, is a better knowledge of the weaknesses exhibited by a student in his or her silent reading. These weaknesses will indicate to the trained diagnostician how to proceed logically with the diagnosis, once the informal reading inventory has been completed. The purpose of the diagnostic flow chart, on the following pages, is to show you where to go in the diagnostic procedure once you have finished administering the *Ekwall Reading Inventory.* And most important, it will help you to determine how to do the diagnosis in the most efficient way.

On the pages that follow you will first find Figure 1 which shows the first steps recommended by the author in doing a diagnosis of a student with reading difficulties. You will note that Step 3 includes the administration of an informal reading inventory. As a result of the information gained in the administration of an informal reading inventory you would be likely to proceed in any one, or more, of five directions, depending upon the difficulties noted by the diagnostician while the inventory was being administered. In Figures 2, 3, 4, and 5 you will find a detailed explanation of each of five possible sequential procedures that might be followed based upon the information derived from the administration of the *Ekwall Reading Inventory.* Finally, you will find, in Figure 6, the total diagnostic sequence as detailed in Figures 1, 2, 3, 4, and 5.* A very brief explanation of each step follows:

Step 1. This consists of a short interview. If you are doing a detailed diagnosis, there will be a number of points that you may wish to cover. If, however, you are only going to administer an informal reading inventory, then you may only wish to make sure the student being tested is comfortable, talk briefly with the student to put him or her at ease in the testing situation, and proceed to Step 2 or Step 3.

Step 2. If you are doing a detailed diagnosis, you may wish to test the student using one of the vision screening devices. Since some studies indicate that nearly 50 percent of the students that are referred for remedial reading have some sort of visual problem, this is a necessary part of a diagnosis for a student who has not had an eye test by an eye doctor in a period of a year or less. The administration of an eye examination is also a good way to establish rapport with the student since it would generally not be a threatening situation. If the student showed no signs of difficulty, then the diagnosis would move to Step 3. If the student showed signs of visual difficulty, then the student would be referred to a vision specialist or eye doctor as indicated in Step 10.

Step 3. Nearly any informal reading inventory, including the *Ekwall Reading Inventory,* uses a graded word list to establish a beginning point

* A more detailed explanation, along with a list of assessment devices, may be found in the following reference: Ekwall, Eldon E. & Shanker, James L. *Diagnosis and remediation of the disabled reader,* 2 ed. Newton, MA: Allyn and Bacon, Inc., 1983, Chap. 13.

for the passages of the informal reading inventory. The informal reading inventory is usually started at the student's independent reading level as shown by the results of the graded word list. The *Ekwall Reading Inventory* includes the *San Diego Quick Assessment Word List* for this purpose. It is helpful when administering a graded word list to write phonetically any wrong responses given by the student as this information will often enable the diagnostician to see particular problems that the student may encounter with word attack skills.

Step 4. This step includes the administration of the informal reading inventory. This will enable the diagnostician to derive an oral and silent independent, instructional, and frustration level for the student being tested. If the student does not read up to grade level on either or both of the oral or silent passages, the diagnostician should give the student a listening comprehension test, as described on page ERI 9 of the *Ekwall Reading Inventory*. This will enable the diagnostician to determine whether there is a discrepancy in the student's ability to comprehend and what he or she has comprehended on the oral and/or silent reading passages. If the listening comprehension level is a grade level or two above the student's comprehension on the oral and/or silent passages, then this will be an indication that the student's potential to comprehend will be higher than that indicated by the oral and/or silent reading passages. This, of course, might be a result of the student's inability to decode rapidly and/or the result of a low sight vocabulary in relation to the actual grade placement of the student.

The steps following #4 would depend upon the information derived from the informal reading inventory. They will be explained and illustrated in numerial order as shown on the diagnostic flow chart. In describing certain of these steps, two coded reading passages are shown that are typical of that of students with reading error patterns illustrating which direction the flow chart might indicate would be the next logical step in the diagnostic procedure. These coded passages appear on pp. ERI 32–33 and will be referred to, at times, in the step-by-step explanations that follow.

Step 5. The diagnostic procedure to be used in Steps 5 through 9 may be accomplished by using the *Assessment of Letter Knowledge* found in Appendix A, pp. 223–227. The diagnostician would proceed to this step in the diagnosis if the student knew very few words even at the pre-primer level. It would also be done if the student had a tendency to reverse letters, even if that student did know a considerable number of sight words. The performance of student #1 (Ramon) shown on page ERI 32 is an example of the type of performance by a reader that might lead the diagnostician to believe that an assessment of letter knowledge would be appropriate.

Step 6. This procedure consists of having the student name the upper and lower case letters from a stimulus sheet. The diagnostician may also wish to have the student write the alphabet in both upper and lower case, although this would not be as directly related to the reading task as the identification of letters. This would be Task 1 on the *Assessment of Letter Knowledge* found on p. 226. It should be remembered that knowledge of the alphabet is not an absolute prerequisite for learning to read;

however, students who do not know the alphabet by the middle or end of grade one will often be those who are also encountering problems in reading. If the student can identify correctly all letters in both upper and lower case (Task 2 on the *Assessment of Letter Knowledge* found on p. 226), the diagnosis in this area would cease. If the student was unable to accomplish this task, then the diagnostician would proceed to Step 7.

Step 7. In doing this activity the student would be asked to point to letters in scrambled order as they are given orally by the diagnostician. This would be Task 3 on the *Assessment of Letter Knowledge* found on p. 226. If the student could do this step, then the diagnosis would cease and the diagnostician would move in another direction. If the student could not do this task, then the diagnostician would move to Step 8.

Step 8. In doing this activity the student would be asked to match a lower case letter with the corresponding upper case letter, or vice versa. This step is Task 4 on the *Assessment of Letter Knowledge* found on p. 226. If the student could accomplish this task, then the diagnostician would cease the assessment in this area and move in another direction. If the student could not do this task, then the diagnostician would move to Step 9.

Step 9. This is Task 5 on the *Assessment of Letter Knowledge* found on p. 226. This consists of having the student match a letter, written in lower case, with another letter that looks exactly the same. If the student could do this task, then the diagnosis would cease in this area and the diagnostician would move in another direction. If the student could not do this task, then the diagnostician may wish to move to Step 10.

Step 10. A student who failed Step 9 and who had not had a test by an eye doctor in a year or less should probably be referred to a vision specialist as indicated in this step. A student who failed one of the tests on the visual screening instrument used in Step 2 would, of course, also be referred to a vision specialist.

Step 11. The diagnostician who noted a student who either had problems with sight words (meaning both basic sight words and/or sight words in general) and/or problems in phonetic word attack or structural analysis word attack would then proceed to this step in the diagnostic flow chart. After examining the errors, as explained below, the diagnostician would proceed to either or all of Step 12, Step 12-a (see Figure 6 for this step), Step 13, Step 24, and Step 26.

Step 12. If the student had difficulties in the analysis of new words that were obviously caused from a lack of knowledge of sound-symbol correspondence or lack of knowledge of vowel rules and syllable principles, then the diagnostician would have to consider the evidence gained so far. If the student was at third grade, or below, and could not pronounce a number of words because he or she did not know how to use phonetic or structural analysis word attack skills, then the diagnostician would logically proceed to Step 13. If a student was at third grade reading level, or below, then there would be no need to administer the *Quick Survey Word List* since the words on it are only for more advanced readers to determine whether they do or do not have a problem with phonics or structural analysis. A student who performed somewhat similar to Student #2 (Theresa) shown on p. ERI 33 would be typical of a student for whom

Step 12-a would be omitted. This student was only at the third grade level and missed some phonetically regular words at the first grade level. Therefore, one would not expect her to be able to pronounce the words on the *Quick Survey Word List,* and giving it would only be a waste of time for the diagnostician and frustrating for the student. On the other hand, if a student was at the fourth grade level, or above, and read quite well and the diagnostician suspected that the student had problems with phonetic or structural analysis skills, then he or she might want to give the student the *Quick Survey Word List.* If the student could pronounce all of the words rather quickly and easily, the entire procedure shown on Diagnostic Sequence, p. ERI 36, could be omitted and a great deal of time would be saved. However, if, after giving the student the words on the *Quick Survey Word List,* it was found that the student had considerable difficulty with the words, then the complete diagnostic procedure as outlined in Steps 13 through 22 might be carried out.

If, in giving the informal reading inventory, it was found that the student had problems with words that should have been known by sight (either basic sight words or sight words in general), then the diagnostician might proceed to Step 23 and give the *Quick Check for Basic Sight Words.** If the student knew all of these words rather rapidly, the diagnostician would stop the diagnosis of basic sight words. On the other hand, if the student did not know one or more of these words, then he or she would proceed to Step 24.

Step 13. This involves the administration of a phonics test. The need for an assessment of phonics knowledge would be indicated by such behaviors as a student reading up to a word and then pausing and finally mispronouncing the word. It would also be indicated by a student mispronouncing the vowel sounds in words or placing the wrong beginning, middle, or ending sounds on words. If the student did not do well on this test, then the diagnostician would proceed to Step 14.

Step 14. If a student performs extremely poorly on a phonics test, then one might wonder if the reason for this poor performance was that the student could not hear the differences between certain phonemes that sound nearly alike such as the slight differences between those heard in the words "shake" and "shape." This author, however, believes that, in most cases, the administration of an auditory discrimination test tends to be a waste of time. This is partly because students often fail an auditory discrimination test, but when the same student is given a second test, he or she usually passes the test. Therefore, it would seem that the results of any one test cannot be depended upon to be accurate. Furthermore, it is somewhat doubtful that training in auditory discrimination is helpful in improving a student's ability to use phonics.

Step 15. This step involves the administration of an auditory acuity test. If a student did poorly on an auditory discrimination test, then there are two possible reasons for this failure. One would be that the student simply needed to learn to discriminate between various "minimal pairs." The other reason why a student would fail would be that the student could not hear the difference between minimal pairs. Therefore, if a stu-

* The *Quick Check for Basic Sight Words* may be found in the following reference: Eldon E. Ekwall, *Locating and correcting reading difficulties,* 4th ed. Columbus, Ohio: Charles E. Merrill, 1985, pp. 200–203.

dent does extremely poorly on an auditory discrimination test, it would seem logical to check that student's ability to hear these differences in sounds.

Step 16. This step involves the referral of a student, who was found to have a problem with auditory acuity, to an audiologist or speech pathologist.

Step 17. If the student passed the auditory acuity test, or it was found that the student had no difficulty in hearing, then the logical process would be to teach the student how to discriminate between minimal pairs. In this case the diagnostician may wish to identify exactly which phonemes or which minimal pairs the student is having difficulty with and list them so that they can be taught.

Step 18. A student who is found to have problems in pronouncing multisyllable words and who is also found to know all of the initial consonants, consonant digraphs, consonant blends, vowel sounds, vowel controlled sounds, etc., would probably be experiencing this difficulty because he or she had problems with the longer sound units of the language that are often referred to as structural analysis or morphology.

Step 19. Some students experience difficulty because they do not use the information that they already possess to attack new words systematically.

Step 20. If a student knew the individual vowel sounds in one-syllable words and yet tended to mispronounce them in multisyllable words, then it would be logical to advance to this step and check the student's knowledge of vowel rules. This may be done by using the materials in Appendix E, pp. 261–270.

Step 21. A student, such as the one described above, who knew the vowel sounds in one-syllable words but who did not seem to know them in multisyllable words should be checked for knowledge of syllable principles. A knowledge of where to break a word into syllables is essential so that the student will know the position of the vowel(s) in each syllable. The student will then know what sound to give each vowel. A check for a student's ability to use syllable principles may be done using the materials in Appendix E, pp. 264–270.

Step 22. If a student is found to know the pronunciation of the vowels in one-syllable words and also knows the vowel rules and syllable principles and yet does not properly attack a word, it is perhaps because the student does not "systematically" use this knowledge. It can be determined if this is the case by giving students multisyllable words and asking them to break the words into syllables and pronounce each one in order. Many students simply need practice in using what they already know about the skills tested in Steps 20 and 21, i.e., *application* of the vowel rules and syllable principles.

Step 23. If a student is found who substitutes one basic sight word for another or who misses an occasional basic sight word, the diagnostician may wish to give the student the *Quick Check for Basic Sight Words.** This involves asking the student to pronounce words from a short list of

* The *Quick Check for Basic Sight Words* may be found in the following reference: Eldon E. Ekwall, *Locating and correcting reading difficulties,* 4th ed. Columbus, Ohio: Charles E. Merrill, 1985, pp. 200–3.

basic sight words. If the student gets them all correct, it can usually be assumed that the student would not need to be given the entire basic sight word test.

Step 24. If a student fails the *Quick Check for Basic Sight Words,* or, that is to say, misses one or more words on that assessment instrument, then it would be logical to administer the entire basic sight word test. It would also be logical to omit the *Quick Check for Basic Sight Words* if it was shown by a student's reading that he or she did not know a number of basic sight words. In such a case the student would be given the entire basic sight word test, providing the student had reached the end of second or middle of third grade where he or she would definitely be expected to know all of the words.

Step 25. If it was found, after a student was tested on the basic sight words, that the student paused at words that one would expect that student to know instantly, then it would be logical to give the student a test on sight words in general that should be known at his or her grade level.

Steps 26 and 27. If a student tends to hesitate before certain basic sight words but usually is able to pronounce all of them, the diagnostician may wish to give the student a flash presentation of each of the basic sight words using flash cards or by programming them on a computer so that they are presented at a rate of one every one and three-fourths seconds. This will enable the diagnostician to know if the student has instant recognition of the words.

Step 28. If a student is found to know all of the basic sight words instantly, then the diagnostician may wish to give the student a flash presentation of certain words that are not basic sight words but that should be known instantly.

Step 29. This step involves the observation of a student while he or she is reading orally to determine whether the student seems to be encountering difficulty in using context clues.

Step 30. If a student seems to be encountering difficulty in the use of context clues, the diagnostician may wish to administer a test for the use of context clues.* If the student does not do well on this test, then the student would need to be taught to be more aware of the use of context clues.

Step 31. If it is noted that the student has difficulties with comprehension in either oral or silent reading, then the diagnostician would proceed to this step which involves a diagnosis of the student's ability to comprehend.

Step 32. This step involves either examining the results of a group or individual standardized test or the administration of the same.

Step 33. In examining the results of the group or individual standardized test the diagnostician can easily determine whether the vocabulary score is below, at, or above grade level. If it is found to be above grade level, then the diagnosis for vocabulary would cease. If it was found to be below grade level, then the diagnostician would proceed to Step 34.

Step 34. This involves the administration of an oral vocabulary test. If a student did not have sufficient word attack skills or a sufficient sight

* An assessment device for checking students' ability to use context clues may be found in the following source: Eldon E. Ekwall, *Locating and correcting reading difficulties,* 4th ed. Columbus, Ohio: Charles E. Merrill, 1985, pp. 213–28.

vocabulary to read and understand the material on a group or individual standardized test, then it would be logical to give the student an oral vocabulary test. This would help the diagnostician determine whether the student actually had a larger vocabulary than he or she appeared to have on the group standardized test that would, of course, involve a certain amount of reading.

Step 35. If the student was found to have a lower than normal score on a group standardized test, but also had a score on an oral vocabulary test that was average or above, then the diagnostician would probably want to check on the student's word attack or word analysis skills. In this case the diagnostician would move to Step 12.

Step 36. This step involves the administration of an intelligence test. If the student was below grade level on both the oral vocabulary test and the group standardized test, then the diagnostician may wish to know if the student is below normal in intelligence, which could logically be considered to be the cause of these low scores.

Step 37. If the student was found to be considerably below normal in intelligence, then the diagnostician may wish to refer the student to a psychologist or another appropriate person for further testing to determine whether the student would be eligible for placement in a particular classroom designed for this type of student.

Step 38. If a student's score on a standardizing reading achievement test is found to be below normal, the diagnostician may wish to check on the student's performance on a sustained silent reading task such as reading a textbook or reading a novel.

Step 39. This step involves checking the student's reading rate in sustained silent reading as noted in Step 38. A student's reading rate in silent reading may be checked by timing the student as he or she reads from the silent reading passages of the *Ekwall Reading Inventory.* Times considered to be slow, average, and fast are given for each silent reading passage. If the student's reading rate is considerably below normal, then the diagnostician may conclude that part or all of the student's problem with comprehension on group standardized tests was because the student could simply not read rapidly enough to finish the test in the given amount of time. This would of course, cause the student to receive a score that would be below that of what the student could achieve in reading something that was untimed.

Step 40. This step involves checking on the student's ability to read for a specific purpose such as reading to make inferences or to find main ideas, etc. Since research studies in the area of reading comprehension have tended to show that it is nearly impossible to identify any reading subskills with the exception of "vocabulary," then it seems somewhat doubtful that this can be done with any accuracy.

STUDENT #1—Ramon, 2d Grade, 8 yrs. old

	Oral	Silent
Independent Level	Grade ND*	ND
Instructional Level	Grade ND	PP
Frustration Level	Grade PP	1
Listening Comprehension Level	3rd grade	

*Indicates that this level was not determined.

1. The diagnostician would probably want to check Ramon's knowledge of letters using the *Assessment of Letter Knowledge*. A student who is in the second grade and reading this poorly is also likely to have some difficulty with the alphabet, although this would not be a foregone conclusion.
2. This student needs to be given a basic sight word test since he missed a number of words that are not just sight words but basic sight words. There would also be no need to give this student the *Quick Check for Basic Sight Words* since it is evident that a great number of basic sight words will not be known. Giving the *Quick Check for Basic Sight Words* would only be a waste of time.
3. One might want also to give Ramon an oral vocabulary test to see if he might possibly have a language problem involving oral vocabulary. However, the fact that the listening comprehension test showed that he had a listening comprehension level at least one year beyond his actual grade placement would mean that he has a strong potential for comprehending the English language if his sight vocabulary and word attack skills were improved.

(Jan) ~~has~~ had a dog.

The dog's || name is (Pat.)

He can ~~run~~ ran (fast.)

One (day) Pat ran (away.)

Jan look(ed) for him.

~~The~~ A dog want(ed) to (eat.)

(Soon) he ~~came~~ can (home.)

STUDENT #2—Theresa, 3rd Grade, 9 years. old

		Oral	Silent
Independent Level	Grade	ND	PP
Instructional Level	Grade	1	1-2
Frustration Level	Grade	2	3
Listening Comprehension Level		Not determined	

* Indicates that this level was not determined

1. Theresa would need to be given a phonics test since she is in the third grade and has difficulty pronouncing some words that are phonetically regular such as "picnic." Therefore, it would be logical to begin at Step #13 since she is in the 3rd grade. Since she could not pronounce the word "picnic" it would follow that she would not be able to pronounce any of the words on the *Quick Assessment Word List* (Step 12-b); therefore, giving her the *Quick Assessment Word List* would be a waste of time rather than possibly saving time.
2. The diagnostician would probably want to give Theresa the *Quick Check for Basic Sight Words* since she missed only one of the the basic sight words and this was a meaningful substitution. That is to say, she may actually know nearly all, or all, of the basic sight words, and if she could pronounce accurately all of the words on the *Quick Check for Basic Sight Words*, then it would be unnecessary for the diagnostician to administer the entire basic sight word list.
3. Since this student was reading at grade level in the silent passages, she would not need to be given a listening comprehension test and nothing further would need to be done with comprehension at this time.

Tuff was a big brown bear. He lived in a big park. He liked to eat honey // best of all. He also liked to eat bread.

Some people were in the park having a picnic. They were sitting by a big table. Tuff went to the (picnic) too. When the people saw him they were (afraid.) They all jumped up and ran away. Then the bear ate all of ~~their~~ the food.

Diagnostic Sequence

1

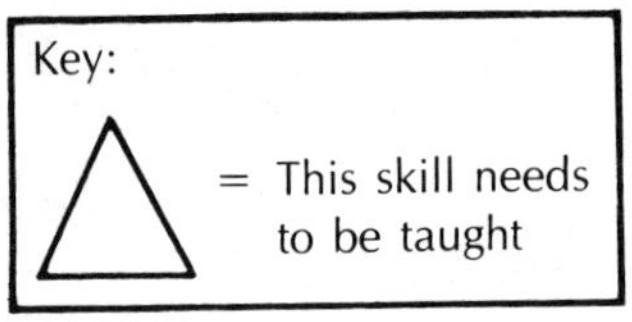

Key:
= This skill needs to be taught

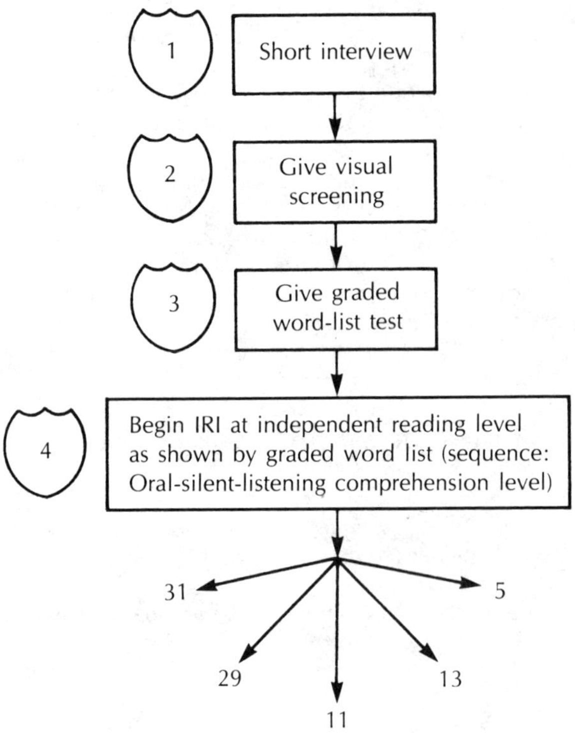

1
Short interview
2
Give visual screening
3
Give graded word-list test
4
Begin IRI at independent reading level as shown by graded word list (sequence: Oral-silent-listening comprehension level)
31
5
29
13
11

2

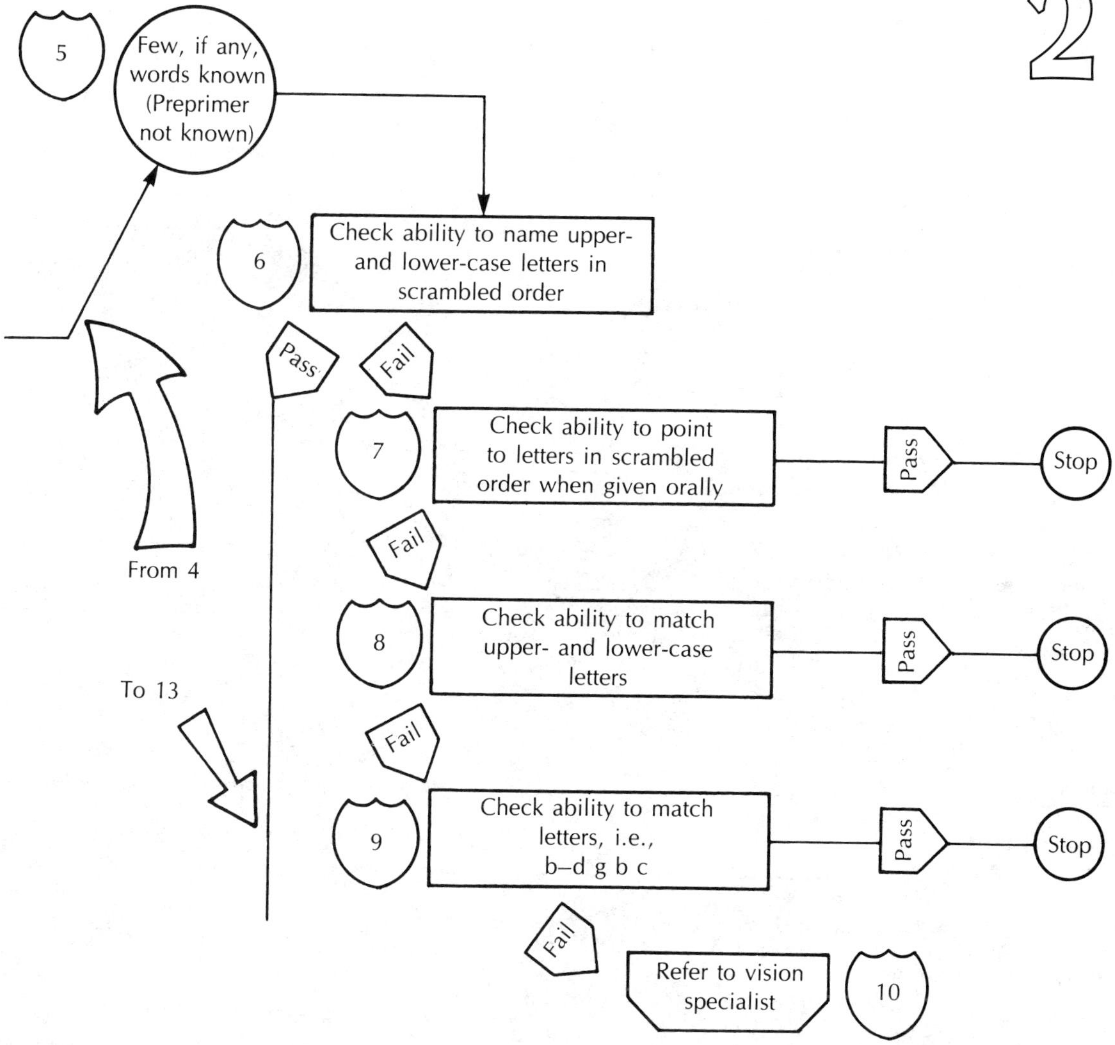
5
Few, if any, words known (Preprimer not known)
6
Check ability to name upper- and lower-case letters in scrambled order
Pass
Fail
7
Check ability to point to letters in scrambled order when given orally
Pass
Stop
Fail
8
Check ability to match upper- and lower-case letters
Pass
Stop
Fail
9
Check ability to match letters, i.e., b–d g b c
Pass
Stop
Fail
Refer to vision specialist
10
From 4
To 13

3

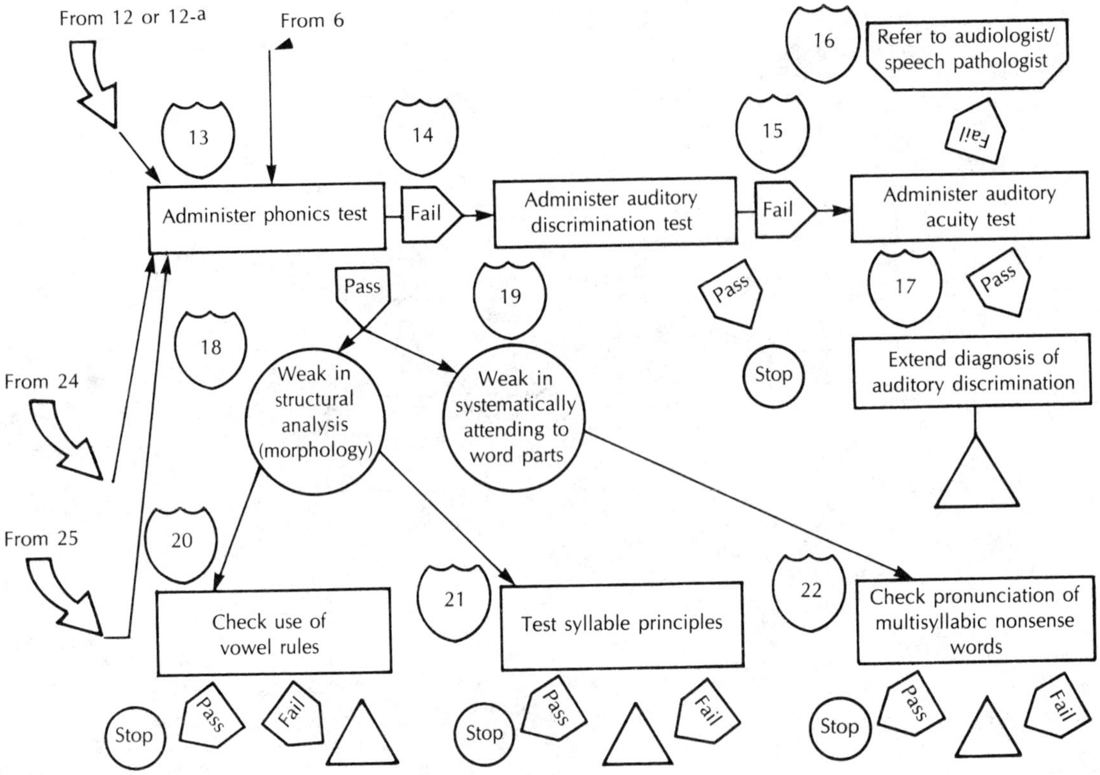
From 12 or 12-a
From 6
16
Refer to audiologist/ speech pathologist
13
14
15
Fail
Administer phonics test
Fail
Administer auditory discrimination test
Fail
Administer auditory acuity test
Pass
19
Pass
17
Pass
18
From 24
Weak in structural analysis (morphology)
Weak in systematically attending to word parts
Stop
Extend diagnosis of auditory discrimination
From 25
20
21
22
Check use of vowel rules
Test syllable principles
Check pronunciation of multisyllabic nonsense words
Stop
Pass
Fail
Stop
Pass
Fail
Stop
Pass
Fail

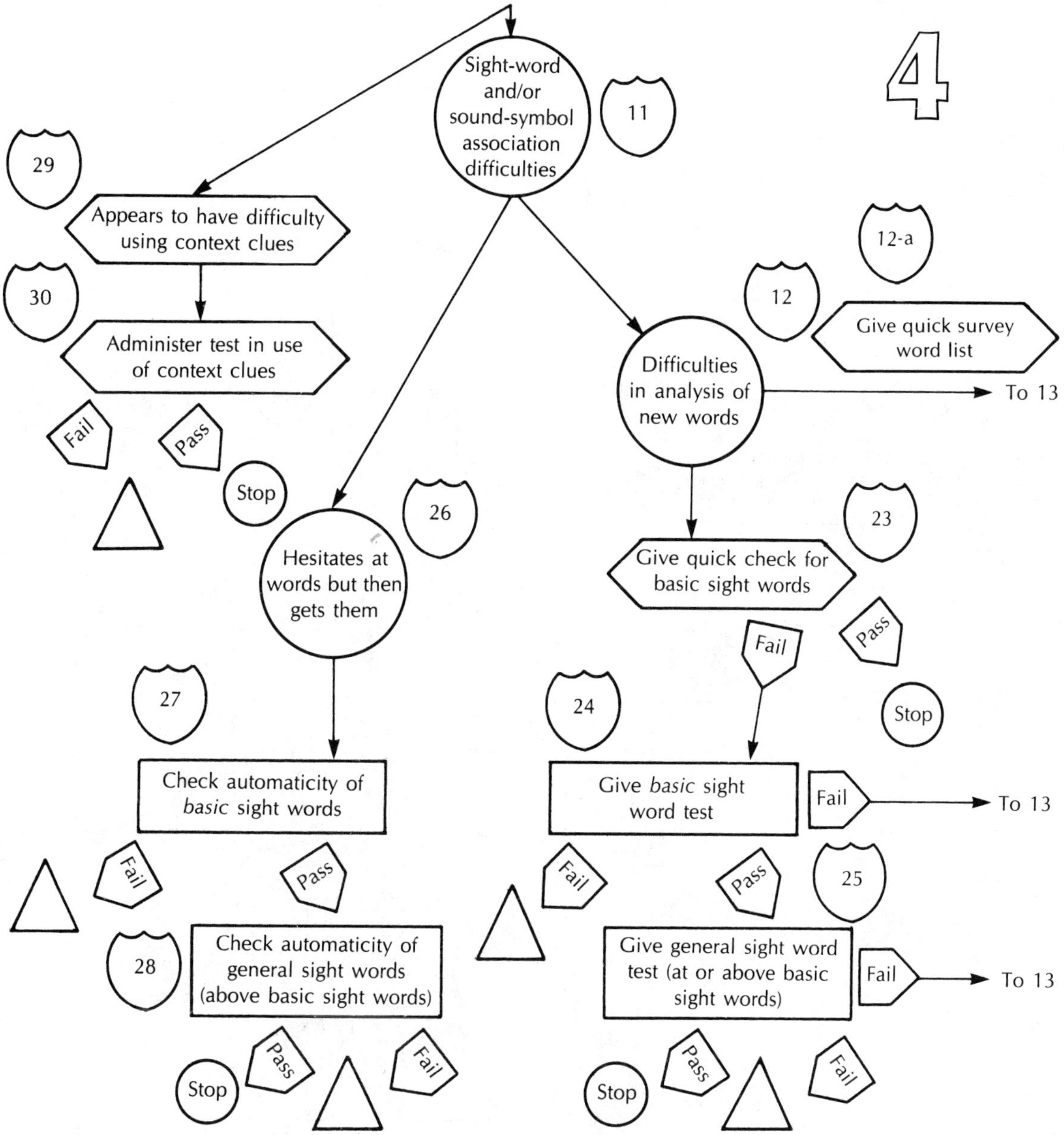
4
Sight-word and/or sound-symbol association difficulties
11
29
Appears to have difficulty using context clues
30
Administer test in use of context clues
Fail
Pass
Stop
12-a
12
Give quick survey word list
Difficulties in analysis of new words
To 13
26
Hesitates at words but then gets them
23
Give quick check for basic sight words
Fail
Pass
Stop
27
Check automaticity of *basic* sight words
Fail
Pass
24
Give *basic* sight word test
Fail
To 13
Fail
Pass
25
28
Check automaticity of general sight words (above basic sight words)
Give general sight word test (at or above basic sight words)
Fail
To 13
Stop
Pass
Fail
Stop
Pass
Fail

5

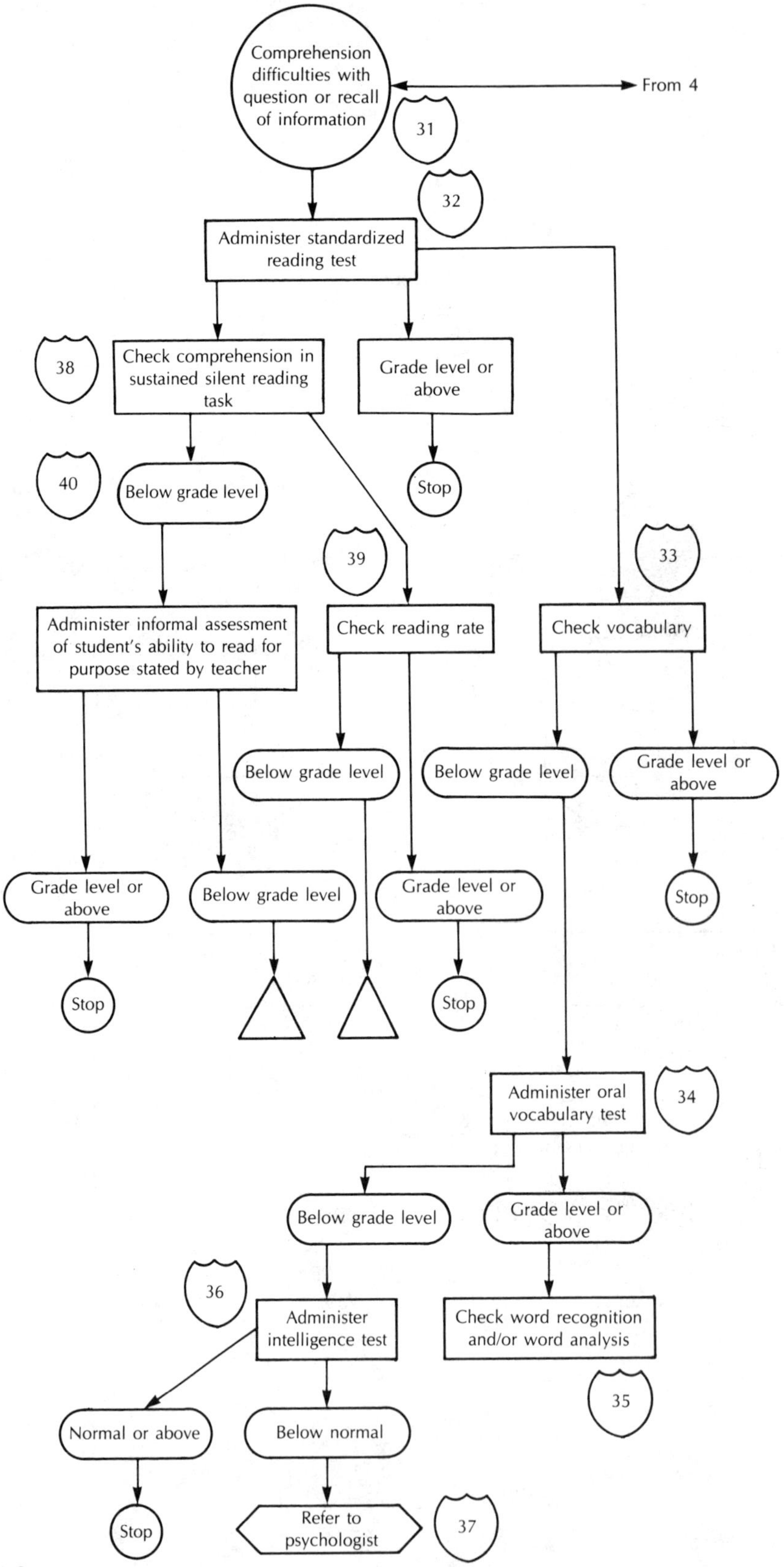
Comprehension difficulties with question or recall of information
From 4
31
32
Administer standardized reading test
38
Check comprehension in sustained silent reading task
Grade level or above
Stop
40
Below grade level
39
33
Administer informal assessment of student's ability to read for purpose stated by teacher
Check reading rate
Check vocabulary
Below grade level
Below grade level
Grade level or above
Grade level or above
Below grade level
Grade level or above
Stop
Stop
Stop
Administer oral vocabulary test
34
Below grade level
Grade level or above
36
Administer intelligence test
Check word recognition and/or word analysis
35
Normal or above
Below normal
Stop
Refer to psychologist
37

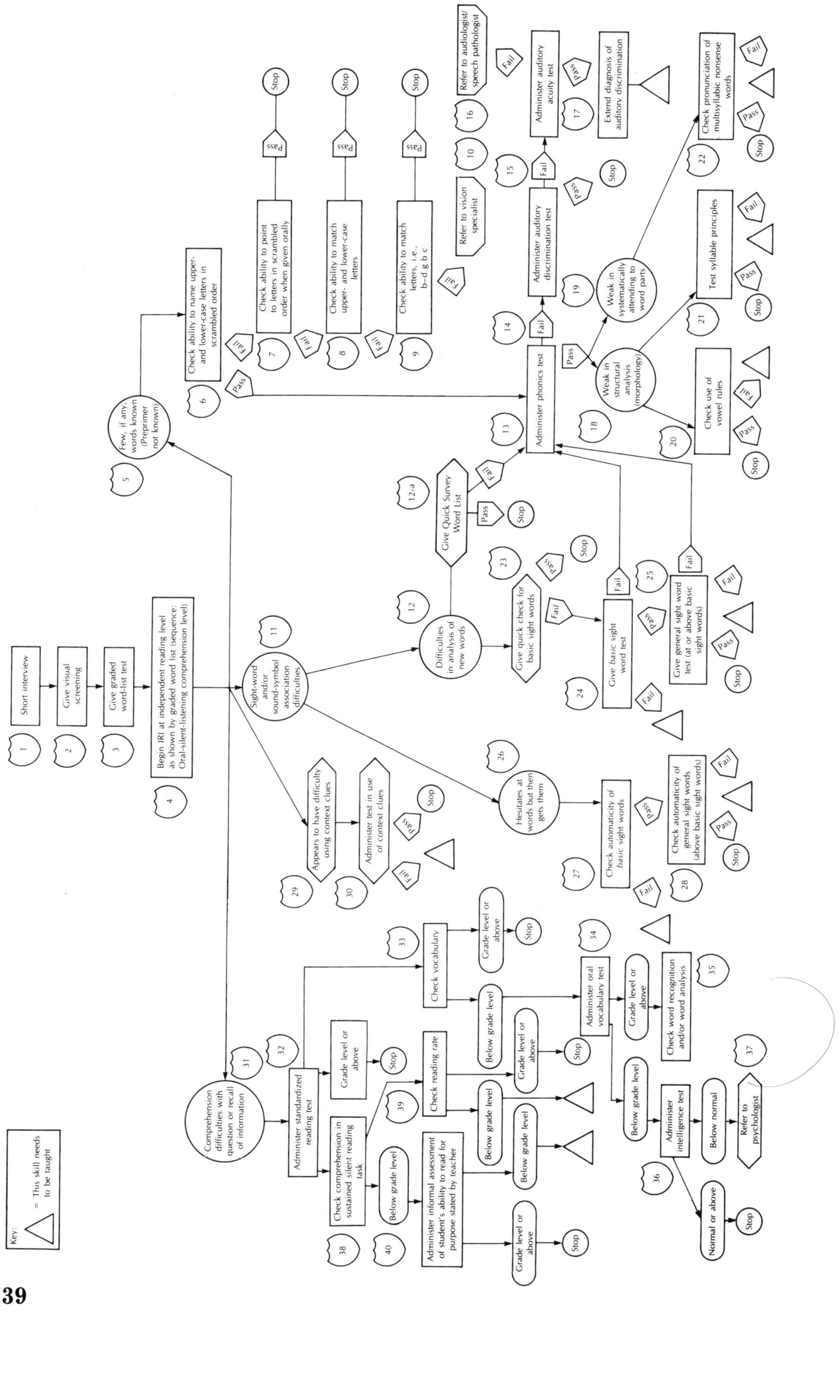
Short interview
Give visual screening
Give graded word-list test
Begin IRI at independent reading level as shown by graded word list (sequence: Oral-silent-listening comprehension level)
Few, if any, words known (Preprimer not known)
Check ability to name upper- and lower-case letters in scrambled order
Check ability to point to letters in scrambled order when given orally
Check ability to match upper- and lower-case letters
Check ability to match letters, i.e., b–d g b c
Refer to vision specialist
Refer to audiologist/ speech pathologist
Administer phonics test
Administer auditory discrimination test
Administer auditory acuity test
Extend diagnosis of auditory discrimination
Weak in systematically attending to word parts
Weak in structural analysis (morphology)
Check use of vowel rules
Test syllable principles
Check pronunciation of multisyllabic nonsense words
Sight-word and/or sound-symbol association difficulties
Difficulties in analysis of new words
Give Quick Survey Word List
Give quick check for basic sight words
Give basic sight word test
Give general sight word test (at or above basic sight words)
Hesitates at words but then gets them
Check automaticity of basic sight words
Check automaticity of general sight words (above basic sight words)
Appears to have difficulty using context clues
Administer test in use of context clues
Comprehension difficulties with question or recall of information
Administer standardized reading test
Check vocabulary
Administer oral vocabulary test
Check word recognition and/or word analysis
Check reading rate
Check comprehension in sustained silent reading task
Administer informal assessment of student's ability to read for purpose stated by teacher
Administer intelligence test
Refer to psychologist
Grade level or above
Below grade level
Normal or above
Below normal
Pass
Fail
Stop
Key: = This skill needs to be taught

ERI 39

Student Reading Passages
Forms A & B

SAN DIEGO QUICK ASSESSMENT LIST*

PP	P	I	∟	⊔	□
see	you	road	our	city	decided
play	come	live	please	middle	served
me	not	thank	myself	moment	amazed
at	with	when	town	frightened	silent
run	jump	bigger	early	exclaimed	wrecked
go	help	how	send	several	improved
and	is	always	wide	lonely	certainly
look	work	night	believe	drew	entered
can	are	spring	quietly	since	realized
here	this	today	carefully	straight	interrupted

□ I	□∟	□ ⊔	□□	□□ I
scanty	bridge	amber	capacious	conscientious
business	commercial	dominion	limitation	isolation
develop	abolish	sundry	pretext	molecule
considered	trucker	capillary	intrigue	ritual
discussed	apparatus	impetuous	delusion	momentous
behaved	elementary	blight	immaculate	vulnerable
splendid	comment	wrest	ascent	kinship
acquainted	necessity	enumerate	acrid	conservatism
escaped	gallery	daunted	binocular	jaunty
grim	relativity	condescend	embankment	inventive

* From Margaret LaPray and Ramon Ross, "The Graded Word List: Quick Gauge of Reading Ability," *Journal of Reading,* January 1969, pp. 305–7. Reprinted with permission of the International Reading Association and the authors.

PPA

Jan has a dog.

The dog's name is Pat.

He can run fast.

One day Pat ran away.

Jan looked for him.

The dog wanted to eat.

Soon he came home.

PPB

Bob likes to play ball.

He plays with Sam.

They play at school.

It is far away.

The boys ride a bus.

It takes them to school.

It also takes them home.

☐ | A

The elephant is the largest animal in the world that lives on land. A full-grown elephant may have a weight of about four tons and may be nine feet tall. Because elephants are so large, they have no natural enemies other than man. Since elephants have so few enemies, they are usually easy to get along with and almost always act friendly.

Elephants usually live in herds with around thirty members of all ages. A female, or lady elephant, is called a cow. The herd usually has a cow as its leader, who is in charge of all the other elephants. During the hottest part of the day the herd will huddle together and attempt to find shade. Near sundown the entire herd usually goes to a nearby river or lake for a drink. Elephants normally continue to stay together in a herd for most of their lives.

The first aircraft that man invented was the balloon. The first balloon was sent into the air by experimenters in France in 1783. It was a large bag made of paper and went about 6,000 feet into the air. It had been filled with hot air and smoke from a fire made by burning straw. A balloon rises into the air because it is filled with a gas that is lighter than the air outside.

Some balloons carry engines that turn a propeller, which drives them through the air. This type of balloon can be driven by a pilot and is called a dirigible or an airship.

For quite a long period of time airships were used to carry passengers. Because airships are rather slow and often dangerous, they are now used very little for transportation. Many people enjoy riding in balloons as a sport because it is so thrilling.

□L A

The beaver is the largest rodent in North America. The weight of an adult may range from 35 to 70 pounds. The hair or coat of the beaver is dense and waterproof, which allows it to swim in cold water without getting cold.

A beaver has sharp teeth that wear away as it uses them to cut down trees. These teeth keep growing as long as the animal lives. The back feet of a beaver are webbed, which help make it a good swimmer. Because of its large lungs that carry oxygen, it can stay submerged in water for as long as 15 minutes. The tail of a beaver is wide and flat and is covered with a scaly skin. When danger approaches, a beaver will warn the others by slapping the surface of the water with its tail.

The dams and canals made by beavers are useful in conserving both water and soil.

☐L B

One of the most useful insects that can be made to work for man is the bee. Two of the most important ways in which the bee benefits us are in the making of honey and the growing of fruit and flowers.

The three types of bees in each hive are the workers, the queen, and the drones. Probably the most interesting members of the bee colony are the workers. The workers do several interesting jobs such as cleaning the hive, acting as nurses, and protecting the hive from enemies. When the worker bees are about ten days old they begin to make short excursions away from the hive. When they first leave they learn to find their way back by becoming familiar with landmarks such as trees and houses. During these trips from the hive the bees learn to gather nectar from flowers. The nectar from the flowers is then made into honey.

One man discovered that bees do a certain kind of dance to inform other bees where flowers with nectar are located.

□⊔A

There are four types of poisonous snakes in North America. One of these is the rattlesnake, which belongs to a family that is often called pit viper. This family of snakes has a deep pit between the eye and nostril on each side of its face. Inside the pit there is a membrane that is sensitive to heat. This membrane enables the snake to locate and strike at any animal with warm blood.

A rattlesnake coils itself into a loop and then strikes with lightning speed. It kills by sinking its poison fangs into its prey.

A rattlesnake gets its name from a series of loosely fitted rings at the end of its tail. A new ring or rattle is formed each time a snake sheds its skin. After the snake sheds its skin the first time, a rattle is formed, which is called a button.

□⊔B

One of the most useful animals in the world is the camel. The camel has helped men living in deserts for thousands of years. One advantage of using camels is that they can travel for great distances without needing water. Because the camel can carry heavy loads of freight, it is sometimes referred to as the "ship of the desert."

The camel is ugly and stupid and has a bad temper. When a camel is loaded for work, it will often show its disapproval by bellowing loudly and by kicking and biting.

There are two kinds of camels; these are the single-humped and the two-humped. The hump contains a great deal of fat and does not have any bone in it. When a camel is required to go without food, the fat in its hump can furnish it with energy for several days.

The main reason camels can go without water for so long is that they do not sweat.

□□A

The most prominent feature in the sky at night is the moon, which is the earth's natural satellite. An astronomer, however, might think our moon is small and insignificant. He would be likely to feel our moon is small because the moons of other planets are so much larger.

Man began to study lunar geography when the telescope was invented. One of the earliest of these astronomers was Galileo, who began looking at the moon in 1609. Later researchers found large craters, mountains, plains, and long valleys on the surface of the moon.

Manned vehicle landings were made on the moon in 1969. These were attempted because men were not satisfied with the information they had obtained by looking through telescopes. Rock samples taken from these explorations of the moon's surface have provided us with a great deal of knowledge about the age of the moon.

Because of man's natural curiosity, few people would be willing to predict what man may accomplish in space.

□□B

No substance has been more eagerly sought after than gold. Because it is rare and durable, gold has been widely accepted as money. In past years gold coins were circulated, but this practice ceased in 1934. Gold is still kept by many nations because they know it will retain its value.

Another important use of gold is in the making of jewelry and metalwork. When gold is made into jewelry, it is usually mixed with another metal to form an alloy. Alloys of gold are used because in its pure form gold is too soft to withstand the wear caused from regular usage.

Tiny quantities of gold occur in most soils and rocks throughout the world. However, in most cases the amount of gold is so small that it is not worth extracting. Gold is often found in association with metals such as copper.

□□| A

There are approximately 3,000 types of lizards, which vary considerably in such characteristics as size, color, shape, and habits. For example, some of these unusual creatures may range from a minimum of merely two to three inches, while some huge varieties may ultimately grow to a maximum length of twelve feet.

Some of these reptiles have startling habits such as the ability to snap off their tails if they are seized. Some species may rear up on their hind legs and scamper away if they become frightened.

Most lizards benefit mankind by eating unwanted insects that, in most cases, are harmful to mankind. Although numerous superstitions abound concerning these strange creatures, only two types are definitely known to be poisonous.

Some lizards lay eggs that have a tough, leathery shell, while others bear living young. The eggs are typically laid where they may be incubated by the warmth emitted from the sun.

Since lizards are cold-blooded animals, they cannot stand extreme variations in temperature. If the sun becomes extremely hot, the lizard must pursue the solace of an overhead shelter such as a rock or bush.

☐☐ | B

The boomerang is perhaps the most remarkable weapon invented by any of the primitive tribesmen of the world. This unusual piece of equipment is fashioned from hardwood and is designed in various shapes and sizes. Most models are smooth and curved and range from two to four feet in length. They are normally flat on one side and convex on the opposite side. It is believed that the first prototype of this strange weapon was designed by the native tribes of aborigines in Australia.

There are two main types of boomerangs commonly used by men and women in sports and in war today. These are classified into two categories, which are the return and nonreturn types. The return type is principally used for sport and amusement and is seldom used by professionals for hunting purposes. The nonreturn type is used for hunting and is capable of doing great damage to an animal for distances up to 400 feet.

With very little formal practice even a novice can become adept at using a return type boomerang.

Student Reading Passages

Forms C & D

SAN DIEGO QUICK ASSESSMENT LIST*

PP	P	I	L	⊔	□
see	you	road	our	city	decided
play	come	live	please	middle	served
me	not	thank	myself	moment	amazed
at	with	when	town	frightened	silent
run	jump	bigger	early	exclaimed	wrecked
go	help	how	send	several	improved
and	is	always	wide	lonely	certainly
look	work	night	believe	drew	entered
can	are	spring	quietly	since	realized
here	this	today	carefully	straight	interrupted

□ I	□L	□ ⊔	□□	□□ I
scanty	bridge	amber	capacious	conscientious
business	commercial	dominion	limitation	isolation
develop	abolish	sundry	pretext	molecule
considered	trucker	capillary	intrigue	ritual
discussed	apparatus	impetuous	delusion	momentous
behaved	elementary	‘blight	immaculate	vulnerable
splendid	comment	wrest	ascent	kinship
acquainted	necessity	enumerate	acrid	conservatism
escaped	gallery	daunted	binocular	jaunty
grim	relativity	condescend	embankment	inventive

* From Margaret LaPray and Ramon Ross, "The Graded Word List: Quick Gauge of Reading Ability," *Journal of Reading*, January 1969, pp. 305–7. Reprinted with permission of the International Reading Association and the authors.

PPC

Sam is a boy.

He has a dog.

The dog's name is Tim.

Tim is a black dog.

He has a pink nose.

Sam goes to school.

The dog stays at home.

PPD

Mary lives in a house.

She has a kitten.

The kitten’s name is Tab.

Tab sleeps with Mary.

He likes to play ball.

The ball is yellow.

Mary and Tab have fun.

| C

Dave and Tom live in a large city. They live with their father and mother. Their house is near a park. Many boys play football in the park.

Dave and Tom like to play football there too. Dave can run faster than Tom.

Dave and Tom's mother goes to school. She is going to be a teacher. Her school is far from their home. She goes to school in a car.

| D

Ann's class went to visit a fire station. One of the firemen was at the door. He said he was happy to see the class.

He showed the class a big fire truck. Then he showed them a car. The car and truck were both red. The big truck had a long ladder on it.

Then the class went back to school. They were very happy. They told their teacher they wanted to go again.

LC

Dale lives on a large animal farm with his father and mother. His father has many cows, horses, sheep, and pigs on the farm. One of the animals belongs to Dale. It is a pet pig. The pig is black with a white ring around its back. It has a very short curly tail.

When Dale goes for a walk, the pig likes to walk with him. Sometimes when Dale goes to school his pig will follow him. The children at school all laugh when they see the pig with Dale. Many of the boys and girls say they would like to have a pet pig too.

└D

Emily has a little black dog with curly hair. The little dog's name is Chester. He has long ears and a short tail. He lives in a little house behind Emily's big house. Sometimes when he is extra good he gets to come in the big house.

The dog does not like cats. Sometimes when he sees a cat he will run after it. The cat can run faster than the dog, so he does not catch it.

When the dog is hungry he begins to bark. When Emily hears him barking she brings him some food.

☐C

Judy's class was going on a trip to visit an airport. Before they left they read some books about airplanes and airplane pilots. Everyone in the class was excited when it came time to go.

The class rode to the airport in a big yellow bus. After the bus stopped, the first person to get off was Judy's teacher. She told the class that they must all stay together so that none of the students would get lost.

First, they visited the ticket counter and learned how passengers buy their tickets. Then a pilot came and told them he would take them on a large airplane. After they were inside the airplane everyone was surprised because it was so large. When Judy's class got back to school they all said they wanted to visit the airport again.

D

Many people would like to live on a farm so they could be around animals. If you have ever lived on a farm, you would know that life is often not easy. Most farmers have to get up very early. In the morning a farmer has to feed and milk his cows. After doing this, the farmer has to go to his fields and work long hours plowing his land or planting his crops. After working hard all day, the farmer has to come home and milk his cows again.

In the winter when it is cold the farmer does not have to work in his fields. But when it is cold he has to work hard at keeping his animals warm.

Today's farmer has to learn how to do many things. He has to know how to care for animals, repair machines, and make the best use of his time.

☐ C

A desert is a place where the weather is dry and often hot. Some people think it is a place where there is nothing but sand. This is true sometimes, but some deserts have many kinds of plants and animals living in them. The kinds of plants and animals living there usually do not require much water. For example, some desert plants can store water in their leaves and exist for long periods of time without rain.

Some animals that live in the desert get all of the water they need by eating the leaves of plants that have water in them. People who have been lost in the desert have died because they had no water to drink. Some of these people would not have died if they had known how to survive. People who know how to survive in such a dry place often know how to obtain water from cactus plants.

A person may enjoy living in the desert because he thinks it is beautiful, but another person may think the same place is not pretty at all.

☐D

One of the biggest jobs ever started was the building of the Panama Canal. The Panama Canal was known as "The Big Ditch." It was called "The Big Ditch" because it was a ditch with water in it and carried ships from one side of Panama to the other side, or from one ocean to another. By going through the Panama Canal, ships did not have to sail all the way around the continent of South America to get from one ocean to another.

When men first started building the Panama Canal there were many dangers from disease. People were getting Yellow Fever, which is a disease carried by a certain kind of mosquito. One man was a hero while the Panama Canal was being built. He discovered a way to get rid of the mosquitoes that were carrying Yellow Fever. After these insects were killed, Yellow Fever was no longer spread from one person to another. By the time the Panama Canal was finished, very few people were dying from Yellow Fever.

☐ IC

There are about a hundred different kinds of monkeys. Some may be as large as a big dog, while others are so small that you could hold them in your hand. Some monkeys have bright-colored faces and when they become excited these colors become brighter. Certain types of monkeys live in pairs or sometimes in clans of up to a hundred or more. Many monkeys can be tamed when they are young, but they have bad tempers when they grow old. The night or owl monkey is so named because it sleeps in the daytime and roams about at night.

Some monkeys are like humans because they make sounds to indicate they are angry. The howler monkey produces a sound that can be heard for a distance of two miles. This type has a boss that is usually the strongest and largest male of the group. When the "boss" loses his job, he may be forced to leave the group and wander alone.

☐ |D

Potatoes, along with wheat and rice, are one of the most important food crops in the world. Nearly every year the world grows about 10 billion bushels of potatoes. In some countries potatoes are used as food for animals as well as for people. In America they are usually consumed only by humans. The potatoes that people eat are almost always baked, boiled, or fried.

Potatoes are often grown in places where it is not quite warm enough for corn. In the far Eastern countries, few are grown because the climate is too warm and because rice has more food value.

When the Spanish first came to South America they found the Indians growing potatoes. It was not until many years later that this new food became popular with the Spanish.

A king in France made this food popular by wearing the flowers of the plant in his buttonhole.

□LC

A mole is a small animal about six inches long. Moles have a long snout like a pig, a short thick neck, and a pink tail. Their ears are not visible but are concealed in their fur.

If a mole is placed on the ground it will begin to scramble about looking for a soft spot to dig. When it begins to dig, it will disappear in less than a minute. Moles often ruin lawns and gardens by making ridges in them caused from their burrowing through the ground.

Most of a mole's life is spent in darkness because it lives underground. A mole's home is usually a nest made from grasses and leaves. Its home is nearly always located beneath something like a rock, tree stump, or stone wall, which gives it more protection.

Moles are most commonly found in the northern half of the world.

OLD

Cottontails and jackrabbits are two of the most commonly known wild animals in the world. Most people do not realize that certain animals such as the jackrabbit and snowshoe rabbit are actually not rabbits but hares. A hare is an animal with longer ears and it is heavier and larger than a rabbit.

A mother rabbit spends considerably more time in building her nest than a mother hare. The female hare, which is called a doe, has two or three litters of young during the year. There are usually four to six babies born in each litter. Young hares are born with their eyes open and can care for themselves in a few days. The infant rabbit is born with his eyes closed and does not see for about a week.

Both the rabbit and the hare are well equipped to detect their enemies. They have long sensitive ears for excellent hearing and eyes that enable them to see in every direction.

Among the animals of the world, one of the most talented is the spider. With its silken webs it can construct suspension bridges, beautiful designs, and insect traps. The spider might be thought of as one of nature's greatest engineers.

Spiders can be found in all parts of the world except where it is extremely cold. They can not survive in cold or polar regions covered with snow because of a lack of food.

People sometimes mistakenly refer to spiders as insects. Unlike insects, which have six legs and three body segments, spiders have eight legs and two body segments.

Although there are many different kinds of spiders in the United States, only two of these are considered dangerous. These are the Black Widow and the Brown House Spider. Spiders are useful to man because they destroy many kinds of harmful insects.

□ ⊔D

Millions of cats have homes, but there are many who are strays. They are still the second most popular type of pet in America. People who raise cats and enter them in shows are called members of the "American Cat Fancy." A cat must have earned four winner's ribbons to become a champion.

Cats are meat eaters and are equipped with special teeth to tear meat into chunks. Once the meat has been torn into small chunks, it is swallowed without chewing. Cats are excellent hunters and can jump as high as seven feet in the air. One purpose of a cat's tail is to enable it to balance itself when it jumps. If a cat is turned upside down and dropped, it will always turn over and land on its feet.

Some cats have been known to live to be 19 or 20 years old; however, the average life of a cat is about 14 years.

□□C

The ostrich, which roams wild in Africa, is the biggest living bird. A fully developed male is extremely large, often standing as tall as seven or eight feet. The eggs from which the young are hatched are also quite large, with a weight of about three pounds.

Most humans consider this giant bird to be awkward and ugly. Although it is not a beautiful bird, it was once highly prized for its fluffy feathers or plumes. Knights of long ago used them as decorations on their helmets and their ladies used them to adorn their dresses.

The ostrich is a flightless bird; however, in running it may attain speeds of up to fifty miles per hour. This large bird often roams over the plains with other animals such as zebras and antelopes. If it fears danger, it is likely to dash off, warning other animals. If it is forced to defend itself, it will often kick using its strong legs and sharp claws.

□□D

There is no other natural substance that has the ability of rubber to stretch or bend and then snap back into shape. This ability makes this important product very useful in modern transportation.

Most of the natural rubber is obtained from the rubber tree. The inner bark of the rubber tree secretes a milky fluid called latex. There are a number of other tropical vines and shrubs that secrete a substance similar to latex, but it is of little economic value.

Most of the trees that produce rubber are grown in an area close to the equator. Rubber trees are normally found in countries with a low altitude. Some of these trees may grow as fast as nine feet per year. When a rubber tree has obtained a growth of about six inches in diameter, it is ready to be tapped for latex.

Although some materials have replaced rubber, it is still one of the most widely used products in the world.

□□ |C

A rather unusual fish that can fly through the air for relatively extensive distances is called the flying fish. It may fly distances of merely a few feet, but may also soar through the air for distances ranging up to 200 yards. This particular type of fish usually only flies when it is pursued by a predator. The peculiar flying fish may stay aloft only momentarily, but it may remain airborne for a duration of up to ten or fifteen seconds. Among the creatures of the ocean who prey on the flying fish are tuna, sharks, dolphins, and porpoises.

If the flying fish is endangered, it is able to use its tail to strike a sharp blow on the water's surface to give it added momentum in making its ascent. When the fish makes its exodus from the water, it may attain speeds of up to 35 miles per hour. Once the fish is airborne, it spreads its pectoral fins and proceeds to use them as wings. These fins are not actually wings but elastic membranes that enable them to be flexible.

There are approximately 65 species of this unique fish, which commonly inhabit only the warm waters of the Atlantic Ocean.

One of our most important and familiar forms of energy is light. Some researchers believe that millions of years ago the sun was responsible for the various chemical reactions that led to the beginning of life. Light is instrumental in photosynthesis, which is a process by which plants utilize light to form chemical compounds necessary for their survival. A large percentage of the living organisms on earth are dependent on photosynthesis for their food supply.

Light is also important in providing the earth's surface and atmosphere with warmth, which is important in maintaining a proper temperature range for habitation. Without a source of light, the temperature of the earth would be so low that survival for man would be impossible.

If an object is to be visible, light must travel from that object to the eye, which then senses that light. An object that provides a source of light in itself is said to be luminous. The moon is typical of an object that is not luminous in itself but is only seen because it reflects light from the sun. In contrast, the sun and other stars emit their own light energy and would be classified as luminous.

Passages to Be Duplicated for Teacher Use

Forms A & B

EKWALL READING INVENTORY
Summary Sheet • Forms A & B

STUDENT'S NAME ____________________ DATE ____________________

GRADE IN SCHOOL ____________________ EXAMINER ____________________

Results of Graded Word List:

Independent Reading Level	Grade ____	(Highest level at which one or no words were missed)
Instructional Reading Level	Grade ____	(Two words missed)
Frustration Reading Level	Grade ____	(Lowest level at which three or more words were missed)

Results of Reading Passages:

		Oral	*Silent*
Independent Reading Level	Grade	____	____
Instructional Reading Level	Grade	____	____
Frustration Reading Level	Grade	____	____
Listening Comprehension Level	Grade	____________	

Word Analysis Skills

____ Adequate in all areas
____ Use of context clues adequate
____ Aware of context clues but needs improvement
____ Little or no use of context clues
____ Guesses at words by first letter only
____ Attempts to sound letter by letter
____ Lacks knowledge of consonants
____ Lacks knowledge of consonant clusters
____ Lacks knowledge of vowel sounds
____ Lacks knowledge of common phonograms (Word families)
____ Unable to blend adequately
____ Appears unaware of common syllable division
____ Appears unaware of common vowel rules (VCE, CV, CVC)
____ Unaware of configuration
____ Guesses by general configuration only
____ Calls words without association of any word attack skills (context, configuration, morphology, phonics)
____ Some contractions not known

Comprehension

_____ Adequate for grade level
_____ Below grade level
_____ Difficulty with factual (F) questions
_____ Difficulty with vocabulary (V) questions
_____ Difficulty with inference (I) questions

Oral versus Silent Reading

_____ Comprehends *better* in *oral* reading
_____ Comprehends *better* in *silent* reading
_____ Comprehends approximately the *same* in *oral* and *silent* reading

Sight Vocabulary

Basic Sight Words
(*Words of high utility*)

_____ No difficulty with Basic Sight Words
_____ *Some* Basic Sight Words not known
_____ *Many* Basic Sight Words not known
_____ *Few* or *no* Basic Sight Words known

Sight Words in General

_____ No difficulty with sight words at or below grade level
_____ *Some* sight words not known
_____ *Many* sight words not known
_____ *Few* or *no* sight words known

Oral Reading Errors

_____ Omissions
_____ Insertions
_____ Partial Mispronunciations
_____ Gross Mispronunciations
_____ Substitutions
_____ Repetitions
_____ Self-corrected errors
_____ Inversions

Characteristics of the Reader

_____ Head movement
_____ Finger pointing
_____ Disregard for punctuation
_____ Loss of place
_____ Does not read in natural voice tones
_____ Word-by-word reading
_____ Poor phrasing
_____ Lack of expression
_____ Pauses
_____ Voicing or lip movement

Rate of Reading

_____ Silent rate fast for grade level
_____ Silent rate high average for grade level
_____ Silent rate average for grade level
_____ Silent rate low average for grade level
_____ Silent rate slow for grade level
_____ Oral rate fast
_____ Oral rate adequate
_____ Oral rate slow
_____ High rate at expense of accuracy

Semantic-Syntactic Abilities

_____ Made meaningful substitutions
_____ Made nonmeaningful substitutions
_____ Meaningful substitutions reflected student's dialect

Listening Comprehension

_____ Understanding of material heard is *below* grade level
_____ Understanding of material heard is *at* or *above* grade level

SAN DIEGO QUICK ASSESSMENT LIST: ANSWER SHEET

NAME ____________________ DATE ____________________

SCHOOL ____________________ TESTER ____________________

PP	P	I
see ______	you ______	road ______
play ______	come ______	live ______
me ______	not ______	thank ______
at ______	with ______	when ______
run ______	jump ______	bigger ______
go ______	help ______	how ______
and ______	is ______	always ______
look ______	work ______	night ______
can ______	are ______	spring ______
here ______	this ______	today ______

2 └	3 ⊔	4 □
our ______	city ______	decided ______
please ______	middle ______	served ______
myself ______	moment ______	amazed ______
town ______	frightened ______	silent ______
early ______	exclaimed ______	wrecked ______
send ______	several ______	improved ______
wide ______	lonely ______	certainly ______
believe ______	drew ______	entered ______
quietly ______	since ______	realized ______
carefully ______	straight ______	interrupted ______

5 □ |

scanty ________
business ________
develop ________
considered ________
discussed ________
behaved ________
splendid ________
acquainted ________
escaped ________
grim ________

6 □ L

bridge ________
commercial ________
abolish ________
trucker ________
apparatus ________
elementary ________
comment ________
necessity ________
gallery ________
relativity ________

7 □ ⊔

amber ________
dominion ________
sundry ________
capillary ________
impetuous ________
blight ________
wrest ________
enumerate ________
daunted ________
condescend ________

8 □□

capacious ________
limitation ________
pretext ________
intrigue ________
delusion ________
immaculate ________
ascent ________
acrid ________
binocular ________
embankment ________

9 □□ |

conscientious ________
isolation ________
molecule ________
ritual ________
momentous ________
vulnerable ________
kinship ________
conservatism ________
jaunty ________
inventive ________

3A (⊔)

Kathy had always wanted to go for a ride on an airplane. One day her father told her that she could ride on an airplane to visit her grandmother and grandfather. She was very happy and could hardly wait to get started.

When the time came to go, her father went to the ticket counter and paid for the airplane ticket. Her mother helped her get on the airplane. Then a lady told her to buckle her seat belt and she even helped her with it.

Soon the airplane was going very fast down the runway. Kathy was afraid at first but soon the airplane was in the air. Kathy peered out of the window at the ground below, where the houses and cars looked very small. The lady gave Kathy something to drink and a sandwich to eat.

(139 Words) (Number of word recognition errors _____)

Questions:

F 1. _____ What had Kathy always wanted to do? (Go for a ride on an airplane)

F 2. _____ Who told Kathy that she could ride on an airplane? (Her father)

F 3. _____ Whom was Kathy going to visit? (Her grandmother and grandfather)

F 4. _____ How did Kathy feel about going? (She was very happy, happy, and/or she could hardly wait to get started)

F 5. _____ Who helped Kathy get on the airplane? (Her mother)

F 6. _____ What did the lady tell Kathy when she got on the airplane? (To buckle her seat belt)

F 7. _____ How did Kathy feel when the airplane started going very fast? (She was afraid)

V 8. _____ What did the word "peered" mean when it said, "Kathy peered out of the window?" (She looked, or she looked out of the window)

I 9. _____ Why did the houses and cars look small below? (Because they were up in the air, far away, or high up in the air)

F 10. _____ What did the lady give Kathy? (A drink and a sandwich) (Student must get both)

Number of Questions Missed	Number of Word Recognition Errors: 0–2	3–4	5–7	8–10	11–13	14
0	+	*	*	*	*	×
1	+	*	*	*	×	×
2	*	*	*	×	×	×
3	*	*	×	×	×	×
4	*	×	×	×	×	×
5+	×	×	×	×	×	×

	Reading Level	
⊞	Independent	☐
⊡	Instructional	☐
☒	Frustration	☐

3B (⊔)

Dick and his father liked to go camping. Dick asked his father if they could go camping in the woods. His father told him they would go the next Saturday.

When Saturday came, they got up early and rode in the car until they found an excellent place to camp. Father decided that they would put up their tent by a small river. They put up their tent and then gathered some wood to start a fire. After the fire was burning, Father got some food ready and Dick helped him cook it over the fire.

After they finished eating they watched the fire until it was time to go to sleep. When Dick and Father had gone to sleep something made a terribly loud noise and woke them up. Dick was afraid but Father laughed because it was only an airplane flying over them.

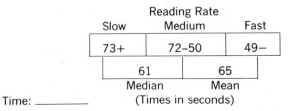

(145 Words)

Reading Rate

Slow	Medium	Fast
73+	72–50	49–

Median	Mean
61	65

(Times in seconds)

Time: ________

Questions:

F	1.	_____	What did Dick and his father like to do? (Go camping)
F	2.	_____	What did Dick ask his father? (If they could go camping)
F	3.	_____	What did his father tell him? (That they could go the next Saturday)
F	4.	_____	How did they get to the place where they camped? (They rode in the car, or in a car)
V	5.	_____	What did it mean when it said they found an "excellent" place to camp? (A good place to camp)
F	6.	_____	Where did they put up their tent? (By a small river, or by a river)
F	7.	_____	What did they do with the wood they gathered? (Started a fire)
F	8.	_____	Why did they start a fire? (To cook some food, or to cook with)
F	9.	_____	What woke them up? (An airplane, or a loud noise)
I	10.	_____	What did Father do that would make you think he was not afraid? (He laughed)

Number of Questions Missed		***Reading Level***	
0–1	Independent	Independent	☐
2–4	Instructional	Instructional	☐
5+	Frustration	Frustration	☐

4A (□)

Some people enjoy exploring the many caves in this country. This can be a lot of fun but it can also be dangerous because you might get lost. Many people have been lost in caves because they did not know what to do to find their way out.

One thing that people who explore caves often take with them is a ball of string. The string serves an important purpose in keeping them from getting lost. They tie one end of the string to a stake outside the cave and unroll the string as they walk along. This way, when they want to leave the cave, all they have to do to find their way out is to follow the string.

Some caves may appear small at the opening, but when you get inside, there may be many giant rooms or caverns in them. One of the largest known caves in the world is Mammoth Cave in Kentucky. It contains enormous caverns and underground rivers, and may take up as much space as 78 square miles.

(176 Words) (Number of word recognition errors _____)

Questions:

F 1. _____ What do some people enjoy doing? (Exploring caves)
F 2. _____ Why can exploring caves be dangerous? (Because you might get lost)
F 3. _____ Why have many people been lost in caves? (Because they did not know how to find their way out, or because they did not use string to follow)
F 4. _____ What do people who explore caves often take with them? (A ball of string) (Tell student if he or she does not know)
F 5. _____ What is the string tied to outside the cave? (To a stake)
F 6. _____ How do they use the string to find their way out? (They follow it, or follow the string that has been unrolled)
V 7. _____ What is a cavern? (A large room in a cave, or a cave)
F 8. _____ Where is one of the largest known caves? (In Kentucky)
F 9. _____ What else does Mammoth Cave contain besides enormous caverns? (Underground rivers, or rivers)
I 10. _____ Why would someone who explored caves need to be brave? (Because it is dangerous, or because one might get lost)

Number of Questions Missed	Number of Word Recognition Errors: 0–2	3–6	7–9	10–13	14–16	17
0	+	*	*	*	*	×
1	+	*	*	*	×	×
2	*	*	*	×	×	×
3	*	*	×	×	×	×
4	*	×	×	×	×	×
5+	×	×	×	×	×	×

Reading Level

⊞ Independent □
⊛ Instructional □
⊠ Frustration □

4B (☐)

One of man's best friends in North America is the bird. Birds are valuable to the farmer and gardener because they eat insects and weed seeds. Birds are also important to the hunter because they provide meat for his table.

When man first came to this country there were many game birds. However, when the white man started hunting birds for sport, some kinds of birds were nearly all killed off. We now have much smaller numbers of wild turkey than we had in the past. In fact, some birds such as the passenger pigeon had all been killed or died by 1914.

In England a man might have been put in prison for taking wild birds' eggs from land owned by another man. A man might have even been hanged for killing a deer on someone else's land. The Indians in North America only killed wild game to eat.

(150 Words)

Reading Rate

Slow	Medium	Fast
66+	65–43	42–

Median	Mean
52	58

(Times in seconds)

Time: ________

Questions:

F 1. ____ What is one of man's best friends in North America? (Birds, or the bird)

V 2. ____ What does the word "valuable" mean in this reading passage? (Worth a lot, or similar synonym)

F 3. ____ Why are birds valuable to the farmer and gardener? (Because they eat insects and weed seeds)

F 4. ____ Why are birds valuable to the hunter? (Because they provide meat, or because they provide meat for the table)

F 5. ____ What happened to many birds when the white man started to hunt them for sport? (They were nearly all killed)

F 6. ____ What kind of bird do we still have but in much smaller numbers than we did in the past? (Wild turkeys)

F 7. ____ What birds had all been killed or died by 1914? (The passenger pigeon)

F 8. ____ What might have happened in England to a man who took wild birds' eggs from a man who owned the land they were on? (He might have been put in prison)

F 9. ____ What might they have done to a man who killed a deer on someone else's land? (Hanged him, or killed him)

I 10. ____ Why do you think the Indians would not have killed off most of the wild game in North America? (Because they only killed game to eat)

Number of Questions Missed		***Reading Level***	
0–1	Independent	Independent	☐
2–4	Instructional	Instructional	☐
5+	Frustration	Frustration	☐

5A (□ |)

The elephant is the largest animal in the world that lives on land. A full-grown elephant may have a weight of about four tons and may be nine feet tall. Because elephants are so large, they have no natural enemies other than man. Since elephants have so few enemies, they are usually easy to get along with and almost always act friendly.

Elephants usually live in herds with around thirty members of all ages. A female, or lady elephant, is called a cow. The herd usually has a cow as its leader, who is in charge of all the other elephants. During the hottest part of the day the herd will huddle together and attempt to find shade. Near sundown the entire herd usually goes to a nearby river or lake for a drink. Elephants normally continue to stay together in a herd for most of their lives.

(148 Words) (Number of word recognition errors _____)

Questions:

F 1. _____ What is the largest animal in the world that lives on land? (The elephant)

F 2. _____ How heavy might a full-grown elephant be? (About four tons)

F 3. _____ Why do elephants have no natural enemies other than man? (Because they are so large)

F 4. _____ Why are elephants almost always easy to get along with or why do they act friendly? (Because they have no or few enemies or because they are so large)

V 5. _____ What is a herd? (A group of something, a group of elephants, or a good synonym)

F 6. _____ How many elephants usually live in a herd? (About thirty)

F 7. _____ Who is usually the leader of an elephant herd? (A cow, a female, or a lady elephant)

F 8. _____ What do elephants do during the hottest part of the day? (They huddle together and/or attempt to find shade)

F 9. _____ What do elephants usually do near sundown? (Go to get a drink or go to a nearby river or lake)

I 10. _____ What did it say that would make you think elephants usually like each other? (They stay together for most of their lives, they stay together, or they stay in a herd)

		Number of Word Recognition Errors							*Reading Level*	
		0–2	3–5	6–8	9–11	12–14	15			
Number of Questions Missed	0	+	*	*	*	*	×	⊞	Independent	□
	1	+	*	*	*	×	×	⊡	Instructional	□
	2	*	*	*	×	×	×	⊠	Frustration	□
	3	*	*	×	×	×	×			
	4	*	×	×	×	×	×			
	5+	×	×	×	×	×	×			

5B (☐ |)

The first aircraft that man invented was the balloon. The first balloon was sent into the air by experimenters in France in 1783. It was a large bag made of paper and went about 6,000 feet into the air. It had been filled with hot air and smoke from a fire made by burning straw. A balloon rises into the air because it is filled with a gas that is lighter than the air outside.

Some balloons carry engines that turn a propeller, which drives them through the air. This type of balloon can be driven by a pilot and is called a dirigible or an airship.

For quite a long period of time airships were used to carry passengers. Because airships are rather slow and often dangerous, they are now used very little for transportation. Many people still enjoy riding in balloons as a sport because it is so thrilling.

(151 Words)

Reading Rate

Slow	Medium	Fast
59+	58–42	41–

Median	Mean
52	53

(Times in seconds)

Time: ______

Questions:

F 1. ______ What was the first aircraft invented by man? (The balloon)
F 2. ______ When did experimenters send the first balloon into the air? (In 1783)
F 3. ______ What was the first balloon made of? (Paper)
F 4. ______ What was the first balloon filled with? (Hot air, or hot air and smoke)
F 5. ______ Why are engines sometimes put on balloons? (To turn a propeller, or to drive them through the air)
F 6. ______ What is a balloon that can be driven by a pilot called? (A dirigible, or an airship)
F 7. ______ What were airships used for, for quite a long period of time? (To carry passengers, or for transportation)
V 8. ______ What does the word "transportation" mean? (A means of carrying people, or a means of carrying things from place to place)
F 9. ______ Why are airships no longer used for transportation? (Because they are slow and/or dangerous)
I 10. ______ Why do you think balloons may still be used for a long time? (Because they are thrilling, or because people still enjoy riding in them)

Number of Questions Missed		***Reading Level***	
0–1	Independent	Independent	☐
2–4	Instructional	Instructional	☐
5+	Frustration	Frustration	☐

6A (☐L)

The beaver is the largest rodent in North America. The weight of an adult may range from 35 to 70 pounds. The hair or coat of the beaver is dense and waterproof, which allows it to swim in cold water without getting cold.

A beaver has sharp teeth that wear away as it uses them to cut down trees. These teeth keep growing as long as the animal lives. The back feet of a beaver are webbed, which help make it a good swimmer. Because of its large lungs that carry oxygen, it can stay submerged in water for as long as 15 minutes. The tail of a beaver is wide and flat and is covered with a scaly skin. When danger approaches, a beaver will warn the others by slapping the surface of the water with its tail.

The dams and canals made by beavers are useful in conserving both water and soil.

(154 Words) (Number of word recognition errors _____)

Questions:

F 1. _____ What is the largest rodent in North America? (The beaver)
F 2. _____ How much might an adult beaver weigh? (From 35 to 70 pounds)
F 3. _____ What is it about the coat or hair of a beaver that allows it to swim in cold water without discomfort? (It is dense and/or waterproof)
F 4. _____ What happens to a beaver's teeth as it cuts down trees? (They wear away)
I 5. _____ How do you know that a beaver's teeth never completely wear away? (Because it said they keep growing as long as the animal lives)
F 6. _____ What is it about a beaver's back feet that enables it to be an excellent swimmer? (They are webbed)
V 7. _____ What does the word "submerged" mean in this passage? (Staying under, or going under water)
F 8. _____ What does the tail of a beaver look like? (It is broad and flat and covered with a scaly skin) (Student must give at least two facts)
F 9. _____ How does a beaver warn other beavers that danger is near? (It slaps the surface of the water with its tail)
F 10. _____ Why are the dams and canals built by beavers useful to man? (Because they help to conserve water and soil)

Number of Questions Missed	Number of Word Recognition Errors: 0–2	3–5	6–8	9–11	12–14	15
0	+	*	*	*	*	×
1	+	*	*	*	×	×
2	*	*	*	×	×	×
3	*	*	×	×	×	×
4	*	×	×	×	×	×
5+	×	×	×	×	×	×

Reading Level

⊞ Independent ☐
⊛ Instructional ☐
⊠ Frustration ☐

ERI 103

6B (□L)

One of the most useful insects that can be made to work for man is the bee. Two of the most important ways in which the bee benefits us are in the making of honey and the growing of fruit and flowers.

The three types of bees in each hive are the workers, the queen, and the drones. Probably the most interesting members of the bee colony are the workers. The workers do several interesting jobs such as cleaning the hive, acting as nurses, and protecting the hive from enemies. When the worker bees are about ten days old they begin to make short excursions away from the hive. When they first leave they learn to find their way back by becoming familiar with landmarks such as trees and houses. During these trips from the hive the bees learn to gather nectar from flowers. The nectar from the flowers is then made into honey.

One man discovered that bees do a certain kind of dance to inform other bees where flowers with nectar are located.

(175 Words)

Reading Rate

Slow	Medium	Fast
66+	65–50	49–

Median	Mean
57	58

(Times in seconds)

Time: ________

Questions:

F 1. ____ What is one of the most useful insects that can be made to work for man? (The bee)

F 2. ____ What are two of the most important ways in which the bee benefits us? (In making honey and in the growing of fruit and/or flowers)

F 3. ____ What are the three types of bees in each hive? (The workers, the queen, and the drones) (Students must get at least two)

F 4. ____ What type of bee is probably the most interesting? (The worker)

F 5. ____ What are some jobs of the worker? (Cleaning the hive, acting as nurse, protecting the hive, and making honey) (Students must get at least two)

V 6. ____ What does the word "excursions" mean in this reading passage? (Trips, or any other appropriate synonym)

F 7. ____ When bees first leave the hive, how do they find their way back? (By becoming familiar with landmarks, or by watching for trees and houses)

F 8. ____ What do bees do on their trips from the hive? (Look for nectar, or gather nectar)

F 9. ____ How old are the worker bees when they first begin to make short excursions away from the hive? (Ten days old)

I 10. ____ How do we know that bees can communicate with each other? (Because it said they do a dance to tell the other bees where flowers, or flowers with nectar, are located)

Number of Questions Missed		***Reading Level***	
0–1	Independent	Independent	□
2–4	Instructional	Instructional	□
5+	Frustration	Frustration	□

7A (□ ⊔)

There are four types of poisonous snakes in North America. One of these is the rattlesnake, which belongs to a family that is often called pit viper. This family of snakes has a deep pit between the eye and nostril on each side of its face. Inside the pit there is a membrane that is sensitive to heat. This membrane enables the snake to locate and strike at any animal with warm blood.

A rattlesnake coils itself into a loop and then strikes with lightning speed. It kills by sinking its poison fangs into its prey.

A rattlesnake gets its name from a series of loosely fitted rings at the end of its tail. A new ring or rattle is formed each time a snake sheds its skin. After the snake sheds its skin the first time, a rattle is formed, which is called a button.

(146 Words) (Number of word recognition errors _____)

Questions:

F 1. _____ How many types of poisonous snakes are there in North America? (Four)

F 2. _____ To what family of snakes does the rattlesnake belong? (The pit viper) (Tell the student if he or she does not know)

F 3. _____ Why is it called pit viper? (Because it has a pit between the eye and nostril on each side of its face, or because it has a pit on its face)

F 4. _____ What is inside the pit? (A membrane that is sensitive to heat, something that senses heat, or a membrane)

F 5. _____ What is the purpose of the heat-sensitive membrane? (It helps the snake locate warm-blooded animals, or warm things)

I 6. _____ Why do you think you might not be able to get away from a snake when it strikes? (Because it said it strikes with lightning speed, or because it strikes so fast)

V 7. _____ What does the word "prey" mean? (What the rattlesnake kills, or something the rattlesnake eats)

F 8. _____ Where does the rattlesnake get its name? (From the series of loosely fitted rings at the end of its tail, or from the rattles on its tail)

F 9. _____ When is a new rattle formed? (Each time the snake sheds its skin)

F 10. _____ What is the first rattle that is formed called? (A button)

Number of Questions Missed	*Number of Word Recognition Errors* 0–2	3–5	6–8	9–11	12–14	15	*Reading Level*	
0	+	*	*	*	*	×	⊞ Independent	□
1	+	*	*	*	×	×	⊡ Instructional	□
2	*	*	*	×	×	×	⊠ Frustration	□
3	*	*	×	×	×	×		
4	*	×	×	×	×	×		
5+	×	×	×	×	×	×		

7B (□ ⊔)

One of the most useful animals in the world is the camel. The camel has helped men living in deserts for thousands of years. One advantage of using camels is that they can travel for great distances without needing water. Because the camel can carry heavy loads of freight, it is sometimes referred to as the "ship of the desert."

The camel is ugly and stupid and has a bad temper. When a camel is loaded for work, it will often show its disapproval by bellowing loudly and by kicking and biting.

There are two kinds of camels; there are the single-humped and the two-humped. The hump contains a great deal of fat and does not have any bone in it. When a camel is required to go without food, the fat in its hump can furnish it with energy for several days.

The main reason camels can go without water for so long is that they do not sweat.

(162 Words)

Reading Rate

Slow	Medium	Fast
56+	55–40	39–

Median	Mean
48	51

(Times in seconds)

Time: ______

Questions:

F 1. ____ What is one of the most useful animals in the world? (The camel)
F 2. ____ How long has the camel been helping man? (For thousands of years)
F 3. ____ What is one of the advantages of using camels? (They can travel great distances without water, can go for a long time without water, or can carry heavy loads)
F 4. ____ Why is the camel sometimes called the "ship of the desert?" (Because it can carry heavy loads, or heavy loads of freight)
I 5. ____ Why do you think you might not like working with camels? (Because they are ugly, stupid, bad-tempered, and they bite and kick) (The student should name at least two reasons)
V 6. ____ What does the word "bellowing" mean in this reading passage? (Making a loud noise)
F 7. ____ What are the two kinds of camels mentioned in this passage? (The single- or one-humped and the two-humped)
F 8. ____ What does the hump contain a great deal of? (Fat)
F 9. ____ Where does a camel get its energy, when it is required to go without food for several days? (From the fat in its hump, or from its hump)
F 10. ____ What is the main reason camels can go without water for so long? (They do not sweat)

Number of Questions Missed		***Reading Level***	
0–1	Independent	Independent	□
2–4	Instructional	Instructional	□
5+	Frustration	Frustration	□

8A (☐☐)

The most prominent feature in the sky at night is the moon, which is the earth's natural satellite. An astronomer, however, might think our moon is small and insignificant. He would be likely to feel our moon is small because the moons of other planets are so much larger.

Man began to study lunar geography when the telescope was invented. One of the earliest of these astronomers was Galileo, who began looking at the moon in 1609. Later researchers found large craters, mountains, plains, and long valleys on the surface of the moon.

Manned vehicle landings were made on the moon in 1969. These were attempted because men were not satisfied with the information they had obtained by looking through telescopes. Rock samples taken from these explorations of the moon's surface have provided us with a great deal of knowledge about the age of the moon.

Because of man's natural curiosity, few people would be willing to predict what man may accomplish in space.

(164 Words) (Number of word recognition errors _____)

Questions:

F 1. _____ What is the most prominent feature in the sky at night? (The moon)

F 2. _____ Why might an astronomer think our moon is small and insignificant? (Because the moons of other planets are so much larger)

V 3. _____ What does "lunar" mean in this passage? (It refers to the moon)

F 4. _____ Who was one of the earliest astronomers? (Galileo)

F 5. _____ When did Galileo begin to study the moon? (In 1609)

F 6. _____ What did later researchers find on the surface of the moon? (Craters, mountains, plains, and valleys) (Students must name at least two)

F 7. _____ When did man make the first manned vehicle landings on the moon? (In 1969)

F 8. _____ Why did man make the first manned landings on the moon? (Because he was not satisfied with the information he had obtained by looking through telescopes)

F 9. _____ What did the rock samples taken from the moon's surface provide us with? (Information about the age of the moon)

I 10. _____ Why do you think many more space explorations may be made in the future? (Because of man's curiosity)

Number of Questions Missed	Number of Word Recognition Errors: 0–2	3–5	6–8	9–12	13–15	16
0	+	*	*	*	*	×
1	+	*	*	*	×	×
2	*	*	*	×	×	×
3	*	*	×	×	×	×
4	*	×	×	×	×	×
5+	×	×	×	×	×	×

Reading Level

⊞ Independent ☐

⊡ Instructional ☐

☒ Frustration ☐

8B (☐☐)

No substance has been more eagerly sought after than gold. Because it is rare and durable, gold has been widely accepted as money. In past years gold coins were circulated, but this practice ceased in 1934. Gold is still kept by many nations because they know it will retain its value.

Another important use of gold is in the making of jewelry and metalwork. When gold is made into jewelry it is usually mixed with another metal to form an alloy. Alloys of gold are used because in its pure form gold is too soft to withstand the wear caused from regular usage.

Tiny quantities of gold occur in most soils and rocks throughout the world. However, in most cases the amount of gold is so small that it is not worth extracting. Gold is often found in association with metals such as copper.

(144 Words)

Reading Rate

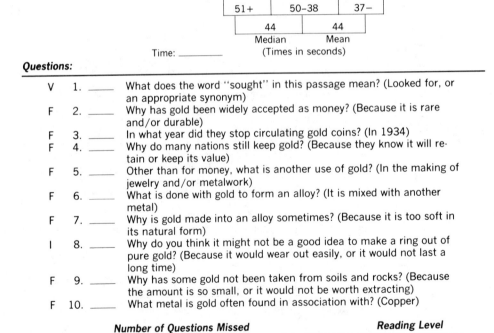

Slow	Medium	Fast
51+	50–38	37–

Median	Mean
44	44

(Times in seconds)

Time: ______

Questions:

V 1. ____ What does the word "sought" in this passage mean? (Looked for, or an appropriate synonym)

F 2. ____ Why has gold been widely accepted as money? (Because it is rare and/or durable)

F 3. ____ In what year did they stop circulating gold coins? (In 1934)

F 4. ____ Why do many nations still keep gold? (Because they know it will retain or keep its value)

F 5. ____ Other than for money, what is another use of gold? (In the making of jewelry and/or metalwork)

F 6. ____ What is done with gold to form an alloy? (It is mixed with another metal)

F 7. ____ Why is gold made into an alloy sometimes? (Because it is too soft in its natural form)

I 8. ____ Why do you think it might not be a good idea to make a ring out of pure gold? (Because it would wear out easily, or it would not last a long time)

F 9. ____ Why has some gold not been taken from soils and rocks? (Because the amount is so small, or it would not be worth extracting)

F 10. ____ What metal is gold often found in association with? (Copper)

Number of Questions Missed		***Reading Level***	
0–1	Independent	Independent	☐
2–4	Instructional	Instructional	☐
5+	Frustration	Frustration	☐

9A (☐☐ |)

There are approximately 3,000 types of lizards, which vary considerably in such characteristics as size, color, shape, and habits. For example, some of these unusual creatures may range from a minimum of merely two to three inches, while some huge varieties may ultimately grow to a maximum length of twelve feet.

Some of these reptiles have startling habits such as the ability to snap off their tails if they are seized. Some species may rear up on their hind legs and scamper away if they become frightened.

Most lizards benefit mankind by eating unwanted insects that, in most cases, are harmful to mankind. Although numerous superstitions abound concerning these strange creatures, only two types are definitely known to be poisonous.

Some lizards lay eggs that have a tough, leathery shell, while others bear living young. The eggs are typically laid where they may be incubated by the warmth emitted from the sun.

Since lizards are cold-blooded animals, they cannot stand extreme variations in temperature. If the sun becomes extremely hot, the lizard must pursue the solace of an overhead shelter such as a rock or bush.

(186 Words) (Number of word recognition errors _____)

Questions:

F 1. _____ In what ways do lizards vary? (In size, shape, color, and habits) (Students must get at least three)

F 2. _____ What is the maximum length you might expect a lizard to be? (Twelve feet)

F 3. _____ What happens to some lizards if they are seized by the tail? (It snaps off)

F 4. _____ Why might some lizards rear up on their hind legs and scamper away? (Because they are frightened, or scared)

F 5. _____ How do some lizards help us? (By eating harmful insects, or by eating insects)

I 6. _____ Why do you think that most lizards would not harm us? (Because there are only two kinds that are poisonous)

F 7. _____ What is the shell of a lizard's egg like? (Tough and/or leathery)

V 8. _____ What does the word "incubated" mean? (Hatched, or an appropriate synonym or explanation)

F 9. _____ What characteristic of lizards keeps them from being able to stand extreme variations in temperature? (They are cold-blooded)

F 10. _____ What would a lizard be likely to do if it became extremely hot? (Pursue the solace of a rock or bush, go where it was not hot, or go where it was cool)

Number of Questions Missed	Number of Word Recognition Errors: 0–2	3–6	7–10	11–13	14–17	18
0	+	*	*	*	*	×
1	+	*	*	*	×	×
2	*	*	*	×	×	×
3	*	*	×	×	×	×
4	*	×	×	×	×	×
5+	×	×	×	×	×	×

Reading Level

⊞ Independent ☐

[*] Instructional ☐

☒ Frustration ☐

9B (☐☐ |)

The boomerang is perhaps the most remarkable weapon invented by any of the primitive tribesmen of the world. This unusual piece of equipment is fashioned from hardwood and is designed in various shapes and sizes. Most models are smooth and curved and range from two to four feet in length. They are normally flat on one side and convex on the opposite side. It is believed that the first prototype of this strange weapon was designed by the native tribes of aborigines in Australia.

There are two main types of boomerangs commonly used by men and women in sports and in war today. These are classified into two categories, which are the return and nonreturn types. The return type is principally used for sport and amusement and is seldom used by professionals for hunting purposes. The nonreturn type is used for hunting and is capable of doing great damage to an animal for distances up to 400 feet.

With very little formal practice even a novice can become adept at using a return type boomerang.

(175 Words)

Reading Rate

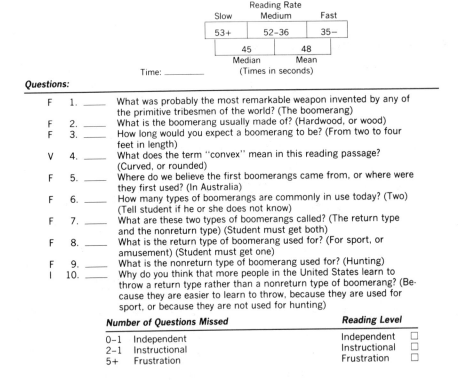

Slow	Medium	Fast
53+	52–36	35–

Median	Mean
45	48

(Times in seconds)

Time: ________

Questions:

F	1.	____	What was probably the most remarkable weapon invented by any of the primitive tribesmen of the world? (The boomerang)
F	2.	____	What is the boomerang usually made of? (Hardwood, or wood)
F	3.	____	How long would you expect a boomerang to be? (From two to four feet in length)
V	4.	____	What does the term "convex" mean in this reading passage? (Curved, or rounded)
F	5.	____	Where do we believe the first boomerangs came from, or where were they first used? (In Australia)
F	6.	____	How many types of boomerangs are commonly in use today? (Two) (Tell student if he or she does not know)
F	7.	____	What are these two types of boomerangs called? (The return type and the nonreturn type) (Student must get both)
F	8.	____	What is the return type of boomerang used for? (For sport, or amusement) (Student must get one)
F	9.	____	What is the nonreturn type of boomerang used for? (Hunting)
I	10.	____	Why do you think that more people in the United States learn to throw a return type rather than a nonreturn type of boomerang? (Because they are easier to learn to throw, because they are used for sport, or because they are not used for hunting)

Number of Questions Missed		***Reading Level***	
0–1	Independent	Independent	☐
2–1	Instructional	Instructional	☐
5+	Frustration	Frustration	☐

Passages to Be Duplicated for Teacher Use

Forms C & D

EKWALL READING INVENTORY
Summary Sheet • Forms C & D

STUDENT'S NAME: ______________________ DATE: ______________________

GRADE IN SCHOOL: ______________________ EXAMINER: ______________________

Results of Graded Word List:

Independent Reading Level	Grade ____	(Highest level at which one or no words were missed)
Instructional Reading Level	Grade ____	(Two words missed)
Frustration Reading Level	Grade ____	(Lowest level at which three or more words were missed)

Results of Reading Passages:	Oral	Silent
Independent Reading Level	Grade ____	____
Instructional Reading Level	Grade ____	____
Frustration Reading Level	Grade ____	____
Listening Comprehension Level	Grade ______________	

Word Analysis Skills

____ Adequate in all areas
____ Use of context clues adequate
____ Aware of context clues but needs improvement
____ Little or no use of context clues
____ Guesses at words by first letter only
____ Attempts to sound letter by letter
____ Lacks knowledge of consonants
____ Lacks knowledge of consonant clusters
____ Lacks knowledge of vowel sounds
____ Lacks knowledge of common phonograms (Word families)
____ Unable to blend adequately
____ Appears unaware of common syllable division
____ Appears unaware of common vowel rules (VCE, CV, CVC)
____ Unaware of configuration
____ Guesses by general configuration only
____ Calls words without association of any word attack skills (context, configuration, morphology, phonics)
____ Some contractions not known

Comprehension

____ Adequate for grade level
____ Below grade level
____ Difficulty with factual (F) questions
____ Difficulty with vocabulary (V) questions
____ Difficulty with inference (I) questions

Oral versus Silent Reading

_____ Comprehends *better* in *oral* reading
_____ Comprehends *better* in *silent* reading
_____ Comprehends approximately the *same* in *oral* and *silent* reading

Sight Vocabulary

Basic Sight Words
(Words of high utility)
_____ No difficulty with Basic Sight Words
_____ *Some* Basic Sight Words not known
_____ *Many* Basic Sight Words not known
_____ *Few* or *no* Basic Sight Words known

Sight Words in General
_____ No difficulty with sight words at or below grade level
_____ *Some* sight words not known
_____ Many sight words not known
_____ *Few* or *no* sight words known

Oral Reading Errors

_____ Omissions
_____ Insertions
_____ Partial Mispronunciations
_____ Gross Mispronunciations
_____ Substitutions
_____ Repetitions
_____ Self-corrected errors
_____ Inversions

Characteristics of the Reader

_____ Head movement
_____ Finger pointing
_____ Disregard for punctuation
_____ Loss of place
_____ Does not read in natural voice tones
_____ Word-by-word reading
_____ Poor phrasing
_____ Lack of expression
_____ Pauses
_____ Voicing or lip movement

Rate of Reading

_____ Silent rate fast for grade level
_____ Silent rate high average for grade level
_____ Silent rate average for grade level
_____ Silent rate low average for grade level
_____ Silent rate slow for grade level
_____ Oral rate fast
_____ Oral rate adequate
_____ Oral rate slow
_____ High rate at expense of accuracy

Semantic-Syntactic Abilities

_____ Made meaningful substitutions
_____ Made nonmeaningful substitutions
_____ Meaningful substitutions reflected student's dialect

Listening Comprehension

_____ Understanding of material heard is *below* grade level
_____ Understanding of material heard is *at* or *above* grade level

SAN DIEGO QUICK ASSESSMENT LIST: ANSWER SHEET

NAME ______________________	DATE ______________________
SCHOOL ______________________	TESTER ______________________

PP	P	I
see ________	you ________	road ________
play ________	come ________	live ________
me ________	not ________	thank ________
at ________	with ________	when ________
run ________	jump ________	bigger ________
go ________	help ________	how ________
and ________	is ________	always ________
look ________	work ________	night ________
can ________	are ________	spring ________
here ________	this ________	today ________
2	**3**	**4**
our ________	city ________	decided ________
please ________	middle ________	served ________
myself ________	moment ________	amazed ________
town ________	frightened ________	silent ________
early ________	exclaimed ________	wrecked ________
send ________	several ________	improved ________
wide ________	lonely ________	certainly ________
believe ________	drew ________	entered ________
quietly ________	since ________	realized ________
carefully ________	straight ________	interrupted ________

5 □ |

scanty ____________

business ____________

develop ____________

considered ____________

discussed ____________

behaved ____________

splendid ____________

acquainted ____________

escaped ____________

grim ____________

6 □L

bridge ____________

commercial ____________

abolish ____________

trucker ____________

apparatus ____________

elementary ____________

comment ____________

necessity ____________

gallery ____________

relativity ____________

7 □ ⊔

amber ____________

dominion ____________

sundry ____________

capillary ____________

impetuous ____________

blight ____________

wrest ____________

enumerate ____________

daunted ____________

condescend ____________

8 □□

capacious ____________

limitation ____________

pretext ____________

intrigue ____________

delusion ____________

immaculate ____________

ascent ____________

acrid ____________

binocular ____________

embankment ____________

9 □□ |

conscientious ____________

isolation ____________

molecule ____________

ritual ____________

momentous ____________

vulnerable ____________

kinship ____________

conservatism ____________

jaunty ____________

inventive ____________

PPC

Sam is a boy.

He has a dog.

The dog's name is Tim.

Tim is a black dog.

He has a pink nose.

Sam goes to school.

The dog stays at home.

(32 Words) (Number of word recognition errors ______)

Questions:

F 1. ______ Who is Sam? (A boy)
F 2. ______ What does Sam have? (A dog)
F 3. ______ What is the dog's name? (Tim)
F 4. ______ What color is the dog? (Black, or black with a pink nose)
F 5. ______ Where does Sam go? (To school)

		Number of Word Recognition Errors			
		0	1	2–3	4
Number of Questions Missed	0	+	*	*	×
	1	*	*	×	×
	2	*	×	×	×
	3	×	×	×	×
	4	×	×	×	×
	5+	×	×	×	×

Reading Level

⊞	Independent	☐
⊡	Instructional	☐
⊠	Frustration	☐

2D (L)

Emily has a little black dog with curly hair. The little dog's name is Chester. He has long ears and a short tail. He lives in a little house behind Emily's big house. Sometimes when he is extra good he gets to come in the big house.

The dog does not like cats. Sometimes when he sees a cat he will run after it. The cat can run faster than the dog, so he does not catch it.

When the dog is hungry he begins to bark. When Emily hears him barking she brings him some food.

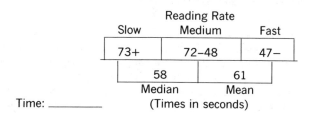

(97 Words)

Reading Rate

Slow	Medium	Fast
73+	72–48	47–

Median	Mean
58	61

(Times in seconds)

Time: ________

Questions:

F	1.	_____	What does Emily have? (A dog, a little dog, or a little black dog)
F	2.	_____	What does he look like? (He is black, has curly hair, long ears, and a short tail) (Student must get at least two answers)
F	3.	_____	Where does the dog live? (In a little house, or behind Emily's house)
F	4.	_____	When does the dog get to come in the big house? (When he is good, or when he is extra good)
F	5.	_____	What does the dog not like? (Cats)
F	6.	_____	What does he sometimes do when he sees a cat? (He runs after it)
F	7.	_____	Why can't the dog catch the cat? (It runs faster than the dog)
F	8.	_____	What does the dog do when he is hungry? (He barks)
F	9.	_____	What does Emily do when she hears the dog barking? (She brings him food)
I	10.	_____	Why do you think cats do not like the dog? (Because he chases them, or runs after them)

Number of Questions Missed		***Reading Level***	
0–1	Independent	Independent	☐
2–4	Instructional	Instructional	☐
5+	Frustration	Frustration	☐

3C (⊔)

Judy's class was going on a trip to visit an airport. Before they left they read some books about airplanes and airplane pilots. Everyone in the class was excited when it came time to go.

The class rode to the airport in a big yellow bus. After the bus stopped, the first person to get off was Judy's teacher. She told the class that they must all stay together so that none of the students would get lost.

First, they visited the ticket counter and learned how passengers buy their tickets. Then a pilot came and told them he would take them on a large airplane. After they were inside the airplane everyone was surprised because it was so large. When Judy's class got back to school they all said they wanted to visit the airport again.

(137 Words) (Number of word recognition errors ______)

Questions:

F 1. ______ Where was Judy's class going? (To visit an airport)

F 2. ______ What did they do before they left? (They read some books, or they read some books about airplanes and airplane pilots)

F 3. ______ How did the class feel when it was time to go? (They were excited)

F 4. ______ How did the class get to the airport? (They rode in a bus, or in a big yellow bus)

F 5. ______ Who was the first person to get off the bus? (Judy's teacher, or the teacher)

F 6. ______ What did the teacher tell the class when they first got off the bus? (That they must stay together, or that they must stay together so they would not get lost)

F 7. ______ What did they visit first? (The ticket counter)

V 8. ______ In this story it said the students learned how the passengers buy their tickets. What is a passenger? (Someone who rides on an airplane, or someone who rides something)

F 9. ______ When the pilot came to meet the class, what did he tell them? (He told them he would take them on an airplane, or on a large airplane)

I 10. ______ What did the class say that would make you think they liked their visit to the airport? (They said they wanted to visit the airport again)

Number of Questions Missed	0–2	3–4	5–7	8–10	11–13	14
0	+	*	*	*	*	×
1	+	*	*	*	×	×
2	*	*	*	×	×	×
3	*	*	×	×	×	×
4	*	×	×	×	×	×
5+	×	×	×	×	×	×

(Columns: ***Number of Word Recognition Errors***)

Reading Level

⊞ Independent ☐

⊛ Instructional ☐

⊠ Frustration ☐

3D (⊔)

Many people would like to live on a farm so they could be around animals. If you had ever lived on a farm, you would know that life is often not easy. Most farmers have to get up very early. In the morning a farmer has to feed and milk his cows. After doing this, the farmer has to go to his fields and work long hours plowing his land or planting his crops. After working hard all day, the farmer has to come home and milk his cows again.

In the winter when it is cold the farmer does not have to work in his fields. But when it is cold he has to work hard at keeping his animals warm.

Today's farmer has to learn how to do many things. He has to know how to care for animals, repair machines, and make the best use of his time.

(151 Words)

Reading Rate

Slow	Medium	Fast
81+	80–59	58–

Median	Mean
65	71

(Times in seconds)

Time: ________

Questions:

F 1. _____ Why do many people think they would like to live on a farm? (So they could be around animals)

F 2. _____ When do most farmers get up? (Early, or very early)

F 3. _____ What kind of work do many farmers have to do in the morning? (Feed and/or milk their cows)

F 4. _____ What do many farmers often work long hours doing during the day? (Either or both—plowing their fields, or planting their crops)

F 5. _____ What do many farmers have to do after working all day in their fields? (Milk the cows again)

F 6. _____ When does the farmer not have to work in his fields? (In the wintertime)

F 7. _____ What does the farmer have to do with his animals when it is cold? (Try to keep them warm)

F 8. _____ What are some of the things a farmer has to know today? (How to care for animals, repair machines, and make the best use of his time) (Student must name at least two)

I 9. _____ Why do you think today's farmer does not have much free time? (Because he has to spend so much time working)

V 10. _____ This reading passage said that the farmer has to know how to repair machines. What does "repair" mean? (To fix, or a proper synonym)

Number of Questions Missed		***Reading Level***	
0–1	Independent	Independent	☐
2–4	Instructional	Instructional	☐
5+	Frustration	Frustration	☐

4C (☐)

A desert is a place where the weather is dry and often hot. Some people think it is a place where there is nothing but sand. This is true sometimes, but some deserts have many kinds of plants and animals living in them. The kinds of plants and animals living there usually do not require much water. For example, some desert plants can store water in their leaves and exist for long periods of time without rain.

Some animals that live in the desert get all of the water they need by eating the leaves of plants that have water in them. People who have been lost in the desert have died because they had no water to drink. Some of these people would not have died if they had known how to survive. People who know how to survive in such a dry place often know how to obtain water from cactus plants.

A person may enjoy living in the desert because he thinks it is beautiful, but another person may think the same place is not pretty at all.

(181 Words) (Number of word recognition errors _____)

Questions:

F 1. _____ What do we call a place that is dry and often hot? (A desert)

F 2. _____ What do some people think a desert is? (A place where there is nothing but sand, or a place that is beautiful)

F 3. _____ What do some deserts have living in them? (Plants and animals)

F 4. _____ What is it about some plants and animals that enables them to live in the desert? (They do not need much water)

F 5. _____ Where do some desert plants store water? (In their leaves)

F 6. _____ Where do some animals that live in the desert get their water? (From the leaves of plants)

F 7. _____ What has sometimes happened to people who have been lost in the desert? (They have died, they had no water to drink, or they have died because they had no water to drink)

V 8. _____ What does the word "survive" mean? (To live, or stay alive)

F 9. _____ Why did it say someone might enjoy living in the desert? (Because it is beautiful, or because the person thought it was beautiful)

I 10. _____ Why do you think it would be a good idea to learn how to survive in the desert? (So that you would not die if you were lost, or a similar answer)

Number of Questions Missed	*Number of Word Recognition Errors* 0–2	3–6	7–10	11–13	14–17	18
0	+	*	*	*	*	×
1	+	*	*	*	×	×
2	*	*	*	×	×	×
3	*	*	×	×	×	×
4	*	×	×	×	×	×
5+	×	×	×	×	×	×

Reading Level		
⊞	Independent	☐
⊛	Instructional	☐
⊠	Frustration	☐

4D (☐)

One of the biggest jobs ever started was the building of the Panama Canal. The Panama Canal was known as "The Big Ditch." It was called "The Big Ditch" because it was a ditch with water in it and carried ships from one side of Panama to the other side, or from one ocean to another. By going through the Panama Canal, ships did not have to sail all the way around the continent of South America to get from one ocean to another.

When men first started building the Panama Canal there were many dangers from disease. People were getting Yellow Fever, which is a disease carried by a certain kind of mosquito. One man was a hero while the Panama Canal was being built. He discovered a way to get rid of the mosquitoes that were carrying Yellow Fever. After these insects were killed, Yellow Fever was no longer spread from one person to another. By the time the Panama Canal was finished, very few people were dying from Yellow Fever.

(173 Words)

Reading Rate

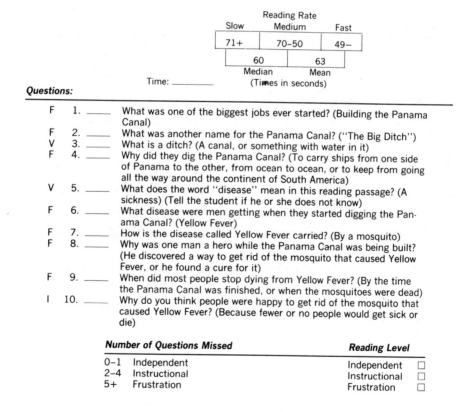

Slow	Medium	Fast
71+	70–50	49–

Median	Mean
60	63

(Times in seconds)

Time: ______

Questions:

F 1. ______ What was one of the biggest jobs ever started? (Building the Panama Canal)

F 2. ______ What was another name for the Panama Canal? ("The Big Ditch")

V 3. ______ What is a ditch? (A canal, or something with water in it)

F 4. ______ Why did they dig the Panama Canal? (To carry ships from one side of Panama to the other, from ocean to ocean, or to keep from going all the way around the continent of South America)

V 5. ______ What does the word "disease" mean in this reading passage? (A sickness) (Tell the student if he or she does not know)

F 6. ______ What disease were men getting when they started digging the Panama Canal? (Yellow Fever)

F 7. ______ How is the disease called Yellow Fever carried? (By a mosquito)

F 8. ______ Why was one man a hero while the Panama Canal was being built? (He discovered a way to get rid of the mosquito that caused Yellow Fever, or he found a cure for it)

F 9. ______ When did most people stop dying from Yellow Fever? (By the time the Panama Canal was finished, or when the mosquitoes were dead)

I 10. ______ Why do you think people were happy to get rid of the mosquito that caused Yellow Fever? (Because fewer or no people would get sick or die)

Number of Questions Missed		***Reading Level***
0–1	Independent	Independent ☐
2–4	Instructional	Instructional ☐
5+	Frustration	Frustration ☐

5C (☐ |)

There are about a hundred different kinds of monkeys. Some may be as large as a big dog, while others are so small that you could hold them in your hand. Some monkeys have bright colored faces and when they become excited these colors become brighter. Certain types of monkeys live in pairs or sometimes in clans of up to a hundred or more. Many monkeys can be tamed when they are young, but they have bad tempers when they grow old. The night or owl monkey is so named because it sleeps in the daytime and roams about at night.

Some monkeys are like humans because they make sounds to indicate they are angry. The howler monkey produces a sound that can be heard for a distance of two miles. This type has a boss that is usually the strongest and largest male of the group. When the "boss" loses his job, he may be forced to leave the group and wander alone.

(164 Words) (Number of word recognition errors _____)

Questions:

F 1. _____ How many different kinds of monkeys are there? (About a hundred, or a hundred)

F 2. _____ How big are some of the biggest monkeys? (As large as a big dog)

F 3. _____ What happens to some monkeys' faces when they become excited? (They become brighter)

V 4. _____ What does the word "clan" mean in this passage? (A group, or appropriate synonym)

F 5. _____ What happens to monkeys if they are not tamed before they grow old? (They get bad tempers, or become mean)

F 6. _____ Why is one kind of monkey called the night or owl monkey? (Because it sleeps in the daytime and/or roams about at night)

F 7. _____ How did this reading passage say some monkeys are like humans? (They make sounds to indicate they are angry)

I 8. _____ How do you know that some monkeys can make loud sounds? (Because they can be heard for two miles)

F 9. _____ What is the largest and strongest male of the group called? (The boss)

F 10. _____ What happens to the boss if he loses his job? (He may be forced to wander alone, to go off alone, or to be by himself)

		Number of Word Recognition Errors							Reading Level	
		0–2	3–5	6–8	9–12	13–15	16			
Number of Questions Missed	0	+	*	*	*	*	×	⊞	Independent	☐
	1	+	*	*	*	×	×	⊡	Instructional	☐
	2	*	*	*	×	×	×	⊠	Frustration	☐
	3	*	*	×	×	×	×			
	4	*	×	×	×	×	×			
	5+	×	×	×	×	×	×			

5D (☐ |)

Potatoes, along with wheat and rice, are one of the most important food crops in the world. Nearly every year the world grows about 10 billion bushels of potatoes. In some countries potatoes are used as food for animals as well as for people. In America they are usually consumed only by humans. The potatoes that people eat are almost always baked, boiled, or fried.

Potatoes are often grown in places where it is not quite warm enough for corn. In the far Eastern countries, few are grown because the climate is too warm and because rice has more food value.

When the Spanish first came to South America they found the Indians growing potatoes. It was not until many years later that this new food became popular with the Spanish.

A king in France made this food popular by wearing the flowers of the plant in his buttonhole.

(149 Words)

Reading Rate		
Slow	Medium	Fast
61+	60–64	43–

Median	Mean
50	52

(Times in seconds)

Time: ________

Questions:

F 1. ____ What three crops are among the most important in the world? (Potatoes, wheat, and rice) (Student must get at least two)

F 2. ____ How many bushels of potatoes does the world grow each year? (10 billion)

F 3. ____ In some countries potatoes are used for food for people and what else? (Animals)

V 4. ____ What does the word "consumed" mean in this reading passage? (Eaten or used)

F 5. ____ What are some ways that potatoes are prepared when they are eaten by humans? (They are baked, boiled, or fried) (Student must get at least two)

F 6. ____ This reading passage said potatoes are often grown where it is not warm enough for what crop? (Corn)

F 7. ____ Why are few potatoes grown in far Eastern countries? (Because the climate is too warm, or because it is too warm and because rice has more food value) (Student must get one of the two)

F 8. ____ Whom did the Spanish find growing potatoes when they came to South America? (The Indians)

I 9. ____ How do we know that potatoes were not already a popular food with the Spanish when they found the Indians growing them? (Because the reading passage said they did not become popular until many years later)

F 10. ____ How did a king in France make potatoes popular? (By wearing the flowers of the plant in his buttonhole)

Number of Questions Missed		***Reading Level***	
0–1	Independent	Independent	☐
2–4	Instructional	Instructional	☐
5+	Frustration	Frustration	☐

6C (☐L)

A mole is a small animal about six inches long. Moles have a long snout like a pig, a short thick neck, and a pink tail. Their ears are not visible but are concealed in their fur.

If a mole is placed on the ground it will begin to scramble about looking for a soft spot to dig. When it begins to dig, it will disappear in less than a minute. Moles often ruin lawns and gardens by making ridges in them caused from their burrowing through the ground.

Most of a mole's life is spent in darkness because it lives underground. A mole's home is usually a nest made from grasses and leaves. Its home is nearly always located beneath something like a rock, tree stump, or stone wall, which gives it more protection.

Moles are most commonly found in the northern half of the world.

(147 Words) (Number of word recognition errors _____)

Questions:

F 1. ____ About how long is a mole? (Six inches)

F 2. ____ What does a mole look like? (It has a long snout, a short thick neck, and a pink tail) (Student must name at least two)

V 3. ____ What does "concealed" mean in this reading passage? (Hidden)

F 4. ____ What will a mole do if it is placed on the ground? (It will begin to scramble and/or look for a place to dig, or look for a soft spot)

F 5. ____ How long will it take a mole to disappear when it is placed on the ground? (Less than a minute)

I 6. ____ Why do you think people might not like moles? (Because they ruin lawns and/or gardens)

F 7. ____ Where does a mole spend most of its life? (In darkness and/or underground)

F 8. ____ What does a mole usually use to make its nest? (Grasses and leaves)

F 9. ____ Why do moles usually build their homes beneath rocks, tree stumps, or stone walls? (To give them more protection, or to make them more safe)

F 10. ____ Where are moles most commonly found? (In the northern half of the world)

Number of Word Recognition Errors

Number of Questions Missed	0–2	3–5	6–8	9–11	12–14	15
0	+	*	*	*	*	×
1	+	*	*	*	×	×
2	*	*	*	×	×	×
3	*	*	×	×	×	×
4	*	×	×	×	×	×
5+	×	×	×	×	×	×

Reading Level

⊞ Independent ☐

⊛ Instructional ☐

☒ Frustration ☐

6D (□ L)

Cottontails and jackrabbits are two of the most commonly known wild animals in the world. Most people do not realize that certain animals such as the jackrabbit and snowshoe rabbit are actually not rabbits but hares. A hare is an animal with longer ears and it is heavier and larger than a rabbit.

A mother rabbit spends considerably more time in building her nest than a mother hare. The female hare, which is called a doe, has two or three litters of young during the year. There are usually four to six babies born in each litter. Young hares are born with their eyes open and can care for themselves in a few days. The infant rabbit is born with its eyes closed and does not see for about a week.

Both the rabbit and the hare are well equipped to detect their enemies. They have long sensitive ears for excellent hearing and eyes that enable them to see in every direction.

(162 Words)

Reading Rate

Slow	Medium	Fast
61+	60–47	46–

Median	Mean
54	56

(Times in seconds)

Time: ________

Questions:

F 1. ____ Name two of the most commonly known wild animals in the world. (Cottontails and jackrabbits, or hares, and rabbits)

F 2. ____ In this passage it said that jackrabbits and snowshoe rabbits are not actually rabbits. What are they? (Hares)

F 3. ____ In their looks, what is the difference between a hare and a rabbit? (A hare has longer ears and/or is larger and heavier than a rabbit)

I 4. ____ Why do you think a mother rabbit takes better care of her young than a mother hare? (Because she spends more time in building her nest, *or* because young hares are born with their eyes open and can care for themselves in a few days, *or* because the infant rabbit is born with its eyes closed and does not see for about a week)

F 5. ____ What is a female hare called? (A doe)

F 6. ____ How many babies does a female hare usually have? (Four to six, *or* four, five, six)

F 7. ____ How long is it before a young hare can care for itself? (A few days)

V 8. ____ What does the word "infant" mean? (A baby, or a very young rabbit)

F 9. ____ How long does it take for a baby or infant rabbit to open its eyes? (About a week)

F 10. ____ Why are hares and rabbits able to detect their enemies? (They have long sensitive ears for hearing and/or can see in every direction, *or* they can hear and/or see well)

Number of Questions Missed		***Reading Level***	
0–1	Independent	Independent	□
2–4	Instructional	Instructional	□
5+	Frustration	Frustration	□

7C (☐ ⊔)

Among the animals of the world, one of the most talented is the spider. With its silken webs it can construct suspension bridges, beautiful designs, and insect traps. The spider might be thought of as one of nature's greatest engineers.

Spiders can be found in all parts of the world except where it is extremely cold. They can not survive in cold or polar regions covered with snow because of a lack of food.

People sometimes mistakenly refer to spiders as insects. Unlike insects, which have six legs and three body segments, spiders have eight legs and two body segments.

Although there are many different kinds of spiders in the United States, only two of these are considered dangerous. These are the Black Widow and the Brown House Spider. Spiders are useful to man because they destroy many kinds of harmful insects.

(142 Words) (Number of word recognition errors _____)

Questions:

F 1. _____ What might be considered as one of the most talented animals in the world? (The spider)

F 2. _____ What are some things that spiders are able to construct with their webs? (Suspension bridges, beautiful designs, and insect traps, or bridges, designs, and traps) (Student must name at least two)

I 3. _____ Why might the spider be thought of as one of the world's greatest engineers? (Because it is able to build so many things, or because of its ability to build)

F 4. _____ Where would you not expect to find spiders? (Where it is extremely cold)

V 5. _____ What does the word "talented" mean in this reading passage? (Skillful, able to do many things, gifted, or an appropriate synonym)

F 6. _____ What do people often mistakenly call spiders (Insects)

F 7. _____ How are spiders different from insects? (Spiders have eight legs while insects have six, and spiders have two body segments while insects have three) (Students must explain at least one difference)

F 8. _____ How many kinds of poisonous spiders are there in the United States? (Two)

F 9. _____ What are the two kinds of dangerous spiders in the United States? (The Black Widow and the Brown House Spider)

F 10. _____ Why are spiders useful to man? (Because they destroy many harmful insects, or because they kill insects)

Number of Questions Missed	*Number of Word Recognition Errors* 0–2	3–5	6–7	8–10	11–13	14
0	+	*	*	*	*	×
1	+	*	*	*	×	×
2	*	*	*	×	×	×
3	*	*	×	×	×	×
4	*	×	×	×	×	×
5+	×	×	×	×	×	×

Reading Level

⊞ Independent ☐

⊛ Instructional ☐

⊠ Frustration ☐

7D (□ ⊔)

Millions of cats have homes, but there are many who are strays. They are still the second most popular type of pet in America. People who raise cats and enter them in shows are called members of the "American Cat Fancy." A cat must have earned four winner's ribbons to become a champion.

Cats are meat eaters and are equipped with special teeth to tear meat into chunks. Once the meat has been torn into small chunks, it is swallowed without chewing. Cats are excellent hunters and can jump as high as seven feet in the air. One purpose of a cat's tail is to enable it to balance itself when it jumps. If a cat is turned upside down and dropped, it will always turn over and land on its feet.

Some cats have been known to live to be 19 or 20 years old; however, the average life of a cat is about 14 years.

(157 Words)

Reading Rate

Slow	Medium	Fast
54+	53–40	39–

Median	Mean
47	49

(Times in seconds)

Time: ________

Questions:

V	1.	____	What is meant by a "stray?" (Something without a home, or a cat without a home)
I	2.	____	How do you know from reading this passage that cats are not the most popular type of pet in America? (Because it said that cats are the second most popular type of pet in America)
F	3.	____	What must a cat have to become a champion? (Four winner's ribbons)
F	4.	____	For what purpose do cats have special teeth? (For tearing meat into chunks)
F	5.	____	What do cats do with meat once it has been torn into chunks? (Swallow it, or swallow it without chewing it)
F	6.	____	How high can cats jump? (Seven feet)
F	7.	____	What is one purpose of the cat's tail? (To enable it to balance while it jumps, or to enable it to balance)
F	8.	____	What will happen to a cat if it is turned upside down and dropped? (It will turn over and land on its feet, or it will land on its feet)
F	9.	____	How long have some of the oldest cats been known to live? (For 19 or 20 years)
F	10.	____	How long is the average life of a cat? (About 14 years)

Number of Questions Missed		***Reading Level***	
0–1	Independent	Independent	☐
2–4	Instructional	Instructional	☐
5+	Frustration	Frustration	☐

8C (☐☐)

The ostrich, which roams wild in Africa, is the biggest living bird. A fully developed male is extremely large, often standing as tall as seven or eight feet. The eggs from which the young are hatched are also quite large, with a weight of about three pounds.

Most humans consider this giant bird to be awkward and ugly. Although it is not a beautiful bird, it was once highly prized for its fluffy feathers or plumes. Knights of long ago used them as decorations on their helmets and their ladies used them to adorn their dresses.

The ostrich is a flightless bird; however, in running it may attain speeds of up to fifty miles per hour. This large bird often roams over the plains with other animals such as zebras and antelopes. If it fears danger it is likely to dash off, warning other animals. If it is forced to defend itself, it will often kick using its strong legs and sharp claws.

(163 Words) (Number of word recognition errors ______)

Questions:

F 1. _____ What is the largest living bird? (The ostrich)

F 2. _____ How tall might we expect a fully developed male ostrich to be? (Seven to eight feet)

F 3. _____ How much might we expect an ostrich egg to weigh? (About three pounds)

F 4. _____ What do most humans think of the ostrich? (They think it is awkward and/or ugly)

F 5. _____ Why was the ostrich once highly prized? (For its fluffy feathers or plumes, *or* for its feathers and/or plumes)

F 6. _____ For what purpose were ostrich feathers once used? (For decorations for clothing and/or for knights to use in their helmets)

V 7. _____ What does "flightless" mean? (Unable to fly)

F 8. _____ What other animals might one expect to find ostriches with? (Zebras and antelopes)

I 9. _____ Why might other animals like to have ostriches around them? (To warm them of danger)

F 10. _____ How do ostriches defend themselves? (By kicking, or by using their sharp claws)

		Number of Word Recognition Errors					
		0–2	3–5	6–8	9–12	13–15	16
Number of Questions Missed	0	+	*	*	*	*	×
	1	+	*	*	*	×	×
	2	*	*	*	×	×	×
	3	*	*	×	×	×	×
	4	*	×	×	×	×	×
	5+	×	×	×	×	×	×

Reading Level

⊞ Independent ☐

⧆ Instructional ☐

⊠ Frustration ☐

8D (☐☐)

There is no other natural substance that has the ability of rubber to stretch or bend and then snap back into shape. This ability makes this important product very useful in modern transportation.

Most of the natural rubber is obtained from the rubber tree. The inner bark of the rubber tree secretes a milky fluid called latex. There are a number of other tropical vines and shrubs that secrete a substance similar to latex, but it is of little economic value.

Most of the trees that produce rubber are grown in an area close to the equator. Rubber trees are normally found in countries with a low altitude. Some of these trees may grow as fast as nine feet per year. When a rubber tree has obtained a growth of about six inches in diameter, it is ready to be tapped for latex.

Although some materials have replaced rubber, it is still one of the most widely used products in the world.

(162 Words)

Reading Rate

Slow	Medium	Fast
51+	50–40	39–

Median	Mean
45	47

(Times in seconds)

Time: ______

Questions:

F 1. ______ What are some of the abilities of rubber that no other natural substance has? (Stretch, bend, and snap back into shape) (Student must name at least two)

F 2. ______ In what part of industry do these abilities make rubber very useful? (In modern transportation, or in transportation)

F 3. ______ From what do we get most of our natural rubber? (From the rubber tree)

F 4. ______ What is the milky fluid collected from rubber trees called? (Latex)

V 5. ______ What does the word "secrete" mean? (To give off, or a similar synonym)

F 6. ______ Where are most of the trees that produce rubber grown? (In an area close to the equator, or close to the equator)

F 7. ______ Rubber trees are usually found in countries with what types of altitude? (Low)

F 8. ______ How fast might we expect some rubber trees to grow? (Nine feet per year)

F 9. ______ How large in diameter must a tree be before it is tapped for latex? (Six inches)

I 10. ______ From what you read in this passage, why do you think it would be hard to do without rubber? (Because it is one of the most widely used products in the world, or because it is so important in transportation)

Number of Questions Missed		***Reading Level***	
0–1	Independent	Independent	☐
2–4	Instructional	Instructional	☐
5+	Frustration	Frustration	☐

9C (☐☐|)

A rather unusual fish that can fly through the air for relatively extensive distances is called the flying fish. It may fly distances of merely a few feet, but may also soar through the air for distances ranging up to 200 yards. This particular type of fish usually only flies when it is pursued by a predator. The peculiar flying fish may stay aloft only momentarily, but it may remain airborne for a duration of up to ten or fifteen seconds. Among the creatures of the ocean who prey on the flying fish are tuna, sharks, dolphins, and porpoises.

If the flying fish is endangered, it is able to use its tail to strike a sharp blow on the water's surface to give it added momentum in making its ascent. When the fish makes its exodus from the water, it may attain speeds of up to 35 miles per hour. Once the fish is airborne, it spreads its pectoral fins and proceeds to use them as wings. These fins are not actually wings but elastic membranes that enable them to be flexible.

There are approximately 65 species of this unique fish, which commonly inhabit only the warm waters of the Atlantic Ocean.

(202 Words) (Number of word recognition errors ______)

Questions:

F 1. ______ What is the name of the unusual fish in this reading passage? (Flying fish)

F 2. ______ What is the longest distance this fish may be able to soar through the air? (Up to 200 yards, or 200 yards)

F 3. ______ When does this particular fish usually fly? (When it is chased, or when it is pursued by a predator)

F 4. ______ How long can this fish stay in the air if it wants to? (From ten to fifteen seconds, or either ten or fifteen seconds)

F 5. ______ What kinds of ocean creatures prey on the flying fish? (Tuna, sharks, dolphins, and porpoises) (Student must get at least three)

F 6. ______ What does the flying fish do to give it added momentum in its ascent? (It strikes its tail on the water)

V 7. ______ What does the word "exodus" mean in this reading passage? (Leaving, or taking off from the water)

F 8. ______ What does the flying fish use its pectoral fins for? (To fly, or as wings)

F 9. ______ What are the fins made of that allow them to be flexible? (An elastic membrane)

I 10. ______ Why would we not expect to find this fish in the cold waters around the polar regions? (Because it lives only in the warm waters of the Atlantic Ocean, or because it lives in warm water)

Number of Questions Missed	Number of Word Recognition Errors: 0–3	4–7	8–11	12–15	16–19	20
0	+	*	*	*	*	×
1	+	*	*	*	×	×
2	*	*	*	×	×	×
3	*	*	×	×	×	×
4	*	×	×	×	×	×
5+	×	×	×	×	×	×

Reading Level

⊞ Independent ☐

⊡ Instructional ☐

☒ Frustration ☐

9D (☐☐ |)

One of our most important and familiar forms of energy is light. Some researchers believe that millions of years ago the sun was responsible for the various chemical reactions that led to the beginning of life. Light is instrumental in photosynthesis, which is a process by which plants utilize light to form chemical compounds necessary for their survival. A large percentage of the living organisms on earth are dependent on photosynthesis for their food supply.

Light is also important in providing the earth's surface and atmosphere with warmth, which is important in maintaining a proper temperature range for habitation. Without a source of light, the temperature of the earth would be so low that survival for man would be impossible.

If an object is to be visible, light must travel from that object to the eye, which then senses that light. An object that provides a source of light in itself is said to be luminous. The moon is typical of an object that is not luminous in itself but is only seen because it reflects light from the sun. In contrast, the sun and other stars emit their own light energy and would be classified as luminous.

(198 Words)

Reading Rate

Slow	Medium	Fast
58+	57–40	39–

Median	Mean
46	51

(Times in seconds)

Time: ______

Questions:

F 1. ______ What is one of the most important and familiar forms of energy? (Light, or the sun)
F 2. ______ What do some researchers believe was responsible for the chemical reactions that led to the beginning of life? (The sun)
F 3. ______ What is the process called in which plants utilize light to form chemical compounds necessary for life? (Photosynthesis)
F 4. ______ Other than causing chemical reactions, what does light do that is important for maintaining habitation on the earth? (It helps maintain a proper temperature)
F 5. ______ What would happen to man if it were not for the light source that we have? (He could not inhabit the earth, or it would get too cold to live)
F 6. ______ In order for an object to be visible what must happen? (Light must travel from that source to the eye)
F 7. ______ What is the word that refers to an object that provides its own source of light? (Luminous)
F 8. ______ What object was mentioned that is not luminous? (The moon)
V 9. ______ What does the word "emit" mean? (To send out, give off, or a similar synonym)
I 10. ______ Why do you think the moon does not provide us with a great deal of energy? (Because it does not emit or give off light, or because it is not luminous)

Number of Questions Missed		***Reading Level***	
0–1	Independent	Independent	☐
2–4	Instructional	Instructional	☐
5+	Frustration	Frustration	☐

Index

Admission, Review, and Dismissal Committee (IEP), 114
Allington, Richard, L., 117
Alphabet knowledge, 24, 196
Anderson, Richard C., 87
Annual Review (IEP), 115
Appreciation, 6
Audiovisual aids, 106, 177, 178

Babbs, Patricia, 82, 83
Barrett, Thomas, 5–7
Basic sight words, 2–3, 11, 18
  computer testing of, 182
  diagnosing knowlege, 24–25
  remediation procedures, 27–31
  utility of, 30
Berg, David N., 99
Blending, 56–57
Brozo, William G., 88
Buss, Ray R., 3, 5

Cassettes, 188
Child Study Committee, 113
Children's books, 24
Chunking, 88
Cloze procedure, 95
  developing, administering, and scoring, 80–82
  matching student to materials, 79–80
  reliability, 82
  use of computer with, 183
  vocabulary building and, 106
Cohn, Marvin, 90–91
Commercial informal reading inventories, 71, 115
Comprehension, 3, 5–7, 29
  computer programs for, 198–200
  developing, 82–99
    changing reading speed, 83
    metacognition and, 83–86
    modeling teacher's questions, 84–91, 92
    obtaining mental images, 83–84, 97
    paragraph study, 93–95
    predicting, 84, 97
    purpose for reading, 85, 90, 95
    questioning strategies, 88–90
    request procedure, 91–92
    schemata theory, 87–88
    SQ3R, 92–93
    with story frames, 86
    structured comprehension, 90–91
  diagnosis by computer, 178
  learning activities, 95–99
  mastery of, 11
  material read (*see also* Reading levels; Reading materials), 69
  questions, 75, 78
  reader knowledge, 68–69
  scoring and interpreting, 76–79
  teaching by computer, 180
  testing, 70–79, 115, 182–183
Computer hardware (*see also* Microcomputers; Software):
  evaluation, 188–190
  factors to consider, 188–189
  IRA guidelines, 191
Computer magazines, 195
Computer programs. *See* under name of skill (e.g., Vocabulary); Microcomputers: Software
Computer technology. *See* International Reading Association guidelines; Microcomputers
Computer terminology, 215–219
Configuration clues, 7
Consonants (*see also* Vowel rules):
  consonant cluster, 61
  exercises with, 51–54
Content area reading, 197
Context clues, 102, 104
  diagnosing knowledge, 40
  exercises, 45–46
  increasing difficulty, 44–45
  picture context clues, 41, 42, 45
  remediation procedures, 41–44
  semantic clues, 41, 43–44
  syntactic clues, 41, 43–44
  using tape recorder, 41–42
Contractions, 48, 63–64
Critical reading:
  computer programs for, 201

Dale-Chall Readability Formula, 181
Davis, Frederick B., 3
Diagnosis (*see also* under reading areas (e.g., Basic sight words)):
  continual, 20
  procedures, 14–16
Diagnostic-referral procedure, 16
Dictionary skills, 2, 7
Diphthongs, 54

Disabled reader (*see also* Remedial reading; Remedial reading class):
  defined, 110–111
  early identification, 111, 119
  IQ test, 110–111
  mainstreaming, 111, 115
  measuring progress, 117–118
  referrals, 111–113
  selection of students, 111–116
  stories for, 97–98
  tests for screening, 113–116
  younger students, 116
Dolch List, 2, 11, 24
Durr, William, 24

Educational diagnostician, 113, 122
Ekwall Basic Sight Word List, 2, 24
Ekwall, Eldon E., 27, 90–93, 118
Ekwall Reading Inventory, 25, 68, 71, 102, 115
El Paso Phonics Survey, 48
Evaluation, 5–6

Factor analysis, 3, 7
Flash presentations, 31, 182
Fowler, Gerald W., 86
Frustration reading level, 19, 80, 183
  criteria for, 73, 76, 78, 115
Fry Graph, 181
Fry list, 2

Giordano, Gerard, 89
Group diagnostic tests, 15
Group standardized achievement tests, 70, 99–101, 103, 117–118

Hard and Soft *C* and *G* rules, 54–56
Harris-Jacobson List, 2, 24
Heckelman, R. G., 29–30
Hyman, Ronald T., 89–90

Implementation-Instruction Plan (IEP), 114
Independent reading level, 25, 79–80, 183
  criteria for, 73
Individual intelligence tests, 101, 110–111
Individual standardized achievement tests, 70–71
Individualized Education Program (IEP), 111, 113–115
Inference, 5, 11
Instructional reading level, 19, 79–80, 183
  criteria for, 73, 79
International Reading Association:
  guidelines for using computers, 190–193

Joag-Dev, Chitra, 87
Johnson, Dale D., 3, 5
Johnson, Marjorie, 72, 73

Kinesthetic approach, 34–35
Kress, Roy, 72, 73

Language-experience approach, 27–29
Letter knowledge, 26–27
Life skills, 184
Literal meaning, 5
Look-alike words, 32, 46

Mainstreaming, 111, 115
Manzo, Anthony, 91–92
Metacognition, 68, 82–83
Microcomputers (*see also* Computer hardware; Software):
  categories of materials, 177
  compatible software, 176–177, 188, 191
  determining needs, 176–179, 180, 190
  International Reading Association guidelines, 190–193
  record-keeping and, 182
  teaching procedure, 177–178
  use with disabled readers, 180–184
  voice synthesizer and, 177–179
Moe, Alden, 82, 83
Morphology, 48

Neurological impress method, 27, 29–30
  use of computer, 183–184
Neutral questions, 75

Oral reading, 74–76, 179
Oral vocabulary tests, 102–103

Paragraph structure, 93–95
Passage-dependent questions, 89
Phonics, 18, 54
  testing, 48–50, 179–180
Phonograms, 56
Picture context clues, 41, 42, 45
Picture dictionaries, 51
Picture vocabulary file, 104
Picture vocabulary tests, 103
Platt, Jennifer M., 82–83
Public Law 94-142, 111, 113–115

Questioning:
  request procedure, 91–92
  strategies, 88–90
Quick Survey Word List, 48

Radio Shack Pocket Computer (PC-2), 182
Ratio-of-learning, 118
Readability formulae, 69, 72, 181

Readence, John E., 106
Reading (*see also* Reading levels), 72
  competencies, 7, 11–12
  critical, 201
  silent or free, 103–104
Reading inventories, 102
Reading Level Calculator, 77–79
Reading levels:
  frustration, 19 (*see also* Frustration reading level
  independent, 25 (*see also* Independent reading level)
  instructional, 19 (*see also* Instructional reading level)
  oral and silent, 68 (*see also* Oral reading)
Reading materials (*see also* Software):
  Cloze procedure for matching, 79–80
  evaluating, 152–153
  main kinds, 185
  programs for critical reading, 201
  recommended books, 153–173
  teacher-made informal inventories and, 72–74
  teacher's manual, 152–153
Reading skills (*see also* Basic sight words; Context clues; Word attack skills), 2–3
  levels of development, 12
  scope and sequence, 11
  subskills, 3–7, 100
Reading vocabulary (*see also* Vocabulary development), 100
Recall, 5, 89
Recognition, 5
Reinforcement, 178, 185, 187
Remedial reading (*see also* Disabled reader; Public Law 94-142):
  awareness of progress, 18–19
  follow-up, 22, 119
  forms for communication, 122–124
  individualized program, 16, 19, 111, 113–115
  materials, 19
  recognizing the problem, 18
  skills taught, 7
  summarizing, 21
  teacher's attitude, 20–21
Remedial reading class (*see also* Disabled reader; Individualized Education Program):
  length of program, 118–119
  length of sessions, 116
  size, 116
  subjects displaced, 117
Rinehart, Steve D., 82–83
Robinson, Francis, 92
R-, *W-*, and *L*-controlled vowels, 56

San Diego Quick Assessment List, 25, 115
Schemata theory, 87–88
Schmelzer, Ronald V., 88
Schwa (a) sound, 61
Seafross, Lyndon W., 106
Self-instruction, 21
Semantic mapping, 99
Sentence length, 69
Shanker, James L., 27, 90–93, 118
Sight word lists, 25
Sight words (*see also* Basic sight words), 2–3
  diagnosing knowledge, 25–26
  remediation procedures, 27–31
    using computer, 36, 183
    using tape recorder, 35–36
    word games, 31–34
Signal words, 95
Sinatra, Richard C., 99
Software (*see also* Computer hardware; Microcomputers):
  compatibility, 176–177, 188, 191
  deficiencies, 178–180
  evaluation, 184–188
  feedback characteristics, 187
  graphics, 187
  peripheral requirements, 188, 189
  program characteristics, 186
  purchasing, 185–186, 190–191
  teacher's manual, 186
  user control and friendliness, 186–187
Software directories, 176, 188, 193–194
Software publishers, 213–215
Software reviews, 194
Sound-symbol correspondence, 51–54
Spache, Evelyn, 90
Spache, George, 90
Special learning classroom (*see also* Remedial reading class), 16
Speed reading courses, 83
Spelling:
  computer programs for, 202–203
  use of computer, 184
Spires, Hillar A., 88
SQ3R, 92–93
Stahl-Gemake, Josephine, 99
Stefferson, Margaret, 87
Stevens, Kathleen C., 88
Stewart, Oran, 83
Story frames, 86
Strange, Michael, 87
Structural analysis skills, 48–50
Study skills, 2, 7
  computer programs for, 204, 206–207
Syllabication principles:
  remediation procedures, 60–63
  syllable principles, 62
Synonyms, 96, 106
Syntax, 69

Teacher-made informal reading inventories, 71–79, 115
marking oral reading errors, 74–78
matching student with materials, 72–74
Tei, Ebo, 83
Toms-Bronowski, Susan, 3, 5
Total Service Plan (IEP), 114

Vocabulary card file, 104–105
Vocabulary development, 7
computer programs for, 205
strategies for increasing, 103–106
Vocabulary measurement, 99–103
group standardized achievement tests, 99–101
individual intelligence tests, 101
informal reading inventories, 102
oral tests, 102–103
picture vocabulary tests, 103
Voice synthesizer, 177–179, 184, 188, 193
Vowel exercises, 52–54
Vowel rules, 12, 61
AU, AW, OU, OL, OY rules, 60
EE, EA, OA, AY, AI rule, 58–59
final *E* rule, 58
OO rules, 60
OW sounds, 59
syllabication and, 61–62
Y rules, 59

Wechsler Intelligence Scale for Children—Rev., 101
Word attack skills, 2–3, 101, 103
computer programs for, 208–210
use of computer, 183
Word awareness, 84–86, 104
Word endings, 64–66
Word games, 116
apple words, 57
for comprehension, 95–99
for contractions, 63–64
for sight word learning, 31–34
for sound-symbol correspondence, 52–54
for word endings, 65–66
Word processing:
creative writing and, 181
Words in context (*see also* Context clues), 32, 34
Writing:
computer programs for, 211–212